BEFORE THE
MELTING POT

BEFORE THE MELTING POT

SOCIETY AND CULTURE IN COLONIAL NEW YORK CITY, 1664–1730

JOYCE D. GOODFRIEND

PRINCETON UNIVERSITY PRESS

PRINCETON, NEW JERSEY

Library of Congress Cataloging-in-Publication Data

Goodfriend, Joyce D.
Before the melting pot : society and culture in colonial New York
City, 1664–1730 / Joyce D. Goodfriend.
p.   cm.
Includes bibliographical references and index.
ISBN 0-691-04794-4
ISBN 0-691-03787-6 (pbk.)
1. New York (N.Y.)—History—Colonial period, ca. 1600–1775.
2. New York (N.Y.)—Ethnic relations.   3. Ethnicity—New York
(N.Y.)—History.   I. Title.
F122.G643 1991 974.7'102—dc20 91-19094

This book has been composed in Linotron Galliard

Princeton University Press books are printed
on acid-free paper and meet the guidelines for
permanence and durability of the Committee on
Production Guidelines for Book Longevity
of the Council on Library Resources

First Princeton paperback printing, 1994

Printed in the United States of America

10 9 8 7 6 5 4 3 2

For I.S.G. and S.M.G.

PARENTS *EXTRAORDINAIRE*

One does not need to claim everything for the Dutch . . .
to recognize the Dutch background as an
important and peculiar factor in the social growth
of New York and the nation.
—Dixon Ryan Fox, *Yankees and Yorkers*

The Dutch, the founders of the city, had been
reduced to a kind of spectral eminence.
—Jan Morris, *Manhattan '45*

CONTENTS

ILLUSTRATIONS

TABLES

ACKNOWLEDGMENTS

W HEN I WAS a child growing up in Manhattan, names such as Beekman, Schuyler, and Stuyvesant conjured up telephone exchanges, not Dutch families. Only years later, after embarking on research into New York's colonial past as a graduate student in California, did I begin to comprehend the magnitude of the Dutch imprint on the city. Armed with this insight and dissatisfied with prevailing Anglocentric interpretations of the colonial city's social and cultural development, I resolved to retell New York City's early history in a way that would make visible all the peoples who had been actors in that history. In so doing, I have also ventured to cast new light on the nature of pluralism in early America.

Many individuals have offered counsel, references, and encouragement during the time I have spent piecing together the puzzle of New York City's formative decades. I welcome this opportunity to thank Gary Nash, John Murrin, Pat Bonomi, Mike McGiffert, Roy Ritchie, Oliver Rink, Jessica Kross, Michael Kammen, Randall Balmer, David Cohen, Steve Bielinski, and Tom Burke for their contributions to my work.

I am grateful to a number of people for granting me access to the resources of their institutions: Phyllis Barr of the Archives of the Parish of Trinity Church, Elizabeth Moger of the Haviland Records Room of the New York Yearly Meeting, Natalie Naylor of the Long Island Studies Institute of Hofstra University, and Barbara Stankowski of the Holland Society of New York. Robert Williams of the Collegiate Reformed Protestant Dutch Church of the City of New York went out of his way to arrange for photographing the church's portrait of Rev. Gualterus Du Bois. Charly Gehring, Nancy Zeller, Peter Christoph, and Florence Christoph of the New Netherland Project at the New York State Library were consistently generous with ideas and information. I am also indebted to the staffs of the New-York Historical Society, the New York Public Library, the Historical Documents Collection at Queens College, the New York State Archives, and the New York State Library for their help.

Portions of chapters 5 and 9 appeared previously in *The William and Mary Quarterly*.

At the University of Denver, the assistance of Carol Taylor of the Faculty Computer Lab and May Smith of the Interlibrary Loan Department of Penrose Library was invaluable.

I would like to express my appreciation to the Holland Society of New York for a grant to help with publication costs.

Gail Ullman of Princeton University Press has strongly supported this endeavor from the outset for which I thank her.

I am most grateful to my mother and father for their abiding faith in me and my work.

BEFORE THE
MELTING POT

INTRODUCTION

WHEN CHARLES LODWICK observed in 1692 that New York City was "too great a mixture of nations and English the least part," he was articulating the sentiments of not only an influential group of contemporaries but scores of later commentators who believed that ethnic diversity threatened the social fabric.[1] In recent years, scholars have offered a more sanguine assessment of colonial New York City's pluralistic social order, one that emphasizes the enrichment of experience that results from cultural variety. Never in dispute, however, has been the fact that the propinquity of diverse peoples from Europe and Africa in the compact settlement at the tip of Manhattan Island indelibly shaped the social and cultural evolution of the city during the seventeenth and eighteenth centuries.

The three generations following the English conquest of New Netherland in 1664 were singularly important in New York's history. As the city was brought under imperial governance—its economy reoriented and its ethnic demography altered by an influx of European and African immigrants—a multifaceted process of transformation was set in motion that took decades to unfold. Because Leisler's Rebellion has seemed to epitomize the complexity of New York's development, scholars have tended to regard politics as the key to understanding the city's early history. Their attempts to unravel the tangled strands of political life, ranging from pioneering efforts to construct a narrative of events to far more sophisticated analyses of political behavior, invariably paid homage to the heterogeneity of the populace.[2] But not until recent years has ethnicity been integrated into the conception of the political process in a uniform way. While historians such as Patricia Bonomi, Robert Ritchie, Thomas Archdeacon, Gary Nash, John Murrin and Adrian Howe do not agree on precisely how cultural groups expressed their values in political action, collectively they have proved that New York City's politics in the decades stretching from the English conquest to the middle third of the eighteenth century cannot be explained without reference to ethnicity.[3]

In all these works, however, the treatment of ethnicity is an auxiliary concern. Data on ethnic groups are marshaled in order to interpret political alignments, not to assess the overall imprint of ethnic diversity on New York City society. A similar emphasis characterizes discussions of the city's economy.[4]

It has fallen to social historians to explore the ramifications of cultural coexistence in an ethnically diverse society. The approaches taken have been varied and fruitful. A cluster of studies dating from the turn of the century, commonly dismissed as antiquarian because of their impression-istic rendering of the minutiae of everyday life among the Dutch and En-glish colonists, can now be appreciated for their insights into folklore and material culture.[5] The later work of Thomas Jefferson Wertenbaker, though colored by the stereotypes of the 1930s, delineated the interplay of ethnic interests in New York with surprising sensitivity.[6]

But it was not until the advent of the "new social history" in the 1960s that historians set out in earnest to explore the impact of ethnic diversity on New York City's society and culture. Galvanized by the proliferation of monographs focusing on the homogeneous communities of colonial New England, they embarked on research aimed at illuminating New York's far more differentiated social landscape. Yet, along with historians of other diverse societies in seventeenth- and eighteenth-century America, they lacked models to guide their inquiries. As one scholar commented in 1982, "despite our recognition of the salience of cultural pluralism in the middle colonies, we have never had a theoretical framework for ethnore-ligious research there."[7] The few empirical examinations of heterogeneous colonial communities raised pertinent questions, but did not address the distinctive aspects of New York City's history.[8] Scores of studies of ethnic groups in nineteenth-and twentieth-century America as well as the bur-geoning sociological literature on assimilation and pluralism confirmed the importance of investigating multiethnic societies, but caution had to be exercised in applying concepts derived from later periods to the pre-national era.[9]

Research on colonial New York's complex ethnic history has proceeded along several distinct lines. Topical inquiries directed toward ascertaining the part played by ethnicity in shaping inheritance patterns, gender roles, and educational practices have convincingly demonstrated the ways in which social institutions reflect cultural values.[10]

The experiences of the separate groups in New York City's ethnic mo-saic have captured the attention of other historians. Most notable has been the renaissance of interest in the colonial Dutch.[11] Provocative overviews by Alice Kenney and Gerald de Jong, a revisionist history of New Nether-land, and ambitious efforts to interpret the material culture of the colonial Dutch have not only broadened our knowledge of the values and institu-tions of early settlers of Netherlands descent but have underlined the en-during legacy of Dutch colonization in New York.[12]

Jon Butler's masterful survey of the city's Huguenots and the author-itative work of David and Tamar de Sola Pool on the Jews help fill in the picture of urban ethnic groups. But, astonishingly, there have been no in-depth investigations of the English, Scots, Scots-Irish, Irish, or Germans in colonial New York City.[13] The same cannot be said for the city's Afri-can-Americans. Intensive research on slaves and free blacks of African descent has heightened awareness of New York's biracial character.[14] Donald Meinig has pointed out that the complex form of pluralism that evolved in New York City was distinctive not only for the variety of cultures found in the European population but for the strong representation of persons of African descent.[15] This telling insight has yet to be explored in a history of the city's ethnic groups.

Scholars have been much more successful in disentangling the threads in colonial New York City's religious tapestry. Major studies by Randall Balmer and Richard Pointer have made plain the importance of religion in defining the social identity of colonial New Yorkers.[16] Nevertheless, viewing the city's pluralistic social order from the perspective of the religious denomination skirts the question of the relationship between ethnicity and religion, an issue of overriding importance in the context of New York history.[17]

Two quantitative historians—Thomas Archdeacon and Bruce Wilkenfeld—have done much to illuminate the structural underpinnings of New York City society in the seventeenth and eighteenth centuries.[18] Employing an array of social indicators to chart the position of the Dutch, English, French, and Jews in the social structure at different points in time, they reached different conclusions about the pace of social change or "Anglicization." Archdeacon pointed to the diminution in Dutch wealth and power in late seventeenth-century New York City as English and French immigrants infiltrated the top echelons of local society. Wilkenfeld, however, argued that the Dutch remained entrenched in the city's social structure well into the eighteenth century.

The pitfalls of relying too heavily on quantitative analysis are apparent in these studies. Comparing the characteristics of social aggregates at stated intervals cannot explain the processes of social and cultural change in New York City. What is needed to capture the social experience of early New Yorkers is a multidimensional approach that explores the consequences of contact between ethnic groups from the perspective of the individual and the group as well as the society.

Despite the great strides researchers have made in deciphering colonial New York City's evolving social patterns, no one yet has traced the city's distinctive social and cultural history during this critical era with the acuity and precision the subject warrants. To do so, it is essential to keep in mind four fundamental ideas.

First, New York City had a unique sequence of development among American colonial cities which cannot be understood without recognizing the enduring impact of the Dutch on society and culture. As a "charter group" the Dutch introduced institutions, laws, and customary practices, altered the landscape, set the pattern for interaction with native peoples and imported Africans, and selectively transplanted their culture.[19] But just as they were beginning their metamorphosis into a creole group, they were forced into the subordinate status of a conquered people when New Netherland passed into English hands. Submission to English rule, the virtual cessation of immigration from the Netherlands, and the influx of English, French, and other Europeans did not entail the wholesale divestiture of the Dutch way of life in New York City. In varying degrees, Dutch settlers maintained their institutions, social forms, and values as they gradually adapted to the altered context of their lives.

Second, the concept of "Anglicization," which has come to dominate the historiography of colonial New York City, is limited in its explanatory power. Focusing exclusively on the pace and timing of Dutch assimilation to English ways not only diverts attention from assimilative processes that worked the other way—what John Murrin refers to as "Batavianization"—but compresses the variety of social adaptations and cultural permutations into a monolithic mold.[20] Analyzing the complex social and cultural evolution of New York City during the late seventeenth and early eighteenth centuries requires unraveling the multiple strands of experience that collectively constitute the city's history and confronting the often contradictory evidence of continuity and change.

Third, New York was a biracial city from the outset. Social life and cultural forms reflected African as well as European influences. Though historians have been quick to point to the slave revolt of 1712 as proof of the volatility of New York City's social mixture, no one has yet examined the city's sizable black community in counterpoint to the European subcommunities that composed the city's white society. Only by doing so can the nature of colonial New York City's pluralism be appreciated.

Fourth, the central expression of culture in early New York City was religion. Until recently, scholars have charted the city's history primarily in secular terms, focusing on the role of ethnicity in political and economic developments. But without defining the relationship between ethnic identity and religious identity in this milieu, it is impossible to comprehend how individuals defined themselves or how communities functioned. Heightened ethnic consciousness, largely predicated on religious identity, formed the basis for group life in early New York City.

The research design for this book incorporates three distinct levels of analysis—family, immigrant group, and society. Whereas previous research has centered on the city as a whole, offering static pictures of the apportionment of ethnic or religious groups in the social and political structure at various points in time, my inquiry moves beyond these baseline findings to probe the ways in which old settler families, European immigrants, and persons of African background adapted to the changing urban environment. The different components of the city's population are treated not just as statistical aggregates in analyses of wealth distribution and officeholding, but as social groups with distinctive histories. A longitudinal study tracing the occupational, marital, and religious histories of members of the largely Dutch old settler families over three generations provides an abundance of biographical data with which to test current hypotheses concerning the pace and timing of social and cultural change after the English conquest. Detailed social profiles of the major European immigrant groups (English, Scots, Scots-Irish, Irish, French, Germans, and Jews) and the city's large African-American group supply much-needed information on patterns of migration to early New York City, enhance our understanding of the range of cultures represented in the city, and illuminate the process of ethnic group formation in preindustrial America. Taken together, these three perspectives on the social and cultural evolution of New York City between 1664 and 1730 contribute to a substantially altered interpretation of the period's history.

The book's central thesis is that a pluralistic social order structured around Dutch, English, and French ethnoreligious communities emerged in late seventeenth-century New York City as a consequence of the juxtaposition of new immigrants and old settlers. By furnishing individuals with an institutional base in the increasingly heterogeneous society, these ethnic communities fostered a tenuous equilibrium in the city. After 1700, the ethnic basis of community life began to fracture, notwithstanding the tenacity of Dutch women in clinging to their ancestral faith. It was not until the mid-eighteenth century, however, that other forms of social identity superseded ethnicity. The success of Europeans in creating ethnic preserves in New York's fluid society is brought into relief by considering the problems blacks encountered in fabricating the bonds of community.

The book is essentially topical in nature, though it proceeds along a basically chronological line. It is organized in what is best described as a contrapuntal fashion, with chapters on society as a whole alternating with chapters on particular social groups: old settler families, European immigrants, and African-Americans.

Chapter One

NEW AMSTERDAM BECOMES NEW YORK CITY

W HEN THE ENGLISH acquired New Amsterdam in 1664 they obtained a small but vital urban community of enormous strategic and commercial potential. They also acquired a town with a unique cultural makeup and a distinctive historical evolution. Founded as a trading post of the Dutch West India Company about 1625, the settlement at the mouth of the Hudson river grew haltingly over the years, reaching a population of 1,000 in 1656 and 1,500 in 1664.[1] Despite its small size, New Amsterdam was the province's nexus of trade and government because of its location. During the almost forty years of company rule, patterns were delineated and precedents established that influenced the colonial city's subsequent course of development. Surveying the history of New Amsterdam forms a necessary prelude to constructing a profile of the local society at the time of the English takeover.[2]

The centrality of company government in molding life in New Amsterdam is incontrovertible. In the economic, political, and social realms, the omnipresent hand of the Dutch West India Company determined the parameters of legitimate activity. The Dutch West India Company was one of the great European trading companies of the seventeenth century.[3] Its commercial interests extended from the Amsterdam headquarters to distant corners of the world, its preeminent concern being the African slave trade. The colony of New Netherland was just one small component in an interdependent global empire. Despite the isolation of their colonial possessions and the primitive state of communications, the directors of the Dutch West India Company exercised close supervision over the everyday affairs of New Netherland. Local company officials reported directly to Amsterdam on a wide variety of matters and were held to account for deviations from company policy. Diplomacy and warfare were closely intertwined with commercial rivalry in the seventeenth century and consequently the ramifications of colonial administration extended far beyond the sphere of economic activity. Still, economic success was the paramount concern in the eyes of the company directors.

Since profit making was the major focus of colonial administration, the fluctuating fortunes of the company's imperial interests rather than the particular needs of New Amsterdam's economy and community guided the formulation of policy. Amsterdam officials opposed rigid economic controls even though the idea was advocated by the community's local representatives for the good of the community as a whole. The directors wished to encourage New Amsterdam merchants to engross large profits which would benefit the company.[4] The Dutch West India Company's control of the participation of New Amsterdam merchants in the slave trade similarly was geared to reaping advantage for the company.

The enhancement of company interest was accomplished not only through economic regulation but through the imposition of a centralized form of government that was authoritarian in nature. Local residents had little input into the governmental system. Decisions on issues ranging from petty to the most fundamental were handed down by the colony's director-general. On occasion, citizen advisory groups were created to bolster the government's authority at critical junctures. But these temporary advisory bodies had no regular status in the governmental hierarchy. New Amsterdam's legitimate rulers were men whose authority came from the Dutch West India Company and not from the community. Even after the privilege of municipal government was granted in 1653, the central government of the company still retained ultimate power over local affairs.[5] The company assured its supremacy in New Amsterdam by maintaining a military garrison as well as a slave labor force in the town. These tangible symbols of the coercive potential of company rule served as vivid reminders to the denizens of New Amsterdam of the limits of their freedom.

The life of New Amsterdam's inhabitants was also circumscribed by the uncertainties of imperial politics. Though powerless to control the outcome of remote struggles between England and the Netherlands, the town's residents were very much a part of the ongoing Anglo-Dutch rivalry for the prizes of the Atlantic empire.[6] The presence of the expanding New England colonies on the perimeters of Dutch territory, as well as the incorporation of English towns on Long Island within the jurisdiction of New Netherland, demonstrated the numerical superiority of the English. Tension over Indian relations periodically energized the latent distrust between New Englanders and the Dutch. Although the New Netherland government attempted to pursue a conciliatory policy toward its New England neighbors, the precarious position of the weaker Dutch settlements was apparent to the residents of New Amsterdam.[7] Whatever the balance of power in Europe, on the North American continent the subjects of the Netherlands were in a disadvantaged position.

Although for the majority of its existence New Amsterdam was not a discrete political entity, it still possessed a separate history as a society. For the first twenty years or so of its existence, the New Amsterdam settlement was not much more than a primitive trading post providing basic services. Under the administrations of Peter Minuit (1626–1632), Bastiaen Jansen Krol (1632–1633), Wouter van Twiller (1633–1637), and Willem Kieft (1638–1647), little progress was made toward establishing a permanent community. Kieft's disastrous Indian policy kept the town in perpetual turmoil for most of his administration and retarded social development even further. It was only with the advent of Petrus (Peter) Stuyvesant, whose tenure in office extended from 1647 until the English conquest in 1664, that steps were taken to buttress the local social order and give it a measure of stability. Greater interest in New Netherland on the part of the Dutch West India Company, the expansion of commerce, and the influx of new immigrants, particularly after 1657, all combined to usher New Amsterdam into a new era.[8] Citizens' recognition of the achievement of a semblance of permanence in the community prompted independent political activity designed to obtain representation in the governmental process. The company's grant of municipal government in 1653, however minimal its power, marked the maturation of New Amsterdam society.

New Amsterdam's social patterns reflected the fact of company control. The makeup of the population as well as the institutional framework of the community were both products of company decisions. The Dutch West India Company's perpetual need for settlers for the colony was responsible for the diversity of New Amsterdam's population. The relatively satisfactory conditions of life in the Netherlands in the mid-seventeenth century resulted in a dearth of prospective emigrants to New Netherland, impelling the company to accept colonists of other European nationalities.[9] Expediency rather than devotion to principle dictated the tolerance of diversity in New Amsterdam.[10] In this respect, New Amsterdam mirrored old Amsterdam, which was noted in the seventeenth century as a refuge for persons of diverse backgrounds and creeds.[11] Petrus Stuyvesant's plan to expel the Jews from New Amsterdam was countermanded by the Amsterdam directors, who argued that population increase would lead to greater profits and therefore was more important than social exclusiveness.[12]

The company's need for labor also prompted the institutionalization of slavery in New Amsterdam. The Dutch West India Company was a primary purveyor of African slaves in the seventeenth century and the transplantation of slave labor to New Netherland is explicable in light of the inadequate supply of European workers.[13] Inaugurated under company auspices, slaveholding soon permeated the private sector of the community. At the time of the English conquest in 1664, New Amsterdam's African population, which by then included some free blacks, composed between 20 and 25 percent of the local population.[14]

The expansion of Dutch settlement on Manhattan Island also was responsible for the obliteration of the island's native population. Prior to Dutch occupation, Manhattan was inhabited by two Indian bands of the Algonquian family. The upper part of the island was inhabited by the Rechgawawanc and the lower tip of the island by the Canarsee.[15] Dutch-Indian conflict marked New Amsterdam's history and the highpoint of Dutch aggression against the Indians was Kieft's War of 1643–1646.

However, by the time the English took over New Amsterdam in 1664, the local Indian population no longer posed any threat to European settlers.

Decisions made by the Dutch West India Company determined the institutional contours of New Amsterdam society. The company's official sponsorship of the Dutch Reformed church set the community's religious life within a traditional framework of church-state cooperation.[16] This interlocking relationship between company administration and church formed the basis for governance in New Amsterdam. The regulation of morality was a joint task of both church and state. Yet the church in New Amsterdam was not subordinate to the state. Even though it received financial support from the Dutch West India Company, the colonial church was under the jurisdiction of the Classis of Amsterdam, and its ministers were subject to that body. During the period of Dutch rule, five "Dominies" served the church in New Amsterdam. The church was organized in 1628 by Jonas Michaelius, who served till 1632. He was followed by Everardus Bogardus (1633–1647), Johannes Backerus (1647–1649), Johannes Megapolensis (1649–1670) and Samuel Drisius (1652–1673).[17] These clergymen played a crucial role in the community, not only as spiritual advisers but as functionaries performing the necessary services of communal life. Charitable and educational activities also fell within the purview of the clergy.

Despite the diversity of New Amsterdam's population, religious institutions other than the Dutch Reformed church were denied official status. For over a decade, Lutherans sought leave to worship openly, only to have their efforts thwarted by the intransigent stance of Petrus Stuyvesant and the Dutch Reformed clergy, whose policies were supported by authorities in Amsterdam. The Lutheran church in the Netherlands, its own status insecure, proved ineffective in aiding its coreligionists overseas.[18] After they held services in their homes in 1655, they were barred from doing so in the future; and when a pastor was sent by the Lutheran consistory in Amsterdam in 1657, he was prevented from carrying out his duties and ultimately deported.[19] The discouragement felt by the town's numerous Lutherans after years of strife was captured by a recent immigrant who wrote to the Lutheran Classis of Amsterdam in 1663.

> Having come here a little over two years ago . . . I found here a large congregation adhering to our Christian Unaltered Augsburg Confession, and although hope among us has not lessened, . . . the fact is, alas, that many of the congregation begin to stray like sheep and that they do not come together here to offer any sign of devotion, much less trust themselves jointly to sign a petition to your honors, for fear of being betrayed.[20]

New Amsterdam's Jews, though detested by Stuyvesant and the Dutch Reformed clergy, were more successful in gaining the limited freedom to worship in their own homes. The first arrivals of 1654 and subsequent newcomers, never numbering more than fifty, gradually won permission from the grudging Stuyvesant to trade, to participate in various facets of town life, and to hold religious services in private.[21] In this case, the pressure brought to bear on company officials by influential Amsterdam Jewish merchants was the decisive factor.[22]

At the time of the English conquest, most inhabitants of New Amsterdam lacked a strong identification with the company government. Dissatisfaction with the company's policies, personnel, and system of government, as well as the growing perception of the tenuous position of the colony vis-à-vis the English, fostered an attitude of pragmatism toward the ruling authorities. Loyalty to the company administration was also tempered by the materialistic orientation of the town dwellers. That a shift in allegiance was not problematic for New Amsterdam's residents is demonstrated by the fact that the local citizenry was unwilling to bear arms to defend the sovereignty of the Dutch West India Company in 1664.

Yet if ties to the company government were attenuated, the same cannot be said for ties to the homeland and to the local community. Although it had never been a homogeneous society, New Amsterdam had always existed under the aegis of the Dutch and had been dominated by men, ideas, and institutions imported from the Netherlands.[23] A variant of Dutch culture had indeed taken root and was flourishing in New Amsterdam. Although the sources of transatlantic replenishment were curtailed in subsequent years, the imprint of Dutch society and culture was not eradicated at the advent of English rule. Links with the Netherlands remained an important facet of life in the city.

Ties to the local community were even stronger as they were undergirded by economic foundations and family connections. An embryonic social order had developed in New Amsterdam and local families had a large stake in preserving their way of life. The English assumption of power under the proprietary grant given the Duke of York by his brother, King Charles II, created an unprecendented situation for the local residents, threatening not only their material interests but their social and cultural hegemony.[24]

The boundaries of chronology serve to impose order on the great mass of evidence that constitutes the raw material of historical inquiry. Yet chronological demarcations present hazards for the student of continuity and change, for the signal events that shape historical periodization, whether military, political, or economic, cut across the fundamental social processes that structure the ongoing life of any community. Confronted by the task of reconciling the occurrence of great events with the relentless stream of everyday life, most historians have chosen to focus on either events or social processes. The resulting disjunction between public and private worlds in historical works often makes it difficult to understand decisive episodes in past societies.

An altered perspective—that of people experiencing events—enables us to achieve a more rounded view of social change. The rationale for this approach proceeds from the proposition that the most basic chronological unit, the human lifetime, transcends all categories predicated on sequences of signal events. Though biographers have recognized the possibilities inherent in the life span as a framework for ordering the flow of events, investigators of societies undergoing change persist in emphasizing institutions rather than people.[25] The history of seventeenth-century New York City illustrates this tendency.

The transformation of New Amsterdam into an English city in the late seventeenth century traditionally has been viewed in the light of institutional modification. Generalizations on the substitution of English customs and structures for preexisting Dutch ones inform all historical treatments of the subject, yet the evidence on which such interpretations rests is seriously limited because the definition of change used is restricted to the study of formal institutions. No scholar has traced the careers of the inhabitants of New Amsterdam after imperial reorganization was begun. In what ways did the alteration in government influence the future of those caught in the middle of this moment? How did the changes initiated at the top by the new rulers impinge on the life patterns of those most intimately affected by the shift in the locus of authority? By centering attention on the men and women who lived through this episode of crisis, a fuller perspective on the problem is attainable. The following profile of the men of New Amsterdam at the outset of the English period establishes the base for measuring change and continuity in New York City society after the English assumption of power in 1664.

When the English captured New Amsterdam in 1664, the population of the city was approximately 1,500, as estimated by a group of the residents themselves in a petition to the director-general and council urging capitulation to the invaders.[26] This number probably did not include the approximately 300 African slaves and 75 free blacks in the city.[27] However, the figure of 250 able-bodied men can be adjudged fairly accurate, for it is possible to recover the names of most of these men. Dubbed for shorthand purposes the "conquest cohort,"[28] this group supplies the core for the following analysis of the configuration of New Amsterdam society in 1664 as well as the starting point for a longitudinal study of the future life patterns of these men and their descendants. The procedures employed in obtaining the names of the cohort members require explanation.

Preserved in the New York records are three roughly contemporaneous listings of inhabitants of New Amsterdam / New York City in 1664–65. The first of these, dated September 5, 1664, is the above-mentioned petition, signed by 93 men. The second list contains 251 names of men who took the oath of allegiance to the English in October 1664. These men were primarily residents of New Amsterdam, though some signers came from other areas in the colony. The third roll of inhabitants is a tax list of April 1665 which gives graduated assessments for 254 people in New Amsterdam, including women householders. The tax was instituted to pay for the quartering of the English troops brought to New York.[29]

Using these three lists as the sources for identifying the conquest cohort, a master list was compiled that eliminated duplications of names. After careful cross-checking, the total number of persons mentioned emerged as 350.[30] The master list of 350 persons was then subjected to further refinement in order to remove two categories of persons. Eliminated first were those persons whose primary residence was outside New Amsterdam but whose names appeared on one or more of the lists. Twenty people were placed in this category, although it is probable that a number of those later designated as unidentifiable actually fall into this classification. Next, fifteen women were removed from the list in order to preserve the uniformity of the definition of the cohort and to make possible later comparative studies of fathers, sons, and grandsons. All of these women, many of them widows, appeared on the tax list of 1665. The master list of 315 individuals was then denoted as the conquest cohort of adult males in New Amsterdam at the time of the English takeover. The contemporary figure of 250 able-bodied men, presumably an underestimate because of the nature of the document, comports well with the figure of 315 arrived at here.

All members of the conquest cohort could not be identified and it seemed best to separate out those for whom little or no information was retrieved at the outset. Difficulties of Dutch nomenclature, compounded by the frequency with which certain names were used, explain many of these cases.* Other instances were probably due to the presence of transients or strangers in the community. And, of course, the layers of time have successfully obliterated the traces of other individuals. Keeping in mind all these qualifications, the proportion of identifiable men is still very high. Of 315 men, 222 (71 percent) were identified in enough essential respects to be retained in the cohort group. This sample of 71 percent of the conquest cohort forms the basis of all subsequent generalizations concerning the composition and characteristics of the cohort. In other words, when the conquest cohort is referred to hereafter it is actually these 222 men who are being studied.[31]

Who were these men living on the island of Manhattan in 1664? How had they come to share this episode in the Anglo-Dutch contest for em-

---

* Variations in the spelling of Dutch names in this book reflect customary practice.

pire? Were they recent arrivals, caught by chance in the confrontation, or men with a substantial stake in the community? Despite frequent assumptions that this outpost of the West India Company was subject to a high degree of population turnover, the evidence points in another direction. A large number of men in the conquest cohort had deep roots in the society. Ninety-seven men, almost 44 percent of the cohort, had been in New Amsterdam for ten years or longer. Seventeen were truly pioneers, having moved to the colony before 1640, while another 45 had come during the 1640s. Among these early settlers were surgeon Hans Kierstede, brewer Isaac de Forest, cooper Jan Janszen Bresteede, glazier Evert Duycking, and merchant Johannes de Peyster. The first couple married in the Dutch Reformed Church at New Amsterdam on December 11, 1639, Egbert van Borsum, from Embden, and Annetje Hendricks of Amsterdam, still resided in the town. Earlier a ship captain for the Dutch West India Company, Van Borsum was now a ferrymaster. At least four of his sons—Hermanus, Cornelis, Hendrick, and Tymon—baptized in the Dutch church between 1640 and 1651, would remain in the city, marry, and raise families of their own. A few cohort members had actually been born in New Amsterdam. Stephanus van Cortlandt, the eldest son of Oloff Stevensen van Cortlandt, had been baptized in the New Amsterdam church on May 10, 1643, and had just come of age to witness the Dutch loss of New Netherland with his father.

Of the 56 percent (125 men) of the cohort who arrived in the nine years preceding the conquest, the greatest number (84) came between 1656 and 1660. Men such as baker Laurens van der Spiegel, blacksmith Cornelis Clopper, tailor Boele Roelofsen, mason Paulus Turck, and sword cutler Hendrick Bosch cast their lot in New Amsterdam during these years.

Most of the members of the cohort were married and many were in the process of raising families. Though a good number of the cohort members were already married at the time of their arrival in the colony, many wed after establishing residence in the community. Some of these were remarriages of men whose wives had died while residing in New Amsterdam. But 98 (44 percent) of the 222 cohort members were married for the first time in the local Dutch church in the period through 1665. This fact alone suggests that there was no dearth of single women in New Amsterdam and that a sufficient supply of potential marriage partners was available for both single men and widowers. The children of these unions were baptized in the Dutch church also. Yet marriage and baptism in the church was possible without membership in the communion.

The Dutch Reformed Church, New Amsterdam's established church, by no means included the entire community in its membership. Fewer than half of the men in the cohort were admitted as members of the New Amsterdam congregation in the years through 1665. Of the 222 cohort members, 104 (47 percent) were church members when the English assumed control. Another 23 became communicants subsequent to the conquest, but almost half of the men never joined the church. Of this group of nonmembers, however, 17 were acknowledged Lutherans and one was a Jew. Thus, 145 men in the conquest cohort (65 percent) were religiously affiliated during their residence in the city. Additionally, the wives of 19 of the nonmembers were admitted to church membership either before or after the conquest. Therefore, 164 (74 percent) of the cohort families were represented by at least one member in a local religious body.

Church membership was not congruent with ethnic identity in New Amsterdam. Admission to the Dutch Reformed church was never restricted to persons from the Netherlands and the register of communicants includes scores of people born in other parts of Europe as well as several people of African descent. The ethnic origins of cohort members were similarly diverse. Of the 222 men in the group, 168 (76 percent) were Dutch, 24 (11 percent) were German, 15 (7 percent) were French, and 10 (4.5 percent) were English. The remaining five men included three Scandinavians (a Swede, a Norwegian, and a Finn), a Jew, and an Irishman. The fact that nearly one-quarter of the cohort was not Dutch in origin is not surprising in light of systematic research on the geographical background of immigrants to New Netherland that demonstrates the heterogeneity of the incoming population.[32] Two points must be kept in mind, however. The fluidity of political boundaries in the seventeenth century most likely caused some culturally Dutch immigrants to be categorized as members of other nationalities.[33] Moreover, the seventeenth-century Netherlands, as the most open society in Europe, was a magnet for refugees as well as the restless and ambitious.[34] Some of the foreign-born men who ultimately settled in New Amsterdam had first tried their fortunes in Holland and emigrated from there, having already gained familiarity with Dutch culture. Theophilus Ellsworth, a mariner, was born in Bristol, England, but moved to Amsterdam, where he married in 1647 and his first child was born.[35] About 1650, the young family headed to New Amsterdam.

Dutch culture and institutions held sway in the town and foreign-born residents tended to adopt the ways of the majority.[36] As the only church with official standing, the Dutch Reformed church played an integrative role in the community, registering marriages and baptisms for nonmembers. Germans, Scandinavians, French, and English no doubt attended Dutch-language services in the Reformed church on occasion since alternative forms of worship were prohibited. The dissemination of Dutch in the small settlement is attested to by the fact that when the Lutherans, many of whom were German, requested a pastor in 1653, they asked for a Hollander "inasmuch as the Dutch language is most commonly used here and our children are also instructed therein."[37] The linguistic homogenization of the population facilitated ties across cultural boundaries.

Intermarriage also served to counteract potential ethnic friction resulting from the dissimilar origins of the inhabitants. Though endogamous marriage might have been the ideal, unions between members of different ethnic groups were not uncommon in New Amsterdam. Samuel Edsall of Reading, Berkshire, England, married Jannetje Wessels of Arnhem, Gelderland, the Netherlands, in 1655 in the town's Dutch Reformed Church. In the same year, a young German named Nicholas de Meyer, of Hamburg, took as his wife Lydia van Dyck of Utrecht. Analysis of the marriages of the conquest cohort performed in the Dutch church at New Amsterdam through 1665 discloses that 28 of 110 (25 percent) were exogamous. The West India Company's continual need to attract immigrants to the colony of New Netherland had resulted in the presence of a substantial number of non-Dutch in the colony and specifically in New Amsterdam. This de facto state of ethnic pluralism was reflected in the marriage patterns of the community. Ethnic solidarity, while theoretically desirable, was not possible in New Amsterdam. The company's willingness to tolerate all nationalities in its colony was paralleled by the acceptance of ethnic intermarriage in New Amsterdam as a necessary way of life.

While New Amsterdam was a highly differentiated community with respect to ethnicity, its economic structure was still fairly simple. The primary staple of the colony was the fur trade, with agriculture as an important adjunct activity. The proliferation of merchants and traders in the small town of New Amsterdam reflected the commercial orientation of the port as well as the potential opportunities for enrichment afforded by the fur trade. The prominence of private traders such as Govert Loockermans and Cornelis Steenwyck (figure 1), however, did not diminish the role of the company as controller of the economy.[38] The intrusion of both the company and local administration into the labor market was a defining feature of the town's economic life. The large number of workers and soldiers employed by the agencies of government illustrates the interdependence of economy and government in this preindustrial society. The occupations of the conquest cohort, consolidated into major classifications, are presented in table 1–1.[39]

Insight into the wealth structure of New Amsterdam is restricted by the limitations of source material. No assessment roll covers the entire conquest cohort. The only available gauge of the distribution of wealth in the city is the 1665 tax list which gives graduated assessments for 254 people, including fifteen women. The distribution of wealth based on this tax list is seen in table 1–2. The highest tax assessments, those of 4 and 3 florins, were applicable to slightly less than 10 percent of the community. This elite controlled the major portion of the city's wealth. On the other end of

Figure 1. Cornelis Steenwyck (1626–1684), a leading New Amsterdam merchant, served as burgomaster under the Dutch and mayor under the English. Though possessed of a great fortune at his death, Steenwyck left no children. Courtesy of The New-York Historical Society, N.Y.C.

the spectrum, more than 20 percent of the persons rated were assessed nothing at all, pointing to the large number of inhabitants living at the subsistence level. Another index of wealth in New Amsterdam is slave ownership. The members of the economic elite were accustomed to using slave labor. Of the 25 persons in the top 10 percent of the wealth structure, at least fourteen (56 percent) were slaveowners. Slaveowners among the other 230 taxed inhabitants were far less numerous proportionately,

TABLE 1–1
Occupations of the 222 Conquest Cohort Members

Occupation	Number (and percent of cohort members)	Occupation	Number (and percent of cohort members)
Merchants & retailers	35 (16)	Cloth & leather workers	22 (10)
Merchants	22	Shoemakers & tanners	9
Small traders	13	Saddlers	1
Professionals	31 (14)	Tailors	9
Surgeons	4	Hatters	3
Ministers	3	Wood, metal, & stone workers	40 (18)
Lawyers	1	Carpenters	17
Schoolmasters	2	Turners	3
Notaries public	2	Coopers	4
Clerks	3	Masons	7
Company officials	5	Blacksmiths	5
Measurers, etc.	5	Glaziers	4
Soldiers	4	Laborers	19 (8)
Service trades	44 (20)	Carmen	4
Tavernkeepers	11	City laborers	9
Bakers	11	Messengers, etc.	6
Brewers	8	Unknown	7 (3)
Butchers	4		
Farmers	7		
Millers	3		
Maritime trades	24 (11)		
Mariners	17		
Ship carpenters	5		
Fishermen	2		

Note: All tables in this book are for New York City.

TABLE 1–2
Distribution of Wealth Based on the
1665 Tax List

Tax Rate (in florins)	Number of Taxpayers (out of 254 total)	Percentage
4.00	14	5.5
3.00	10	4.0
2.10	9	3.5
2.00	72	28.0
1.10	13	5.0
1.00	82	32.0
– fl.	54	21.0

although some are unknown because of fragmentary records. Only 16 (7 percent) have been identified.[40] The occupational makeup of the economic elite reflected the commercial aspect of the society as 16 of the 24 men (two-thirds of the group) in the upper tenth of society have been identified as either merchants or traders. Three men were government officials, two were in the professions, two were brewers, and the occupation of one is unknown.

Since New Netherland was the possession of a commercial company, the governmental structure differed from other colonies. At New Amsterdam, company officials and agents coexisted with local officers. Ultimate authority lay with the director-general and council of New Netherland, who were directly responsible to the directors of the Dutch West India Company in Amsterdam. In 1653, the privilege of a separate municipal administration had been granted to New Amsterdam. The major offices of burgomasters and *schepens* roughly paralleled those of mayor and aldermen under the English system. These officers were appointed by the director-general from a slate of nominees presented by the incumbents themselves. Two burgomasters and five *schepens* held office each year from 1653 through 1664, thus creating a possible 84 positions. The holders of these offices composed the political elite of New Amsterdam. A total of 28 men occupied all the burgomaster and *schepen* offices from 1653 through 1664, making the average tenure of office three terms during this twelve-year time span. Whether because officeholders were appointed or the local population was unstable, there was a significant amount of rotation in office in New Amsterdam.

Of the 28 men who constituted New Amsterdam's political elite, 23 were members of the conquest cohort. Twelve of these 23 men were also members of the economic elite. Moreover, twelve of the 24 men in the economic elite were members of the political elite. In short, there was a considerable overlap between these two groups of men, and given the somewhat arbitrary nature of the definitions imposed here, it seems safe to say that about 35 men wielded power in the local society.

The members of the conquest cohort were at various stages of their lives when the English captured New Netherland. Some had spent many years in New Amsterdam and were approaching old age. Others were young, vigorous men with aspirations for fortune and power, willing to chance any new administrative order. Still others were men of middle years, set in their ways, with families, interests, and responsibilities. Most had ties across the Atlantic and were in communication with family and friends through various means. A number had made trips back to "Fatherland," but had returned to New Amsterdam. What the future portended for these men was not made clear by the immediate context of surrender. The leniency of the terms imposed by the English belied the possible disruption that might result from a new government. However peaceful the cession of territory or conciliatory the articles of capitulation, the imposition of an alien executive power alters the entire matrix through which activities must be conducted. At a deeper level, an entirely distinct order of changes might also follow the transfer of sovereignty. The social counterparts of institutional change would emerge in rates of population turnover, patterns of marriage, church membership, and population composition, and in the nature of the society's stratification system. Scrutinizing the subsequent careers of cohort members, their sons, and grandsons lays the groundwork for a comprehensive picture of the development of New York City society in the seventeenth and early eighteenth centuries, and thus renders explicit the degree of continuity and change in these years. From the perspective of Whitehall Palace in London, the transformation of New Amsterdam into an English community was accomplished as soon as the capitulation of Petrus Stuyvesant had been recorded. For the local inhabitants, the process of transformation took many years to unwind in all its manifestations. The emergence of a distinctive provincial society at New York City in the eighteenth century was the result of three generations of confrontation and accommodation.

Chapter Two

THE SECOND GENERATION

CAUGHT UP in the crosscurrents of Anglo-Dutch rivalry, the inhabitants of New Amsterdam at the time of the English conquest in 1664 were faced with the choice of remaining in the small settlement on Manhattan Island or removing elsewhere. Since the right to leave the new English colony was guaranteed by the articles of surrender, a viable alternative existed for these settlers, contingent only on economic ability and personal option. Political pressures were not determinative in the decision-making process, as the experience of former Director-General Petrus Stuyvesant illustrates. Despite his removal from power and the need to undertake a journey to Holland to explain and defend his behavior at the surrender, Stuyvesant chose to return to New York City and make it his permanent home. No more cogent testimony of the prevailing atmosphere of toleration under the early English administrations is available. Yet although the circumstances of the conquest did not require any massive uprooting of the settled population, some residents of New Amsterdam decided to depart. The fact that the majority of New Amsterdam's inhabitants chose not to uproot themselves, however, is more significant for understanding the development of New York City society in the last third of the seventeenth century. The old settlers who stayed in New York City constituted a bridge between the Dutch and English eras in the city's history. Both for residents and newcomers, these preconquest families stood as islands of stability in a shifting social mosaic. In this chapter, the conquest cohort members and their sons form the core of an analysis of the structural basis of continuity in New York City in the latter third of the seventeenth century.

Though the conquest cohort is an extremely large and undoubtedly representative sample of the adult male population of New York City in 1664, for a number of reasons it cannot be viewed as an all-inclusive category. Failure to appear on one of the three lists used to delineate the cohort, and thus the subjects for longitudinal analysis, resulted from a variety of possible circumstances. Temporary residence elsewhere in New Netherland might have entailed absence from the listings. For example, Balthazar Bayard, who by all standards was a preconquest New Yorker, was omitted from the cohort because for a few brief years around 1664 he was living in the newly founded Dutch town of Bergen, later part of New Jersey.

Balthazar, a brewer, and the brother of cohort member Nicholas Bayard, had come to New Amsterdam with his mother and brothers in 1647 and had grown up there. In 1664 he married Marritje Loockermans, the daughter of cohort member Govert Loockermans, a wealthy merchant. By 1672, Balthazar had resumed residence in New York City, but his brief time in Bergen eliminated him from the cohort.

Another category of persons not included in the cohort consists of the underaged sons of New Amsterdam settlers who had died prior to 1664. Raised in the town either by widowed mothers or court-appointed guardians, these second-generation sons were certainly preconquest New Yorkers, even though they did not appear on any of the lists. The Delanoy brothers, Abraham and Peter, exemplify this pattern. Their father, Abraham Delanoy, had died before the conquest. In 1663 their widowed mother had remarried Frederick Gysbertszen van den Bergh, a member of the conquest cohort. Although born in Harlem in the Netherlands, both boys had been in New Amsterdam at least since 1657, when their father was registered as a burgher. In 1680, Peter Delanoy married the widow of Isaac Bedloo, a cohort member, and in 1681 his brother Abraham married the widow of Evert Duycking, Jr., the son of cohort member Evert Duycking, Sr. One other young man who falls into this category was Albertus Ringo, the son of Philip Janszen Ringo, an early town resident. Native to New Amsterdam, Albertus had been baptized in the Dutch church on July 9, 1656, and was a cordwainer by trade. In 1679 he married another native New Yorker, Jannetje Stoutenburg, daughter of cohort member Pieter Stoutenburg. Neither his deceased father, nor eight-year-old Albertus, could have been on the cohort list, yet by all accounts Albertus Ringo was a second-generation New Yorker.

New immigrants to New Amsterdam may have avoided representation on the contemporary listings of inhabitants because of their recent arrival in the community. Other persons may simply have escaped the scrutiny of officials. In addition, the lack of a surname at this time may prevent the proper identification of certain individuals. For example, Peter Jansen Mesier, a ship carpenter, had resided in New Amsterdam as early as 1659, when his daughter Annetie was baptized in the Dutch church.[1] Yet there is no way of knowing which, if any, of the Peter Jansens on the cohort lists was the Peter Jansen Mesier who is found on subsequent New York City rolls. Thus, omission of preconquest New Yorkers from the cohort sample was both possible and inevitable. It deserves renewed emphasis, then, that the conquest cohort is an analytic concept rather than an exact replication of social reality. With these strictures in mind, the following analysis of cohort fathers and sons is designed to probe the foundations of continuity in the society of New York City.

How many cohort members remained in New York City following the

English accession to power in 1664? In the dozen years between 1664 and 1676, the size of the cohort diminished rapidly as a result of emigration and mortality. In successive decades, gradual and expected attrition further reduced the size of the cohort, so that by the end of the century, only a small number of the conquest generation was still alive in New York City.

In 1676, twelve years after the English conquest, at least 127 members of the 222 members of the conquest cohort (57 percent) were still resident in New York City. Moreover, 45 cohort members (20 percent) had died between 1665 and 1676. Of the 20 persons unaccounted for, some had undoubtedly died, others most likely were still in the community but are not traceable, and the remainder was probably among the group of emigrants from New York City. At least 26 cohort members (12 percent) are known to have departed from the city after 1664, some to Europe and others to various colonial regions. Since emigration from New York was a viable option under the peace terms, certain individuals were bound to avail themselves of it. Evaluation of the evidence on emigration during this period, however, suggests that out-migration from New York City was not a dominant force in reshaping the city's social structure.

The major stimulant to emigration in this era of New York City's history was the instability of the governmental structure. Although the English captured New Netherland in 1664, the colony reverted to the Dutch in 1673–74.[2] This brief phase of renewed Dutch control and the subsequent English reoccupation may have catalyzed proclivities toward migration that had remained dormant during the first era of English administration. The Reverend William van Nieuwenhuysen reported to the Classis of Amsterdam on July 26, 1674, that "during the last four weeks, in apprehension of a change of governors, certain of our members have moved away, as some of your Rev. Body will have learned from the letters of dismission exhibited to you by them."[3]

Prior to 1674, however, currents of emigration were equally discernible. A list of passengers returning to Holland at the end of 1664 on the ship *Unity* contains the names of 24 men, some accompanied by families and servants. While six cohort members appear on this list, the majority of travelers presumably resided in other areas of the colony.[4] Attractive prospects in the newly opened colony of Carolina may also have lured a few New York City residents southward. At the end of 1671, Governor Francis Lovelace issued a proclamation relating to proposed emigration to Carolina with an order that emigrants obtain passes before leaving the colony. There is extant one list of passengers permitted to sail to Port Royal in Carolina consisting of eighteen men with dependents and Negroes.[5] Only two names are those of New York City residents although it is possible that other New Yorkers did relocate in Carolina. John Locke, whose interest in promoting Carolina colonization may have influenced his estimates, reported in November 1671 that two hundred families were ready to leave New York for Carolina if they had convenient transportation. By January 1672 Locke noted that "70 persons from Barbadoes and New York come to settle, and others to view the country. The New York people planted on a creek 8 miles from Charles Town, nearer the mouth of the Ashley River." Furthermore, he stated that "six hundred people [were] resolved to come from New York," primarily because of the taxes and the climate.[6] Investigating the experiences of those cohort members who left New York City during these early years elucidates patterns of emigration from New York City.

Emigration was not confined to any portion of the social spectrum, as both wealthy persons and people of modest circumstances departed from the city. However, cohort members who returned to Europe were likely to come from the topmost levels of the social structure. Although lack of evidence concerning obscure individuals may be partially responsible for this conclusion, the biographies of those persons known to have emigrated to Holland locate most of them in the upper ranks of New Amsterdam society. Men with a great deal at stake or with strong ties to the Dutch West India Company were most inclined to seek the familiar security of European homes. Of the fifteen cohort members who returned to Europe, only two were neither company employees nor merchants.

Denys Isacksen van Hartogvelt, a house-carpenter from Wyck bij Duurstede, arrived in New Amsterdam in 1659, married the same year, and began to raise a family. In 1667 his name was added to the membership rolls of the local Dutch church. Yet sometime shortly thereafter, the whole family moved to Amsterdam, where Hartogvelt died about 1681. When Hartogvelt's widow passed away in 1688 in Amsterdam, some friends recorded a deposition in behalf of the couple's three orphaned sons, Joannis, aged 17, Steven, aged 14, and Jacobus, aged 11. A search of New York City baptismal records reveals that none of these children was born there. It can be inferred then that by 1671 the Hartogvelts had left New York City for the Netherlands. The deposition made for these sons in fact states that their parents first lived in "New York on Manhattan (then called Nieuw Amsterdam) and later in Amsterdam."[7]

One of those persons testifying in support of the Hartogvelt children was "Annetje Minnes, 55 years old, wife of Jacob Danielse Pontianes, sergeant." As this deponent had known the Hartogvelts in New Amsterdam, there is no difficulty in identifying her as the widow Annetje Minnen who had married Jacob Danielsen, a widower, in the New Amsterdam Dutch church in 1661. Moreover, Jacob Danielsen (minus surname) was in fact a member of the conquest cohort. He resided in New York City until 1669 when his imminent departure is noted in the city records because of another man's desire to have his job: "Jacob Barentsen Kool requests by petition, that as Jacob Daniels, at present porter at the Weigh house is about to depart in the ship ready to sail, he the petitr. may be Admitted in his place as City labourer."[8]

Hartogvelt and Danielsen were not representative of the emigrants to the Netherlands. The other thirteen men who left New York City for Holland had much greater prestige and standing in the community. One was Samuel Megapolensis, a minister, and the son of the venerable local minister, Johannes Megapolensis. Extensively educated, both at Harvard and in the Netherlands at Utrecht and Leyden, young Samuel, who was 30 years old at the time of the conquest and only recently returned from his educational venture abroad, declined to cast his lot with the settlers on Manhattan Island and departed for Europe in 1669. Envisioning a more distinguished career in the homeland, Samuel occupied the pastorate at Wieringerwaerd, where his father had served, and from 1685 to his death in 1700 was minister of the Scotch Church at Dordrecht. Another emigrant who was tied to the Dutch West India Company was Cornelis van Ruyven, the former provincial secretary, who returned to Holland after the second English occupation.

Paulus Leendertsen van der Grift and Jeronimus Ebbingh, two members of the community's political and economic elite, also departed for the Netherlands, Van der Grift in 1671 and Ebbingh about 1676. Van der Grift, a ship captain and merchant who had been in New Amsterdam since 1647, was among the wealthiest citizens in town and had held the highest political office of burgomaster six times between 1657 and 1664. He became an ironmonger in Amsterdam where he died about 1680. Although he chose to leave New York, Van der Grift never severed his ties to the city. Both of his daughters were married to city residents. Maria van der Grift was the wife of Gerrit van Tricht, a merchant, and a member of the conquest cohort. Her sister, Margrietje, was married to Jacob Maurits, a skipper in the transatlantic commerce between Amsterdam and New York. Jacob's brother-in-law, Gerrit van der Grift, a mariner, sailed with him on a few voyages to New York, but signed on as a second mate with the Dutch East India Company in 1682 and perished soon after in the East Indies. Leenard and Johannes, the other two sons of Paulus Leendertsen van der Grift, resided in the Netherlands. However, Jacob Leendertsen van der Grift, the brother of Paulus, and also a cohort member, remained in New York City after the English takeover and was still living there in 1686.

Jeronimus Ebbingh, another wealthy and successful merchant, was born in Hamburg in 1614 and came to New Amsterdam about 1657, shortly before his marriage to Johanna de Laet, the widowed daughter of Johannes de Laet, who before his death had been a director of the Dutch West India Company as well as one of the partners in the colony of Rensselaerswyck. After the second period of English rule commenced, the Ebbinghs decided to relocate in Amsterdam where some of Mrs. Ebbingh's children by her former marriage were living. Jeronimus Ebbingh continued as a merchant in Amsterdam, where he died in 1691. Until 1686 he had retained a piece of property at Albany.

The majority of emigrants to the Netherlands were of some stature in the community, whether by virtue of wealth or ties to the West India Company government. The same cannot be said for those cohort members who resettled elsewhere in New York or in another colony. Their removal stemmed more from personal motivation than dissatisfaction with the new political order. In some cases, preexistent interests, whether family or business ties, dictated their moves. In other instances, either restlessness or ambition seems the primary impetus for migration. Family ties prompted the relocation of Claes van Elslandt, Jr., court messenger and undertaker. Claes moved to Albany in the early 1670s to be near his sister Catalyntie and brother-in-law, Jacob Abrahamsen van Deursen, a cooper. The death of Claes van Elslandt, Sr., at about this time suggests that the rationale for Claes Jr.'s move was a desire to be near his kinfolk. The yearning for a more secure and peaceful existence seems to have been the uppermost consideration in the mind of Hendrick Jansen van der Vin, who removed to the village of Harlem on upper Manhattan Island about 1670. Although he had been a merchant and had served two terms as a *schepen* of New Amsterdam in 1657 and 1659, Van der Vin elected to retreat from the mainstream of city life. At Harlem, he served as town clerk from 1672 until his death in 1684. Martinus Hoffman, a younger man who tried various occupations, first removed to Albany and then to Kingston, where he settled and rose to prominence. Hoffman typifies the emigrant who was searching for challenging opportunities in a less restricted atmosphere.

The migration from New York City that occurred in the years between 1664 and 1676 was far from a mass phenomenon. Individual decisions premised on realistic assessment of possibilities in the altered environment resulted in various instances of relocation. This pattern is best defined in terms of two small "waves" of emigration following each of the English takeovers in 1664 and 1674, with individual cases of migration spaced out at intervals between these years. The size of the emigration was not considerable, as no more than 15 percent of the cohort group could have left the city. The potential for uprooting oneself from the community was greatest during this period and the likelihood that a cohort member would move from New York City after 1676 was slight. Decisions concerning emigration were taken during this era. After 1676, the time for change had passed for the men of the cohort.

If the years from 1664 to 1676 were critical in defining the scope and pattern of cohort emigration from New York City, then they were equally significant in another respect. At least 20 percent of the cohort died during this time, a greater number than was lost through emigration. The mortality among cohort members can be linked to two interrelated factors, the epidemics of 1668 and 1669, and the age structure of the cohort population.

In 1668 and again in 1669, epidemics of unidentified fevers invaded the small community of New York City. The seriousness of the 1668 outbreak, which may have been typhoid or malaria, can be inferred from the decision of Governor Lovelace to proclaim "days of humiliation" on September 8 and 22, 1668, to atone for the sins that he believed had brought the epidemic on the populace. Lovelace's description of the illness is brief but illuminating:

> Not onely the Land in Generall but this Citty of New yorke in perticuler lyes now groaning undr the afflicting hand of Gods just Judgment in suffering his Minister of death with an unusuall sicknesse to enter amongst us, whereby some are dayly swept away & many more lying on their languishing bedds, expecting each houre their dissolution.[9]

Sickness again returned to New York City the following year as Samuel Maverick wrote Colonel Richard Nicolls in October 1669: "The flux, agues, and fevers, have much rained, both in cittie and country, & many dead, but not yett soe many as last yeare."[10] Apparently the mortality was higher in the 1668 outbreak than in that of 1669.

Whatever the dimensions of the epidemics of 1668 and 1669, it is probable that they hit the population selectively since the very young and the aged were more likely to succumb to such diseases when they occurred. Of the 53 cohort members for whom reliable age data is available, 18 or slightly more than a third were 50 years or older in 1664. This fact is critical for explaining the cohort mortality in the next decade or so. Many of the men who died between 1664 and 1676 were early settlers of New Amsterdam and were past middle age. Among them were these men whose age in 1664 is given: Reynier Rycken, 42; Govert Loockermans, 47; Thomas Hall, 50; Hans Kierstede, Sr., 52; Egbert van Borsum, 55; Cornelis Aertsen, 57; Johannes Megapolensis, 61; Teunis Cray, 63; Samuel Drisius, 64; and Claes van Elslandt, Sr., 64. Most of these men, then, passed away at reasonably advanced ages for the era, some undoubtedly the victims of the epidemics of 1668 and 1669.

Fevers and fluxes probably caused a significant proportion of the deaths in New York City during this time period, but other causes of death were unrelated to epidemiology. A well-to-do young merchant named Walraven Claerhout had the misfortune to drown shortly after he married in 1668: "On the 21th of June [1670], the Boddy of Walraven Claerhout (who being fallen overboard from Claes Lock's Sloop at her last going up and drounded) was brought up at Esopus and . . . Visited, but found no Wound or bruise on the sd Boddy."[11] Accidental death, whether caused by carelessness or involvement in situations of conflict, claimed at least a few victims.

The substantial mortality within the cohort group in the period up to 1676 contributed to the diminution of the adult male segment of the preconquest population. The further depletion of cohort ranks through emigration and the mortality of successive decades set the stage for the assumption of adult responsibilities by the sons of preconquest New Yorkers. In some cases, early inheritance of estates smoothed the course of development. For other sons, whose fathers were still alive, the demands of the labor market may have spurred their early entry into the practice of their trades. Not forced to wait for the acquisition of land, these urban youth stepped into the void and shouldered the burdens of life in the new social world of New York City.

As all but a handful of cohort members were married, the replacement of cohort fathers by their sons would be expected to compensate for attrition in the cohort in the years after 1664. Yet only slightly more than half of the 222 cohort members are known to have had sons who survived to adulthood. Gaps in evidence may partially explain this low figure, but evaluation of the information collected on the families procreated by cohort members suggests that the high mortality in the city in the years following the conquest may have influenced the survival rate of cohort children as well.

Of the 222 cohort members, 113 (51 percent) had surviving adult sons. An additional 46 men in the cohort had at least one son baptized in the local Dutch church, but none of these sons is known to have survived to adult years. Some may have reached adulthood after leaving the town at an early age with their families or as youths seeking opportunities elsewhere. Other cohort sons born in New York City may have remained rooted there for at least a part of their adult lives but are not traceable due to the nature of Dutch nomenclature. The use of surnames in one generation but not in the other can prevent accurate linkage of members of the same family. All of these possibilities help to explain the dearth of surviving sons among these 46 cohort fathers, but it is likely that the majority of cases were caused by the high incidence of mortality among infants and young children in the city.

Because of their timing, the epidemics of 1668 and 1669 probably claimed a large number of cohort children among their victims. The multiple assignment of the same given name in the baptismal records of cohort families graphically illustrates the incursions of death in those families. Lucas Andrieszen and his wife had fifteen children baptized between 1656 and 1682, but used only ten names, indicating that at least one-third of their children died at an early age. Two of these 46 cohort members suffered the decimation of their entire families. Peter Jansen van Langestraet had seven children by two wives, none of whom survived beyond childhood.

The most notable case of family mortality concerns the prominent merchant and mayor of New York City, Cornelis Steenwyck. Steenwyck had married Margareta de Riemer in 1658 in the New Amsterdam Dutch church. In the years between 1659 and 1676, six sons and one daughter were born to the couple and baptized in the church. The doleful details of the children's premature deaths at ages ranging from 16 days to 12 years are found in the Bible record of Margareta de Riemer.[12] No wonder the joint will of the Steenwycks (made in 1684, the year that Cornelis died) mentions none of these children as heirs to the very large estate. All had predeceased their father.

Another thirteen cohort members are not known to have produced any sons although they all had daughters, some of whom survived to adulthood. Cornelis Barentsen van der Cuyl, a corn measurer, and his wife Lysbeth Arents had been married in Holland, but they still were childless when they left the Netherlands in 1654. There are two baptisms recorded for Cornelis and his wife in the New Amsterdam Dutch church, that of Marritie in 1655, and that of Neeltie in 1660. Both of these daughters, apparently the Van der Cuyls's only children, are mentioned in their father's 1696 will. When baker Hendrick Willemsen drafted his will in 1692, he provided for his three daughters baptized in the church at New Amsterdam. Both van der Cuyl and Willemsen had surviving offspring, but not male heirs.

Altogether, then, 59 cohort members (27 percent) had children, but no known surviving adult sons. A group almost as large, comprising 50 cohort members, seems to have been childless. No baptisms are entered in local church records for these men, who constituted 23 percent of the cohort group. Some of them may have had children, but the records of their birth, whether in New York, another colony, or Europe, have not been discovered.

Firm evidence exists for several cohort couples who were childless. Trader Peter Jacobs Marius, who had been in New Amsterdam since 1647, married Marritje Pieters in the New Amsterdam Dutch church in 1655. Yet throughout their lives in New York City, no children were ever baptized for the Mariuses. When Peter Jacobs Marius made his will in 1701, the beneficiaries included his sisters in Holland, his niece and nephew, his cousin, and a whole set of his deceased wife's relations. The 1679 will of Sybout Claesen, a carpenter, also confirms the fact of a childless marriage indicated by the lack of recorded baptisms. After the death of his wife, Claesen's estate was to be divided among his wife's two daughters by a former husband. Sybout Claesen and his wife had been married since 1645, yet their only children were those of his wife from a previous marriage. Another union which produced no children was that of Simon Janszen Romeyn, Gentleman. Romeyn's 1702 will directed that upon the death of his wife Sophia, whom he had married in 1671, all his estate was to descend to his wife's nearest relations. Sophia Romeyn made her own will in 1715 and included her brother and sister as beneficiaries as well as a number of other people.

Whether through infertility or high infant and child mortality, the proportion of cohort members who had sons who survived to adulthood cannot have exceeded 60 percent. Furthermore, not all the adult sons of cohort members chose to reside in their hometown. Of the 237 known adult sons of cohort members, 56 (24 percent) settled outside of New York City. Apprehensive of the potentially adverse effects of the English presence in the city, most moved to places with a high concentration of Dutch inhabitants. Fourteen men moved to Albany, thirteen to the area of Kingston in Ulster County, seven to the Dutch towns of Kings County, Long Island, six to New Jersey, and two to Staten Island. Five men departed for the Netherlands and one for the Dutch West Indies. The remainder traveled to Pennsylvania, Delaware, Maryland, and Connecticut. Thus, a combination of reasons—attrition in the cohort group through death and emigration, a relatively limited crop of second-generation cohort sons reaching maturity, and the relocation of almost one-quarter of these sons—created a situation at New York City in which the early maturation of the second generation was not only feasible but desirable.

The group of 181 cohort sons (76 percent) who remained in New York City for a substantial portion of their lives embodied the strands of continuity in late seventeenth-century New York City society. Ties between generations, as well as intermarriage among the preconquest families, created a substantial segment of the local population that was linked to the city. This nucleus of families, some already entering the third generation in the late seventeenth century, constituted the stable center of a community that was to undergo increasing penetration by newcomers as the years passed. Examining the maturation of second-generation cohort sons, their marriage choices, and the kinship ties formed by these marriages illuminates the distinctive nature of New York City's social structure in the latter part of the seventeenth century.

The maturation of the second generation in New York City, as measured by the date of first marriage, occurred over an extended period of time. Due to the wide variation in age of cohort members, the coming of age of their children was spaced over the period from 1654 through 1726. However, 75 percent of the first marriages of cohort sons and daughters took place during the last quarter of the seventeenth century and more than half

TABLE 2–1
Chronological Distribution of Marriages of
Second-Generation Cohort Sons and
Daughters

	Number of Marriages	
Years	Sons	Daughters
Through 1665	2	10
1666–1670	8	8
1671–1675	16	18
1676–1680	23	16
1681–1685	28	35
1686–1690	31	37
1691–1695	18	19
1696–1700	18	19
1701–1705	6	4
1706–1710	4	2
After 1711	1	2
TOTAL	155	170

of these unions were solemnized between 1676 and 1690 (see table 2–1). The median year for first marriages was 1686 for sons and 1685 for daughters. By the final decade of the century, the mature second generation was drawing even with the cohort members still present in the community. The amorphous line separating the distinctive hegemony of the first and second generations of cohort families ran through these years. Only the children of the youngest cohort members and the youngest children of other cohort members had yet to reach maturity in the 1690s.

A society in which the assumption of adult responsibilities at an early age was desirable would be expected to develop a pattern of early age at first marriage for sons. Social conditions in New York City favored early marriage. Nearly two-thirds of the 132 cohort sons for whom data is available married before they were 25 and fewer than 4 percent waited until they were 30 before marrying.[13] (See table 2–2.) The mean age at marriage for these men was 23.8, approximately the same age as native-born men in late seventeenth-century Maryland, but three to four years younger than their counterparts in rural New England.[14] The urban youth of seventeenth-century New York City started families of their own at an early age and had marshaled the economic resources to do so.

How much influence was exerted by cohort fathers on their sons' decisions concerning marriage is uncertain. If fathers wished to delay the marriage of their sons, economic leverage was their most potent tool. A son apprenticed in a trade, however, was capable of striking out on his own

TABLE 2–2
Age at First Marriage of Second-Generation Males
and Females

Age	Men (and percent of total)		Women (and percent of total)	
Under 21	16	(12.1)	60	(40.0)
21 to 24	70	(53.0)	63	(42.0)
25 to 29	41	(31.1)	20	(13.0)
30 and over	5	(3.8)	6	(4.0)
TOTAL	132	(100.0)	149	(99.0)
24 and under	86	(65.1)	123	(83.0)
25 and over	46	(34.9)	26	(17.0)

given the appropriate market conditions and therefore may not have been
dependent on the good will of his father. On the other hand, fathers may
actually have promoted the early independence of their sons by substantial
support in the early years of a son's career. When Coenraet Ten Eyck, Sr.,
a shoemaker and tanner, drafted his will in 1686, he specified his method
of apportioning financial aid to his sons:

> I leave to my son Matthias 2,000 guilders, wampum value, to be paid out of
> the sum which shall come from the sale of my houses, and to make his profit
> therewith without paying any interest for the term of four years, and then he is
> to bring it into the common estate. My son Tobias is to have one year's rent of
> my two houses, because my other children have a long time had the benefit of
> my money and have made their profit therewith.[15]

During his lifetime Coenraet Ten Eyck, Sr., had materially aided most of
his children and his will was designed to give support to those sons who
had not yet benefited from their father's benevolence. All of Ten Eyck's six
sons were married before 1680 and the ages at marriage of the four sons
whose baptismal dates are known suggest that parental aid was crucial in
sustaining early marriage. Coenraet Ten Eyck, Jr., married in 1675 at the
age of 20; his brother Hendrick Ten Eyck was wed in 1676 at 19; Tobias
Ten Eyck was 25 years old when he married in 1678; and Matthys Ten
Eyck entered into marriage in 1679 at the age of 21.

The size of a man's estate determined the type of aid he could offer his
sons. Stephanus van Cortlandt, a merchant and member of New York's
ruling elite, had eleven children for whom to provide when he made his
will in 1700. Fortunately, his estate was ample enough to bear the strain.
Like Ten Eyck, Van Cortlandt also had a systematic plan for aiding his
children: "He leaves to each of his children who are not already provided

for in that manner, a lot of ground in the city of New York, for the building of a convenient dwelling house, and to each of his children not already provided for, £150."[16]

Few children were as well taken care of as the Van Cortlandt offspring, but parents did what they could within their means to assist their progeny in the early years of adult life. Although mariner Simon Barentsen was the stepson of Jurian Blanck, Sr., also a mariner, he still received substantial assistance from him. When Simon's widowed mother Catherine Blanck made her will in 1698, she bequeathed her son only 30 shillings, because

> he [had] been sufficiently provided for, during the life of my husband, Jurian Blanck; having received one half of a sloop, a wedding dinner, 2 wedding suits, a cloak, a fine red broad cloth waist coat, with silver thread buttons, one half dozen fine Holland shirts, one half dozen striped Calico neck cloths, an oyen brigg [sic] feather bed, two new blankets, and had his diett, for two years after he was married.[17]

While most parents willingly helped to outfit their young at this crucial stage of life, a disagreement between father and son over the choice of a mate could have disastrous economic consequences for the son. In one instance, a son's marriage so displeased his father that it resulted in his disinheritance. Allard Anthony boldly stated in his 1685 will, "I leave to my son Nicholas Anthony, for that he hath proved disobedient to me, in his marriage with Angie, his now wife, and for other reasons to me best known, 1 shilling, in full, for all his portion."[18] Nicholas Anthony, an only child, had left New York City to marry and settle in Ulster County. Presumably his father wished him to remain in close proximity to home in order to care for his parents as they aged.

In individual cases the selection of a mate reflects a variety of personal considerations. In the aggregate, however, the characteristics of the marriage partners chosen by a whole generation tell us a great deal about the nature of a society. That the majority of the group of 151 cohort sons for whom information is available married into other local preconquest families indicates not only the presence of a sufficient number of females of marriageable age but a predisposition among these sons to use marriage as a means of strengthening one's roots in the community. The marriage patterns of the second generation ensured the continuance of a stable and firmly rooted old-settler segment in the city of New York throughout the seventeenth century.

Of the 151 cohort sons whose first marriages have been analyzed, only ten married widows.[19] Virtually all were able to find single women for mates. Bricklayer Tobias Stoutenburg typifies the majority of second-generation men who selected women born in New York City for life partners. In 1684, he wed Annetie van Rollegom, a cohort daughter who was born in the city in 1665. Of the 141 new brides wed by cohort sons, 86

Figure 2. Isaac de Peyster (1662–1728), one of four brothers in the second generation of a prominent Dutch mercantile family, became a member of the Dutch Reformed Church in 1696. Courtesy of The New-York Historical Society, N.Y.C.

were natives of New York City and, in fact, more than a third (57) of the 151 marriages contracted by cohort sons were intra-cohort marriages— that is, the sons of cohort members marrying with either the daughters or granddaughters of other cohort members.

Most of the remaining second-generation men wed women who origi- nated in the region. Twelve brides were born on Long Island (eight in Kings County, four in Queens County), seventeen came from Albany County, two were from Dutch towns in New Jersey, and one was from Tappan in New York. Ship carpenter Isaac Brasier, son of Henry Brasier, one of the few English members of the cohort, married Aeltje Colevelt of Breuckelen in Kings County in 1690. Merchant Isaac de Peyster (figure 2) wed Maria van Balen of Albany in 1687. In addition, one bride was born in Brazil and 22 had birthplaces in the Netherlands. Many of these women, at least before the 1680s, however, were members of preconquest families and had come to New Amsterdam as children. Dirck Ten Eyck's wife, Aefje Boelen, the daughter of cohort member Boele Roelofszen, was born in Amsterdam about 1656, and sailed to New Amsterdam with her family on *De Trouw* in 1659.[20] Though four cohort sons married English or part-English women, all of these women were born in the colony of New York.[21] The predominant tendency, then, was for second-generation sons to marry within the community, or when this was not the case, to choose brides from places originally settled as part of New Netherland.

Though the majority of cohort daughters also selected mates who belonged to preconquest families, whether natives of the city, the surrounding region, or the Netherlands, these women were more likely to select outsiders for their spouses than their brothers. Of the 163 cohort daughters whose husbands' birthplaces are known, 18 (11 percent) wed men born in the British Isles.[22] The arrival of young single men from overseas in the decades following the conquest widened the pool of potential husbands for local women and predictably some chose foreigners for their mates. Jannetie van Dyck married John Cooley of London in 1665, and in 1692 Vrouwtie van Hoeck married George Walker from Ireland.

More typical of second-generation women, however, were Aefje Roos and Sarah van der Spiegel, who both married in the 1680s. Aefje, the daughter of carpenter Gerrit Jansen Roos, along with 64 other cohort daughters, chose as her groom a young man born in New York City—Johannes van Gelder, the son of cohort member Jan van Gelder. Sarah van der Spiegel (figure 3), whose father was baker Laurens van der Spiegel, married Rip van Dam, a newcomer from Albany who was destined to play a major role in New York's trade and government over the next half century. Van der Spiegel and 35 other cohort daughters found their life partners among men raised in the region.[23] Aefje Roos and Sarah van der Spiegel were typical of second-generation women in another respect—they were both 21 years old when they wed, close to the mean age at marriage for cohort daughters of 21.7. Practically all second-generation female residents of New York City in the late seventeenth and early eighteenth centuries married and most (83 percent) did so by the time they were 24 (see table 2–2). By contrast, in Amsterdam in the year 1676–77, only 44.4 percent of women were married before the age of 25.[24] Compared to their counterparts in other American colonies in the same time period, however, New York City's women tended to be slightly younger than New Englanders when they embarked on marriage but about three years older than native-born females in Maryland.[25]

The cohort sons and daughters who remained in New York City, for the most part, chose mates with similar roots in the community or at least

Figure 3. Sarah van der Spiegel van Dam (1663–1736), the daughter of a New Amsterdam baker, joined the Dutch Reformed church at the age of eighteen, two years before she married Rip van Dam, an Albany-born merchant who served for many years on the New York Council. Courtesy of The New-York Historical Society, N.Y.C.

ties within the colony. Married at an early age to partners who were familiar with their way of life, second-generation men and women found added security in the presence in the community of members of their parents' generation. Through their marriages, the cohort sons and daughters further elaborated the kinship networks that already threaded the community at all levels.

An in-depth look at the kinship network uniting four cohort families—the Boelens, the Clocks, the De Milts, and the Vanderheuls—makes plain the bonds that knitted second-generation families together in a coherent social universe within the changing urban environment. These four families became interlocked through a series of ten intra-cohort marriages that took place in the local Dutch church in the years between 1679 and 1687. Two brothers, Marten (Martin) and Albert Clock, the sons of carpenter Abraham Clock, married two sisters, Lysbeth (Elizabeth) Vanderheul and Tryntje Vanderheul, the daughters of fellow carpenter Abraham Jansen Vanderheul. Previously, Catharina Clock, Marten and Albert's sister, had married Jacob Boelen, the son of tailor Boele Roelofszen.[26] After these couples had married, Maria Vanderheul, the sister of Lysbeth and Tryntje, chose for her husband Peter de Milt, the son of baker Anthony de Milt. With these marriages, the second-generation members of four cohort families became part of a much wider circle of kin in the community.

Graphic testimony of the durability of the kinship structure initiated by the four marriages is found in Martin Clock's will, made in 1728. Though Martin Clock and Elizabeth Vanderheul had been married for forty-six years, they had no children. Thus, when 72-year-old Martin Clock composed his will, he ticked off his closest kin who were to be the beneficiaries of his estate following the death of his wife. After Elizabeth Clock's death,

> all is to be divided into two parts, and one part is to be given to my nearest relations, namely, to my sisters Sarah Rapalye, widow of Daniel Rapalye, deceased, Catharine Boelen, wife of Jacob Boelen, of New York, goldsmith, and the children of my brother Albert Clock, late deceased. And the other part to my wife's nearest relations, To wit, Johannes Vanderheuil, and the children of Tryntie Clock deceased, late wife of my brother, Albert Clock, deceased, and to Mary De Milt, widow of Peter De Milt, deceased, and to Femetye Wynkoop, wife of Benjamin Wynkoop, of New York, goldsmith, and to the children of Hendrick Vanderheuil, late of New York, deceased.[27]

In 1728, Martin Clock's sister Catherine and her husband Jacob Boelen were both still alive, but Martin's brother Albert and his wife Tryntie Vanderheul Clock were deceased. Martin's sister-in-law, Maria Vanderheul de Milt, was alive, but her husband, Peter de Milt, had died. Therefore, five of the eight parties to the marriages of almost half a century earlier were still involved in a functioning kin network.

Observing the Boelen family as it faced grave problems discloses how kinship ties operated in times of stress. When gunsmith Hendrick Boelen died in 1691 at the age of 30, he left a wife and son to be watched over by other members of his family. He gave instructions in his will for the education of this son and appointed four tutors and overseers for the boy: Boele Roelofszen, his father; Jacob Boelen, his brother; and Dirck Ten Eyck and Willem (William) Hellakers, his two brothers-in-law. The year after Henry's death, his widow, Anneken Cours, married Abraham Keteltas, the grandson of cohort member Evert Pietersen Keteltas. Henry Boelen had left a legacy of £125 for his son in case his wife remarried, and young

Abraham Boelen's three uncles and his grandfather were there to ensure that he received it when his mother married into the Keteltas family. The appointment of close relatives as trustees of estates and guardians of underaged children reflected the primacy of the kin network in dealing with issues affecting family welfare.

An even greater crisis occurred for the Boelen clan when the 1702 yellow fever epidemic in New York City claimed the lives of both Catharine (Tryntje) Boelen and her husband, ship carpenter Willem Hellakers.[28] The official records depict the role of the kin network in absorbing the unfortunate orphaned children of the Hellakers.

> Whereas William Hellaker, lately deceased, leaving behind him a will, declaring his wife Katharine sole executrix, which said Katherine has lately died, since the decease of her husband, and without proving the said will, Therefore Jacob Boelen, silversmith, and Dirck Ten Eyck, cordwainer, uncles and guardians of Katherine, Meritie, and Aphia, children of said William Hellaker, by Katherine his wife, deceased, are made administrators, during the minority of the children, October 1, 1702.[29]

Only these three of the Hellakers' nine children outlived their parents.

The marriages contracted by second-generation cohort sons and daughters formed a kinship network comprising Boelens, Clocks, De Milts, and Vanderheuls, as well as representatives of other cohort families. In addition to the lateral ties within this one generation, the young married couples had the benefit of the counsel, if not material aid, of three of the progenitors of these families for a substantial period of time. Although Abraham Clock died almost immediately after the 1664 conquest, Anthony de Milt survived until 1689 and both Boele Roelofszen and Abraham Jansen Vanderheul were still alive as late as 1701. Thus intergenerational ties enhanced the interconnections of these families and further rooted them to the community.

As time passed and New York City grew from a town of 1875 at the time of the conquest to a city of almost 5,000 in 1698, the stable family groupings among old settler families such as the Boelens, the Clocks, the De Milts, and the Vanderheuls gave a sense of continuity to young people growing up in the new social order. A heavy burden was placed on these kin networks as they mediated between the old and the new in the community, whether through the incorporation of newcomers or the maintenance of group solidarity under pressure. In the face of altered institutional forms and the gradual erosion of cultural certainties, the cohort families sustained themselves as well as others in the changing society of seventeenth-century New York City.

Chapter Three

NEWCOMERS IN SEVENTEENTH-CENTURY
NEW YORK CITY

WHEN VIEWED within the broad context of colonial immigration during the late seventeenth century, the flow of newcomers to New York colony was a relatively minor current. The attractiveness of other potential destinations, coupled with the instability of the political settlement in New York, ensured that the majority of immigrants to the British colonies after the Restoration would settle elsewhere. Although the British West Indian colonies, as well as Virginia and Maryland, still claimed large numbers of new immigrants, the planting of the Carolinas, and especially the Jerseys and Pennsylvania, during this period probably played a more important part in deflecting immigrants from New York. Indeed, some New Yorkers uprooted themselves to seek greater opportunities in New Jersey and Pennsylvania. Other persons, who might have settled in New York, were lured to these neighboring colonies by visions of plentiful land and religious freedom. Consequently, immigration to New York during the latter third of the seventeenth century, when the English were establishing control over their new possession, was hardly as impressive as that to other British colonies.[1]

Despite New York's undistinguished record in attracting new settlers in the seventeenth century, a body of immigrants did come to the colony during these years and New York City received a significant share of them. The people who came to New York City did so not because of any consistent immigration policy implemented by either Crown or local officials, but as a result of a complex of factors relating both to dislocating forces in their prior homes and the contours of society in seventeenth-century New York City. In order to comprehend the patterns of immigration to the city in the late seventeenth century, one must isolate the defining characteristics of the city's incoming population.

The group of immigrants drawn to New York City in the late seventeenth century was just as diverse in composition as the resident population of the city. Ethnically, linguistically, and religiously mixed, representing a broad spectrum of economic levels and occupational skills, these prospective New Yorkers emanated from European, West Indian, and colonial communities. Far from homogeneous in terms of external attributes, they were also differentiated experientially. British soldiers from Ireland, exiled French Huguenot merchants and artisans, and Dutch farmers' sons from rural New York all interacted in the social environment of seventeenth-century New York City.

Why they chose to cast their lots in New York City can never be answered in full, as decisions concerning migration proceed from an enigmatic blend of primary social forces and the most intimate of personal reasons. Still, it is possible to postulate the basic causes of the immigrant influx to New York City in the latter years of the seventeenth century. The lure of economic and political opportunity associated with the developing commercial life of the port of New York impelled numerous individuals to enter into the life of the city. For some persons, the choice was relatively simple because of kinship ties to urban residents. A propitious marriage between a rural colonist and the daughter of a city family may also have prompted a decision to relocate. Another powerful reason for moving to New York City in the late seventeenth century centered around the relatively tolerant religious climate of the city. In the face of religious prejudice and persecution elsewhere, French Huguenots, as well as Jews and Quakers, all found enough freedom and security within New York City to settle there.

Although these reasons account for numerous individual cases of migration to New York, one additional factor merits consideration when explaining the particular patterns of immigration during this period. Awareness of the city's multiethnic structure predisposed non-English immigrants to choose New York City as their home. The knowledge that clusters of compatriots had already carved out a niche in this society spurred migrants to settle where they might take advantage of the support and sentiment of their own people. In this way, the pluralistic nature of New York City's social structure virtually assured a similarly heterogeneous immigrant population.

Immigration to New York City is best viewed in terms of its ethnic groups. From this perspective, the expansion of the city's population occurred through accretions to preexistent nuclei of ethnic communities. In turn, each ethnic community was shaped to some degree by the character of the population reinforcements it received in the late seventeenth century. The extent to which each ethnic community was molded by the influx of newcomers varied, however. The Dutch group was most impervious to external influences, while the French and English enclaves experienced the impact of new settlers much more profoundly. The Jews in the city were virtually all newcomers, the New Amsterdam Jewish community having almost completely dispersed prior to the conquest. In essence, the

English, French, and Jewish groups in late seventeenth-century New York City were primarily immigrant communities, while the Dutch population consisted largely of native colonials.

One of the distinctive features of New York City society in the seventeenth century was the central position of the Dutch in the social order. Numerically predominant, with a firm institutional base in the Dutch Reformed church, the Dutch also had the strongest historical ties to the city. With roots planted during the regime of the Dutch West India Company, many of the city's old Dutch families were still represented in the city in the last decade of the century. Yet, throughout the period of English rule in the seventeenth century, the Dutch community continued to absorb newcomers, thereby augmenting the core of old settler families. These additions to the community bolstered the New York City Dutch group at a time when substantial infusions of non-Dutch peoples threatened to undermine Dutch hegemony. Nevertheless, the city's Dutch in the seventeenth century were primarily persons who were either native to New York City or were members of old city families. The Dutch migrants who joined their fellows in New York City entered a well-established community with the resources to integrate newcomers on its own terms.

Although the proportion of newcomers in the city's Dutch community varied at different points in time between 1664 and 1700, newcomers were always a minority segment of the group. The backgrounds of 242 (71 percent) of the 343 Dutch men on the New York City tax list of 1695 have been ascertained. Of these, 167 (69 percent) were either born in New York City or were members of old city families. The other 75 (31 percent) have been identified as migrants to the city between 1665 and 1695 from various colonial communities and the Netherlands. Thus, less than a third of this sample of the New York City Dutch community in 1695 consisted of newcomers.

Even more significant than the fact that newcomers composed only a minority of the city's Dutch population is the fact that the majority of these newcomers were hardly alien to New York provincial society. Of the 75 Dutch newcomers on the 1695 tax list, 45 (60 percent) emanated from the New York–New Jersey area and most of these were members of old New Netherland families.[2] Analysis of the membership records of the New York City Dutch Reformed Church reveals that more than three-quarters of the new church members between 1684 and 1700 were of local origin.[3] (See table 3–1.) A close examination of the sources and causes of Dutch migration to New York City in the latter third of the seventeenth century clarifies the relative importance of internal and external migration in producing the pattern suggested by these statistics.

TABLE 3–1
Places of Origin of Dutch Newcomers to New York City in the
Seventeenth Century

Place of Origin	Dutch Men on 1695 Tax List (and percent of total)	Dutch Men & Women Admitted to the Dutch Reformed Church with Certificate, 1684–1700 (and percent of total)
Netherlands	29 (39.0)	36 (17.0)
Dutch West Indies; Brazil	1 (1.0)	9 (4.0)
New York; East Jersey; West Jersey	45 (60.0)	164 (76.0)
Other	0	6 (3.0)
TOTAL	75 (100.0)	215 (100.0)

Note: If a husband and wife from the same place were admitted to the church concurrently, then two people were entered in the appropriate category.

The surrender of New Netherland to the English in 1664 forestalled
any substantial Dutch migration from the Netherlands to New York after
that date.[4] The cumulative efforts of the Dutch West India Company to
transplant Netherlanders to its American colony were abruptly terminated
with the transfer of sovereignty. Nevertheless, individual Dutch residents
of the Netherlands were free to relocate in New York after 1664 as long as
they had the means to do so. The immediate postconquest years produced
some residual immigration to New York City as a consequence of family
or commercial obligations, since the vagaries of imperial politics did not
inevitably disrupt the plans of individual colonists. Additionally, the brief
interlude of the Dutch reconquest of New York in 1673–74 created a
spasm of renewed interest in settlement in the province. The introduction
of military personnel into the area resulted in some instances of soldiers or
sailors staying in the community. Dutch immigration from the Netherlands was heavier in the first decade after the English takeover than in successive years. But throughout the seventeenth century, a trickle of Dutch
persons continued to leave the Netherlands to seek homes in the former
Dutch town of New York.[5] One such immigrant was Samuel Meynardt, a glover from Utrecht, who arrived in New York City about 1686.
He and his wife, Annetje Everts, joined the Dutch Reformed Church there
in 1686 with a certificate of attestation from their former church in
Utrecht. In his will made in 1695, Meynardt mentions his two brothers
living in Utrecht. Another Dutch newcomer, Bartholomeus Vonck, was a

tailor. He and his wife were admitted as members of the local Dutch church in 1695 with a certificate from their home church in Amsterdam.

Kinship ties or commercial arrangements induced individual Dutchmen to migrate to New York City. Jacob Marius Groen was a young silversmith who came to New York City about 1696 from Holland, obviously at the urging of his uncle, cohort member Peter Jacobs Marius, who was childless. Groen joined the city's Dutch Reformed Church in 1700 and married there in 1701. His uncle, a merchant, died in 1702, naming Groen as one of his beneficiaries. Channels of communication between the New York City Dutch and their countrymen in the Netherlands were not disrupted by the alteration in governmental authority. Through the medium of church and family, as well as through partners in trade, ties with the homeland were perpetuated long after the surrender.[6] Under these conditions, a small but steady flow of immigration from the Netherlands to New York City persisted during the seventeenth century. This immigration is best characterized as a movement of individuals or families whose motives for relocating in New York City proceeded from their own personal histories rather than from any clearly defined social issue.

Although personal factors also influenced intracolonial mobility, the flow of Dutch internal migration to New York City was connected to discrete causal factors that assumed salience in the waning years of the seventeenth century. The largest single body of internal migrants to the city in the seventeenth century came from Albany. Of the 164 migrants from New York and the Jerseys found in the church membership records, 116 (71 percent) came from Albany. Of the 45 internal migrants on the 1695 tax list, 31 (69 percent) also came from Albany. This movement of people out of the Albany area was concentrated in the years of King William's War, when the dangers of life on the northern frontier of New York colony prompted an exodus from the area. An official document labeled "The Christians departed from the Citty and County of Albany since the beginning of ye Warr" disclosed that 142 men, 68 women, and 209 children had left Albany between 1689 and 1697.[7] Although these refugees were free to move anywhere in the region, a sizable segment of the group chose New York City as the site for a new home. Of the 116 new church members from Albany admitted to the Dutch Reformed Church of New York City between 1684 and 1700, 94 (81 percent) joined the church during the years between 1689 and 1697, when the stream of migrants was at its peak. Prior kinship or economic links to the city, coupled with the sense of security associated with New York City's protected position, produced the influx of settlers from Albany.

Among the migrants from Albany during this critical era were a carpenter, a brewer, and two merchants of the same family. These men and their wives all joined the New York Dutch Reformed church with certificates of attestation from the Albany church. Born into a New York City cohort family, carpenter Salomon Fredericksen Boog had moved to Albany, where he married Annetie Bratt in 1686. The couple resettled in New York City, where they joined the Dutch church in 1692. Fellow Albany congregants Harmen Rutgers and his wife Catharina de Hooges joined the New York City church in 1696. Rutgers was a brewer. Willem Teller, Sr., and Willem Teller, Jr., both merchants, also migrated from Albany. The younger Willem Teller and his wife Rachel Kierstede, a native of New York City, joined the local church in 1689, and the elder Willem Teller and his wife Maria Verleth joined in 1692.

In addition to out-migration because of wartime exigencies, Dutch settlers in New York colony uprooted themselves from communities on western Long Island in response to mounting population pressure on the limited supply of land. The densely settled towns of Kings County had been experiencing emigration ever since 1664, but the pace of emigration began to accelerate in the last decade of the century.[8]

Of the 164 internal migrants on the church membership list, 16 (10 percent) emanated from these towns. Similarly, 7 (15.5 percent) of the 45 internal migrants on the 1695 tax list also came from the Dutch towns of Kings County. Gerrit Hendricksen Brasser, who was born in New Amersfoort, moved to New York City early in the 1690s. He and his wife Catharina Hardenbroeck joined the local Dutch Reformed church in 1693 with a certificate from the Dutch church in Midwout (Flatbush). Annetje van Tuyl, the wife of Cornelius Vandeventer, a carpenter, became a member of the New York City Dutch Reformed Church in 1703 with a certificate of attestation from the church in New Utrecht. Vandeventer was already resident in the city in 1699. While the bulk of this migration out of Kings County in the late seventeenth and early eighteenth centuries was directed toward areas in New Jersey, where land was accessible to new settlers, the small number of Kings County residents who selected New York City as their future home deserves notice because they composed a well-defined segment of the city's incoming Dutch population.

The few Dutch immigrants who arrived at New York City by way of the Dutch West Indian possessions represented a type of immigrant that was more notable among the French and English newcomers.[9] These individuals had tried their luck in the islands and had decided to move on to the mainland in search of better opportunities. Marinus de Vos, who joined the New York City Dutch church in 1693 with a certificate from Curaçao, and Martinus Lamberits, who became a church member in 1695 with the attestation of the church in Surinam, are representative of this group of migrants. That denizens of the Dutch West Indies would select New York City as a destination in the seventeenth century is plausible in view of the well-established commercial connections that had linked New York City and the Dutch islands since the days of New Netherland. In most respects, these immigrants were already familiar with the contours of the colonial world.

A majority of the Dutch newcomers who settled at New York City in the latter third of the seventeenth century were born in or were members of families with roots in the old communities of New Netherland. Although these individuals were certainly strangers to New York City society, they had sufficient knowledge of the provincial social order, and especially the native Dutch subsociety, to function effectively in the city soon after arrival. When one recalls that only 29 (12 percent) of the 242 Dutch men studied on the 1695 tax list were natives of the Netherlands, then the overwhelmingly colonial character of the New York City Dutch community is evident.

In contrast to the Dutch community, the Jewish, French, and English communities of late seventeenth-century New York City were predominantly immigrant in makeup. The Jewish community was essentially reconstituted in the decades following the transfer of sovereignty, since only a handful of New Amsterdam's Jews remained in the city. Asser Levy, "the best known Jewish link between the Dutch and English periods," arrived on Manhattan Island in 1654 and pursued a wide-ranging career in trade for nearly thirty years.[10] But most of his fellow Jews had left for greener pastures by 1663, when formal religious services ceased in New Amsterdam.[11]

The hospitable climate under the new English administration as well as the precedent of earlier Jewish settlement encouraged a small number of Jews to migrate to the city. Whereas there was only one Jew on the 1665 tax list—Asser Levy—four Jews appear on the 1676 tax list. One scholar has estimated that there were "at least ten householders or families in town" in 1678, the year that Governor Edmund Andros noted the presence of "some Jews" in New York.[12] Religious services began at the latest in 1682 and a synagogue was in existence by 1695.[13] The names of eight Jews are found on the 1695 tax list and fourteen on the 1699 tax list. It is estimated that in 1695 there were twenty Jewish families in New York City and by 1700 between 100 and 150 Jews.[14]

Early Jewish settlers made their way to the city from a variety of places including England, the West Indies, and Surinam.[15] Among them were merchants Joseph Bueno and Isaac Rodriguez Marques and butcher Joseph Isaacs. However diverse their origins, the Jewish faith brought these migrants together in seventeenth-century New York City.

New York City's French community was distinctive in the way that it was shaped by the influx of newcomers in the last decade and a half of the century. While persons of French background had been present in the city for the entire period of settlement, both under the Dutch and the English, the French group prior to the 1680s was amorphous, with no clear center. A few French immigrants entered New York City in the postconquest years, but it was only with the arrival of the Huguenots after 1685 that the French united as a community of refugees, with an institutional base in the refugee church founded in 1688. Formerly integrated into the larger Dutch society, the French developed a viable community life as the Huguenots poured into the city. From a scattered handful of non-Dutch, the French became a clearly identified minority group in a multiethnic society.

Among the immigrants to New York City in the late seventeenth century, the French Huguenots were unique in their prior experience of persecution and exile. Bonded together by their decision to leave Louis XIV's France in order to preserve their Protestant faith, they had abandoned their homes and sought sanctuary throughout Europe. Those French Protestants who eventually settled at New York City in the late 1680s and 1690s comprised but a small sample of this much larger displaced population whose rationale for emigration flowed from religious conviction rather than the desire for material improvement. Despite the centrality of religious values in the Huguenot experience, other defining characteristics served to differentiate these immigrants and played a significant role in their integration into alien societies. The community of exiled French Protestants in New York City, which was spiritually united in the Eglise Françoise à la Nouvelle York, founded in 1688, was not uniform in its social makeup. Distinctions in regional background, channels of dispersion, age and marital status, occupation, property holding, and prestige all transected the monolithic religious character of the group. A profile of the French refugee community in late seventeenth-century New York City must recognize both its religious homogeneity and its social diversity.

Of the estimated 160,000 Protestants who left France in the years surrounding the revocation of the Edict of Nantes in 1685,[16] the vast majority remained in Europe, primarily in England, Ireland, the Netherlands, Germany, and Switzerland.[17] Not many of the French exiles crossed the ocean to America and the number who settled in the British continental colonies did not exceed 2,000.[18]

Those Huguenot refugees who did migrate to the British continental colonies found homes in widely scattered areas from New England to South Carolina. Moreover, many of these exiles were forced or chose to move from their original residences in the colonies, thus making it especially difficult to ascertain the size of the Huguenot population in America. Some scholars believe that the largest Huguenot population was located in South Carolina and that this group consisted of no more than 500 people in 1700.[19]

By the end of the seventeenth century, there were about 400 Huguenots in New York City, or almost 9½ percent of the 1698 white population of 4,237. Huguenot men numbered 67 (11 percent) of the city's male taxpayers in 1695 and 69 (10 percent) in 1699. The total number of Huguenot households, including female-headed households and the households of nontaxpayers, must have been about 80. Assuming that each household contained about five members produces the figure of 400.[20]

A much higher estimate of the city's Huguenot population was developed by John A. F. Maynard, the historian of the French church in New York City, based on a count of pastoral acts (baptisms, marriages, and funerals). Maynard hypothesized that the size of the New York City parish was about 250 in 1688–89, 450 in 1692, and between 700 and 800 in 1700.[21] However, these figures are inflated, in part because they include previously resident French, and, more likely, because significant numbers of Dutch Reformed adherents chose to worship with the Huguenots in the aftermath of the Leislerian crisis. Disillusioned with the pro-English stance of Reverend Henricus Selyns, they found a temporary home in the French church.[22] In any case, Huguenots constituted a sizable portion of New York City's population in the latter years of the seventeenth century.

The paths by which these refugees traveled to New York City were various. One of the earliest groups on the scene was the contingent of French Protestants that reached New York City in 1686. Writing in November 1686, Governor General Denonville of New France indicated that a reliable informant who had recently returned from a trip to Manhattan had told him that "within a short time fifty or sixty men, Huguenots, arrived there from the Islands of St. Christophers and Martinique, who are establishing themselves at Manat [Manhattan] and its environs."[23] Governor Thomas Dongan's 1687 report on the state of New York colony corroborates Denonville's intelligence: "Of French there have been since my coming here several families come both from St. Christophers and England, and a great many more expected."[24]

Of the refugees who came to New York City from the French islands, the majority had sought homes in the West Indies prior to the revocation of the Edict of Nantes. However, it is possible that a few of the island refugees were among those who had been forcibly transported to the French Antilles by Louis XIV's government.[25]

Governor Dongan's 1687 report also reveals that French immigrants had been arriving at New York from England. As might be expected, prospective immigrants to the British colonies more than likely had spent some time in England. It is possible to trace a number of the Huguenots who eventually settled in New York City in English records, although denization and naturalization records must be used with care.[26] Many of the French Protestant refugees had petitioned for denization before embarking from England to America and these persons are listed on the English rolls of the period. Others petitioned for denization after reaching their

destination, as the dates of denization coincide with the time of their settlement in the colonies. In addition, some refugees petitioned to colonial
authorities for denization or naturalization once in the colonies. As a
means of locating migrants in time and space, therefore, the denization
and naturalization records are of limited value.

More useful in tracking these peripatetic individuals during their odys-
seys are English church registers for the years of the late seventeenth century. The catalogue of French Protestant refugees who were aided by the
Threadneedle Street Church of London between 1681 and 1687 includes
a number of persons who ultimately settled in New York City. Augustus
Grasset, who later became weighmaster in New York City, received charitable grants for himself and his family between 1681 and 1683 amounting
to over £30. Other beneficiaries of charity included François Bouquett, a
mariner, Josué David, a shipwright, and François Vincent, a sailmaker.[27]

Some Huguenot refugees spent a number of years in England before
continuing their travels overseas, while others merely halted for a brief
spell en route to the colonies. During their sojourns in England, some refugees married or had children baptized. Widower Elie Boudinot, Sr., married Suzanne Papin, a widow, in London in 1686. Boudinot, a merchant,
was admitted as a freeman of New York City in 1688 and he and his new
wife presented a daughter for baptism in the Eglise Française à la Nouvelle
York in July 1689. André Laurent, ancestor of Henry Laurens of South
Carolina, was wed to Marie Lucas in London in 1688. Both Laurent and
his brother-in-law, Augustus Lucas, resided in New York City before
moving on, Laurent to South Carolina, Lucas to Rhode Island. John Mag-
non, a tailor who emigrated to New York City about 1698 and later relocated at New Rochelle, was married in the French church at Bristol, England, in 1695 and had a son baptized there in 1697.[28] Of the Huguenots
who left the refugee communities in England to seek more salutary environments in the American colonies, a sizable number ended up in the city
of New York.

A few French Protestants spent time at Boston before moving on to
New York City.[29] One of these individuals was Benjamin Faneuil, a prominent merchant, who relocated at New York City in 1699, where he married and raised a family and eventually died.

The group of settlers involved in building the French town in the Narragansett country of Rhode Island contributed more substantially to the
population of New York City.[30] Upon the demise of that settlement which
had been started in 1686 and was abandoned by 1691, most of the Huguenots turned toward New York City. One of the few French colonists
who persevered in Rhode Island recalled over a decade later that "some of
[our] principale Persons went to Boston & York to seek out new Habitations where ye Govermtts had Compassion of them & gave them relief. &

help to their wives & Children Subsistance only two familys moveing to Boston & they rest to New York."[31] The existence of church records for this Rhode Island colony, as well as other documentary material, makes it possible to trace many of the Narragansett settlers who did move on to New York City. Jacob Rattier, a mariner who died in New York in 1702, had married Jael Arnaut, a widow, in Rhode Island in 1689. Their son Jacob was baptized there in 1690. In 1701, Rattier voted in the city's East Ward and also had an indenture of apprenticeship registered in the municipal records. Another mariner, Elie Rambert, was a member of the French settlement at Narragansett, Rhode Island. He and his wife Jeanne Coulombeau had their son Paul baptized there in 1689. However, by 1692, the Ramberts were resident in New York City, where their son Samuel was baptized. Three more children were baptized for the Ramberts in the Eglise Française à la Nouvelle York by 1698, when Madame Rambert apparently died. Elie Rambert remarried Marthe Moreau in 1699 in New York City and two more children were born to him by 1703. Rambert died in New York in 1706. Other Huguenots who arrived at New York City by way of Rhode Island include members of the David, Targée, Many, Lafon, and Grazillier families.

While incomplete documentation prevents us from tracing the movements of more than a portion of New York City's French refugees prior to their arrival, the major sources of these immigrants are not in doubt. Some came by way of the French West Indies, others transplanted themselves directly from England, a few moved from Boston, and a group emanated from the Narragansett country of Rhode Island. A handful of individuals also arrived from the Netherlands and South Carolina. Auguste Jay (figure 4), the son of a wealthy La Rochelle merchant and the ancestor of revolutionary statesman John Jay, originally sailed to South Carolina, but soon moved to New York City.[32]

Although the Huguenots who eventually located in New York reached the city by various paths, most of them originated in a fairly circumscribed area of France. Of 128 men studied, the original homes of 91 (71 percent) have been identified with some degree of reliability. Of these, 71 (78 percent) emanated from three seaboard provinces of western France—Aunis, Saintonge, and Poitou. The city of La Rochelle, located in the province of Aunis, was itself the home of 22 of the Huguenot refugees who settled in New York City. Only 8 (9 percent) refugees had roots in northern provinces of France such as Normandy or Picardy, while but 9 (10 percent) came from southern and eastern provinces such as Languedoc and Guyenne. Three refugees (3 percent) started from the Netherlands, England, and the French West Indies. The great majority of New York Huguenots had initially lived in areas of substantial Protestant strength in France and their emigration to the colonies by way of England was facilitated by the proximity to the sea of their native places.[33]

Figure 4. Auguste Jay (1665–1751), one of the city's most successful Huguenot merchants, was born in La Rochelle, France. Married in the Dutch Reformed church in 1697 and an elder of the French church in 1704, by the 1720s he had affiliated with Trinity Church. Courtesy of The New-York Historical Society, N.Y.C.

Once in New York City, the French newcomers coalesced into a discrete community bound together by ties of language, heritage, and religion. Their experience differed markedly from that of the English immigrants to seventeenth-century New York City.

Reconstructing the history of the English newcomers to New York City requires a familiarity with the peculiar nature of the city's English community in the seventeenth century. Despite the continual presence of English people in New York City from the time of the 1664 conquest, any semblance of a cohesive English community failed to emerge until the very end of the seventeenth century. Two interrelated characteristics of the English population were responsible for this time lag in creating a viable ethnic community. First, a high rate of population turnover among English settlers in the seventeenth century produced a marked lack of continuity in the group. Second, the English settlers in the city were strikingly diverse in terms of role in the community, religious background, and geographical origin. Coupled with the absence of a stable nucleus, this pronounced internal differentiation impeded the evolution of an ethnically unified English community in the seventeenth century.

English immigrants had streamed into New York City ever since the 1664 takeover, but their high rate of turnover guaranteed that at the end of the seventeenth century the English community, unlike the Dutch, would still consist primarily of newcomers.[34] The first dozen years of English administration of New York colony witnessed a sizable influx of English immigrants into the city. From ten men (4.5 percent) in the cohort group, the number of English men in the city rose to 110 out of 387 (28 percent) in 1676–77. Seven of the ten cohort Englishmen still resided in the city but they were surrounded by newcomers.

Many of the early immigrants were ambitious young men of the colonial world attempting to carve out places for themselves in the newly appropriated city. New York's first governor, Richard Nicolls, recognized the lack of perseverance of some of the early English immigrants in 1666 when he wrote that "new comers of our owne nation, who at first (as we find by experience) are blowne up with large designes, but not knowing the knack of trading here to differ from most places, they meet with discouragements and stay not to become wiser."[35] In a sense, these men were but the first of a series of waves of transplanted Englishmen who sought to capitalize on the commercial opportunities and political patronage symbolized by the city of New York. Merchants such as John Robinson, who was assessed over £2,500 in 1676, came to reap the advantages of the port's newly opened trade. To consolidate his ties in the city, Robinson married Grietie, the daughter of cohort member Hendrick Willemsen, a baker, in 1678. Robinson's wife was noted as a member of the local Dutch Reformed Church in 1686. The couple was mentioned in Willemsen's will made in 1692.

The promise of political appointments also enticed Englishmen to New York City. Philip Johns, a young man from London, was commissioned "Haven Master" of New York City by Governor Nicolls in 1665. He married a local Dutch woman in 1668 and died about 1675. Before leaving England to take up his post, Governor Thomas Dongan met Michael Vaughton "who hapning to bee in London when I came away offered his service to come along with mee, whom finding a pretty ingenious young man & out of employment I promised to help him with a little money when hee stood in need of it for to put him into some way." As Dongan's protégé, Vaughton, who married Susannah Leisler in 1687, was the recipient of both favors and appointments.[36] Other early English immigrants boasted less prestigious employments, but nevertheless attempted to seize the opportunities afforded to men of their nation in the city. James Matthews, an innkeeper, John Ray, a pipemaker, and William Boyle, a shoemaker, were representative of this group of English newcomers.

Few links existed between the English residents of New York City during Benjamin Fletcher's administration (1692–1698) and those who had inhabited the city under Edmund Andros's rule (1674–1680). Of the 110 English men on the 1676–77 city tax lists, only 15 (14 percent) were present on the 1695 tax list. In comparison, 69 (26 percent) of the 261 Dutch men on the 1676–77 lists were found on the 1695 list. Severe smallpox epidemics in 1679–80 and 1690, as well as an unidentified illness in 1689, undeniably took a toll on members of both groups.[37] On Saturday, June 8, 1680, Jasper Danckaerts reported that "there was a training and muster to-day, which had not taken place before in two years, because the small-pox had prevailed so much the last year."[38] Nine years later, Stephanus van Cortlandt announced the presence of disease in New York City again: "Many persons are quickly taken out of this world. Since November more than fifty persons have died and not one was sick more than five days. Those who lie [ill] longer generally recover."[39] In an account penned in 1692, Charles Lodwick noted that "2 years ago ye Small Pox, which was very mortal, especially to grown people, a sort of pleurysye, (not cured but increasing by bleeding,) and violent fevers took away a great many."[40]

But the vacuum created in the Dutch community when individual Dutch men succumbed to disease was soon filled as kinfolk and longtime neighbors took their place. At least another 109 Dutch men on the 1695 list were natives of New York City or members of old city families. At a minimum, then, 178 (52 percent) of the 343 Dutch men in New York City in 1695 had solid ties to the city. The same cannot be said for the English. Cordwainer William Hyer was one of the few second-generation English men on the 1695 tax list. His father, Walter Hyer, a laborer who worked as a porter for the city, had arrived in the city not long before November 1668, when he married a Dutch woman in the local Reformed church.[41] The Hyers were the exceptions in an English community that did not have very deep roots. While the proportion of English men in New York City was virtually the same in 1695 (30 percent) as it had been in 1676–77 (28 percent), the members of these groups were for the most part unrelated.

Given the high rate of turnover, the English population failed to grow in the seventeenth century. Early English immigrants to New York City obviously were reluctant to persevere under unfavorable conditions, but specifying the particular reasons that prompted any individual to relocate is possible only in isolated cases. Nevertheless, the causes of the out-migration of English settlers are clear—tax burdens, limited access to land, denial of political liberties, religious pluralism, and the attractiveness of other colonial opportunities. However, these liabilities were not sufficient to deter numerous other English migrants from choosing New York City as their prospective home in the same time period.

The English settlement in seventeenth-century New York City was continually losing members but just as consistently being replenished by newcomers eager to try their luck. In the absence of statistics, one cannot plot the course of immigration to the city with precision. However, it is certain that substantial numbers of English headed to New York immediately after the conquest and also after the subsequent repossession of the colony from the Dutch in 1674.[42] That there was a lull in English immigration in the 1680s is suggested by Governor Dongan's 1687 comment that "for these 7 yeares last past, there has not come over into this province twenty English Scotch or Irish familys."[43] However uneven the flow, English migration to New York persisted throughout the seventeenth century, thereby creating a sufficient demographic base for the development of a viable ethnic community. But the lack of continuity manifested in this group of English settlers made it unlikely for any sense of ethnic solidarity to crystallize during these years.

The inability of New York City's English immigrants to coalesce into a cohesive ethnic unit until very late in the seventeenth century also relates to the composition of the group. Despite the linguistic and cultural ties that bound them together, the English were unlike in many respects. This diversity was reflected in the institutional vacuum that existed in New York City for most of the seventeenth century until the Anglican Trinity church was established in 1697. Members of the city's English community were cognizant of their unique predicament. Writing in 1699, the church-wardens and vestry of the new Trinity Church stated:

> The English nation for above Thirty Yeares had been possessed of these Countreys without any place for public worship of Almighty God, in this City, except the Chapel in the Fort built by the Dutch so that though the English grew numerous, the government in their hands and the national laws took place, yet for want of a Temple for the public Worship according to the English Church, this seemed rather like a conquered Foreign Province held by the terrour of a Garrison, than an English Colony, possessed and settled by people of our own Nation.[44]

The fact that no English religious institution existed in the city for more than three decades after the conquest, except for a very small Quaker meeting, calls attention to the divisions among the English. While all the city's immigrant communities were internally stratified, the English newcomers were dissimilar to the others because a gulf existed between servants of the Crown and ordinary settlers. As recipients of royal subsidies in a variety of forms, the Crown's representatives in New York were all dependent on the machinery of imperial politics.

The English garrison, while connected to the civil administration, was a separate entity, with its own internal hierarchy.[45] Though the size of the military contingent in New York City varied during the seventeenth century, royal troops were located in the city for the entire period of English rule. Officers and soldiers alike shared the opprobrium reserved for occupying forces in any community. Yet the gradations in status that proceeded from the military ranking system fragmented this group of English newcomers as well. The deplorable conditions under which the common soldiers were forced to serve further alienated them from their commanders and from the society at large.

One cannot always draw a precise line between those men who came to New York City in an official capacity and those who migrated as private citizens. Servants of the Crown were frequently engaged in private enterprises at the same time as they performed their official duties. In a similar way, members of the private business community often were involved with colonial officials in a variety of matters touching upon the public domain. Some merchants and attorneys enjoyed the favor of the government and used their connections to augment their private fortunes.[46] Nevertheless, specifying the primary roles of English migrants to New York in the seventeenth century helps to distinguish those individuals who came under the auspices of the Crown from those who migrated independently. Questions of motivation become more complex in dealing with that segment of the English community that undertook the journey to New York independent of any government support. Though more than a few immigrants counted on exploiting ties to the English administration, most people probably ventured out with only the desire to improve their prospects and perhaps a vague connection to somebody in New York.

The English private citizens who immigrated to New York City in the seventeenth century included merchants, professionals, artisans and laborers. Yet one category of immigrant was notably absent—the indentured servant. Whether in response to the institutionalization of slavery in New York or the pressing labor requirements of other colonies, the vast majority of indentured servants in the late seventeenth century were bound to masters in other locations.[47] Scrutinizing extant lists of servants bound from English ports for the American colonies in the latter part of the seventeenth century reveals only a scattered few individuals destined for New York colony.[48] A list of persons departing from Barbados in 1679, most of them servants, includes just 34 individuals headed for New York out of a total of 593 passengers.[49] One surviving contract from 1678 records the indenture of George Renals, a laborer of Barbados, to Thomas Gibbes, a New York City merchant for "3 years service in New York in exchange for 270 pounds of good Moscov[   ] sugar (already paid) & his passage & sufficient Meate drinke and App[   ]ll during his said time."[50]

The bulk of English persons who came to New York City in the seventeenth century, then, migrated independently, without using the device of indentured servitude to pay for their transportation. However, upper-class English newcomers did bring personal retainers with them to New York and members of the elite occasionally imported servants after their arrival. In 1696, "in Consideration of her Passage on board the Barquentine Called the Antegua (Capt William Kidd late Owner) in the late voyage from the Kingdom of England to this port of New Yorke," Elizabeth Morriss, "Att Present of ye Citty of New Yorke Spinster," bound herself as a servant to Captain Kidd for four years to commence from "the day of her Arrival here from the Kingdom of England."[51]

The foundation for a viable English community in New York City was unsteady throughout the seventeenth century as powerful centrifugal forces further fragmented the immigrants. English newcomers lacked the unity that common religious identity supplied for the Dutch and French communities in New York City. While the Dutch and French groups were essentially ethnoreligious communities, the English constituted an ethnic group with discrete religious subcommunities. With the exception of the Quakers, these religious subcommunities did not possess institutional bases for most of the seventeenth century. Consequently, discovering the religious orientation of early English settlers is a prodigious task. At best, one can identify the constituent elements that made up the English religious spectrum in seventeenth-century New York City.

A very small group of Roman Catholics was present in the city during the seventeenth century, finding especially congenial conditions during the administration of Governor Thomas Dongan, an Irish Catholic. Governor Benjamin Fletcher submitted a list of the ten Roman Catholics in the city of New York in June 1696 to the Lords of Trade.[52] Adherents of both Congregational and Presbyterian forms of worship presumably were present in New York City during the seventeenth century, but their numbers were insignificant.[53] Whether Puritans from Long Island or Presbyterians from Scotland or Ulster, they were unable to organize a church to meet the needs of dissenters. A Presbyterian meeting was not started in New York City until 1716.[54]

Even though their form of worship had official sanction in England, New York City's Anglicans were not able to found a church until 1697.[55] Since the conquest, Anglican residents of the city had attended services in the Dutch church with English chaplains officiating. The Labadist missionary, Jasper Danckaerts, who visited New York in 1679, commented pointedly on the abysmally low attendance at the Anglican service as well as its formalistic character:

> We went at noon to-day to hear the English minister, whose services took place after the Dutch was out. There were not above twenty five or thirty people in the church. The first thing that occurred was the reading of all their prayers and ceremonies out of the prayer book, as is done in all Episcopal churches. A young man then went into the pulpit and commenced preaching, who thought he was performing wonders; but he had a little book in his hand out of which he read his sermon which was about a quarter of an hour or half an hour long. With this the services were concluded, at which we could not be sufficiently astonished.[56]

By the late 1690s, the city's Anglicans had mobilized sufficient strength to found Trinity Church with official support and firm legal guarantees. The establishment of Trinity Church supplied a necessary measure of organizational coherence to the city's English community and provided the focus for political activity as well.

The only other English religious institution founded in New York City during the seventeenth century was the Quaker meeting. Missionaries from the Society of Friends had visited the city in 1671 and 1672, but the official beginning of the meeting is recorded as 1681.[57] During the seventeenth century, Flushing, Long Island, was the center of the colony's Quaker community and relatively few Quakers resided on Manhattan.[58] Merchants such as Miles Forster, Richard Jones, William Bickley, and James Mills predominated among the small group of city Friends.[59] Tailors, a carpenter, a cooper, and a mariner were also found among the members.[60] The New York City meeting may have included a few non-English people as well. Quaker missionary James Dickinson, who came to the city in 1696, described "a large meeting; in which we opened the principles of Truth, by and through the demonstration and power of God, and wiped off the reproaches which George Keith, and those who ran out with him, had cast upon us. Many hearts were deeply affected and tendered, both among the Dutch and English."[61]

Regional background, as well as religion and role in the community, divided the city's English immigrants in the seventeenth century. Though defined as a single group because of linguistic unity, British newcomers did not share a common geographical or cultural heritage. Very few immigrants came to the city by way of other continental colonies or other parts of New York. One who did was famed printer William Bradford. Born in Leicestershire, England, Bradford initially settled in Philadelphia, where he set up his printing press. After a dispute with authorities, Bradford transferred his base of operations to New York City in 1693, becoming the colony's official printer and later the publisher of the *New-York Gazette*.[62]

The vast majority of immigrants, however, emanated directly from the British Isles or the British West Indies. Using the birthplaces of 75 British grooms enumerated in the marriage records of the city's Dutch Reformed Church in the years between 1664 and 1699 as an indicator, it is likely that the majority of British newcomers in the seventeenth century came directly from England, a measurable group from Scotland, and small numbers from Ireland, the British West Indies, and other mainland colonies.[63] Close to half of the English immigrants may have originated in London.[64] John Sharpe, an attorney who accompanied Governor Richard Nicolls to the colony, "formerly lived at the Sign of the Ramme, at the end of Ramme Alley, in Flleete Street," and Thomas Delavall, an early office-holder and merchant, testified before the High Court of Admiralty that he was born in "the City of London."[65] Quaker merchant Richard Jones identified himself as the son of "Richard Jones of the City of London, Taylor" when he married in 1688.[66]

Londoners were joined in New York City by men from many different parts of England—Walter Hyer, the laborer, from Surrey; Walter Thong, a merchant, from Hartfordshire; Gabriel Ludlow, clerk of the New York Assembly, from Somerset; and Matthew Clarkson, the provincial secretary, from Yorkshire.[67] The birthplace of Robert Walters, a merchant who married a daughter of Jacob Leisler in 1685, was Plymouth.[68] Another merchant, Thomas Wenham, a prominent opponent of Leisler, was born in Hailsham, Sussex.[69] Innkeeper Roger Baker left no doubt about his origins, stating in his will that he was "the son of Roger Baker living in a house called Paradise, in the Parish of Yordly, in the County of Worcestershire, in Old England."[70] The father of Caleb Heathcote (figure 5)—merchant, landowner, mayor of New York City, and staunch supporter of Trinity Church—was the mayor of Chesterfield in Derbyshire.[71]

Though the Duke of York's efforts to promote emigration from Scotland to New York in the 1660s were fruitless, Scots nevertheless appeared in the city during the seventeenth century.[72] Several had been exiled for their religious beliefs. David Jamison, who taught a Latin school after his arrival in 1685 and later practiced as an attorney, had, according to Governor Robert Hunter, belonged to "that multitude which in the end of King Charles ye seconds reign, were called by the name of sweet singers, and were then distinguished from the rest of that distracted party by their renouncing the use of arms, and who were for burning every book except the bible. . . . He was in company with others of that sort when taken prisoner . . . while they were a worshiping after their manner brought to Edenburgh and with them put into Bridewell . . . so far were they from being condemned, that they never had any Tryal, but one Lockhart who had a ship boun[d] for America was ordered by the Government to go to

Figure 5. Caleb Heathcote (1666–1721), who arrived from England in 1692, prospered as a merchant and was appointed to the New York Council. A loyal Anglican, he played a key role in the founding of Trinity Church in New York City. Heathcote also owned an estate in Westchester County. Courtesy of The New-York Historical Society, N.Y.C.

the house w[h]ere they were kept, and know of them whether they would voluntary go on Board with the rest."[73] Other immigrants whose religious views forced them to leave Scotland were cordwainer William Jackson and merchant John Spratt.[74]

David Vilant, a Scotsman whose share of the proprietary lands in the Scottish settlement of East New Jersey undoubtedly influenced his decision to cross the ocean, registered for the freemanship in New York City in 1695 as a schoolteacher, but called himself a merchant in his 1707 will.[75]

Several English newcomers arrived by way of the West Indies. Lawrence Reade, a merchant and the father of two prominent eighteenth-century merchants—John and Joseph Reade—arrived from Barbados about 1691.[76] In short, New York City's English community coalesced from a number of distinctive sources.

In contrast to the relative homogeneity of the Dutch, French, and Jewish newcomers to New York City in the seventeenth century, the incoming English population constituted a much more diverse offshoot of seventeenth-century British society. Finding a niche in New York City society was made difficult because of this fact. Moreover, the volatility of this immigrant population further hindered its effective integration into the local social order. At the end of the seventeenth century, the English remained predominantly an immigrant community still struggling to establish a foundation in the city.

Each of the ethnic communities in New York City at the end of the seventeenth century possessed distinctive attributes. The Dutch subsociety was the largest and most rooted, with a long-established church constituting its organizational nucleus. The Dutch also formed the most homogeneous group in the city, as the majority of Dutch newcomers shared a colonial background with the city's old settler families. Though composed almost entirely of immigrants who had taken diverse paths to reach New York City, the French community was also quite homogeneous. Originating in a geographically circumscribed region of France, the members of this group were drawn together by common religious belief and the powerful experience of persecution. The refugee church, founded contemporaneously with the major influx of immigrants, stabilized the French group once it had coalesced in New York City. Similarly, a shared religion supplied unity for the small Jewish community that had assembled from diverse sources.

The English subsociety, also primarily an immigrant community, was the least rooted and most heterogeneous group in New York City. Population turnover within this sector of society was undoubtedly accelerated by the frequent changes of governmental administration during the seventeenth century. Diverse in terms of the social background and religious orientation of its members, the English group lacked a central institutional base akin to the churches that unified the Dutch and French communities. Ironically, the English possessed the least cohesive ethnic community in the city that they ruled.

Chapter Four

ETHNICITY AND STRATIFICATION IN
SEVENTEENTH-CENTURY NEW YORK CITY

WHEN VIRGINIA planter William Byrd visited New York City in 1685, he found "a prety pleasant towne consisting of about 700 Houses, and a very handsome strong forte wherein is the Governors House, a great Church, Secretary's office, and convenient lodgings for the officers and Soldiers of the Garrison, with other conveniences."[1] If five people lived in each of the houses, then the city's population numbered about 3,500, an increase of two thousand over the 1,500 inhabitants (probably not including blacks) estimated to live there in 1664. By the end of the century, the number of people in New York City was more than triple the number who had been present at the conquest. The census of 1698, which provides the only precise population figures for the city in the seventeenth century, shows a total population of 4,937 persons, of whom 700 were blacks. From about 300 slaves and perhaps 75 free blacks in New Amsterdam in 1664, the number of blacks in New York City and county grew to 700 in 1698. But while the black community approximately doubled in size, the proportion of blacks in the population fell from about 20 percent in 1664 to about 14 percent in 1698. At the same time, decisive changes occurred in the ethnic composition of the city's white population.

Although the settlement on Manhattan Island had included representatives of diverse nationalities from its earliest years under the aegis of the Dutch West India Company, the great majority of the inhabitants of New Amsterdam at the time of the English takeover in 1664 were of Dutch descent. In 1685, William Byrd noted that "the Inhabitants are about six eighths Dutch, the remainder French and English."[2] However, by the end of the seventeenth century, the substantial numerical dominance of the Dutch had clearly receded, as English and French immigrants entered the community, soon constituting sizable components of the city's population. No longer token individual foreigners, these English and French newcomers coalesced into distinct ethnic groups with separate identities. While New York City had always been an ethnically mixed city, the accretions to the English and French blocs in the latter third of the seventeenth century made New York City a plural society in fact as well as in name. The ethnic polarization that achieved expression in the politics of the pe-

TABLE 4–1
Ethnic Composition of New York City's White Adult Male Population, 1664–1703

Ethnic Group	Number of Men for Period Indicated (and percent of total)									
	1664–65[a]		1676–77[b]		1695[c]		1699[d]		1703[e]	
Dutch	196	(88.0)	261	(67.0)	343	(58.0)	394	(55.0)	326	(52.0)
English	10	(4.5)	110	(28.0)	175	(29.5)	235	(33.0)	223	(36.0)
French	15	(7.0)	12	(3.0)	67	(11.0)	69	(10.0)	68	(11.0)
Jews	1	(0.5)	4	(1.0)	8	(1.0)	14	(2.0)	7	(1.0)
TOTAL	222	(100.0)	387	(99.0)	593	(99.5)	712	(100.0)	624	(100.0)

Note: "Dutch" category includes Germans and other miscellaneous nationalities.
[a] Members of conquest cohort.
[b] Male taxpayers.
[c] Male taxpayers.
[d] Male taxpayers.
[e] Male heads of household in census.

riod was clearly adumbrated in the structural changes that occurred in the city in the late seventeenth century. This chapter explains the ways in which the shift in ethnic ratios affected the economic and political structures of the city.[3]

The decline in Dutch strength is evident from the population figures presented in table 4–1. The penetration of New York City society by newcomers is strikingly illustrated, with the non-Dutch group achieving near parity with the Dutch by 1703.[4] The direction of change is pinpointed by following the proportionate representation of the Dutch and English segments of the population over these years. In light of the sizable population turnover that characterized the English in seventeenth-century New York City, the steady growth in the English sector is particularly impressive. While the Jewish community in New York City remained very small throughout this period, significant fluctuations occurred in the demographic profile of the French community. The loss of strength in the years following the conquest is attributable to the lack of any noteworthy immigration plus the expected attrition from the cohort group. The dramatic upswing between 1676–77 and 1695 is obviously a consequence of the current of Huguenot immigration to New York that gathered force in the 1680s and continued throughout the rest of the century. This brief period of thirty-five years, then, witnessed profound changes in the ethnic makeup of the New York City population.[5] These changes, in turn, altered patterns of stratification in the city.

How did ethnicity affect the allocation of power and privilege in late seventeenth-century New York City? Were positions in the social order apportioned equitably to each ethnic group or did an ethnic hierarchy emerge to parallel the city's class hierarchy? Was New York City controlled by an ethnic elite that overlapped its political, economic and social elites or was the city's heterogeneous population fairly represented at the top levels of the social pyramid? Were low status positions associated with a particuar ethnic group? Discovering whether a system of ethnic stratification developed in the city entails analyzing the distribution of ethnic groups in New York City's occupational, wealth, and political structures. By determining the degree to which each ethnic component of the population was over- or underrepresented at the various levels of the social structure, it is possible to evaluate the role of ethnicity in shaping the New York City social structure.

Ascertaining the economic power of a group in society depends upon the choice of appropriate indexes to measure the group's economic position. Neither occupation nor wealth alone is an entirely reliable criterion of economic standing, but in tandem the two provide the best possible gauge of economic position. In the following analysis, wealth is measured along two scales—tax assessment of real and personal property, and incidence of slaveholding. Conclusions about the relative economic power of the Dutch, English, and French in New York City, then, are based on three dimensions of economic standing—occupation, tax assessment, and slaveholding.

The names of 667 taxpayers in the five urban wards were extracted from the city tax list of December 1695, of whom 593 were men and 74 were women.[6] The ethnic identity of the male taxpayers has been determined through an analysis of surnames. The occupations of 446 (75 percent) of the men have been ascertained with reliability. The profile of New York City's occupational structure in 1695 is based upon this sample of 446 men for whom sufficient data was available.

A study of New York City's occupational structure based on the tax list of December 1695 is biased in three ways. Recognition of these distorting factors should lead the way toward a clearer picture of the city's social structure. The first qualification concerns the city's black population. Comprising 700 in 1698 (about 14 percent of the population), blacks were primarily slaves and therefore were not entered on the tax rolls. Locked in a debased status by both law and custom, they formed the bottom layer of the social pyramid. However, New Yorkers of African descent also constituted a sizable component of the city's labor force, and their distribution in the occupational hierarchy is not as clear-cut as their position in the status order. How many blacks were skilled workers and in what crafts cannot be discovered from the available evidence. Slave workers, skilled or unskilled, regularly encountered hostility from white workingmen who resented their competition. However, even when the New York City Common Council passed a law in 1683–84 reserving the occupation of carman exclusively for whites, it acknowledged the importance of black workers in the city's economic life by allowing an exception: "Noe Negro Or Other Slave doe Drive Any Carte within this City under the penalty of Tweenty Shilling, to be payd by the Owner of such Slave for Each Offence, (Brewers Drayes or Carriages for Beer, Only Excepted)."[7] Whether or not laborers and domestic servants outnumbered skilled workers in the black population, it is certain that a greater proportion of blacks than whites were members of the city's laboring population, since black men, women, and children all were put to work by the white slaveowners of New York City.[8]

Though women were listed on the city's tax rolls and indisputably contributed to the city's economy, the 74 female taxpayers (11 percent of 667 taxpayers) have been excluded from this analysis for several reasons. First, it is difficult to identify the productive roles of these women.[9] Also, in many cases, especially those of widows, inherited wealth formed the basis of the tax assessment. It is not always possible to ascertain the marital status of these women. When married or widowed females are identified, one cannot readily discern their ethnic background. Finally, these women do not constitute a comparable group with the male taxpayers, since many of the women did not work regularly. Consequently, the group of women taxpayers has been eliminated from this analysis of economic stratification.

It is also important to consider the defining characteristics of the 147 men (25 percent of male taxpayers) for whom occupations have not been found. The bias lies in two possible directions. Occupations of poor or marginal individuals are always more difficult to find than those of their more prosperous fellow workers, and not surprisingly, a majority of those with unknown occupations were located in the lower tax brackets. Moreover, some poor people may have been omitted from the tax rolls altogether. The occupations of poor people, then, are underrepresented in this study. The other potential distorting factor concerns the ethnic identity of the taxpayers. Did a greater proportion of one ethnic group fall among the unknowns than of any other ethnic groups? Distortions along the lines of ethnicity do not appear to be significant in this study. The occupations of 92 of the 343 Dutch (27 percent) are unknown, 46 of the 175 English (26 percent), nine of the 67 French (13 percent) and none of the Jews. Thus, the proportion of unknowns in both the Dutch and English groups is only slightly higher than the overall proportion of unknowns, while the French and Jewish groups exhibit much better rates of identification.

The task of categorizing occupations is a complex one, involving many pitfalls.[10] For the purposes of this analysis, the forty occupations that were found in New York City in 1695 have been grouped into seven major categories, defined in terms of function. The occupations and ethnic identity of the 446 men studied are presented in table 4–2. In table 4–3, this

TABLE 4–2
Occupations and Ethnic Identity of Male Taxpayers, 1695

Occupation	Dutch	English	French	Jews	Total
Merchants & retailers	46	34	18	7	105
Professionals					
Physicians	6	1	1	—	8
Ministers	1	—	1	—	2
Attorneys	—	3	—	—	3
Government officeholders	6	16	1	—	23
Clerk	1	—	—	—	1
Printer	—	1	—	—	1
Schoolmasters	2	—	1	—	3
Service trades					
Victuallers, tavernkeepers	6	10	5	—	21
Bakers & bolters	20	1	1	—	22
Brewers	4	—	—	—	4
Butchers	—	4	—	1	5
Barber	—	1	—	—	1
Tobacconist	—	—	1	—	1
Combmaker	1	—	—	—	1
Maritime trades					
Mariners	29	23	10	—	62
Ship carpenters	3	6	2	—	11
Sailmakers	—	—	3	—	3
Ropemaker	—	1	—	—	1
Cloth & leather workers					
Cordwainers	30	2	2	—	34
Tailors	4	1	2	—	7
Weavers	1	—	2	—	3
Feltmakers	2	—	—	—	2
Glover	1	—	—	—	1
Wood, metal, & stone workers					
Carpenters	25	4	1	—	30
Joiners	—	4	—	—	4
Turners	3	1	—	—	4
Coopers	14	2	—	—	16
Masons	12	2	1	—	15
Blacksmiths	8	2	1	—	11
Silversmiths	5	1	1	—	7
Gunsmith	1	—	—	—	1
Brazier	1	—	—	—	1
Pavier	—	1	—	—	1
Pumpmaker	—	1	—	—	1
Potmakers	2	—	—	—	2

TABLE 4–2 (*cont.*)

Occupation	Dutch	English	French	Jews	Total
Wood, metal, & stone workers (*cont.*)					
Tallow chandlers	—	1	2	—	3
Glaziers	4	—	1	—	5
Laborers					
Carmen	12	6	—	—	18
Porter, laborer	1	—	1	—	2
TOTALS	251	129	58	8	446

data is consolidated in order to show the ethnic composition of the different occupational categories.

In comparison with the occupational structure of New Amsterdam at the time of the English conquest, New York City in 1695 displayed a somewhat larger range of trades. By the 1690s, the city boasted a printer, a tobacconist, a glover, a combmaker, and several silversmiths. None of these crafts had been practiced in New Amsterdam. On the other hand, the degree of occupational specialization in New York City in the 1690s was still rather limited and the vast majority of the working population was concentrated in the basic occupations. A comprehensive listing of trades practiced in the city of London in 1692 contains 139 different occupations in contrast to the forty occupations found in New York City in 1695.[11] In terms of economic diversity, New York City was still relatively undeveloped.

The central preoccupation of New York City's economy was commerce,[12] and the occupational breakdown illustrated in tables 4–2 and 4–3 confirms this fact.[13] Men in the mercantile and maritime trades accounted for over two-fifths of the city's working force, and when auxiliary trades such as bolter, cooper, and tallow chandler are included, then the predominance of occupations associated with the commerce of the port is evident.

The second largest occupational category in the city, closely following that of merchants and retailers, was that of wood, metal, and stone workers. Though this composite category included a variety of crafts, the building trades were most prominent in it. The importance of the building trades in New York City in the last decade of the seventeenth century is suggested by a notation in the diary of Benjamin Bullivant, who visited the city in 1697. Governor Fletcher "was . . . pleased to walk the town with me and shew me the multitudes of greate & Costly buildings erected since his arrivall about 4 years since to be theyr Gouvernour."[14] Other evidence corroborates this testimony. The growth in population necessitated additional housing and the pace of construction was too slow for some inhabi-

TABLE 4-3
Ethnic Composition of Occupational Categories, 1695

Ethnic Group	Merchants & Retailers	Professionals	Service Trades	Maritime Trades	Cloth & Leather Workers	Wood, Metal, & Stone Workers	Laborers	Proportion of NYC Population
Dutch	44% (N=46)	39% (N=16)	56% (N=31)	41.5% (N=32)	81% (N=38)	74% (N=75)	65% (N=13)	58.0%
English	32% (N=34)	51% (N=21)	29% (N=16)	39% (N=30)	6% (N=3)	19% (N=19)	30% (N=6)	29.5%
French	17% (N=18)	10% (N=4)	13% (N=7)	19.5% (N=15)	13% (N=6)	7% (N=7)	5% (N=1)	11.0%
Jews	7% (N=7)	—	2% (N=1)	—	—	—	—	1.0%
TOTAL	100% (N=105)	100% (N=41)	100% (N=55)	100% (N=77)	100% (N=47)	100% (N=101)	100% (N=20)	99.5%

tants.[15] A British official arriving in the city in 1701 complained, "I have eight in family and know not yett where to fix them, houses are so scarce and dear, and lodgings worse in this place."[16]

During the 1690s two new church edifices were erected in the city, the Garden Street Dutch Reformed Church, completed in 1694, and Trinity Church, built in 1697. Both of these projects employed numerous workmen in the building trades and an extant Trinity Church record of the "board of managers for the building of the church" provides numerous details of the process of construction.[17] The flurry of building activity may even have affected the quality of building materials. Dirck Vanderburgh, a master bricklayer, petitioned the New York Assembly in 1703 concerning the fact that "the Brichmakers in this province, making their Bricks not according to the Standard of England, is prejudicial to this Province."[18] In light of this peculiar request from a man of Dutch background, it is not surprising to learn that Vanderburgh was in charge of the masons' work on Trinity Church, and was responsible for keeping eight or ten workmen on that job.

The expansion of the city, then, as well as its commercial life, accounted for its distinctive occupational profile. While the majority of the working population was involved in some aspect of commerce or construction, numerous men were engaged in those productive activities that are necessary to sustain life in any complex society. Providing food, clothing, and professional services to the community at large, these men played just as vital a role in New York City's economy as those directly involved in the building trades or commercial activity. The city's tavernkeepers also fulfilled an essential function in the community by supplying an appropriate environment for social and political interchanges.

It is essential to point out that the size of the laborers' category in this analysis is too small because of two biases of the taxpayers sample already noted. Many of those men for whom occupations are unknown were probably laborers. In addition, slaves formed an integral part of the city's labor force, but they are not included in this sample based on taxpayers.

Examining the city's occupational structure with an eye to ethnicity reveals no extreme distortions and no evidence that an institutionalized system of ethnic stratification existed. Nevertheless, ethnicity did play a part in shaping the city's occupational configurations. The relationship between occupation and ethnicity in New York City is clarified by examining the ethnic composition of the seven major occupational categories found in the city in 1695 (see table 4–3). Comparing the proportion of each ethnic group in these occupational categories with the proportion of the group in the city's population as a whole enables us to determine if any marked disparities existed in the apportionment of occupations among the major ethnic groups.

While maintaining substantial representation in all the major occupational categories, the Dutch were clearly underrepresented as merchants and retailers, professionals, and in the maritime trades. On the other hand, they were significantly overrepresented as cloth and leather workers and as wood, metal, and stone workers. The French were equitably distributed in all occupational categories, though they were somewhat overrepresented in the maritime trades and as merchants and retailers. The occupational profile of the English reveals some significant divergences from their population profile, however. The English are underrepresented as cloth and leather workers and as wood, metal, and stone workers, while they are overrepresented as professionals and in the maritime trades. The patterns disclosed in this analysis indicate the means by which New York City integrated its newcomers into the economic structure.

During the latter third of the seventeenth century, Dutch control of all the major occupational areas was challenged by the intrusion of non-Dutch newcomers into the various spheres of work. The pace of penetration was uneven, however, and at the end of the century, certain occupations still remained bastions of Dutch strength. On the other hand, a number of key occupations had become ethnically diverse in makeup. The occupations that were dominated by the Dutch consisted primarily of basic productive trades. Why were these occupations so resistant to infiltration by newcomers? Part of the explanation may lie in the fact that the immigrant groups contained few persons skilled in these particular crafts.

Thus, the Dutch majority in particular trades may have come about by default in the absence of skilled immigrant competitors. Although this may have been the case in specific instances, a more likely reason for the situation concerns the traditional basis of these trades, and their perpetuation through the apprenticeship system and more generally through kinship ties. With the exception of bolters and coopers, the Dutch-dominated trades primarily served the local community. Premised upon reputation, handed down in native families, these crafts proved much more difficult for immigrants to break into than occupations connected with overseas trade or the new English government. Indeed, the employment of local Dutch workmen in the construction of Trinity Church testifies to the monopolization of the building trades by the Dutch. While English, French, and African workers also were enlisted in the project, the prominence of the Dutch in construction work guaranteed their involvement in the enterprise.

Immigrants were concentrated in those occupations whose structure had altered in response to the new governmental and economic conditions of the English regime. Familiarity with English legal and institutional forms gave English immigrants a distinct advantage in vying for governmental appointments at all levels. Political connections further assisted English newcomers in finding places in administrative ranks. The participation of Englishmen in the commerce of New York port was facilitated by the reordering of the parameters of trade to benefit the English empire. Prior experience within the boundaries of the English commercial world gave British newcomers the edge in many aspects of trade. French Huguenot merchants and mariners also possessed certain advantages in terms of previous dealings around the globe and some were able to prosper in New York because of this background.

With the planting of significant numbers of non-Dutch in New York City, a demand developed for specialized services to these ethnic communities. Ministers, schoolmasters, retailers, and especially tavernkeepers were required to meet the distinctive needs of English and French newcomers. The establishment of taverns geared to an ethnic clientele signalized the institutionalization of ethnic pluralism in the city.[19] As immigrants took their place in society, the occupational structure of the city began to change. In the face of substantial challenges to their hegemony in the mercantile and maritime trades, the Dutch had retreated, but they held on to the more secure but presumably less profitable basic trades.

What were the implications of these alterations in New York City's occupational configurations for the relative economic power of the three major ethnic groups? Ranking occupations by means of median assessments permits us to focus on the effects of this occupational redistribution on the economic position of the groups. Table 4–4 presents the median assessments computed for twenty-one occupational categories, arranged in four quartiles. Table 4–5 shows the number and proportion of each ethnic group located in each quartile. When interpreted in this way, the occupational profiles of the major ethnic groups point to significant differences in the groups' respective economic power. The Dutch are clearly underrepresented in the top quartile where the other groups are overrepresented. Thus, as New York City's occupational structure was remolded by the infiltration of non-Dutch immigrants, the altered economic profile of the Dutch community began to reflect the concentrated penetration of these newcomers into the top-ranked occupations.

Although the comparative positions of the ethnic groups on this scale suggest that a distinct setback in the economic power of the Dutch had occurred, the precise nature of the changes in New York City's economic structure in the late seventeenth century is made clear through analysis of the patterns of wealth distribution in the city. Measurement of each ethnic community's total wealth, as well as the internal distribution of that wealth, brings into focus the distinctive changes that were occurring in New York City's social structure. The overall distribution of wealth in New York City in 1695 is presented in table 4–6, and the distribution of wealth in each ethnic community is shown in tables 4–7, 4–8, and 4–9.

TABLE 4–4
Median Assessments for Occupations in New York City, 1695

	Occupation	Median Assessment
£75 to £100+	Merchants	£130
£50 to £74	Bakers & bolters	73
	Physicians	65
	Misc. professionals	64
	Misc. wood, metal, & stone workers	55
	Misc. maritime trades	53
	Tavernkeepers	50
	Silversmiths	50
£25 to £49	Coopers	43
	Misc. service trades	43
	Mariners[a]	38
	Blacksmiths	35
	Carpenters	30
	Joiners & turners	30
	Ship carpenters	30
	Government officeholders	30
	Masons	25
	Cordwainers	25
	Misc. cloth & leather workers	25
£0 to £24	Carmen & laborers	18
	Tailors	10

[a] The category of mariners includes both sea captains (who normally would be in the £50 to £74 group) and seamen (who normally would be in the £0 to £24 group).

TABLE 4–5
Ethnic Distribution of Occupations Ranked by Median Assessment, 1695 (in percent)

Ethnic Group	Median Assessments (£)				Proportion of Population
	0–24	25–49	50–74	75–100+	
Dutch	63.0 (N=17)	61.0 (N=139)	57.0 (N=49)	44.0 (N=46)	58.0
English	26.0 (N=7)	29.0 (N=67)	24.0 (N=21)	32.0 (N=34)	29.5
French	11.0 (N=3)	9.0 (N=21)	19.0 (N=16)	17.0 (N=18)	11.0
Jews	—	0.4 (N=1)	—	7.0 (N=7)	1.0
TOTAL	100.0 (N=27)	99.4 (N=228)	100.0 (N=86)	100.0 (N=105)	99.5

TABLE 4–6
Distribution of Wealth Based on the 1695 Tax List

Wealth Bracket (in percent)	Assessments of Persons (in pounds)	Total Assessed Wealth (in pounds)	Percent of Wealth	Cumulative Percent of Wealth
0–10	0–5	298	.57	.57
11–20	5–10	553	1.08	1.65
21–30	10–20	997	1.94	3.59
31–40	20–25	1,530	2.80	6.40
41–50	25–30	2,022	3.90	10.30
51–60	30–50	2,897	5.60	15.90
61–70	50–70	4,092	8.00	23.90
71–80	70–100	6,219	12.10	36.00
81–90	105–150	9,522	18.50	54.50
91–95	150–250	6,786	13.20	67.70
96–100	250–2,610	16,398	32.00	99.70
0–30	0–20	1,848	3.59	
31–60	20–50	6,449	12.30	
61–90	50–150	19,833	38.60	
91–100	150–2,610	23,184	45.20	

Note: The tax list is for the five New York City urban wards and the Bowery Ward (excluding Harlem). The total number of persons on the tax list is 722 (with 72 persons in the top eight brackets and 73 in the bottom two). The total assessed wealth for all 722 persons is £51,314.

TABLE 4–7
Distribution of Wealth for Dutch Men Based on the 1695 Tax List

Wealth Bracket (in percent)	Assessments of Persons (in pounds)	Total Assessed Wealth (in pounds)	Percent of Wealth	Cumulative Percent of Wealth
0–10	0–5	162	.63	.63
11–20	5–15	321	1.25	1.88
21–30	15–20	593	2.30	4.18
31–40	20–25	765	2.97	7.15
41–50	25–33	985	3.83	10.98
51–60	35–50	1,351	5.25	16.23
61–70	50–65	1,883	7.32	23.55
71–80	65–100	2,771	10.77	34.32
81–90	105–155	4,432	17.22	51.54
91–95	160–255	3,295	12.81	64.35
96–100	260–2,610	9,173	35.65	100.00
0–30	0–20	1,076	4.18	
31–60	20–50	3,101	12.05	
61–90	50–155	9,086	35.31	
91–100	160–2,610	12,468	48.46	

Note: The tax list is for the five New York City urban wards and the Bowery Ward (excluding Harlem). The total number of persons on the tax list is 343 (with 34 persons in the top nine brackets and 37 in the bottom bracket). The total assessed wealth for all 343 persons is £25,731.

TABLE 4–8
Distribution of Wealth for English Men Based on the
1695 Tax List

Wealth Bracket (in percent)	Assessments of Persons (in pounds)	Total Assessed Wealth (in pounds)	Percent of Wealth	Cumulative Percent of Wealth
0–10	3–5	70	.58	.58
11–20	5–10	109	.90	1.48
21–30	10–15	213	1.75	3.23
31–40	15–25	390	3.21	6.44
41–50	25–40	594	4.89	11.33
51–60	40–60	844	6.95	18.28
61–70	65–90	1,292	10.64	28.92
71–80	90–130	1,780	14.66	43.58
81–90	130–160	2,420	19.92	63.50
91–95	160–255	1,466	12.07	75.57
96–100	270–640	2,968	24.44	100.01
0–30	3–15	392	3.23	
31–60	15–60	1,828	15.05	
61–90	65–160	5,492	45.22	
91–100	160–640	4,434	36.51	

Note: The tax list is for the five New York City urban wards and the Bowery Ward (excluding Harlem). The total number of persons on the tax list is 175 (with 17 persons in the top five brackets and 18 in the bottom five brackets). The total assessed wealth for all 175 persons is £12,146.

TABLE 4–9
Distribution of Wealth for French Men Based on the
1695 Tax List

Wealth Bracket (in percent)	Assessments of Persons (in pounds)	Total Assessed Wealth (in pounds)	Percent of Wealth	Cumulative Percent of Wealth
0–10	3–5	31	.65	.65
11–20	5–10	53	1.10	1.75
21–30	10	70	1.50	3.25
31–40	10–15	98	2.10	5.35
41–50	15–25	150	3.20	8.55
51–60	25–40	230	4.80	13.35
61–70	45–50	345	7.25	20.60
71–80	60–90	500	10.50	31.10
81–90	130–175	905	19.00	50.10
91–95	190–290	730	15.30	65.40
96–100	455–710	1,645	34.60	100.00
0–30	3–10	154	3.25	
31–60	10–40	478	10.10	
61–90	45–175	1,750	36.75	
91–100	190–710	2,375	49.90	

Note: The tax list is for the five New York City urban wards and the Bowery Ward (excluding Harlem). The total number of persons on the tax list is 67 (with 6 persons in the top three brackets and 7 in the bottom bracket). The total assessed wealth for all 67 persons is £4,757.

New York City in 1695 was far from an egalitarian society. The upper tenth held over 45 percent of the wealth, while the top 5 percent controlled almost one-third of the wealth. Moreover, the people in the bottom half of the wealth spectrum controlled only about 10 percent of the city's total wealth. Yet New York City was not unique among colonial cities in the late seventeenth century. The wealth distribution profiles of Boston and Philadelphia in the same time period are remarkably similar.[20] In Boston in 1687, the top tenth held 46 percent of the taxable property, while in Philadelphia in 1693 people in the same bracket also held 46 percent of the wealth. In New York City in 1695, as noted, the top tenth controlled just over 45 percent of the taxable property. At the same time, the lowest 30 percent on the wealth spectrum controlled 3.59 percent of the wealth, while in Boston in 1687 the comparable group held 2.6 percent of the wealth, and in Philadelphia in 1693 those in the same bracket held 2.2 percent of the wealth. All of these colonial urban societies, then, were highly differentiated. Yet New York City manifested a singular pattern of ethnic differentiation. In order to determine whether a form of ethnic stratification accompanied the economic stratification revealed here, it is necessary to study more intensively the distribution of wealth in each of the city's major ethnic communities.

This analysis of the distribution of wealth in New York City's ethnic communities is based upon the male taxpayers of each ethnic group resident in the city's five urban wards, but also includes property they held in the Bowery ward. Comparing the relative economic power of these groups as a whole reveals a remarkably equitable division of resources among New York's major ethnic groups. Table 4–10 shows the amount and proportion of wealth controlled by each ethnic group in relation to its size in the city.

It is clear that no one group had a monopoly on wealth in New York City. The distribution of wealth closely paralleled the ethnic makeup of the population and no evidence of ethnic stratification is present. Yet the way in which the total wealth of each ethnic group was divided among its members differed considerably, with the distribution of wealth in the Dutch and French communities much more uneven than that in the English community (see tables 4–7, 4–8, and 4–9). The upper tenth of the wealth pyramid in the Dutch and French groups controlled close to one-half of their community's respective wealth, whereas the top tenth of the English group controlled only slightly more than 35 percent of the total wealth of their community. If one employs a narrower definition of the economic elite (the top 5 percent of the wealth pyramid), a similar picture emerges. The upper 5 percent of the Dutch and French groups held just over one-third of their group's wealth but the wealthiest 5 percent of the

TABLE 4–10
Ethnic Distribution of Taxable Property, 1695

Ethnic Group (Males)	Total Taxable Wealth (in pounds)	Proportion of Taxable Wealth (in percent)	Proportion in Population (in percent)
Dutch			
(N = 343)	25,731	59.0	58.0
English			
(N = 175)	12,146	28.0	29.5
French			
(N = 67)	4,757	11.0	11.0
Jews			
(N = 8)	670	1.5	1.0
TOTAL	43,304	99.5	99.5

English group held slightly less than one-quarter of the total wealth of their group.

The relative economic leverage of members of these groups located in other wealth brackets also varied. The French were comparatively in the worst position. While the bottom half of the Dutch and English groups controlled about 11 percent of their community's wealth, the lower half of the French group possessed only 8.5 percent of that group's total wealth. In the 50 to 80 percent brackets, however, the Dutch and English wealth patterns diverged, as the French pattern again closely paralleled the Dutch. The Dutch and French in the combined 50 to 80 percent brackets controlled about 23 percent of the wealth of their respective groups, whereas the English located in the same brackets controlled over 32 percent of the wealth of their community. English men of these upper middle ranks, then, had a considerably greater amount of economic leverage than their counterparts among the Dutch and the French.

Thus, even though the wealth of New York City male taxpayers was distributed closely in proportion to the relative size of the city's major ethnic groups, the distribution of wealth within each ethnic community did not exhibit a uniform pattern. Both the Dutch and French communities were dominated by an extremely wealthy elite, while the English elite was considerably less affluent. The upper middle ranks of the Dutch and French groups were not as well off as the comparable segments of the English group, suggesting that the great wealth of the Dutch and French elites was obtained at the expense of those in the middle levels of the wealth structure. No one in the poorest ranks of New York City's social structure had much economic leverage, but the French poor were the most disadvantaged in relative terms.

In a society that depends on slave labor, the ownership of slaves is a gauge to the economic power of the inhabitants. Whether employed in a craft, a business establishment, as domestic servants, or hired out as day laborers, slaves were a valuable asset in seventeenth-century New York City. The extent and dimensions of slaveholding in the city emerge from an analysis of the data contained in the 1703 census.[21] While 41 percent of the households in New York City held at least one slave in 1703, only 37 percent of the Dutch households possessed slaves. In contrast to this small underrepresentation of Dutch slaveholders, 44 percent of the English, 50 percent of the French, and 75 percent of the Jewish households contained slaves. In a society where slaveholding had been institutionalized under the government of a Dutch trading company specializing in the slave trade, non-Dutch ethnic groups had outstripped the Dutch in slave ownership.

From another perspective, the Dutch were also relatively less involved in slaveholding than the city's other ethnic groups. In table 4–11, the number and proportion of slaveholders in each ethnic group and the number and proportion of the city's slaves owned by the members of each ethnic group is given, along with the proportion of each ethnic group in the city's population in 1703. While the Dutch formed 52 percent of the city's adult male population, they comprised 47 percent of the slaveholders and owned only 45 percent of the city's slaves. The English, French, and Jews, however, were proportionately more involved in slaveholding than their size in the city's population. The Dutch also fell near the bottom of the scale on another index—the size of slaveholdings. The average number of slaves owned by the English was 2.4, by the French 2.3, by the Dutch 2.1, and by the Jews 2.0. Thus, of all the major ethnic groups in New York

TABLE 4–11
Ethnic Distribution of Slaveowners, 1703

Ethnic Group	Proportion of Male Population (in percent)	Number and Proportion of Slaveowners		Number and Proportion of Slaves Owned	
Dutch	52	148	(47%)	314	(45%)
English	36	119	(38%)	285	(40%)
French	11	41	(13%)	93	(13%)
Jews	1	6	(2%)	12	(2%)
TOTAL	100	314	(100%)	704	(100%)

City, the Dutch were in the least advantageous position with respect to slaveholding.

As the eighteenth century began, the New York City Dutch still formed a slight majority of the city's population. Possessed of an extremely wealthy elite and a strong numerical and institutional base, the Dutch were not in danger of wholesale displacement from their traditional place in the city's social structure. Nevertheless, English and French immigrants had carved out niches in the community. New York City had become a plural society in reality, and economic power was shared among all ethnic groups. The division of power in the political structure also signified the institutionalization of pluralism in the city.

The imposition of English rule on the colony of New York had immediate repercussions in the ethnic makeup of New York City's municipal government. Although Englishmen were placed in city offices alongside the Dutch, these appointments reflected English colonial policy rather than changes in the contours of New York City's social structure. With the passage of years, however, the alterations in the composition of the city's Common Council that had been instituted by fiat were legitimized by the patterns of immigration to the city. By the time of the Dongan charter of 1686, which provided for the election of aldermen, assistant aldermen, and constables by ward, the penetration of New York society by non-Dutch newcomers had created the demographic preconditions for a multiethnic slate of municipal officeholders.[22]

In order to ascertain the extent to which New York City's political structure mirrored its ethnic structure, the ethnic background of municipal officeholders over the twenty-year period from 1687 to 1707 has been analyzed.[23] Table 4–12 presents information on the ethnic identity of all officeholders for the city's five urban wards, including assessors and tax collectors, who were not elected but appointed by aldermen in the respective wards. Although cognizant of variations by wards and years, the following generalizations are based on the overall picture of municipal officeholding in this twenty-year time span.

No political office was barred to any major ethnic group, and with a few exceptions, offices along the entire spectrum were distributed roughly in proportion to the relative size of the three groups in the city's population. The Dutch were somewhat overrepresented, while the French were slightly underrepresented. Only in the most important office of alderman were the French clearly disadvantaged, holding only two positions out of 100. The English were grossly underrepresented in the appointed office of tax collector, where the Dutch were greatly overrepresented. Dutch tax collectors undoubtedly were more efficient in a city with a large Dutch population. Moreover, this onerous office would have been especially difficult for a newcomer to fill. The city's political hierarchy, then, was not

TABLE 4–12
Ethnic Distribution of Municipal Officeholders, 1687–1707

Office	Number of Positions Available	Number of Positions Held by			
		Dutch	English	French	Jews
Alderman	100	66 (66%)	32 (32%)	2 (2%)	—
Assistant alderman	100	64 (64%)	28 (28%)	8 (8%)	—
Assessor	190	125 (66%)	49 (26%)	16 (8%)	—
Tax collector	55	46 (84%)	3 (5%)	6 (11%)	—
Constable	100	61 (61%)	32 (32%)	7 (7%)	—
TOTAL	545	362 (66%)	144 (26%)	39 (7%)	—
Proportion of Population (in percent)		58.0	29.5	11.0	1.0

congruent with any form of ethnic hierarchy. One ethnic group did not monopolize the city's powerful and prestigious offices, leaving the least desirable offices to be filled by members of the other ethnic groups. Local political office at any level was not the exclusive prerogative of any particular ethnic group.

While political power at the local level was shared equitably among the city's major ethnic groups, New Yorkers were far more cautious in selecting officeholders on the basis of occupation. As seen in table 4–13, the status of officeholders, as measured by occupation, was clearly related to the level of office held. Merchants filled more and more positions the higher one goes in the political hierarchy, while the opposite is true for artisans. The New York City political hierarchy was calibrated more to the city's occupational hierarchy than to any ethnic ranking system. The political elite was much more of an occupational elite than an ethnic elite.

That leadership in New York City society was not restricted to any one ethnic group is further corroborated by an analysis of the background of the city's militia officers in 1700.[24] The New York City regiment of militia, consisting of 685 men, was led by 31 officers, including three field officers, and the officers of eight foot companies and a troop of horse. Of these 31 officers, 19 (61 percent) were Dutch, 9 (29 percent) were English, and 3 (10 percent) were French. Thus, positions of leadership in the military hierarchy were also allocated roughly in proportion to the ethnic composition of the city's population. The plural nature of New York City society was reflected in its military leadership.

TABLE 4–13
Occupational Distribution of Municipal Officeholders, 1687–1707

Office	No. of Positions Available	Number of Positions Held by						
		Merchants	Professionals & Govt. Employees	Bakers, Bolters, Brewers, Butchers	Tavern-keepers	Artisans	Mariners	Unknown
Alderman	100	65 (65%)	—	17 (17%)	4 (4%)	7 (7%)	7 (7%)	—
Assistant alderman	100	45 (45%)	2 (2%)	10 (10%)	4 (4%)	33 (33%)	6 (6%)	—
Assessor	190	74 (39%)	6 (3%)	9 (5%)	4 (2%)	84 (44%)	9 (5%)	4 (2%)
Tax collector	55	11 (20%)	4 (7%)	6 (11%)	1 (2%)	28 (51%)	1 (2%)	4 (7%)
Constable	100	15 (15%)	3 (3%)	11 (11%)	4 (4%)	57 (57%)	3 (3%)	7 (7%)
TOTAL	545	210 (38.5%)	15 (3%)	53 (10%)	17 (3%)	209 (38%)	26 (5%)	15 (3%)

The distribution of economic and political power in seventeenth-century New York City was far more equitable than might have been expected in a city that had been a pawn in the Anglo-Dutch contest for empire. Although ethnic antagonism flared periodically, this interethnic conflict did not bring in its wake a pronounced system of ethnic stratification in which one group completely dominated the others. The absence of any conspicuous form of ethnic stratification in seventeenth-century New York City, however, does not imply that ethnicity played no part in shaping the city's social structure. On the contrary, the manner in which power and privilege were shared by the major ethnic groups suggests that ethnicity was a very potent factor in New York City's social environment and that consciousness of ethnicity was pervasive. Tracing the development of each ethnic community during the latter third of the seventeenth century will enhance our understanding of the maturation of New York City as a plural society.

Chapter Five

COMMUNITY AND CULTURE IN
SEVENTEENTH-CENTURY NEW YORK CITY

THE IMPRINT of ethnic diversity on seventeenth-century
New York City society was not limited to the shaping of the
city's patterns of stratification. The convergence of three distinct European nationalities within the boundaries of the city also affected
the ordering of community life. Although always heterogeneous in the
makeup of its population, the settlement on lower Manhattan Island did
not possess well-defined ethnic subcommunities during the period of
Dutch rule. By the end of the seventeenth century, in the wake of substantial non-Dutch immigration to the city, an ethnically differentiated society
had emerged, with the crystallization of discrete Dutch, English, and
French communities. Although rigid ethnic compartmentalization was
never totally realized in late seventeenth-century New York, the trend toward separation and heightened ethnic consciousness was unmistakable.
The most telling evidence that a process of differentiation was at work
comes from the altered framework of community life, as institutions serving specific ethnic constituencies were created and existing institutions
were redefined along ethnic lines. Corroborative evidence can be gleaned
from analysis of the the patterns of behavior that characterized New York
City's inhabitants. While explanations must be advanced for contradictory
tendencies, the overall pattern revealed through behavioral evidence
confirms that a structurally and culturally plural society had come into
being at New York City by 1700.

How had a system of social arrangements premised on ethnic differences evolved in seventeenth-century New York City? Theoretically, the
separation of ethnic groups in a society may result from a decision of the
ruling authorities. The coercive power of the state enforces a discrim-
inatory policy against certain groups whose oppression is intellectually
justified. Consequently, separation signifies segregation or ghettoization,
as some groups are singled out as less than equal. The power relationship between groups in society determines the condition of separation,
even though state policy may coincide with group imperatives regarding
autonomy.

In the case of seventeenth-century New York City, ethnic separation
was not the product of external pressure from governmental authority. In-

deed, ethnic consciousness persisted in the face of a contrary English policy. Envisioning a society in which a much greater degree of cultural homogeneity prevailed, the English did not wish the Dutch and French inhabitants of the city to remain apart as separate groups, but instead wanted them to amalgamate with the English people of the city, or at least become Anglicized in culture. Yet realism dictated a policy of toleration, for the English newcomers were themselves a cultural minority in a predominantly Dutch society throughout the seventeenth century.[1] In the early years of their administration, the English pursued a consciously conciliatory policy in the cultural realm, allowing a wide range of practices to persist. Yet at the same time they were committed to transforming New Netherland into an English province, thereby removing the threat of alien influence from within the colony. In this sense, the transfer in governmental authority was only the prelude to the central task of Anglicizing New York society. Cultural coexistence at New York City was a necessary, though temporary, stage in the metamorphosis of New York City into a truly English society. Still, cognizant of historical and demographic factors, the English were moved to acknowledge the legitimacy of a pluralistic social order in New York City, even though they occasionally invoked indirect sanctions to accelerate the process of Anglicization.

Was ethnic separation, then, a result of independent choice on the part of the city's non-English ethnic groups? A voluntaristic explanation for the society's ethnic compartmentalization is also inadequate. The historical precedent of Dutch rule and the prominence of Dutch institutions in New York City precluded "free choice" for most of the city's residents. The Dutch Reformed church, with its place in society rooted in the historical experience of the people, was a force of considerable magnitude in the community. Moreover, its corporate power extended to adjunct charitable and educational activities. The coercive capability of this institutional complex ensured that the maintenance of Dutch culture in New York City rested on much more than a series of individual choices.

With the exception of small covert groups of Lutherans and Jews, whose existence was officially decried but condoned in practice, New Amsterdam's diverse population had been served primarily by the institutional network centered in the Dutch Reformed church and the Dutch West India Company.[2] The religious, educational, and charitable functions essential for the maintenance of community life were provided by complementary activities of company and church. Individuals of any nationality could attend religious services in the Dutch Reformed church and membership was not restricted to persons of Dutch background. Interethnic unions were consolidated through the agency of the church and the offspring of such unions were baptized in the church. Other communal services performed by the church were also available to non-Dutch persons, whether or not they were church members. Although the administration of poor relief involved both civil and ecclesiastical authorities, charity was dispensed to all persons in need by the deacons of the Dutch Reformed church. The church also maintained an almshouse, which served mainly the aged poor, and a poor farm.[3]

Church, company, and local government all combined to meet the educational needs of New Amsterdam's youth. The Dutch placed great value on education and a city school was founded in New Amsterdam as early as 1638. Other educational ventures, including a Latin school and independent classes taught by private schoolmasters, operated at various times during New Amsterdam's history. While local church authorities did not exercise extensive control over these enterprises, the Amsterdam Classis had a substantial influence on the city's educational program.[4] In an environment so supportive of education, it is unlikely that prospective students were barred from attendance at the community's schools because of their nationality. Instructions prepared for schoolmaster Evert Pietersen by the burgomasters of New Amsterdam in 1661 specified that "the poor and needy, who ask to be taught for God's sake he shall teach for nothing."[5] The pragmatic demands of the Dutch West India Company for settlers overshadowed all attempts on the part of Peter Stuyvesant and the Calvinist clergy to enforce orthodoxy in New Amsterdam.[6] The metropolitan Dutch tradition of toleration coupled with the open competitiveness of the frontier environment created a social climate in which cultural differences were subordinated to economic gain. The inclusive nature of the community's institutions merely reflected the larger societal ethos.

The Dutch institutional network was not obliterated at the advent of English rule, the lenient terms of the peace settlement ensuring its continuance. Nevertheless, the legal status of the institutions founded and maintained by the Dutch church and government was changed, leaving the door open for the creation of alternative institutions in the city. The Dutch Reformed church, which had formerly been the established church, lost its privileged position and became in theory, if not in fact, just one church in the community. Similarly, the Dutch city school was transformed into a voluntary enterprise after 1674, when its municipal financial support ceased. The charitable activity of the Dutch Reformed church also acquired a narrower focus, no longer constituting a community-wide system of philanthropy. In response to a complaint of the deacons of the Dutch Reformed church in 1671 "that they are charged with some of the poore of the Lutheran profession notwithstanding a Collection is made for the poore in the said Lutheran Church," the Mayor's Court of New York City ordered that "each Church should for the future Maintaine their owne Poore."[7]

As the domain of the Dutch Reformed church contracted, and its responsibilities toward the inhabitants of the community were redefined, other ethnic groups began to fill the institutional void in the city. Once concentrated in the institutions of the Dutch establishment, the religious, educational, and philanthropic functions of the community were progressively diffused among the city's ethnic groups throughout the remainder of the century. With the development of parallel institutional structures in the latter third of the seventeenth century, culminating in the establishment of the Church of England in 1697, the basis was laid for a pluralistic social order in New York City.

Minority religious sects availed themselves of the opportunity afforded by the English position on toleration to come out into the open. Lutherans, Quakers, and Jews, none of whom had been allowed to worship publicly under the Dutch regime, all were permitted to found congregations in New York City during the seventeenth century. The Lutherans were recognized in 1666 by Governor Nicolls and were already in the process of erecting a church building in 1671–72.[8] Quakers were also present in the city during the first decade of English rule, but the earliest record of a Quaker meeting in New York City is dated 1681.[9] The Jewish congregation, Shearith Israel, was able to worship openly perhaps as early as 1682, but certainly by 1695. A real estate deed of 1700 mentions a house on Mill Street owned by John Harperding as "now commonly known by the name of the Jews' synagogue."[10]

Yet the most significant alterations in the institutional profile of the community were linked to the currents of immigration that revised the ethnic composition of the city's population. Not until the small nuclei of English and French in the city were supplemented by sizable infusions of newcomers were they able to form separate churches. In 1683, English and French clergymen were conducting religious worship in the Dutch church. Henricus (Henry) Selyns, the minister of the Dutch Reformed church, reported that "Rev. John Gordon, has come over from England, to perform service for the English. His English service is after my morning service, and the French service is after my afternoon service."[11] Although a series of chaplains attached to the English garrison ministered to the small number of Anglicans in the city until the foundation of Trinity Church, the French pastor, Peter Daillé, had just arrived in New York in 1683. Within the span of a few years, he was joined by many fellow French Huguenots in exile.

The influx of French Protestant refugees after 1686 prompted the creation of a separate French Reformed church in New York City in 1688. The recency of their flight, the obligation of sustaining their religious beliefs, and their settlement in a multiethnic community, all served to reinforce their sense of separateness as a group. As dissenters from the religious orthodoxy of Louis XIV's Catholic France, the Huguenots undoubtedly felt their innermost sense of identity premised upon their commitment to the Protestant faith. The foundation of the Eglise Françoise à la Nouvelle York almost immediately after numbers of refugees had gathered in New York reflected their pronounced religiosity. Yet the church also provided an organizational nucleus for the city's expanding French community. In addition to conducting marriages, baptisms, and funerals, the church held itself responsible for the support of needy French refugees. Collections for the poor were made at regular services and the new congregation also received special gifts from time to time. Funds were dispensed to a small number of indigent parishioners whose names can be gleaned from the meticulous records kept by the church. Instruction in the basic religious tenets was provided by Pierre Bontecou, a schoolmaster employed by the church as a reader.[12]

In establishing a church in New York City, the exiled French Huguenots not only met the particular needs of their people, but they added to the city's institutional complexity. Yet the process of institution formation in seventeenth-century New York City was not completed until the Anglican church was begun almost a decade later. The English experience of church-founding was quite different from that of the French Huguenots. The bulk of the Huguenots who settled in New York City arrived during the last fifteen years of the seventeenth century and rapidly organized themselves into a discrete and self-sufficient ethnoreligious community with a stable institutional base. In contrast, the English arrival at New York City was not chronologically telescoped. Moreover, the English sector of New York City society lacked the internal unity that so marked the French community. Composed of persons with diverse backgrounds and different religious orientations, the city's English were far from a cohesive ethnoreligious community. Consequently, official intervention was required in order to inaugurate the Anglican church in New York City.

The process of founding Trinity Church occurred during the administration of Governor Benjamin Fletcher.[13] After an extended political struggle catalyzed by the Ministry Act of 1693, Dutch support for an Anglican establishment in New York City was obtained in exchange for a charter guaranteeing legal security for the Dutch Reformed church.[14] The charter was granted in 1696 and Trinity Church was established in 1697. While pressure for a local unit of the Church of England was generated by the official community, sufficient support from the indigenous English society was also essential. That enough English men were willing to involve themselves in the planning and construction of the church demonstrates not only their commitment to the enterprise but their realization that the city's English needed an institutional base. Though total identification of New York City's English community with the new Anglican church was impossible because of the presence of dissenters in the population, the creation of an English church in New York City added an essential component to the city's institutional structure. Auxiliary educational and charitable activities soon supplemented the church's religious functions. Bolstered by the support of the Society for the Propagation of the Gospel in Foreign Parts (S.P.G.) soon after the turn of the century, the Anglican establishment quickly assumed a prominent place in the city's social order.

Between the time of the English conquest and 1700, the English and French, along with a few minority religious sects, created autonomous institutions in New York City that complemented the preexisting Dutch institutional network. These alterations in the community's institutional framework provided the structural basis for ethnic separation in New York City.[15] To ascertain whether the actions of New York City's inhabitants reinforced the structure of ethnic separation rooted in the community's institutional pattern, it is necessary to examine behavioral evidence in conjunction with the evidence on institutional change.

The analysis of responses to situations involving a choice relating to ethnicity enables us to determine the importance attached to the perpetuation of ethnic identity by members of any community. Preserving ethnic solidarity in a heterogeneous urban society required deliberate actions. Unconscious adherence to traditional ways was not enough. Social distance had to be maintained through conscious choices on issues involving ethnic identity. These decisions, which covered such matters as church affiliation, marriage partner, education, apprenticeship, language retention, and philanthropic activity, can be evaluated systematically with reference to ethnicity, thereby affording an insight into the dynamics of the New York City social system that cannot be gained from an overview of the city's institutional framework.

One way of assessing the significance of ethnic consciousness in a community entails analyzing patterns of church affiliation. Though ethnic identity and religious identity are not always identical, they often overlap. That the two were intertwined in late seventeenth-century New York City is made clear by the demarcation of groups in the city's religious spectrum along ethnic lines. The Dutch Reformed church was the religious home of the Dutch, the Eglise Française à la Nouvelle York catered to the French, and the Quaker meeting and Trinity Church served the city's English population. In addition, a small number of Dutch, Germans, and Scandinavians belonged to the Lutheran church and the Jews had their own synagogue. Since the city's religious institutions were essentially ethnic churches, ethnic consciousness could be expressed through identification with an ethnically circumscribed church. Church affiliation, then, forms a reliable indicator of the importance of ethnicity to the city's inhabitants.

To what extent did New Yorkers participate in this ethnically structured religious life? The presence of religious institutions in a community does not necessarily imply a high degree of religiosity nor even a substantial amount of church affiliation. Though no precise figures are available, it is possible to develop an estimate of the proportion of the New York City population that was churched. According to the census of 1698, there were 2,076 white adults in New York City. A contemporary observer put the size of the Dutch Reformed congregation in 1698 at 650 persons.[16] This statistic is plausible in light of a document that enumerates 556 individuals who were church members in 1686[17] and the church admissions list for the intervening years. Maynard's estimate of the size of the parish of the Eglise Françoise à la Nouvelle York—between 700 and 800 in 1700—is too high.[18] If we cut the figure to 400 and divide it in half for the number of adult parishioners, we arrive at 200. Trinity Church had just been established in 1697 and the congregation was quite small at this time. No membership records are extant, but a list of church wardens and vestrymen shows that fifty men served in these offices between 1697 and 1704.[19] Assuming that these officials were not the only members of the church, a figure of 100 Anglicans seems justifiable. The membership of the city's smaller religious bodies—the Lutherans, Jews, and Quakers—combined may have totaled another 100 persons. Thus, approximately 1,050 white adults or 51 percent of the adult white population of New York City in 1698 were church members.

The fact that more than half of the city's adult white population in 1698 was churched suggests that participation in church life was an effective means of sustaining ethnic identity in the diverse milieu of seventeenth-century New York City. A close look at the social composition of New York City's three major congregations illuminates the distinctive features of the city's ethnoreligious communities.

Despite setbacks following the English reconquest and Leisler's Rebellion, the Dutch Reformed church expanded substantially during the seventeenth century—from between 300 and 400 in 1666 to 450 in 1681 and 650 in 1698—and moved from the old church in the fort to a new and larger church on Garden Street in 1694.[20] The upheaval generated by Leisler's Rebellion had an especially severe impact on the church because the Reverend Henricus Selyns chose to side with the English authorities and their allies among the Dutch elite during the conflict, thereby alienating the majority of Dutch residents who saw Jacob Leisler as a heroic figure. Church attendance dipped precipitously in the wake of the rebellion and only gradually recovered. "The people got such an aversion to the public worship, that at first only a tenth part enjoyed the Lord's Supper, and some have to this day not enjoyed the same," partisans of Leisler asserted in 1698.[21] But even with the disruptions triggered by Leisler and his followers, Selyns and his Dutch colleagues in 1692 were already sanguine about the future of their church. "During this year of troubles," they reported to the Amsterdam Classis, "a new church edifice of stone, is in course of erection, outside the fort and larger than the old one. In this we hope to bring to the knowledge of God and Jesus Christ, many, who had a certain antipathy to the church in the fort."[22] By 1694 Selyns was informing the classis that "the troubles are, no doubt, diminishing. The attendance at church services has improved. My salary is better paid; but the arrearages remain unpaid, and I see no prospect of their ever being paid. Our new church (in Garden St.) is finished up to the towers. On Sundays it is too small; on Wednesdays, too large."[23] Though difficulties associated with Leisler's Rebellion resurfaced in 1698, the New York City Dutch church outlasted the crisis.

The core of the congregation was a group of families that now extended into the second and third generations. Dominie Selyns's 1686 enumeration of the 556 members of the church, when analyzed in conjunction with serial membership lists, affords an opportunity to examine the duration of membership.[24] Many communicants had deep roots in the congregation. Of the 430 for whom sufficient data are available, 48 percent had been members for over ten years and 23 percent for over twenty years. Of those persons who joined the church in the ten years before 1686, a substantial number can be identified as children or relatives of members. Kinship ties of all kinds crisscrossed the congregation. Dutch newcomers to the city, primarily from Albany and Long Island but also from the Netherlands and the West Indies, constituted the remainder of the congregation in the seventeenth century.[25]

After 1664, the vast majority of the congregation remained Dutch. Of the 556 communicants in 1686, only twelve can be identified as non-Dutch: five Englishmen, one Frenchman, and six free blacks. The English and French men were married to Dutch women and the black men and women had, in an important sense, become culturally Dutch through long residence in the city.[26] In addition, twenty Dutch women church members were married to English men who were not church members. For example, Margareta Blanck was listed in 1686 as "huysvrouw van Philip Smit." Margareta, the daughter of cohort member Jeuriaen Blanck, had married Philip Smith of Cambridge, England, in the Dutch Reformed Church in 1676. In other words, of the twenty-five English men married to Dutch women who belonged to the church, 80 percent chose not to join a church identified with a different ethnic group. The fact that these twenty English men who married Dutch women in New York remained outside the congregation supports the thesis that the Dutch Reformed church was redefining itself along ethnic lines in the late seventeenth century. Moreover, a few French men who had joined the church in New Amsterdam were no longer listed as members in 1686 and are noted as transferring to the French church in the margins of the church admissions records. Cohort member Paul Richard, whose wife Celetje Jans was listed as a member in

1686, had joined the Dutch Reformed Church in 1663 and had been married there in 1664. Yet he no longer was a church member in 1686.

Not only were the majority of Reformed church members of Dutch ancestry, but the majority of the city's Dutch population in the seventeenth century was affiliated with this church. The 650 members in 1698 composed approximately 57 percent of the Dutch adults in the city.[27] In addition, some Dutch residents belonged to the small congregation of Dutch Lutherans, while others of pietist sympathy may have participated in an informal gathering of Dutch Labadists during the 1680s.[28]

In the late seventeenth century, New York City's Dutch Reformed church was ethnically enclosed but socially inclusive. The 188 male adherents whose names appear on the city tax list of 1695 are found in every tax bracket, although the higher a man's assessment, the greater the chance that he was a communicant (see table 5–1). While only 65 (38 percent) of the 173 men in the lower half of the Dutch wealth spectrum are identifiable as church members, 123 (72 percent) of the 170 men in the upper half were members.[29] In the top three wealth brackets, 80 (78 percent) of 102 men were members, but only 37 (35 percent) of 105 men in the lowest three brackets were members. The elders and deacons were men of stature in the community but by no means were drawn exclusively from the mercantile elite. Of the thirty men who filled these offices from 1701 through

TABLE 5–1
Economic Position of Male Members of Dutch Reformed Church, 1695

Wealth Bracket (in percent)	Assessments of Persons (in pounds)	Number of Persons	Number & Percent of Dutch Reformed Church Members
0–10	0–5	35	9 (24%)
10–20	5–15	35	14 (41%)
20–30	15–20	35	14 (41%)
30–40	20–25	34	10 (29%)
40–50	25–33	34	18 (53%)
50–60	35–50	34	23 (68%)
60–70	50–65	34	20 (59%)
70–80	65–100	34	26 (76%)
80–90	105–155	34	26 (76%)
90–100	160–2,610	34	28 (82%)
		343	188 (55%)

Note: This table is based on information contained in table 4–7 in chapter 4.

1710, ten were merchants, five were bakers, and three each were silver-smiths, physicians, and shoemakers. The remainder included two carpenters, a brewer, a mariner, a cooper, and a glazier.[30]

Though males dominated the church's lay leadership, they were outnumbered by women in the congregation. In 1686, 344 (62 percent) of the 556 communicants were female.[31] Of the 882 persons admitted to the church between 1665 and 1695, 517 (59 percent) were women. Women continued to outnumber men among those entering the church between 1696 and 1730 by a ratio of approximately two to one.[32] This sexual disparity takes on additional meaning when one notes that in 1686, 44 percent of households were represented in the church solely by virtue of a female member. In that year, the membership consisted of 179 married couples, 100 wives (of nonmembers), 34 widows, 33 single men, and 31 single women.[33]

In the late seventeenth century, in sharp contrast to the Dutch Reformed church, whose pews were filled by native-born colonials, Huguenot and Anglican congregations were composed of newcomers. The French Huguenot church, organized in 1688, expanded swiftly to about 400 members at the end of the century.[34] By 1703, the Huguenots found it necessary to build a new and larger church edifice, the minister and elders stating in a petition that "their Congregation is so much Encreased that the said Church is to[o] small to Conteine them and that they are not at present in a Capacity to Divide themselves into two congregations."[35]

The congregation of the Eglise Française à la Nouvelle York was composed mostly of French immigrant families linked together not only by ethnic and doctrinal ties but by experiential bonds, with a sprinkling of earlier French residents who transferred from the Dutch Reformed church. Though no membership list is extant, marriage and baptismal records, as well as other church documents, attest to the exclusively French character of the congregation. A resolution of "Chefs de Fammille" made in 1704 enumerates 38 male heads of household, all French, belonging to the church.[36] The bulk of the city's French population was affiliated with the Huguenot church; only a handful of French persons were associated with the Dutch Reformed church and Trinity Church before 1700.[37] French Protestants on the city's tax list in 1695 ranged through every tax bracket but were concentrated in the highest and lowest segments of the wealth structure.[38]

Trinity Church, founded by Anglicans in 1697 and possessing the privileges of an established church, was composed mainly of recent immigrants.[39] Though Trinity parish comprised the whole city, the congregation counted only a small fraction of the city's population. As late as 1714, when the colony's population was approximately 28,000, Caleb Heathcote, one of Trinity's founders, reported that "frequenters of the English church [in New York colony] were not more than 1,200 and the actual communicants not more than 450."[40] In its early years, Trinity Church was predominantly English in makeup, with only a few French and Dutch adherents. Of the fifty men who served as wardens and vestrymen during the years 1697 to 1704, forty-eight were English and two were French. While most members were English, however, it is not true that most of the English in New York City were affiliated with Trinity. A small number were Quakers, while others, of dissenting sympathies, had no church ties.[41]

Trinity's most visible parishioners came from the privileged segment of society, but the church also had its share of middling as well as poor adherents. While the city's elite provided the majority of Trinity's lay leaders, some church leaders had lesser status. Occupations are known for 57 of the 60 men who served as churchwardens and vestrymen between 1697 and 1708. Of these, 28 were merchants, 9 served in the provincial administration, 6 were attorneys, 4 were innkeepers, 2 were ship captains, and one was a physician. The remainder plied a variety of trades including those of cooper, barber, tailor, printer, saddler, brewer, and silversmith.[42]

The prices and arrangement of family pews in the church reflected social gradations in the congregation. The most favorably situated pews, commanding the highest prices, were purchased by merchants, government officeholders, and lawyers, while artisans and shopkeepers usually occupied the cheaper pews in less desirable locations. In 1718 the vestry ordered that the "front pews [of the new gallery] be Appropriated to Housekeepers & their wives Masters of Vessels & their wives and Schoolmasters & their wives."[43]

Parishioners who could not afford to pay for seating were not turned away. In 1724 the vestry asked the churchwardens "to place all such poor familys as Shall Apply to them for Seats in such vacant places in the Church as they in their discretion Shall think fit & Convenient."[44] Other categories of persons were assigned specially demarcated places in the church. Single men had spaces in the Bachelors Pew, while students of the charity school and other scholars were seated in the gallery. In 1700 the vestry acquiesced in the governor's request that "benches be set in the Isles for Accommodation of the Soldiers that may come to our Church during the vacancy of a Chaplain to the Garrison provided the Church Wardens be consulted in the ordering & placing of said benches."[45]

Differences in social status among Anglicans also emerged in their mode of burial. Affluent members built vaults in the churchyard, while parishioners unable to pay according to the scale of fees were buried gratis, as were soldiers from the garrison.[46] Blacks, though permitted to be baptized and to become communicants, could not be buried in Trinity churchyard.[47]

Of all New York City's religious bodies in the seventeenth century, only three small congregations did not fit the mold of an ethnic church—the Quakers, Jews, and Lutherans. In these groups, the members deepest sense of identity proceeded from religious commitment. The Quaker meeting, whose presence is first officially noted in 1681, was composed of English men and women.[48] Difficult to identify because of the lack of preparative Meeting records, the city's few Friends maintained strong ties with their brethren on Long Island, who were far more numerous.[49] Quakers worshiped in members' homes before finally erecting their own building between 1696 and 1698.[50] New York City's small but diverse Jewish community was able to worship openly perhaps as early as 1682, but certainly by 1695.[51] Sephardim predominated in the congregation, Shearith Israel, during its early years; Ashkenazic Jews joined in growing numbers before the end of the seventeenth century.[52]

Lutherans were strong in New Amsterdam and might have formed a sizable body once granted toleration in 1666, yet this did not prove to be the case.[53] The delayed arrival and improper behavior of the first minister, the necessity of sharing a pastor with the congregation at Albany, and a lengthy period without any minister, coupled with the curtailment of Lutheran immigration from Europe after the English takeover, contributed to an attrition of membership.[54] In 1705 a new minister reported that "our congregation has become dispersed, the young people and many of the older ones have gone over to the so-called Reformed sect."[55]

Though the congregation was under the aegis of the Dutch Lutheran church in Amsterdam and conducted worship in the Dutch language, it was heterogeneous in makeup from its earliest days.[56] In 1704 the Reverend Justus Falckner related that "my few auditors are mostly Dutch in speech, but in extraction they are mostly High-Germans, also Swedes, Danes, Norwegians, Poles, Lithuanians, Transylvanians, and other nationalities."[57] The remarkable diversity of the so-called "Dutch" Lutherans constituted an exception to the prevailing ethnic patterns of church life in seventeenth-century New York City. For most residents, by contrast, ethnic identity and religious affiliation were intertwined.

Church affiliation is not the only index of ethnic consciousness. The question of ethnic identity was posed in an area of behavior where a decision was almost unavoidable—the choice of a marriage partner. The most intimate choice afforded to an individual in terms of primary relationships lies in the selection of a spouse.[58] Given the presence of potential marriage partners of other ethnic or religious groups, the fact that a person chooses to marry within his or her own group reveals a desire on the part of the individual, or the family, to maintain ethnic or religious ties. On the other hand, if a person selects a partner from outside the group, then the importance of ethnic or religious bonds may not be so great. Other values, such as class position or romantic love, have greater weight in such decisions.

Evaluating the data on the marital behavior of New York City's ethnic groups in the late seventeenth century involves three major problems. The first concerns the lack of information on the sex ratio in New York City. It is obvious that a person would have to marry outside the group if not enough potential marriage partners were present in the community. The census of 1698 reports that there were 1,019 adult white males and 1,057 adult white females in New York City. However, since this data is not broken down according to nationality, there is no way of knowing whether this nearly even sex ratio held true for the Dutch, English, and French groups in the city. Moreover, even if one assumes that these groups exhibited relatively even sex ratios in 1698, it is not justifiable to assume that this had been the pattern for the prior thirty years. In light of extant marriage records and the pattern of immigration to New York, it seems likely that there was a dearth of English women in the city until late in the seventeenth century. There might also have been a slight under-representation of women in the French Huguenot migration.

Another problem associated with interpreting the evidence on marital behavior concerns the fact that many newcomers to New York City in the latter third of the seventeenth century were already married prior to their migration to the city. Although some information exists on the ethnic and religious backgrounds of such spouses, these marriages cannot be analyzed in conjunction with the marriages contracted in New York City. Whether they had married in Europe, or in another colonial society, the newcomers had made decisions regarding the choice of a spouse in another milieu. Therefore, these marriages are not comparable to those that were made in the distinctive multiethnic environment of New York City. These strictures concerning marriages contracted prior to arrival in New York City are most applicable to the situation of the French Huguenot immigrants. As the Huguenot migration involved people at all stages of the life cycle, due to the involuntary nature of the movement, the marriage choices of the persons already in the middle of their marriages would reflect conditions in France or in a community of exiles elsewhere, rather than circumstances in New York City. The transplantation of English and Dutch persons to New York in the seventeenth century proceeded from more mundane reasons. Most such newcomers were probably young and unmarried. There were exceptions, however, as in the case of the sizable Dutch removal from the Albany frontier in the 1690s.

In assessing the marriage patterns exhibited by New York City's population, one must also take into account the limitations of the evidence itself. Information on marital behavior is not conclusive due primarily to incomplete data for the English residents of the city. No marriage records survive from Trinity Church for this period and since there was no religious institution serving English dissenters in New York City at this time, evidence concerning the marital behavior of the city's English must be as-

TABLE 5–2
Marriages of Dutch, English, and French Men

Group	Endogamous		Exogamous		Total
English	22	(38%)	36	(62%)	58
French	34	(77%)	10	(23%)	44
Dutch	217	(100%)	2	(1%)	219

sembled from different sources. Quaker records document the marriages of a few English inhabitants of the city, marriage records of the Dutch Reformed church include a number of English persons, and licenses issued for civil marriages cover other English residents. However, there are still New York City English whose marital activities are undocumented and therefore conclusions reached about English marriage patterns are tentative. On the other hand, complete marriage records exist for the Dutch Reformed church and fairly complete records survive for the Eglise Françoise à la Nouvelle York. Coupled with the records of marriages contracted under civil license, these documents provide a reliable basis for generalizations concerning marital behavior in the city.

What was the effect of New York City's multiethnic environment on marriage choices among the three major ethnic groups? The following discussion of New York City marriage patterns is based on analysis of the marriages contracted by 219 Dutch men and 58 English men on the 1695 city tax list and 44 French men on the 1695 and 1699 tax lists and the 1703 census.[59] (See table 5–2.)

Only 44 French men married in New York City during the era of migration, 20 in the French church, 6 in the Dutch church, and 18 by civil license. Thirty-four of the marriages were with French women, 9 were with Dutch women, and one was with an English woman. In contrast, all but one of the 55 French men who wed prior to arrival in New York City were married to French women. The cosmopolitan milieu and perhaps an unbalanced sex ratio prompted a substantial minority of French men to marry outside their group. In the 1690s, 40.8 percent of all the known Huguenot marriages were between Huguenots and English or Dutch spouses.[60] The ethnic cohesion of the French Huguenots in New York City, then, was threatened at an early stage by exogamous marriage patterns.

English men in New York City were more prone than French men to marry exogamously. A clear majority of English men married outside their ethnic group and every one married a Dutch woman. Though some of the English men for whom information is lacking may have been married to

English women, eight of the ten English men whose spouses were identified but who did not marry in the city had Dutch wives. Most of these marriages had been contracted in the colony of New York, where English women were at a premium. The scarcity of English women, then, played a major role in producing this anomalous pattern of behavior among the English in New York City.

Marrying a Dutch woman was probably easiest for those men who themselves were products of English-Dutch marriages, but who have been classified as English on the basis of surname. For example, the sons of the Ellsworths and the Lewises, both cohort families, were among those who married exogamously in New York City. Stoffel (Christopher) Ellsworth was an Englishman by birth who had migrated to the Netherlands as a young man, married a Dutch woman there, and then come to New Amsterdam. His four sons—George, William, Clement, and Johannes—were born in the city and baptized in the Dutch Reformed Church and all married Dutch women there. However, none of the Ellsworth sons joined the church. Thomas Lewis, originally from Ireland, married a Dutch woman in Albany and joined the Dutch Reformed Church in New York City in 1675. His son, Thomas Lewis, married Frances Leisler, the daughter of Jacob Leisler, the German-born leader of the uprising in 1689, and his Dutch wife, by civil license in 1694. Another son, Leonard Lewis, married elsewhere in the colony, but his wife was also Dutch.

Religious persuasion may also have influenced the marriage choices of British immigrants to New York City. Because of the doctrinal similarity between the Presbyterian church and the Dutch Reformed church, dissenters may have found it relatively easy to marry into Dutch families. Three Scottish men, for example, married Dutch women in New York City. William Jackson, a cordwainer from Edinburgh who eventually was active in setting up the Presbyterian church in New York City, married Anna Wessels of New York in the city's Dutch church in 1694. Alexander Lamb, a mariner, also from Scotland, married Elizabeth Koning of New York City in the Dutch church in 1688. Though their wives became communicants of the Dutch church, both Jackson and Lamb remained nonmembers.

Another Scotsman, Robert Sinclair, who married Mary Duycking in the New York City Dutch Reformed Church in 1683, was more fully integrated into Dutch society by his marriage. Sinclair's life history shows how a British newcomer was incorporated into a Dutch kinship network in New York City. In 1679, Sinclair was a young sailor, "a Scotchman, by birth, from the Orkneys, and a Presbyterian by profession," who worked on the ship *Charles*, which brought the Labadist missionary Jasper Danckaerts to New York.[61] One of Sinclair's fellow crewmen was a son of cohort member Evert Duycking. Sinclair married the younger Duycking's

sister Mary in 1683 and settled in New York City, becoming a member of
the Dutch church in 1684. When he died twenty years later, a successful
sea captain, his will included a provisional bequest to the Dutch Reformed
Church of New York City. However, his will is even more revealing because of the precise articulation of the interfamilial ties that Sinclair had
elaborated during his residence in New York City. He remembered his
relatives in Scotland, but his primary loyalty was to the Duycking family
circle in New York:

> After my wife's decease, the estate is to go to my daughter Anna, but if she die
> under age then one half is left to my wife's cousin, Evert Duyckinck, and to my
> wife's brother, Garret Duyckinck, and to the children of my wife's sister Beeltie,
> wife of Jan Byvanck, deceased, To my wife's sister Anna, wife of Johannes
> Hooglandt, To my wife's sister Sytie, wife of Peter Daille, To the children of my
> wife's sister Altie, deceased, wife of Tobias Ten Eyck, and Gerrit Duyckinck and
> his children are to have a double portion of the same. The other half to the
> Dutch Reformed Church of New York, with the condition that if any of my
> brother's children should come here out of Scotland they are to have one half
> of the same.[62]

Not only dissenters, but Anglicans, married into Dutch families in New
York City. A number of the English men who affiliated with Trinity
Church were married to Dutch women. Jeremiah Tothill, a merchant who
was a vestryman of Trinity Church from 1698 through 1705, had married
Janneken de Key in the Dutch Reformed church in 1686. David Jamison,
a Scot who served Trinity Church as both warden and vestryman between
the years 1697 and 1714, also had a Dutch wife, Mary Hardenbroeck. Of
the 48 English men who were wardens and vestrymen of Trinity Church
between 1697 and 1704, 29 had wives whose ethnic background could be
determined. Of these 29 men, 11 were married to Dutch women, one was
married to a French woman, and the remaining 17 were married to English women. It is probable that the majority of the men for whom no
reliable data was procured were married to English women. Anglicans
were perhaps most reluctant to marry exogamously for both doctrinal and
political reasons. However, under the circumstances of life in seventeenth-
century New York City, such marriages were unavoidable. The uneven sex
ratio among the English forced some English men to marry into Dutch
families. Moreover, alliance with a prominent Dutch family was not an
unattractive proposition for an aspiring young English merchant or government official.

Endogamous marriages characterized the small group of English Quakers in seventeenth-century New York City. Subject to harassment by colonial authorities for their pacifist beliefs, the Friends directed their energies
toward safeguarding their marginal position in society. Since they defined

themselves in terms of religion rather than ethnic identity, the Quakers married within their own group as a matter of course. With this exception, British men of all religious persuasions were willing to marry Dutch women in New York City.

Exogamous marriages also occurred at all levels of the class structure. British men in every wealth bracket in 1695 had Dutch wives. Four men in the upper tenth of the English wealth spectrum, Philip French, John Spratt, Thomas Roberts, and Robert Sinclair, all had married Dutch women in the city's Dutch Reformed Church. Members of the English political elite, as well as the economic elite, were married to women of Dutch background. Matthew Clarkson, the provincial secretary, was wed to Catharina van Schayck of Albany. Interethnic unions between English men and Dutch women were not unusual in seventeenth-century New York City nor were they confined to any particular segment of the English community. The inadequate supply of English women and the lure of valuable connections in the Dutch community combined to produce a large number of marriages between English men and Dutch women.

Dutch men had no difficulty in finding mates of Dutch ancestry in seventeenth-century New York City. Since the few single English and French women had a wide range of selection within their own groups, it was unlikely that they would consider marriage to a Dutch man. Whether or not the city's Dutch men were willing to marry non-Dutch women, the uneven sex ratio of the English and French groups prevented most of them from doing so.

It is only by studying the marital behavior of Dutch women that one can determine the strength of the Dutch desire to remain ethnically enclosed. Though the majority of Dutch women in New York City married Dutch men, 45 (17 percent) of the 264 Dutch women studied did marry English or French men. What prompted these exogamous unions? The mere presence of unattached young English men in the community surely disposed some Dutch women to seek the unfamiliar. Knowledge of the prestige associated with English background in the changed political context may also have spurred an interest in English marriage partners. Neither can romantic love be discounted. But it was family opinion that held most weight at this time.[63] It is unlikely that very many young women would contract marriages with men who were unacceptable to their parents, since the economic leverage wielded by parents played a critical part in the choice of a mate. In wealthy families, parental pressure assumed even greater salience. Abraham de Peyster, a prominent Dutch merchant, stipulated in his 1702 will that "if any of my children marry without my wife's consent, they are to forfeit their share of my real estate."[64] Most of the Dutch parents whose daughters married English men must have acquiesced in the selection of the husband.

In some instances, parental wishes were instrumental in fostering an interethnic union. This was probably the case in families such as the De Keys where more than one daughter married exogamously. These families aspired to improve their position in society and used the marriage of their daughters to promising young Englishmen as a means of upward social mobility. Dutch cohort member Jacob Teunis de Key, a baker who was on the fringes of the economic elite in New Amsterdam, had two sons and three daughters who survived to adulthood. In 1680, his eldest son, Teunis, married Helena van Brugh, the daughter of another Dutch cohort member, Johannes van Brugh, a wealthy merchant. By the early eighteenth century, however, the other four De Key children were all married to people of English descent. The second son, Jacob de Key, a merchant, married Sarah Willett of Queens County, Long Island, in 1694 with a civil license.[65] He was one of the very few Dutch men who married English women in the seventeenth century. By 1705, his three sisters had wed English men associated with Trinity Church. Janettie had married merchant Jeremiah Tothill in 1686 as a young woman of twenty. Agnettie married William Janeway, a brewer, after the death of her first husband, Henricus de Meyer, and Mary married Sampson Broughton, a lawyer and son of the colony's attorney-general, following two brief marriages to French Huguenots. The marital alliances knitted by the De Keys suggest a deliberate effort on the part of the family to align with the English sector of New York City society.

Not every Dutch family that permitted a daughter to marry an English suitor envisioned ultimate absorption into the English community. The Duycking family, which included Robert Sinclair, the Scottish mariner, as a son-in-law, was still strongly Dutch in the early eighteenth century. The marriages documented in Sinclair's 1704 will attest to the pervasive ties with other Dutch families. Only one other daughter had married outside the Dutch group in her second marriage. Instead of bringing the Duycking family closer to the fold of British culture, Robert Sinclair was Batavianized by his marriage. Not only did he join the local Dutch Reformed church, but he mentioned the church in his will.

The patterns of ethnic intermarriage delineated here suggest that ethnic consciousness informed decisions regarding the choice of a spouse. Where a sufficient supply of women of the same group was available, as in the case of Dutch men, crossing over ethnic lines was very rare. However, among those groups that displayed an uneven sex ratio—the English and, to some extent, the French—men were permitted to intermarry with Dutch women. The unavailability of women of their own ethnic group prevented these men from expressing ethnic preferences when choosing their spouse. As for the Dutch women who were involved in interethnic unions, their behavior stemmed from personal predilection more than ethnic policy, except in those cases where a distinctive familial pattern of exogamous marriages existed. Another significant aspect of such marriages is their consequences in terms of the ethnic loyalty of the new nuclear family.[66] Did mixed families remain in a marginal position in society or did they gravitate toward one ethnic camp?

Both mixed and homogeneous families were obliged to make decisions concerning the education of their children. If the preservation of ethnic identity was of paramount concern to parents, then one would expect them to ensure that their youngsters' education was ethnically circumscribed. Schooling was a purely voluntary matter in colonial New York City and it is unlikely that very many of the city's 2,161 white children in 1698 received more than a rudimentary formal education. In fact, the most important portions of a child's education occurred outside the institutional setting, in the home or as an apprentice. The family circle was the crucible in which the elements of identity took shape.[67] Exposure to a particular way of life from earliest memories unconsciously molded the child. Additionally, deliberate efforts were made to instill traditional values in the child. The inculcation of religious dogma began at home as did training in customary forms of behavior. Instruction in reading as well as household skills also took place in the context of the family. If a family desired supplementary instruction for its children, the choice of a teacher was made by the parents. For many parents, church-sponsored schools offered the ideal combination of religious training and elementary education.

The Dutch Reformed church sponsored formal instruction in the fundamental tenets of the faith. Soon after his arrival in New York City in 1682, the Reverend Henricus Selyns instituted a new course of study for the congregation's youth: "For the sake of the children, who multiply more rapidly than anywhere else in the world, I hold a catechetical class on Sunday evenings, and it is filled to overflowing."[68]

The following year he elaborated on the nature of his educational program:

> To provide against receiving such into church membership as are hardly yet acquainted with the elements of Christian truth, I instituted a regular course of catechetical instruction with the Compendium of the Heidelberg Catechism, and had about one hundred youth in the class. This is gone through with every three months. Those who are deemed qualified by their knowledge of the truth and who give evidence of piety are then admitted.[69]

In a 1698 report Selyns praised the accomplishments of 65 catechumens (44 boys and 21 girls), ranging in age from seven to fourteen, who had performed in public ceremonies held in the church on the second day of Easter, Ascension Day, and the second day of Pentecost. According to Selyns, "these had learned and repeated, or were ready to repeat, publicly, freely and without missing, all the Psalms, hymns, and prayers in rhyme, in the presence of my Consistory and of many church members."[70]

Since this document contains the names of all the children who recited, it is possible to ascertain the ethnic identity of the students in the Dutch Reformed church school. All but four of the catechumens were Dutch and the four children with English surnames—Johan and Cornelia Spratt, Samuel Pell, and Sara Koeck—were the offspring of interethnic marriages. John Spratt, a Scottish merchant, had married Maria de Peyster, the daughter of Dutch cohort member Johannes de Peyster. Both were members of the Dutch Reformed church and their four children were baptized there between 1688 and 1696. Sara Koeck was also the child of an English father and a Dutch mother. However, her father Thomas Koeck, son of cohort member William Koeck, was himself the product of an interethnic union and his mother was a Dutch woman. Although his wife, Harmentie Dircx, was a church member, he was not. Samuel Pell was the son of Samuel Pell of Oyster Bay and Hester Bording, the daughter of cohort member Claes Bording. His father died when he was a young child and he was raised by his mother, who joined the church as a widow in 1693. John Spratt and Thomas Koeck had also died before 1698, when their children were performing in the Dutch Reformed church school. The education of these half-English children, then, had been ethnically defined by their mothers and they were being raised as members of the Dutch community.

Dutch families also had the option of sending their children to the local elementary school run under the supervision of the church. Deprived of municipal support after 1674, the Dutch school continued to function under the control of the church consistory. The schoolmaster at the time of the English conquest, Evert Pietersen (Keteltas), carried on his duties until 1686, when he was replaced by Abraham Delanoy. Delanoy, who had conducted private classes in the city since 1668, filled the post until his death in 1702.[71] In 1679, the Labadist Jasper Danckaerts had visited a weekly catechizing session held at Delanoy's home where "a company of about twenty-five persons, male and female, . . . mostly young people . . . sang some verses from the Psalms, made a prayer, and answered questions from the catechism, at the conclusion of which they prayed and sang some verses from the Psalms again."[72]

Other city churches also sponsored religious instruction for the children of their members, but none on such an elaborate scale as that of the Dutch Reformed church. Pierre Bontecou, the reader of the Eglise Française à la Nouvelle York and also a schoolmaster, was Delanoy's counterpart in the French community. The smaller religious groups undoubtedly provided appropriate religious instruction for their congregations, though the educational activities of Trinity Church did not officially commence until the early eighteenth century.

Even though education in the seventeenth century was customarily religiously oriented, not all instruction took place under church auspices. Independent schoolmasters formed part of the city's educational spectrum. In addition to their duties at church-associated schools, both Abraham Delanoy and Pierre Bontecou taught students outside the institutional context. Another Dutch schoolmaster, Johannes Schenck, may have held classes briefly in the city at the end of the seventeenth century in between terms of service in Flatbush.[73] There was also one English schoolmaster in New York City during the seventeenth century, William Huddleston, whose later career under the auspices of the S.P.G is discussed in chapter 9.

At the turn of the eighteenth century, then, parents in New York City possessed a number of educational options. Decisions reached concerning the nature of instruction given their children shed light on the value they placed on ethnic identity. In most instances, parents opted for an ethnically bounded education for their youngsters, with formal training reinforcing familial education. When non-English families chose to patronize an English teacher, economic considerations must have outweighed ethnic preferences. Ambitious Dutch and French families sought an English education for their children in order to improve their position in society. However, the connection between formal education and social advancement in the colonial period was tenuous at best. Occupational training played a much more important part in preparation for future success.

The indispensable part of a young lad's education consisted of on-the-job training in a trade. While higher learning was a prerequisite for a small number of professions, such as the law or the ministry, apprenticeships provided the vast majority of males with the skills essential for obtaining a livelihood. Whether formalized through a legal arrangement, or conducted under informal family auspices, personalized instruction in the context of the household supplied the vocational training necessary to function in the preindustrial world of work. In addition to the transmission of specific skills, a term of apprenticeship familiarized the trainee with the structure and values of his occupational group. Since the apprentice learned his craft in the locality where he would practice it, the relationships formed between master, apprentices, and fellow workers during the period of service frequently proved enduring. Ties fostered in the setting of the master's home could influence work arrangements and friendship patterns throughout a lifetime in the community.

Family, rather than education or interest, was the most important element in career choice in the preindustrial community. Various studies stress the role of kinship ties in the determination of occupational roles.[74] Occupations were passed down from fathers to sons or from uncles to nephews. Thus, the range of a boy's occupational choices consisted of those trades represented within his kinship network. In a homogeneous community, the relationship between kinship group and ethnic group was clear. In a multiethnic environment, such as New York City, however, all one's kin might not be circumscribed within one's ethnic group. The study of the ethnic composition of apprenticeship arrangements, then, provides a means of determining the centrality of ethnic identity in formulating career plans for one's children.

The evidence of ethnic clustering in the major productive trades in New York City in 1695 presented in chapter 4 suggests that ethnic factors played a large part in controlling entry into such crafts. Since these trades were dominated by men of Dutch background, however, kinship ties may have been more crucial in producing this pattern. The marriage patterns characteristic of the New York City Dutch community predisposed Dutch craftsmen to transmit their skills to young men of their own nationality. In this instance, kinship and ethnicity were mutually reinforcing.

The ratio of ethnic groups found in a group of 108 indentures of apprenticeship for the period 1694–1707 was not congruent with the proportion of these groups in the city's population in this era.[75] English people, either as masters or apprentices, were involved in 78 (72 percent) of the 108 agreements, while Dutch people were represented in 37 (34 percent), and French people in 23 (21 percent). Recalling that the Dutch formed about 55 percent of the city's population in 1699, the English 33 percent, and the French 10 percent, it is clear that the English were greatly overrepresented, the French somewhat overrepresented, and the Dutch greatly underrepresented in these documents. The English and the French were apt to legalize apprenticeship arrangements, while the Dutch tended more often to use informal channels of vocational education.

As the data on the ethnic composition of apprenticeships presented in table 5–3 shows, all the major groups had a preference for ethnic homogeneity when making apprenticeship arrangements. Of the 108 apprenticeships recorded, 73 (67.5 percent) involved members of the same ethnic group. The ten apprenticeships contracted between Dutch masters and English apprentices merely reflect the Dutch predominance in certain crafts that the English desired to enter. That twelve Dutch apprentices worked under English or French masters, however, suggests that in some cases economic or social factors transcended cultural preferences in placing offspring.

Ethnic solidarity was an important consideration for parents planning their children's education in turn-of-the-century New York City. Since occupational training took place in a familial setting, and moral as well as

TABLE 5–3
Ethnic Composition of 108 Indentures of
Apprenticeship, 1694–1707

Ethnic Background of		Number and Proportion of Apprenticeships
Master	Apprentice	
English	English	51 (47.0%)
Dutch	Dutch	13 (12.0%)
Dutch	English	10 (9.0%)
French	French	8 (7.0%)
English	Dutch	6 (5.5%)
French	Dutch	6 (5.5%)
English	French	4 (4.0%)
French	English	4 (4.0%)
English	Indian/Negro	3 (3.0%)
Dutch	Indian/Negro	1 (1.0%)
Jewish	Jewish	1 (1.0%)
Dutch	French	1 (1.0%)

technological knowledge was imparted, the preference for a fellow coun-
tryman as the teacher of one's child was understandable. When the desire
for occupational advancement conflicted with ethnic attachments, a minority of parents chose masters of another ethnic background for their
youngsters. Since kinship and ethnic ties overlapped in most cases for the
non-English segments of New York City society, decisions regarding the
ethnic aspect of apprenticeship arrangements for one's children may not
have been made very frequently. Similarity of ethnic background between
master and apprentice was taken for granted when ethnic compatriots
dominated all the traditional occupations found in one's kinship circle.

In the course of planning their children's education, New York City's
non-English parents were also forced to make decisions about the language training of their offspring. Whether arrived at automatically by following custom or reached through careful deliberation, the choices made
by parents concerning the maintenance of their native tongue reveal a
great deal about their attitudes toward their ethnic heritage. Since the perpetuation of language is closely linked to the preservation of culture, language behavior offers a sensitive index to beliefs about ethnic autonomy.[76]
The stance of the Dutch and French peoples of New York City on language retention gives additional support to the thesis that these peoples
were intent on sustaining their ethnic identity at the end of the seventeenth century.

Unable to insulate themselves from the English language like the Albany Dutch, the Dutch and French of New York City were regularly faced with options concerning language usage.[77] As the language of public discourse, English had the sanction of an official tongue.[78] Dutch and French men were bound to have some acquaintance with English through their activities in the work world or in the civic arena. Their wives, whose exposure to English was limited, persisted in the native tongue at home. Yet non-English families appreciated the benefits of fluency in the English language, especially when the number of English immigrants in the city was increasing. Moreover, in the early eighteenth century, the Anglicans began to sponsor educational enterprises aimed at promoting linguistic shift as part of the program of religious instruction. Thus, considerable pressure was exerted upon non-English speakers to accommodate themselves to the new linguistic environment of New York City.

On the other hand, powerful forces in the community supported the retention of the Dutch and French languages. The Dutch and French churches expected their communicants to persevere in their native tongues. Religious loyalty and language loyalty were interconnected and services of worship as well as classes of instruction were conducted in the mother tongue. The records of each church were kept in the native language.[79] The historical experience of the Dutch and the French peoples of New York City also favored the retention of their languages. In the case of the French Huguenots, their heightened sense of group identity as a result of persecution and exile made it likely that they would persist in speaking French in their new home. In October 1696, the city's Common Council received "the petition of Lewis Bongrand . . . Setting forth that he was Lately Chosen Constable of the North Ward that he is Above Sixty Years of Age and Cannot understand English, therefore prays this Courte will Consider the Same and Order he be Dismissed from Serving in Such office."[80]

The Dutch, as descendants of the first European settlers of New York, possessed a tradition of legitimacy that attached to their language. In terms of linguistic priority, it was the English who were usurpers. Moreover, much of the basic productive work in the city was carried on by Dutch men who were successful in practicing their trades without mastering the English language. The Dutch language would remain alive as long as these men were not prevented from supporting their families because of their inability to speak English.

In light of these countervailing pressures, the evidence on the language behavior of New York City's non-English inhabitants assumes especial significance. At the end of the seventeenth century, Lord Bellomont, New York's governor, reported that "those that are honest of the Dutch, being formerly kept out of imployment and business are very ignorant, and can neither speak nor write proper English."[81] (See figure 6.) Facility in the

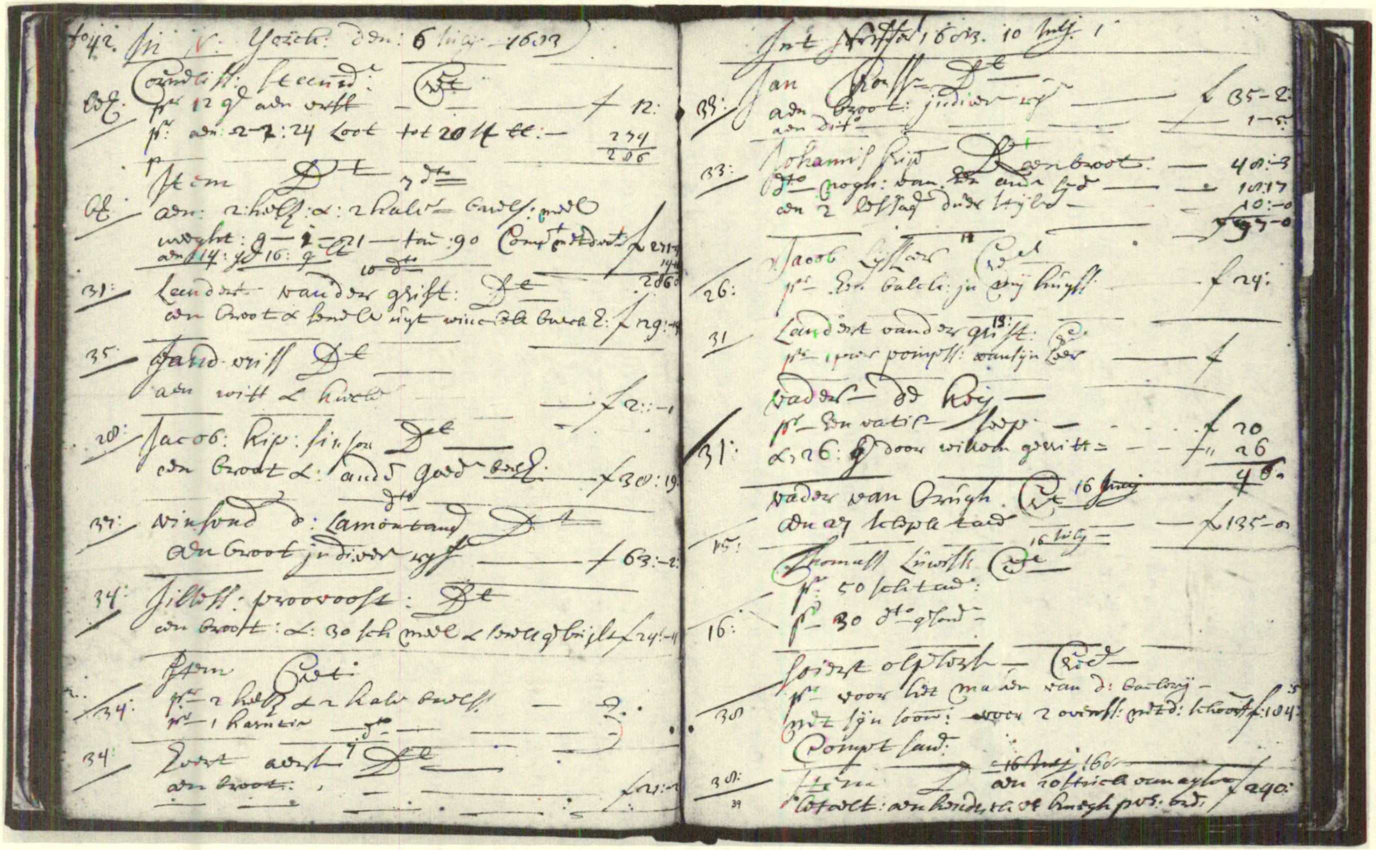

Figure 6. In 1683, merchant Theunis de Key, a second-generation New Yorker, was still keeping his accounts in the Dutch language and calculating his debts in Dutch florins. Johannis Kip, Jacob Lyslaer, and vader van Brugh [Johannes van Brugh, De Key's father-in-law] are among the customers whose names are inscribed on these pages from his account book. Courtesy, New York State Library, Theunis de Key Account Book, Accession number 19532.

English language, however, was not even widespread among Dutch members of the establishment. In commenting on the candidates of the "English party" in the city election of 1699, Bellomont noted that

> three of the four Candidates they set up were as meer Dutch as any are in this Town. Alderman Wenham was the only Englishman of 'em, the other three were Johannes Van Kipp, Rip Van Dam, and Jacobus Van Courtland; the names speak Dutch, and the men scarce speak English.[82]

The tenacity with which the New York City Dutch, many of whom were native-born colonials by the end of the seventeenth century, held to their mother tongue is made clear by their adherence to the forms of nomenclature peculiar to the Dutch people. The reappearance of distinctive names in the baptismal records of the Dutch Reformed church well into the eighteenth century gives evidence of the assertion of ethnic identity through the choice of names for one's children.[83] The expression of cultural identity through the medium of language was not confined to naming children. Personal communication in Dutch between kinfolk and friends also fostered the maintenance of the Dutch language in New York City.

Since language behavior is a valuable index of ethnic consciousness, the perpetuation of the Dutch tongue in the face of mounting pressure to adopt English argues for the existence of a society in which ethnic differentiation was legitimate. The Dutch and French peoples of New York City were not at a great disadvantage at the turn of the eighteenth century because of their linguistic proclivities. They were able to perform satisfactorily in the economic, political, and social life of the city, bolstered by the presence of ethnically defined institutions.

Confirmation of the importance of ethnic consciousness to New Yorkers in this period emerges from the study of another behaviorial index—philanthropic activity.[84] If an individual's charitable gifts are earmarked for a particular ethnic constituency, then the person possesses a heightened sense of ethnic consciousness. If the majority of a community's donations follows ethnic lines, it is likely that ethnic separation is a potent factor in the community's social life. In the case of New York City, we find seemingly contradictory patterns of philanthropy. Yet it is possible to explain the discrepancy in the findings and show that ethnic differentiation marked the city's eleemosynary activity.

Although an embryonic municipal welfare system had emerged in New York City by the end of the seventeenth century, the traditional charitable networks centered in the community's religious institutions still assumed responsibility for needy congregants.[85] The aid bestowed by the churches usually took the form of outdoor relief, though the Dutch Reformed church continued to maintain a poor house. The charitable work of the city's churches depended on the contributions of communicants, both obligatory and voluntary. The testamentary bequests of parishioners formed a part of the voluntary gifts to the city's ethnoreligious communities. The majority of charitable legacies found in twenty-six wills of New York City residents in the period 1675–1725 reflect ethnic preferences. Of the twenty-six donors, six were Dutch, six were English, and fourteen were French. The recent acquaintance of the French Huguenots with privation accounts for their overrepresentation in this set of wills.

With three exceptions, all the legacies were designated for the testator's ethnic group. Each ethnic sample included one testator whose gifts crossed ethnic lines. A prominent member of the Dutch elite, Abraham de Peyster, included in his will of 1702 a provisional bequest of £50 each to the city's Dutch, English, and French churches. While De Peyster's wealth may have been solely responsible for this bequest, one cannot ignore the possible political gains from this magnanimous gesture. Elias Neau, a French Huguenot who converted to Anglicanism and became the S.P.G.'s teacher of Negroes and Indians in New York City, specified in his 1722 will that £20 should be given to Trinity Church and £20 also should be given to "the Poor of the French church being Refugees, residing in the city of New York." Neau's unique life history explains the logic of these bequests.[86] Robert Sinclair, the Scottish mariner whose dissenting background and marriage to a Dutch woman have already been noted, made a provisional bequest in his 1704 will to the Dutch Reformed Church of New York City. Sinclair's incorporation into a Dutch family circle and his membership in the Dutch church account for his gift.

All other bequests were strictly along ethnic lines. Usually, a specific sum was allocated for the poor of a particular church or nationality in the city. François Hulin, in his will proved in 1702, left £10 to "the Poor people of the French Congregation in the city of New York." Sybout Claesen and his wife Susanna Jans, in their joint will of 1678–79, bequeathed "1000 guilders, wampum value, to the Deacons of the Dutch Church for the poor." Sometimes the poor of another locality were designated as the recipients of legacies. William Baker, an English sea captain who made his will in 1690, specified bequests to "the Poor of the parish of Stepney" (his birthplace) and to "the Poor belonging unto the Brownists Church, in Amsterdam, in Holland," in addition to a gift of £40 to the "Poor English of the Towne of New Yorke." A French woman, Magdalena Pelletreau, in her will of 1702, made small gifts to the poor of the French congregations both in New York City and New Rochelle. Individual testamentary bequests, then, conformed to an ethnically differentiated pattern of philanthropy, as 23 of the 26 people studied confined their charitable gifts to their own ethnic group.

Another type of evidence relating to philanthropic activity presents a somewhat different picture of the behavior of city residents. Two community-wide subscriptions for building or improving church edifices in New

TABLE 5–4
Ethnic Identity of Contributors to Church
Buildings

Ethnic Group	Dutch Reformed Church, 1688 (number and proportion)		Trinity Church, 1711 (number and proportion)	
Dutch	262	(89%)	47	(21%)
English	29	(10%)	141	(62%)
French	3	(1%)	33	(14%)
Jews	—		7	(3%)
	294	(100%)	228	(100%)

York City were conducted in this era, one in 1688 for the Dutch Reformed church's new building, and the other in 1711 for the steeple of Trinity Church.[87] Analysis of the ethnic composition of the lists of donors to these projects suggests that supra-ethnic charitable giving was common in New York City. As shown in table 5–4, each of these groups of contributors contained persons of different ethnic backgrounds, while each had a majority of contributors from the ethnic constituency of the church sponsoring the subscription. However, the Dutch preponderance in 1688 was far greater than the English preponderance in 1711. While 89 percent of the donors in 1688 were Dutch, only 62 percent of the donors in 1711 were English. In part, this can be explained by the fact that the number of non-Dutch in the city's population in 1688 was far less than the number of non-English in 1711. Therefore, the number of potential contributors outside the particular ethnoreligious community was far greater in 1711 than in 1688. Still, demographic factors alone cannot account for the more equal ethnic distribution on the 1711 list.

A closer look at the group of contributors composed of ethnic group members other than the primary group in each case suggests an important difference distinguishing the two groups. Most of the non-Dutch contributors in 1688 had kinship ties to communicants of the Dutch Reformed church. William Boyle, a shoemaker who pledged 72 florins in shoes to the church fund, was married to Jannetje Frans, a church member. Another Englishman, Walter Heyer, of Kingston in Surrey, contributed 12 florins to the campaign. Heyer had wed Amsterdam-born Tryntje Bickers, a church member, in the Dutch church in 1668. Kinship ties, however, do not account for most of the non-English donors to Trinity Church in 1711. Many of the Dutch and French men listed were not married to English women and presumably they were not members of Trinity Church. While a few non-English men affiliated with Trinity Church by 1711, a shift in religious allegiance does not account for the 38 percent of the contributors who were either Dutch, French, or Jewish. Indeed, the case of the seven Jewish contributors poses the question most cogently. A separate section at the end of the list labeled "The Jews' Contributions" lists seven men who obviously were not affiliated with the Anglican church. Why, then, did non-Anglicans contribute to the fund for the steeple of Trinity Church?

The pattern of philanthropic activity evident in the Trinity Church steeple fund suggests that a system of mutual accommodation between ethnic groups in New York City had developed by the second decade of the eighteenth century. Recognition of the rights and goals of each ethnic community by the other ethnic communities was the only basis on which order and stability could be achieved in this multiethnic society. That supra-ethnic loyalty to the community-at-large could be mobilized by the early eighteenth century in the form of charitable donations to the Anglican church indicates that a form of pluralism had been institutionalized in New York City. Communal integration had been accomplished by legitimizing the place of ethnic subcommunities in the city's social structure. Donations to a group other than one's own merely ratified the balance of power between the city's ethnic groups. Moreover, at the solemn moment when a person composed his last will and testament, the press of ethnic loyalty was still supreme. The pattern of philanthropic activity revealed by the study of charitable gifts in New York City affirms the importance of ethnic consciousness in the community.

Though they shared a common Western European Protestant background, each of the three major nationality groups in New York City possessed a distinctive history and culture. Transplanted to a setting where insulation was impossible, colonists were exposed to the norms of other cultures. In this particular situation of culture contact, English culture acquired official sanction in a preponderantly Dutch community. Even though a shift toward English norms in the public domain began during the seventeenth century, Dutch culture remained entrenched in New York City at the turn of the century. In 1704, a visitor from Boston singled out the unique costume of the city's Dutch women for special comment:

> The English go very fasheonable in their dress. But the Dutch, especially the middling sort, differ from our women, in their habitt go loose, were French muches wch are like a Capp and a head band in one, leaving their ears bare, which are sett out with Jewells of a large size and many in number. And their fingers hoop't with Rings, some with large stones in them of many Coullers as were their pendants in their ears, which You should see very old women wear as well as Young.[88]

Sartorial modes may have been the most obvious indication of the persistence of a distinctive Dutch way of life in New York City, but abundant evidence confirms the vitality of local Dutch culture at the beginning of the eighteenth century. The Dutch language, as well as religious customs and educational forms, were all flourishing and French culture, transplanted more recently into the city, also remained vigorous.

Nevertheless, the round of daily activities put a premium on mastery of the English language and customs. Affluent Dutch and French men were most apt to familiarize themselves with English legal modes in order to conduct their business affairs successfully. Officeholders in supra-ethnic community instititions learned official governmental procedures to promote their own interests and those of their ethnic constituents. Acculturation was thus accelerated among the Dutch and French elites, whereas those farther down the social scale felt less pressure to acquire the ways of the new culture. For all non-English New Yorkers, the first stage in the process of acculturation was biculturalism, as they absorbed English culture while retaining their native culture. As the years went by, Dutch and French residents gradually became conversant with two cultures—their own and that of the English ruling authorities.

Yet cultural change in seventeenth-century New York City as a whole was slow. Given the accommodationist thrust of English policy, the divergent cultural traditions of the Dutch and French were permitted to exist without harassment. Although various incentives spurred individuals to conform to English norms, coercion was not employed by the government to force citizens to alter their life styles. Not only was English policy conciliatory, but strong counterpressure against acculturation emanated from the Dutch and French churches, especially regarding language behavior. Familial as well as community opinion were arrayed against change. Ethnically enclosed social arrangements also buttressed cultural identity. In assessing the cultural consequences of ethnic interaction in seventeenth-century New York City, then, what is noteworthy is the gradual pace of acculturation as well as the significant amount of cultural autonomy that each group was able to retain. At the beginning of the eighteenth century, New York City's ethnic groups remained structurally and culturally separate.

Chapter Six

AFRICAN-AMERICAN SOCIETY
AND CULTURE

N EW YORK CITY was not only a multiethnic but a biracial society. Though blacks lived in close and continuous contact with whites, their lives were defined by an impermeable color line that sharply limited their chances for individual autonomy and communal action. The cultural distinctiveness that Europeans translated into an institutional bulwark was for blacks suppressed and diluted. Given the constraints of law, the pervasiveness of racial stereotyping, and the pressures to acculturate, community formation presented problems of a different order of magnitude for blacks than for whites. Nonetheless, the city's blacks were not totally lacking in resources to define their identity and improve their daily existence.

People of African descent had a firm foothold on Manhattan Island at the time New Amsterdam passed into English hands. The instititution of slavery was also well established by 1664, though the Dutch had not codified it in law.[1] It was left to English authorities to develop the first legal framework for slavery in the colony. By 1730, a constellation of laws governing the lives of slaves existed, substantially restricting the latitude of black people in New York City.[2]

New York City's importance as an entrepôt in the slave trade grew under the English. Though not all slaves brought to the city remained there, surveying the contours of the trade provides essential background for understanding the composition of New York City's black population. With the Dutch West India Company no longer enjoying the privilege of supplying slaves to the colony, and the Royal African Company (which had been granted a monopoly of the English slave trade) directing its slave cargoes from West Africa to more profitable markets in the West Indies, private traders took the lead in importing slaves to New York. Initially, most slaves arriving in the city came from the English islands of the West Indies. The Royal African Company sanctioned the resale of these slaves in New York: "That Company only pretend to the first empcion [importation] or transportacion of Negroes out of Guiny, and when they are once sold in Barbados, Jamaica etc. by them or their factors, they care not whither they are transported from thence; for the more are carryed of[f], the more againe wilbe wanting; and therefore you need not suspect the

Company will oppose the introduceing of black Slaves into New Yorke from any place (except from Guiny) if they were first sold in that place by the Royall Company or their agents."[3]

Between the time of the English takeover and the end of the seventeenth century, the number of blacks in New York City virtually doubled, increasing from approximately 375 in 1664 to 700 in 1698, the year of the first provincial census.[4] Some of these were the offspring of previous residents, but most were new arrivals. Until the end of the seventeenth century, the importation of slaves to New York was haphazard, the bulk emanating from the West Indies in small shipments. New York merchants and seamen were the primary suppliers of slaves (as opposed to British merchants or the Royal African Company) and their cargoes, as a rule, were small. In 1678, Governor Andros, after noting that there were "very few slaves" in the province, reported that "some few slaves are sometimes brought from Barbados, most for provisions & Sould att abt 30 lb or 35 lb Country pay."[5] Occasional references to the arrival of ships such as the *Anna & Catharina* from Nevis in October 1689 with "a parcell of negroes" only hint at the dimensions of the West Indian slave trade.[6] The correspondence of Jacobus van Cortlandt between 1698 and 1700 clarifies the nature and scale of this trade.[7] Van Cortlandt received individual slaves, along with other commodities, on consignment from several persons in the West Indies. He reported to his correspondents on his success in selling the slaves, including information on the prices received, market conditions, and the types of slaves that were preferred.

Not all slave cargoes coming to New York City during the late seventeenth century originated in the West Indies. The prosecution of Robert Allison in 1687 for illegally trading to West Africa in violation of the Royal African Company's monopoly makes clear that the lure of profits from the traffic in human beings motivated New Yorkers to travel far and wide in search of slaves. Allison was accused of importing "four negroe Servts[,] 2127 . . . pound of Elephants teeth and 107 . . . pounds weight of Bees wax" into New York.[8]

Few slaves were imported illegally from West Africa in comparison to the numbers imported from Madagascar beginning in the 1690s.[9] New York merchants, in league with pirates, sponsored voyages to East Africa that brought hundreds of Malagasay people to New York as slaves. The year 1698 was a banner year for the New York slave trade. In addition to the usual trickle of slaves from the West Indies, Van Cortlandt informed a correspondent in April of "3 vessels Comming in hier whith Slaves two from mardagsr [Madagascar] and one from gieny [Guinea]."[10] Frederick Philipse, the most prominent slave merchant in the city, candidly explained the reason for his participation in high-risk ventures to Madagascar: "It is by negroes that I find my cheivest [chiefest] Proffitt. All other trade I only look upon as by the by."[11] The East India Act of 1698, in combination with the prosecution of persons involved in piracy, deterred New York merchants from pursuing this avenue of trade in subsequent years. However, a vessel illegally carrying 117 Malagasay Negroes did reach New York in 1721.[12]

During the first thirty years of the eighteenth century, the number of slaves brought to New York increased and imports from West Africa became more common, though still sporadic. Lord Cornbury related in 1708 that "Some times we have a vessell or two to go to the Coast of Guinea, & bring Negroes from thence, but they seldom come into this place, but rather go to Virginia or Maryland, where they find a much better market for their negroes than they can do here."[13] In October 1711, the *Boston News-Letter* reported that Captain Jarret's ship had arrived in New York from Guinea with 74 Negroes.[14] Between 1701 and summer 1715, 209 slaves arrived in New York from Africa, compared to 278 from the West Indies. From 1715 to 1730, however, imports from the West Indies far exceeded those from Africa (2,018 to 633). Overall, between 1701 and 1730, 71 percent of the slaves brought to New York came from the West Indies.[15] Typically, these slave shipments were small. On August 2, 1720, Isaac Bobin informed his employer, provincial secretary George Clarke, that "Capt. Vanbrugh . . . arrived here on Sunday last from Barbadoes, he has brought with him four Negroes, two Men & two Women."[16]

Small numbers of slaves were transported to New York from other colonies. This coastal trade accounted for 96 of the slaves who arrived in New York City between 1715 and 1730.[17] Noting that "a great Number of the Inhabitants of the Colony of South Carolina, by reason of the War lately broke out in the said Colony with the Indians, are necessitated to transport themselves and families with their Goods Slaves and Effects into this . . . Colony of New York for refuge and shelter," the New York Assembly in 1715 temporarily exempted these newly arriving South Carolina slaveowners from slave import duties.[18]

Not all ships bearing slaves to New York discharged their cargoes in the city. Slaves routinely were smuggled in from eastern Long Island, Perth Amboy, and Connecticut to avoid New York's import duty on slaves.[19] The impact of the accelerating trade in slaves is shown in the expanding black population of the city in the eighteenth century. Notwithstanding a drop in the number of blacks from 700 in 1698 to 630 in 1703 as a result of the 1702 yellow fever epidemic, the black population grew from 970 in 1712 to 1,362 in 1723, and 1,577 in 1731. Blacks constituted 14 percent of the city's population in 1703, 17 percent in 1712, 19 percent in 1723, and 18 percent in 1731.[20]

New York City's large black population was strikingly heterogeneous, consisting of native-born New Yorkers, "seasoned" blacks from the West

Indies or other mainland colonies, West Africans, Malagasay people from Madagascar, and so-called Spanish Indians. Newspaper advertisments at times mentioned the provenance of slaves offered for sale; individuals were described as "born in this city," "arrived 12 months ago," "a Madagascar slave", or "well seasoned."[21] In 1722/23, Isaac Bobin informed George Clarke that "Captain Munro has a young Negro Wench to dispose off between 16 & 17 years of age born at Jamaica in the West Indies but brought up here since three years old."[22] Commenting on a Negro woman for sale at Perth Amboy, Bobin expressed his surprise at her "very extraordinary price, especially for one that has not been long in the Country, and knows but little."[23]

Among the peoples from West Africa whose presence in New York has been documented are Angolans, Coromantines, and Paw Paws (Popo).[24] Angolans arrived during the Dutch period, probably by way of a Portuguese colony. A 1662 court proceeding noted that Cornelis Steenwyck's slave spoke Portuguese.[25] Coromantines and Paw Paws arrived at a later date, as did the Malagasay people from Madagascar. The increasingly diverse ethnic origins of New York's slaves after the 1690s accentuated language differences within the black community.

Spanish Indian slaves were also found in the city. The *Boston News-Letter* reported in 1704 that a Dutch privateer had arrived in New York City with thirty slaves, Negro and Indian, which they took on the coast of New Spain.[26] Governor Hunter described them in 1712 as "prisoners taken in a Spanish prize this war and brought into this Port by a Privateer, about six or seven years agoe and by reason of their colour which is swarthy, they were said to be slaves and as such were sold among many others of the same colour and country. . . . Soon after my arrival in this government I received petitions from several of these Spanish Indians as they are called here, representing to me that they were free men subjects to the King of Spain, but sold here as slaves."[27]

Indians born in New York or other mainland colonies also were subject to enslavement by white New Yorkers. Municipal and provincial laws regularly referred to Indian slaves, never specifying whether Spanish Indians or local Indians were meant, though presumably it was illegal to enslave native-born Indians in New York.[28] The precarious status of freeborn Indians in New York is illustrated by the 1711 petition of Sarah Robinsa, a freeborn Indian woman. Robinsa stated that she was

> a Native of this . . . Province and was born of ffree parents [and] hath lived [a] great part of her time upon Long Island with One John Parker of Southampton and by him was turned over to One John Week of Bridgehampton . . . who turned her over to Capt. Robert Walters of the City of New York[.] but on what account, she knoweth not The Said Robert Walters

upon the ffirst day of January last caused [her] against her Will to be Transported unto the Island of Madera in Order to be there Sold for a Slave but after her arival . . . upon her Application to the English Consul and declareing that She was a Free Subject the Said Consul So procured that Captain Peter Roland who brought her into the Said Island Should bring her back again to this Colony—She having before refused to be made a Free woman if she would have turned to the Roman Catholik ffaith and be therein Baptized[.]

Fearful that she might in the future be "Craftily conveyed to Some other part of the World under the Notion of a Slave," she asked that "John Parker John Week or . . . Robert Walters may be put to prove their Title to her as a Slave and if they fail therein" then she requested the governor's "Protection whereby She may be Suffered to live quietly and Safely in this her Native Country as a Free born Subject."[29]

Other Indians were less willing to allow the law to determine their fate. In 1717, widow Anna Grevenraedt along with a widow from Kings County, sought the help of provincial authorities in recovering their Indian slaves, Christian and Tom, who had run away in 1715. The widows had been "informed that the said Slaves are amongst the Indian Natives of this Province at a place called Pekkemeck and are there entertained by one of the sachems called melinkamaham who has adopted them [?] for [?] his sonns."[30] A few Indians from the Carolinas were sold in New York. Lutheran church records note the baptism on April 4, 1708, of "Thomas Christian, a Carolina Indian and servant of Mr. Pieter Woglum, who took him to be baptized after previous catechizing. He voluntarily promised, before omniscient God and the Christian congregation that after his baptism he will as faithfully serve his master and mistress as he has done before."[31]

Not only were New York City's blacks ethnically diverse, but their legal status was not uniform. Of the total black population of about 375 in 1664, approximately 75 were free. For the most part men and women who had been emancipated by the Dutch West India Company, they had settled in family units on the outskirts of the city on plots of land granted to them at the time of their manumission.[32] In the 1660s, their titles to this farmland were confirmed by Richard Nicolls, the first English governor.[33] The names of twenty-two free blacks are preserved on a 1673 list of persons residing between the Fresh Water and Harlem.[34] While on a tour of Manhattan Island in 1679, Jasper Danckaerts observed these people:

We went from the city, following the Broadway, over the valley, or the Fresh water. Upon both sides of this way were many habitations of negroes, mulattoes and whites. These negroes were formerly the proper slaves of the (West India) Company, but, in consequence of the frequent changes and conquests of the country, they have obtained their freedom and settled themselves down where they have thought proper, and thus on this road, where they have ground enough to live on with their families.[35]

Free blacks maintained a presence in New York long after the end of Dutch rule. In 1674, Frans Bastiaensz bought a parcel of land from Judith Stuyvesant, the former governor's widow, and in 1685, Anthony John Evertse purchased 100 acres at the Great Kill from Anna Hall.[36] The names of nine blacks were included in a list of twenty-nine persons who petitioned the governor for land on Manhattan Island in 1676.[37] Five free blacks were admitted as communicants of the New York City Dutch Reformed church between 1674 and 1679 and six blacks appear on the 1686 list of church members.[38] One of these free black communicants, Solomon Peters, was a successful farmer on the Bowery who, with his wife Maria Anthonis Portugues, raised four sons and four daughters. In his 1694 will, Peters bequeathed his "houses and lands and household goods" to his wife and left his four sons "all my iron tools and implements of husbandry, and all my guns, swords, pistols, and the like."[39] But Peters's prosperity was exceptional. As settlement on Manhattan Island inched northward, New York's old free black families were caught in an economic squeeze and were compelled to sell their lands to whites.[40] Two free black families, the De Vrieses and the Manuels, followed several other farming families from the Bowery to the new Tappan Patent in New Jersey in 1683.[41] Others were submerged in New York City's expanding population of propertyless blacks.

Under English rule, additions to the city's free black population were few. Between 1664 and 1712, when a restrictive manumission law was enacted, probably not more than a dozen slaves were freed, either in wills or through instruments of manumission.[42] In several cases, the grant of freedom took effect only after a specified time had elapsed. Mary Jansen Loockermans' 1677 will contained instructions that Manuell should serve her daughter until his twenty-fifth year and "that then according to agreement made with his father and mother to bee free and at Liberty having therefore his convenient maintenance."[43] In 1708, Huguenot merchant Benjamin Faneuil emancipated his slave Nero on condition that he serve Faneuil and his heirs for ten years.[44]

One instance of immediate emancipation concerned "a certaine Child named George St. George aged about sixteen months Son of a Spanish mollatta woman named Dianna Belonging to [Lord] Cornbury" who was sold to John Person on December 31, 1707, for five shillings. Two days later, Person, who was noted as one of the "Gentlemen and Servants that came from England with Lord Cornbury" when he became a freeman of the city in 1702, executed a legal document stipulating "I do Remise Release Exonerate manumitt Quitt claim and Discharge him [George St. George] from his . . . Slavery villainage & Servitude for Ever."[45] This favored infant was, in all likelihood, the offspring of an interracial liaison in the governor's household.

A few slaves were manumitted by the free blacks who owned them. In 1724, John Fortune, a free Negro cooper, manumitted Marya, whom he subsequently married, and her son Robin.[46] Peter Porter, a free Negro, executed a manumission instrument in 1720 stipulating that his slave Nanny was to be free after his death.[47]

When New York's legislators placed hurdles in the path of masters wishing to manumit their slaves following the slave rebellion of 1712, the opportunities for acquiring freedom were curtailed and they remained slim even after the law was revised in 1717. Sam, a slave emancipated by butcher George Norton in 1715, encountered almost insurmountable difficulties in holding on to his freedom and to the slave his former master had bequeathed him.[48] In his 1728 will, shopkeeper Marten Clock promised his slave Frank that he would be freed after the death of Clock's wife Elizabeth and given clothing and £25. But the promise stood unrealized for at least sixteen years. When Elizabeth Clock made her own will in 1744, she stated that "my Negro man Frank is to be free."[49]

Despite the thinning out of the old free black population and the paucity of manumissions under the English administration, references to free blacks regularly appear in eighteenth-century records. In 1722, Isaac Solomons, a free Negro laborer of the Out Ward, was brought before the Court of General Sessions for assaulting Isabella Solomons, his wife, and attempting to stab her.[50] In an indenture of apprenticeship dated 1723 "John Fortune A Free Negro Man of the City of New York, Cooper[,] & Maria his wife a Free Negro woman . . . placed and Bound their Daughter Elizabeth Fortune aged Nine Years" to spinster Elizabeth Sharpas for nine years.[51] Several free blacks were listed among Elias Neau's pupils in the catechetical school sponsored by the Society for the Propagation of the Gospel in Foreign Parts.[52] "A Negro Man Called Peter of the City of New York Labourer otherwise Commonly Called Peter the Doctor" was presented before the Court of General Sessions in February 1714/15 for entertaining Negro slaves in his house in the East Ward, and specifically "Sarah, the negro slave of William Walton."[53]

Free blacks were greatly outnumbered by slaves in early eighteenth-century New York City. These slaves were widely distributed among the city's white households. As a rule, white families owned only one or two slaves.[54] But well-to-do New Yorkers had larger slaveholdings. The inventory of innkeeper Roger Baker taken in 1704 listed a Negro named Hector, 2 Negroes Jack and Moll and their child, a Negro named Madagascar Jack, a Negro named Ragow, a Negro woman named Nan and her 2 children, and a Negro woman named Janey.[55] The scale of attorney James Alexander's slaveholdings was inadvertently revealed when he reported on March 26, 1729, that "four of our Negroes have the Measles, & one we are afraid is getting them this day, So that there is but . . . one black wench that I can call well in our family."[56]

The majority of New York City's slaves lived in settings that were not conducive to the formation of nuclear families. Finding mates was difficult because male and female slaves of comparable age were isolated in separate white households. Nevertheless, some slaves were able to form unions with slaves belonging to another master. Evidence of one such relationship emerges from the record of a 1697 episode with tragic consequences. Ordered by John Papin to secure a Negro man called Dick who had run away, Elias Boudinot, Jr., entered the kitchen of George Rescarrick's house "where he saw the said Negro Dick with a Negro woman he calls his wife." A scuffle ensued wherein Dick wounded three men with a knife with which he had been eating bread and butter, one of whom died. Dick claimed that "he was Drunk & knew not what he Did."[57]

Even if city slaves found mates, the permanency of their relationships was in jeopardy since they were always subject to being sold or hired out to different masters. Cadwallader Colden was well aware of the depth of emotional attachments between slaves. His deliberate intention to separate a couple in his household is revealed in his instructions to a slave trader in North Carolina:

> Since you went my Negro Wench tells me that Gabrield [sic] designs to return if he do not like the place but as one reason of my selling him was to keep him from that Wench that I value You must not allow him to return but sell him to the best advantage you can unless you take him to your self & then I shall expect the price I mention'd.[58]

Not only were the living arrangements of slaves detrimental to family life, but their work situations hindered the development of ties with other blacks. Under Dutch rule large groups of blacks had worked together for the Dutch West India Company or on Petrus Stuyvesant's bouwery (farm). But after the English takeover, most slaves worked in close proximity to their white masters rather than in large gangs of blacks. Prized as laborers in a society where European indentured servants were never numerous, slaves were viewed solely in economic terms. Masters aimed at profit, not at giving their black workers the opportunity to associate with their compatriots.

Skilled blacks were vital to the livelihood of New York City's artisans. Few artisan masters explicitly acknowledged the central role slaves played in their acquisition of wealth, but when blacksmith Harmanus Burger's slave Harry was sentenced to death in 1719 for "feloniously taking the Goods of Sundry persons," Burger petitioned for mercy for his slave, stating that he (Burger) was "a very poor Lame and Antient man and having nothing whereby to sustain himselfe but what is procured by the Labour of the said Negro man."[59] Another artisan family's dependence on slave labor is revealed in Richard Elliott's petition for the pardon of his slaves Jack and Mingoe. Elliott, a cooper, based his plea on the fact that he was "now Growne old & Impotent not able in the least to helpe him Selfe, and hath a greate ffamily of Children to Mayntayne. and hath Noe other helpe or Dependence for getting of a Lively hood for them, Butt by the Labour of Two Negroes Slaves the which by much paines he hath Brought up to work at his own Trade."[60] Shortly after Thomas Burroughs, Jr., inherited the tools of the pewterer's trade from his father, he sold a substantial number of them to a local merchant. Enumerated in the bill of sale dated February 1, 1704, along with molds, hammers, soldering irons, and an anvil, was "one negro man named Frank," who presumably was as indispensable to his former master's success as the myriad of specialized tools.[61] In 1715, Governor Hunter recounted the case of butcher George Norton "who by his Will manumitted one of his Negroes who by his faithful and diligent service, had helpt to gain most part of his masters Wealth."[62]

Well-to-do New Yorkers relied on slaves to perform the essential work of their households. "Please to buy mee two negro men about eighteen years of age," wrote Cadwallader Colden to his agent in 1721. "I designe them for Labour & would have them strong & well made Please likewise to buy mee a negro Girl of about thirteen years old my wife has told you that she designes her Cheifly to keep the children & to sow & theirfore would have her Likely & one that appears to be good natured."[63]

When normal work routines failed to fill slaves' time, masters felt no compunction about hiring them out. The city of New York employed slaves to carry out a variety of tasks. In 1712, the Common Council allowed an account for "seaventeen days work of A slave for Clearing and Levelling the street by the weigh house."[64]

Slaves could not have been unaware of their value to their masters. Their appreciation of the leverage they possessed in their dealings with their masters is evident in their efforts to define the pace of work or the variety of tasks performed. Pretending ignorance of a required skill was one strategy employed. "Mr Dupuys Negro Wench . . . is unwilling to be sold, and her Mistress as unwilling to part from her, which makes the Dr [Dupuy] afraid she can do nothing but desires you'll not believe her for she can do every thing belonging to a House, except milking a Cow." The woman's previous master told Isaac Bobin "who ever buys her must have a watchful Eye over her otherwise she will be apt to Idle her time."[65] But enslaved Africans could only protest abuses in their work situations as individuals; the basis for common action was lacking.

Divided by ethnicity, language, and legal status, subject to an increasingly rigid racial code, and living and working under the continuous surveillance of whites, New York City's blacks seemingly possessed few raw materials out of which to knit the cloth of community. But far from being inert victims of their condition, urban blacks were alert, inventive, risktaking people. Sustained by a reservoir of spiritual beliefs, they struggled to affirm their separate and distinct identity while combating the assaults of bondage.

The legacy of New Amsterdam's strong black community, with its nucleus of free blacks—in part, a living legacy—gave newly arrived slaves a vital model for group life. Slaves who had labored side by side for the Dutch West India Company or on Petrus Stuyvesant's bouwery developed a camaraderie that endured after emancipation. Permitted to own land and to pursue a legitimate family life, they stood as a beacon to the enslaved hundreds.[66]

Bonds between blacks were imperiled by the efforts of the new English government to impose constraints on the free blacks who assisted slaves. In 1670/71, the municipal court warned "Domingo and Manuel Angola, free negroes" that complaints had been made "that the free negroes were from time to time entertaining sundry of the servants and negroes belonging to the Burghers and inhabitants of this City to the great damage of the owners." The court then ordered them "not to entertain from now henceforth any servants or helps, whether Christians or negroes on pain of forfeiting their freedom in case it were again found that they shall have harboured any servants or helps of others longer than 24 hours: which they were likewise ordered to communicate to the other remaining free negroes."[67] In December 1680, Jan als Swan, a Negro man, and his wife were complained of for keeping a disorderly house, selling drinks to Negroes and entertaining them at unseasonable hours.[68] Authorities were unsuccessful in curbing the influence of free blacks on the city's slaves, since the Common Council admitted in 1692 that "the frequent randivozing of Negro Slaves att the houses of the free negroes without the gates hath bin occasion of great disordr." Again, measures were taken to discourage the intermingling of slaves and free blacks: "if . . . ffree Negroes doe Entertaine or Shelter in their houses any Slave either Male or female [they] shall forfeit for each Slave so Entertained by them the vallue of Six Shillings halfe."[69] Subsequent instances of free blacks being prosecuted for entertaining slaves in 1714/15 and 1724 indicate that opportunities for blacks to enjoy each other's fellowship were never completely foreclosed.[70]

The concentration of population in the urban setting facilitated communication between blacks. Municipal leaders apprehended the potential social consequences of meetings among blacks and repeatedly sought to curtail such assemblies, especially at night, but occasions to congregate still arose.[71] One night in August 1696, Mayor William Merret confronted a group of "Negro slaves making a great Noise and disturbance in the Street [and] uttering Several Oaths and Execrations."[72] Work assignments sometimes allowed blacks to converse surreptitiously. Since they were required by a 1711 Common Council order "to take up their Standing in Order to be hired at the Markett house at the Wall Street Slip until such time as they are hired," blacks could exchange news as they waited for daily employment.[73]

The Christian Sabbath provided blacks with an occasion to collect outdoors to reinforce their own customs. Frequent injunctions against blacks are found in the city records for profanation of the Christian Sabbath. In 1682, the Court of Assizes condemned the "Many Greate Evills and Inconvenincys . . . Committed and Done by Negroes and Indian Slaves their Frequent Meetings and Gathering themselves together in Great Numbers on the Lords Day . . . useing and Exerciseing Severall Rude and Unlawful Sports and Pastetimes."[74] In 1700, after the Grand Jury noted "the frequent meetings of negroes in tumultuous crowds [on the Sabbath]," municipal authorities admitted that "the Inhabitants of this Citty have neglected to Restrain their Indian and Negro Slaves from Associating together on the holy Sabbath in time of Divine Service to the Great Scandal of the Christian Profession and Religion."[75] Elias Neau remarked in 1703 that "on Sundays while we are at our Devotions, the streets are full of Negroes, who dance and divert themselves."[76] On holidays such as Shrove Tuesday they joined with young whites to engage in illicit activities. In February 1718/19, the Court of General Sessions, citing the "Disorders and Other Mischiefs that Commonly happen within this City on Shrove Tuesday by Great Numbers of Youths Apprentices and Slaves that Assemble together in throwing at Cocks," prohibited this "Cruel Usage and Custom."[77]

When the economic interests of whites transcended their racial prejudice, they willingly provided meeting places for slaves to socialize in defiance of the law. In 1710, Elizabeth Green, the wife of a ropemaker, was brought before the Court of General Sessions for entertaining slaves without their masters' knowledge in her house in the South Ward. She did "Suffer Sundry Negro Slaves to assemble and meet together to feast and Revel in the Night time and . . . did keep and Maintain a disorderly house and with the said Negro Slaves did . . . buy sell and trade and Receive of and deliver to the said Negro Slaves Sundry quantities of Strong Liquors."[78]

In this convivial interracial underworld, blacks could share impressions of masters, contrive ways to circumvent odious rules, and perhaps plan escapes. Slaves and free blacks could plot petty crimes against whites, often with the complicity of other whites, who would purchase stolen merchandise. In 1718, Mary Holst was indicted for entertaining Negro slaves at her house and receiving stolen goods such as silver and gold rings.[79]

Fueled by a desire for material goods, blacks frequently stole from their masters or other whites. An eighteen-year-old mulatto woman who admitted that she stole "as much Bristol Stuff as would make her a Gown and Pettycoat and also a Silk Muslin handkerchief and a Small piece of Callicoe" and brought them to a tailor to make up, explained that "she Stole the said Goods because She was almost Naked & her Mistriss would give her no Clothes."[80] Occasionally slaves banded together to take the goods of whites. In 1699, a group comprised of twelve slaves (including one woman), belonging to eight different masters, was prosecuted for stealing a brass kettle, a pettycoat, and quantities of bread.[81]

Black New Yorkers drank, gambled, danced, and committed petty thefts to make their days in bondage more bearable. But fundamental questions about the meaning of life in their new environment could only be answered by reaching back to the African past or experimenting with unfamiliar European ideas. The persistence of African beliefs and practices among the city's blacks is underlined most clearly in references to polygamy. Anglican chaplain John Sharpe asserted that New York's Negroes were "kept off [from Christianity] because of their polygamy contracted before baptism where none or neither of the wives will accept divorce."[82] Elias Neau, the S.P.G.'s catechist of Negroes, believed that it was "only in order to give more freedom to concupiscence that [blacks] refused to be instructed, because they know that I often insist on the 7th commandment, and that I thunder against polygamy."[83]

Blacks relied on spiritual resources drawn from their African heritage. Funerals were the focal point of black religion in New York City. When blacks assembled to bury a member of their community, the opportunity existed for reinforcing traditional beliefs about death and the afterlife. African religions placed a great emphasis on funerary practices and these customs were transplanted to the Americas.[84] New York City's blacks, according to John Sharpe, "are buried in the Common by those of their country and complexion without the office, on the contrary the Heathenish rites are performed at the grave by their countrymen."[85] The custom of blacks burying their kin at night, evidently a carryover from Africa, caused consternation among white New Yorkers and spurred laws requiring black funerals to be conducted in daylight and restricting to twelve the number of slaves attending a funeral.[86]

Further proof of the presence of African customs in New York emerges from Peter Kalm's account of the poisoning of slaves whose primary loyalties were to whites by their compatriots—evidence of the transplantation of traditional conjuring techniques—and the distinctive black celebrations of the Dutch holiday of Pinkster (Pentecost).[87] When some black New Yorkers told the Anglican catechist that "the god of their country is as great as ours," they were not being presumptuous, as Neau thought, but merely affirming their traditional faith.[88]

Forcible separation from Africa may have provoked some slaves to extreme reactions, even suicide. A slave's adamant refusal to work for a New York City blacksmith in 1677 has the earmarks of a case of passive resistance. Enraged at failing to extract the expected amount of labor from his slave, John Cooley inflicted mortal wounds on the man. His elaborate rationale for his deeds graphically describes the behavior of the bondsman:

> [Cooley] did lately and unfortunately buy a Negro Slave, who as it appeared since was very sick, indisposed and defective; And withall, soe stubborne, sullen, and Layzy, that hee would do neither the Least Chore . . . nor use the Least motion for his Bodely health; In soe much that the Physicians told your Petitioner if he did not constreine or force his said Negro speedily to use or fall to some bodyly Exercise, hee would immediately and of necessity dye; whereupon your Petitioner used all meanes in a quyett and peaceable manner; who had no regard thereunto; Whereupon yor Petitioner was constreyned to give his said Negroe such Lawfull Correction, as was propre for Such a Slave in his present State and Condicon. But . . . the said Negro dyed the 9th day after his Chastisement.[89]

Bristling at the demands placed on them, newly arrived Africans at times chose to flee from European society. Perhaps the Negro man "remarkably scarrified over the Fore head" and branded R N upon the shoulders who ran away from Jasen Vaughan in 1730 had spent his early years in Africa.[90] African-born blacks may also have led the group of runaways who stole from and terrorized Dutch farmers in the settlement of Harlem in 1690.[91]

African culture was not only a basis for affirming personal identity but the mainspring for communal action. The one major instance of collective resistance in New York City before 1730—the 1712 rebellion—was not just a spontaneous reaction to oppression but an act rooted in preexistent cultural bonds.[92] When "some Negro slaves [in New York City] of ye Nations of Carmantee & Pappa plotted to destroy all the White[s] in order to obtain their freedom," they sealed their pact ritualistically, "the Conspirators tying themselves to Secrecy by Sucking ye blood of each Others hands, and to make them invulnerable as they believed a free negroe who pretends Sorcery gave them a powder to rub on their Cloths which made them so confident" they proceeded with their plan.[93]

These slaves, many born in Africa, embarked on a direct and violent course of action to alter their condition. Empowered by their belief in the deities of their home continent, they struck out against the white people who had stripped them of their freedom. The fact that 185 slaves had arrived in New York City from Africa between 1710 and 1712, the years just preceding the uprising, leaves little doubt of the high level of African influence in this signal instance of collective resistance.[94]

African cultural values remained potent in New York City well into the eighteenth century. For some blacks, especially those born in Africa, they remained the primary source of meaning in life. For men and women native to the colonies, traditional beliefs, while honored, became increasingly inadequate in a world dominated by Europeans. Never entirely discarded, they were supplemented by European notions and gradually reshaped to form the basis of an evolving African-American culture. Without institutional props, however, this emerging blend of the old and the new remained an inchoate outlook instead of becoming the cornerstone of a cohesive black community.

Examining the process of acculturation among New York City's blacks in the years before 1730 exposes the dilemma of a people cut off from the wellsprings of tradition yet justifiably cautious about adopting the culture of their captors.

The ability of African-Americans to absorb elements of European culture is beyond question. Not only did slaves acquire the requisite skills to work as carpenters, coopers, tailors, brewers, butchers, and sailors in New York, but they learned to speak the languages of their masters. In October 1730 the *New-York Gazette* carried an advertisement for "a Likely Negro Girl about 18 Years of Age, and a likely Negro Boy about 16 Years, both born in this City, they can speak good English and Dutch and are bred up to all sorts of House-work."[95] Some blacks learned to read and a few even to write. Literacy was a precious tool for blacks, serving not only as a means of amassing knowledge, but as a practical instrument for fabricating false identities. In 1729 James Alexander described his runaway slave Yaff as a 35-year-old man who "was born in this country and reads and writes. He is a sensible cunning Fellow and probably has got a pass forged."[96]

Acculturated slaves did not hesitate to test the limits of the system of slave controls. Demonstrating their knowledge of local customs, they contrived ways to deceive whites or to gain their complicity in schemes to defraud masters. When Abraham Santvoord's slave Tony, "a very good sailor," stowed away on a ship of the Royal Navy in 1710, his master searched for him in vain. However, the clever slave had secured the cooperation of the captain, for once the ship put to sea, he was transferred to another vessel bound for England.[97]

Perhaps the boldest challenge to the authority of a master came from George Elsworth's 32-year-old slave Will, a man whom his owner would not have parted with for £150, "the said slave understanding & speaking very well both the English & Dutch tongues & understanding his Trade of a Butcher." A short while after his slave "absented himself from [his] Service," Elsworth was arrested in the name of "one William Archer (as the said Negro now calls him Self) . . . on a notion Some people had that the Negro was a freeman & now Sued for his wages [during] the time he lived with [Elsworth]." Though Elsworth asserted that Will "had been Sold a Slave to four different persons" before he had bought him, one of the city's eminent attorneys agreed to represent Will in court. Elsworth believed that Will was "privately kept by Some persons that have Encouraged him in the matter" and warned that "if such dealings of Attorneys at Law with Slaves be not discouraged every master may Soon be put to the hazard of being sued by his own slave pretending to be free, if the said slave has had One or more Oportunities to robb his Master of So much money as may suffice to carry on such a suit." Whatever the actual circumstances of the case, Will had obviously become well versed in the intricacies of the legal system and had astutely lined up support among powerful whites.[98]

Acculturation could only proceed so far in early New York City due to the almost universal opposition of whites to incorporating blacks in their communities and the reticence of people of African descent to compromise their fundamental values. Nevertheless, increasing familiarity with European languages and occupational skills led some blacks to reconsider their conception of the cosmos and their ethical principles. The responses of blacks to Christian teachings and teachers provide the best evidence for evaluating the extent of cultural change among African New Yorkers before 1730.

During the initial period of settlement in New Amsterdam, Dutch Reformed pastors welcomed blacks to the church and by encouraging them to marry and baptize their children there, they successfully introduced blacks to European-style family forms and Dutch naming systems.[99] Toward the end of the period of Dutch rule, cultural boundaries became more rigid. Reverend Henricus Selyns impugned the motives of slaves seeking baptism for their children and denied the sacrament to them

> partly on account of their lack of knowledge and of faith, and partly because of the worldly and perverse aims on the part of said negroes. They wanted nothing else than to deliver their children from bodily slavery, without striving for piety and christian virtues. Nevertheless, when it was seemly to do so, we have, to the best of our ability, taken much trouble in private and public catechizing. This has borne but little fruit among the elder people who have no faculty of comprehension, but there is some hope for the youth who have improved reasonably well.[100]

Black participation in the city's Dutch Reformed church waned after the English assumed control of the colony, although a few free blacks remained communicants as late as 1686, "den slave van Capt. Davidt Provoost" was baptized in 1708, and several black couples were married in the church in the late seventeenth century.[101] The disdain in which black worshippers were held in the city's Reformed church is apparent in a 1686 directive instructing the sexton to "restrain with all his might any talking in the Lord's House, and any disorders, whether done by children or negroes during service."[102] Dutch families did not attach a high priority to having their slaves attend worship. In 1719, Elias Neau observed that "Dutch and French masters . . . make their Servants look after their houses and Children while they goe to Church."[103]

New York City's small Lutheran congregation included a few, primarily free, blacks. In 1669, "on Dominica Palmarum, a 50 year old Negro was baptized and named Emmanuel."[104] Maria, the child of "Are and Jora van Guinea, colored people . . . both Christians of our congregation" was baptized on June 24, 1705, with her parents and a white Lutheran as witnesses. In 1726, Jan Louis and his wife, free black people, celebrated their first communion in the Lutheran church.[105] Lutherans seemed genuinely willing to treat these few black church members as spiritual equals.[106]

For the most part, black worshippers were not taken seriously in New York City, and when they did attend services they were relegated to the fringes of the congregation. "The great distance at which they are placed in the Churches (if so much care is taken)," noted John Sharpe, "is inconvenient for hearing."[107] White New Yorkers had never been sanguine about the benefits of religious instruction for slaves. Governor Dongan observed in 1687 that "they take no care of the conversion of their slaves."[108] In 1699, they adamantly opposed efforts to convert non-Christians. "A Bill for facillitating the conversion of Indians and Negroes (which the Kings instructions required should be endeavoured to be pass'd) would not go down withe the Assembly," wrote Lord Bellomont, "they having a notion that the Negroes being converted to Christianity would emancipate them from their slavery and loose them from their service, for they have no other servants in this country but Negros."[109] Even after the New York Assembly passed a law in 1706 stating that "the Baptizing of any Negro, Indian or Mulatto slave shall not be any cause or reason for the setting them at Liberty," slaveowners did not relish the prospect of exposing their slaves to teachings they felt might make them less submissive and more independent.[110]

The Anglican Society for the Propagation of the Gospel in Foreign Parts (S.P.G.) made the only significant effort to convert blacks to Christianity in New York City during the first third of the eighteenth century by sponsoring Elias Neau's catechetical school for Negroes in New York City from 1705 to 1723. Compelled by the logic of their circumstances to question the linkage between religious instruction and conversion postulated by the S.P.G., people of African descent managed to adapt Anglican-sponsored schooling to their own ends.

Only a fraction of New York's blacks attended Neau's school at any one time. In 1706, when he estimated that there were "above 1000 slaves in the city," Neau related that "they do not send me a quarter of ye slaves that are here."[111] In 1707, he reported that "I have now above 100 altho' they never come all at a time."[112] In 1712, John Sharpe asserted that those "who have been Seasoned with principles of Religion . . . are but a small number that come to School in comparison of the many hundred that are in this place. I believe not above ye tenth."[113]

However, the cumulative impact of Neau's instruction was greater than any one set of statistics might indicate, since the number of slaves who had ever been under the schoolmaster's tutelage exceeded those enrolled at any one point in time. Neau, who conscientiously traced the ebbs and flows of attendance, recognized the problem of turnover, admitting that "there are a great many, who came but 2 or 3 times," but he added, "I see almost every time new faces, thus . . . that makes me believe they tell one another that we intend to instruct them."[114] If, as Neau suspected, students shared their impressions of him and his regimen with their kin and friends, then a high level of awareness existed among blacks of the availability of religious instruction.

These students of the Gospel comprised a cross-section of New York City's nonwhite population. Blacks, Indians, and mulattoes, slave and free, male and female, all came to learn from the S.P.G. catechist in the refurbished attic room of his house. Nor were the slave students the exclusive property of English masters, for many belonged to Dutch, French, and even Jewish residents of the city.[115] In fact, Neau asserted that the majority of his pupils came from households headed by Dutch and French persons.[116] After 1710, the makeup of Neau's school diversified even further as "severall white apprentices [came] to . . . School both Dutch & French as well as English."[117]

Surprisingly, in light of the consensus among Anglican clergymen and S.P.G. missionaries that only young slaves born in America were educable, most of Neau's students were adults. In 1719, Neau taught sixty-five adults, ranging in age from 20 to 65, as well as eighteen boys and girls.[118] The commitment and accomplishments of elderly students especially impressed the catechist. "I have severall new Schollars of all Ages," he noted with obvious satisfaction in 1719, "and the old comes chearfully to me to be Instructed."[119] Older pupils who qualified for baptism were singled out for praise: "Col. Nicholson . . . was witness of one of my Catechumens being baptized last Sunday in the Afternoon, he was above 44 Years old."[120] Mature students also were exceptionally loyal to Neau. "I have pupils who come to my school for more than twelve years," he wrote in 1718, "and they are the oldest negroes and negresses who come here the most constantly."[121]

Blacks who knew something of Elias Neau's life history were emboldened to listen to his message. Virtually enslaved by Louis XIV's government for being a Huguenot, Neau had exhibited great courage during his ordeal, drawing strength from his deepening convictions. Converted to Anglicanism through study of a smuggled Book of Common Prayer, Neau embodied Christian piety in a fashion that distinguished him from the nominal Anglicans who surrounded him.[122] "No doubt his being a confessor in the Galleys, and prisons, for the faith he labours to instruct them in, gives him great advantage. They know he was in earnest resisting unto blood for the truths of the Gospel, many of them can remember his seven years absence from his family upon that account, and conclude there must be great comfort in that Religion, which supported him under so great tryals."[123]

Neau's sensitivity to the plight of enslaved human beings enabled him to establish a unique rapport with New York City's slaves: "He has acquainted himself with the tempers of those infidels whereby he is capable of applying himself to them after the most Convincing Manner."[124] Dedicated to his calling, he created a favorable impression in the minds of the city's blacks: "They see him creeping into Garrets, Cellars and other nauseous places, to exhort and pray by the poor slaves when they are sick, and are seriously persuaded he seeks their eternal happiness by such constancy and unweariedness in his labours."[125] Above all, Neau bore witness to the unchristian behavior of New York's slaveowners. The slaves "hear their masters and others confidently assert and upbraid them that they have no souls, and they observe his [Neau's] care and concern for their salvation."[126]

Neau himself may have captured the imagination of black New Yorkers, but the Anglican creed he espoused, with its emphases on beliefs rather than experience, and externals rather than inner transformation, ordinarily failed to inspire African-Americans, who were much more receptive to a religion of the heart. However, certain aspects of Neau's program of instruction sparked the interest of people rooted in an oral culture. Soon after beginning his work, Neau revised his teaching method, adding "prayers & singing of Psalms, that encourage both them and me, for I represent to them that God plac'd them in the world only for his glory and that in praying and singing those divine praises, one doth in part obey his Commands." "I observe with pleasure," he added, "that they strive who shall sing best."[127] Several clergymen also remarked on the affinity of persons of African descent for music and psalmody, causing scholars to sug-

gest that lining out the psalms was similar to the traditional call and response of African culture.[128]

Black New Yorkers became acquainted with the Bible through Neau's
teaching. "I read to them the principal stories of the Holy Scriptures,"
Neau wrote in 1709, "that I may give them an Historical Notion of the
Creation and Redemption of the World."[129] Bible stories typically elicited
spirited responses from enslaved Africans who could identify with the suf-
ferings of biblical figures.

Though Neau endorsed the orthodox Anglican view that Christianity
required slaves to serve their masters faithfully, his embellishments of the
standard curriculum opened a door to his pupils that henceforth remained
ajar. "I conceal nothing from them that is proper to bring them to Salvation."[130] Because his genuine concern for the spiritual condition of his
charges impelled him to present a fuller version of Christianity than that
ordinarily promulgated by his counterparts, his students may have been
able to appreciate the liberating potential of Christianity.

Despite Neau's assumption that the purpose of religious education was
to prepare blacks for entry into New York's Christian community, most
African-Americans presumably felt the effort involved in seeking baptism
was not warranted. In 1707, when he estimated that he had above 100
catechumens, Neau reported that "I have not 8 or 9 of those people who
are baptized, the others are not[,] at least a great many who might be for
asking, I endeavour to make them Comprehend the necessity of Baptism
but their hearts are desperately Corrupted, —nothing but the Efficacy of
God's Grace can convert them."[131] He continued in this vein in 1708/9: "I
observe with sorrow that the knowledge they acquire makes but little Impression on their hearts" but he added "there are some however that seem
to be affected with the Christian Truths, especially when I talk to them of
the immortality and of the reward & punishments of another life."[132]

Some blacks did take Neau's Christian message seriously and sought
baptism: "The blacks who are baptized do everything possible in order to
make sure that their children are also baptized."[133] But the majority rejected his entreaties for a number of reasons. Beyond a personal commitment to study and preparation, slaves were required to have their masters'
permission to be baptized as well as sponsors who were white or free.[134]
This was not just a formality, especially when so many white New Yorkers
were suspicious of Neau's enterprise. John Sharpe's vivid account of a
slave implicated in the 1712 rebellion emphasizes the fact that this slave
"had for two Years Solicited his master for leave to be baptized but could
not obtain it."[135]

The 1706 law declaring that baptism could not affect the worldly condition of a slave dissuaded blacks from placing a premium on baptism. They

may also have shunned association with the white members of Trinity Church who saw nothing wrong in holding slaves and regarded blacks as their inferiors. There is little reason to doubt that William Ricketts considered himself a devout churchgoer. In 1730, he placed a notice in *The New-York Gazette* after his "new Common Prayer Boo[k] cornered and clasped with Silver marked LR. and in the Book wri[tt]en Wm Ricketts" was "taken out of Trinity Church in New-York." Four years later, in his will, he bequeathed "to the poor communicants of Trinity Church, £3 to be paid by my executors, 'the same day that I shall depart this life, every year during the minority of my son William.'" Yet in the same will, Ricketts distributed ten slaves among his heirs.[136]

Blacks were not treated as spiritual equals in Trinity, where a powerful segment of the congregation opposed Neau's school and exerted influence on Reverend William Vesey to curb Neau's enthusiasm.[137] Though blacks continued to be baptized, it appears that only a handful were admitted to communion.[138] Since 1697, blacks had been prohibited from being buried in Trinity churchyard.[139]

In 1715, Neau charged that Reverend Vesey "would not suffer any of them [Neau's black pupils] to have a place in his Church."[140] After the S.P.G. ordered him to take his students to Trinity to be catechized, Neau emphasized their reluctance to go, pointing out that "severall of my Catecumenes are old men and women and don't pronounce well the English Tongue and Some are indifferently Cloath'd which makes them bashfull to appear at Church."[141] Sensitive as he was to the feelings of his black students, he overlooked what must have been a primary reason for their resistance—their anticipation of the hostility they would encounter from the white congregants.

Since incorporation into New York's Anglican church was not their goal, Neau's students must have discerned other benefits from attending classes. For black men and women continuously subject to the demands and surveillance of their masters, going to school marked a welcome break in the monotonous routine of servile employment. But catechism class was much more than a respite from labor. It was a chance to sample an environment in which they, for once, were the center of concern. In Neau's attic school, each slave was recognized as a being with an immortal soul.

If the missionary's classroom was a domain in which slaves were shielded from the pressures of the outside world, the hours of instruction were a time when slaves could think about themselves. Whether they concentrated on the state of their soul and the path to salvation or reflected on their unhappy worldly condition, the mere fact that a portion of the day could be set aside for contemplation of spiritual matters was of enormous importance for their psychological welfare.

Participation in Neau's classes had profound social as well as personal consequences for enslaved New Yorkers. Dispersed among the city's white households, sometimes singly, and not infrequently in groups that bore little resemblance to nuclear family units, blacks undoubtedly yearned for contact with those of similar ancestry and status. Going to school provided an opportunity for blacks to socialize with each other, exchange information, and forge the bonds of community. The hours spent together in Neau's attic not only initiated communication between slaves and free blacks but may also have facilitated the search for marriage partners.

Acculturation of New York's blacks accelerated within the confines of Neau's school. African-born slaves, as well as Dutch and French speakers, honed their skills in English as they struggled to comprehend Anglican doctrine. Learning a common language and a common set of religious precepts served to break down the barriers between the diverse segments of the city's slave population. For some blacks, Neau's school furnished the supremely important tool of literacy. At times, slave pupils had their lessons reinforced at home by their masters' children, who read them the catechism and drilled them on its contents.[142] Since reading simplified the task of religious instruction, Neau was amenable to the idea of slaves learning to read. In 1722, he requested that the Society send him "3 or 400 copies of the Church Catechise [sic], with ye Alphabet in it, that will be a good help to me because Several Negroes learn at home ye catechism & some learn to read."[143] Earlier, he had referred to "several of them who have learned to read, by means of the book that I give them, and who sing the psalms at church, like the whites."[144]

The catechisms that Neau distributed at regular intervals were prized as objects of instrinsic worth by the slaves who came in contact with him. At an early stage in his endeavors, Neau reported with a sense of puzzlement that "there are a great many, who came [to class] but 2 or 3 times and they keep the books notwithstanding."[145] Once literate, black New Yorkers would not only have access to the Bible and other devotional works, but their knowledge of the world around them would increase dramatically, thereby multiplying their opportunities to gain privileges for themselves and perhaps to escape.

Under Elias Neau's auspices, a bold minority of blacks took decisive steps to alter the Afrocentric view of the world that had endured so long. Skeptical of the efficacy of ancient rituals and inspired by visions of a better life, they turned to Christian beliefs as a way of dealing with the feelings of hopelessness and anger engendered by enslavement. By accepting the doctrine that each person, whatever his worldly condition, has a capacity for salvation, they not only bolstered their self-esteem but discovered a way to transcend their situation as slaves.

Elias Neau's work formed the prelude to subsequent Anglican attempts to convert New York City's blacks. That significant numbers of African-Americans had become at least nominal Christians by the latter half of the eighteenth century is suggested by the comments of Reverend Samuel Auchmuty in 1761: "I am very sure there are very few Negro Children born here but what are baptized; . . . For some Years past I have not baptized less than 80, or 90 Negro Children, & often upwards of 100; besides, several Adults. Dr. Barclay has also baptized many, & the Dutch Ministers & the Dissenters dayly do the same, and yet they continue peaceable Slaves."[146]

By 1774, black Anglicans had identified one of their own as a religious leader. Though he fulfilled his duties under strict supervision, the groundwork had been laid for more autonomous religious activity. Reverend Auchmuty reported "Besides the Sunday Evening Lecture . . . I have at the request of a Number of good Christians opened another at the house of an amiable Man, Mr. Gerarde G. Beekman a merchant of opulence among us, on Thursday evening. This lecture I attend occasionally. One of the blacks, a sincere good man, in my absence reads such parts of the Church Service as I have directed, & then such Sermons as I order, best adapted to their Capacities."[147]

While the paths of Africans and Europeans regularly crossed in early New York City, black men and women journeyed through life on a different road than their white neighbors. Barred from creating institutions expressive of their distinctive outlook on life, yet denied acceptance in the white world on equal terms, African–New Yorkers faced both cultural extinction and social exclusion. Some clung tenaciously to the remnants of once-encompassing African traditions, but most adapted to their bondage by fusing elements of European and African culture in their everyday life. The constraints inherent in the system of racial slavery ensured not only that blacks would remain separate from whites in colonial New York City but that they would not have the opportunity to form an African counterpart to the city's various European communities.

Chapter Seven

IMMIGRANTS TO NEW YORK CITY,

1700–1730

I T WAS NOT a political milestone but a demographic crisis
that, shortly after the turn of the century, marked the end of
an era in New York City's history. In the space of approximately
three months in the summer of 1702, a devastating outbreak of yellow
fever halted the community's growth and shattered the solidarity of many
of its family units. The chronology of this epidemic can be reconstructed
from the testimony of contemporaries.

The yellow fever followed on the heels of an outbreak of smallpox. On
May 18, 1702, Lord Cornbury, the governor of New York, asserted that
"the small pox is very much here, but except that the Province is healthy."[1]
In light of the imminent disaster, Cornbury's confidence was ill-founded.
By early July, New York City was in the grips of a catastrophic illness.
James Logan informed William Penn that "at York they are visited with a
mortal distemper . . . which sweeps off great numbers; tis such a visitation
as that place, they say, never knew before, carrying off eight, ten, or twelve
in one day."[2] The epidemic was still virulent in September when another
correspondent of Penn's recounted the situation at New York City:

> after the smallpox had run over the town, a malignant fever ensued, wch has
> carried off several hundreds, among others Col Menville and the Secretary, and
> rages at present at that rate that all communication is broke up with them, but
> by the post most families left the town and settle in the Jerseys and Long Island,
> and my Lord Cornbury forced to keep at Albany.[3]

The exodus from the city was corroborated by the Common Council
which noted on September 29, 1702, that "to Avoid [the] Contagious and
Malignant distemper great Numbers of this Citty have left their usual habitations and Retired into the Country."[4] Governmental functions as well
as individual lives were disrupted by the outbreak, as both the provincial
assembly and the supreme court were forced to hold their sessions at Jamaica on Long Island.[5] Yet these temporary dislocations were insignificant compared to the more lasting effects of the epidemic on the city.

In September, Lord Cornbury relayed the tragic news that "in ten
weeks time the sicknesse has swept away upwards of five hundred people

of all ages and sexes Some men of note."[6] And the yellow fever did not abate until November.[7] The most reliable estimate of the mortality associated with the epidemic places the number of victims at 570 or about 10 percent of the city's population.[8] This substantial loss of lives is reflected in the 1703 census figures where the city's population is recorded at 4,436, compared with 4,937 in 1698.[9] Although no group in the community was untouched by the epidemic, the poor probably felt the impact of the crisis disproportionately, as they were least able to escape the city's deadly environment. The municipal authorities sought emergency aid from the provincial government, explaining that "in the late Calamatous Distemper . . . the number and necessitys of the Poor were much increased."[10] Care for the indigent was but one of the problems facing the city in the aftermath of the epidemic. Officeholders had to be replaced, business arrangements had to be reconstituted, and estates had to be probated. At a more intimate level, relationships between kinfolk had to be redefined in order to compensate for the loss of family members. And for all survivors, there was the harrowing task of reconciling themselves to the vagaries of a fortune that had spared them.

The yellow fever epidemic of 1702 marked much more than a dip in the city's upward spiral of growth. It was a watershed in the history of the people of New York City when the continuity of family lines was broken and generational cycles were telescoped. Plans for the future had to be altered as the city's human landscape was redesigned in one swift stroke. Yet New York City recovered rapidly from the catastrophic yellow fever epidemic of 1702. By 1731, the number of persons of European ancestry in the city was almost 89 percent greater than it had been in 1703.[11] Between 1703 and 1712, the white population climbed from 3,732 to 4,846, an annual growth rate of 3.3 percent. The rate of growth slowed to just under 2 percent between 1712 and 1723, the next census year, when the number of whites stood at 5,886, but accelerated again to 2.5 percent between 1723 and 1731. New York's Europeans numbered 7,045 in 1731, the year when a serious smallpox epidemic caused the death of over 500 people.[12]

That New York City's population was able to increase so steadily between the devastasting epidemic years of 1702 and 1731 can be attributed, in large part, to the absence of any other major outbreaks of disease until a measles epidemic in 1729.[13] Without any exceptional upswings in mortality, the natural increase of the city's white residents swelled the population. But immigrants from Europe and the West Indies, as well as migrants from New York City's hinterland, also contributed substantially to the expansion of the city's population.

New York was not a major destination for British convicts transported to the colonies in the early eighteenth century and few convicts reached

New York City. According to A. Roger Ekirch, between 1718 and 1775 most English convicts transported to the colonies went to Maryland and Virginia and were sold as servants there.[14]

Not only did New York receive few convicts; it received relatively few indentured servants. The great majority of servants traveled to other colonies. Tabulations of indentured servants by David Galenson and John Wareing reveal very few servants headed for New York from England in the early eighteenth century.[15] According to Thomas Truxes, "although the port enjoyed a modest trade in servants [from Ireland], white indentured servitude never displaced slavery in New York, the colonial port which depended most heavily upon black slaves."[16] However, more servants may have disembarked at New York during the first third of the eighteenth century than previously thought. On September 7, 1713, the New York correspondent of the *Boston News-Letter* reported that "the Dolman Galley arrived yesterday from Bristol in 7 weeks and four days . . . she has on board 47 servants."[17] William Grout, who was "lately imported from Barbados and now resident of New York," was apprenticed to Oliver Earle, a leather dresser, in 1720.[18] Between 1728 and 1732, eight boatloads of indentured servants arrived at the city, seven from Ireland and one from England.[19]

Notwithstanding an upward revison in the number of servants arriving at New York City during the first three decades of the eighteenth century, paying passengers undoubtedly accounted for the bulk of European immigrants to New York City between 1700 and 1730.[20]

During the first third of the eighteenth century, the pattern of immigration to New York City differed noticeably from the seventeenth century. With the exception of American-born Dutch men and women from the region, relatively few persons of European ancestry chose New York City for their home during this period. French Huguenots had completed their move across the ocean. Though individual French Protestants made their way to New York after the turn of the century, the Huguenot migration to the American colonies was a discrete phenomenon, confined to the years between 1680 and 1695.[21] The vast majority of Palatine Germans who landed at the port of New York settled in the rural areas of New York and New Jersey and did not appreciably alter the city's ethnic configuration. A small number of Jews and a few other Europeans trickled into New York City.

Since relatively few Europeans migrated to New York City during this period, British immigrants constituted a greater proportion of the newcomer population in the years from 1700 to 1730 than they had in the previous thirty-five years. Moreover their origins were more diverse, as increasing numbers of Scots, Scots-Irish, and Irish joined their compatriots in New York.

The trend toward a migration composed primarily of British nationals does not mean that persons of foreign birth were not found in the city's population after 1700. Men and women born in the Netherlands and France who had migrated to New York in the latter decades of the seventeenth century were very much in evidence during the early decades of the next century. The Naturalization Act of 1715, as well as other naturalization acts, provide the names of scores of foreign-born individuals who had settled in the city.[22] Of the 75 New York City residents on the list of persons enrolled under the provisions of the 1715 act, 27 were Dutch, 25 were French, and 16 were German. Of the remaining seven, five were Jews. Only the Palatine Germans and the Jews had recently taken up residence in the city.

Dutch newcomers emanated primarily from the New York–New Jersey area. The attestations of new communicants of the city's Dutch Reformed church are the best guide to the sources of Dutch migration to New York City in this period.[23] Of the 220 Dutch persons who presented themselves for admission to the church between 1701 and 1730 with certificates from congregations outside New York City, 88 percent came from settlements in either New York colony or East New Jersey. A few individuals came from places such as Stockholm, while 20 (9 percent) came from the Netherlands or the Dutch West Indies. Two immigrants had held official positions in the Dutch colonial empire. Herman Winkler, who "departed this life . . . in the 46 Year of his Age [in 1734] . . . was born in the East Indies and served the States General in several considerable Posts in Surinam and Curaçao." Floris van Taerling, who, along with his wife, joined the city's Dutch Reformed church in 1723, had been the governor of Curaçao.[24] Immigrants from the Netherlands included clergymen and a physician, Dr. Johannes van Beuren, who was appointed head of the city's hospital in 1736.[25]

The greatest number of internal migrants—60 (27 percent)—originated in Kings County. Populated almost exclusively by Dutch farm families, towns such as Flatbush and Breuckelen experienced sustained emigration in the years following 1700 due to the dwindling supply of land.[26] As Lord Cornbury put it in 1708, "King's County is but small and full of people, so as the young people grow up, they are forced to seek land further off, to settle upon; The land in the Eastern Division of New Jersey is good, and not very far from King's County, there is only a bay to crosse."[27] This flow of young Dutch folk was still pronounced in 1716, when Governor Hunter reported that "great numbers of the younger sort leave Long Island yearly to plant in the Jerseys & Pennsylvania."[28] Though East New Jersey, Pennsylvania, and New York's Hudson Valley were the primary destinations of these aspiring farmers, at least some Kings County

Dutch headed toward the city. This urban-directed population movement compels us to revise our understanding of migration patterns in the early eighteenth century.

Ironically, the next largest group of in-migrants emanated from New Jersey, the target of most Kings County Dutch. However, this migration was most likely the result of kinship ties (some of it may have been marriage migration) as was that from Albany—37 people (17 percent).

The dearth of information on British immigrants to New York City is largely attributable to the nature of the migration.[29] New York's British newcomers did not form part of any group migration predicated on idealistic motives. Nor did they travel en masse on ships for which passenger lists have been preserved. British migration to New York City in the years from 1700 to 1730 was essentially an opportunistic migration of individuals who sought to improve their economic position and consequently their status in society. The prime motive of these immigrants was economic betterment of the sort described by Peter Clark and John Wareing in discussions of short-range movement in England during the seventeenth and eighteenth centuries.[30]

During the first third of the eighteenth century, British immigrants streamed into the city not only from England, Scotland, Wales, and Ireland, but from the West Indies, several mainland American colonies, and other towns in New York colony. The majority were people of English background, whether they arrived from the home country or elsewhere. But significant infusions of Scots, Scots-Irish, and Irish differentiated the flow of newcomers and added to the complexity of the city's ethnic mixture.

The largest number of early eighteenth-century English immigrants came to New York City from London. But because few immigrants identified themselves as explicitly as "John Gee, son of Joshua Gee, merchant in London" did in his 1720 will, it is unclear how many people who called themselves Londoners were actually born in the provinces.[31] Migration to the American colonies, according to John Wareing and other scholars, was usually a two-stage process, with young men and women heading to the English capital first and then deciding to move to the colonies.[32]

The trade links between London and New York naturally spurred merchants to try their fortune in the colonial city. When Thomas Davenport, a merchant who became a freeman of New York City in 1701/2, died there in 1716, it was thought that he had died intestate. But it was discovered that "the said Thomas Davenport was formerly a merchant in London, and made his will, dated February 27, 1698 and did appoint William Horsepool, of London, merchant, his executor."[33] Other early eighteenth-century New York City merchants identified as Londoners include Caleb

Cooper, William Glencross, and Thomas Cockerill. Cockerill named his mercantile correspondents—Sir William Ashurst and John Gough of London—in his 1709 will.[34]

Attorneys Jacob Regnier and Barne Cosens also had roots in London. In his 1714 will, Regnier styled himself "of Lincoln's Inn, England, Barrister at Law, now residing in New York."[35] Cosens's father John, a gunmaker, dwelt in London, specifically St. Clements Deans Parish in Middlesex County.[36]

Artisans also were represented among immigrants from London. William Taylor, who called himself a "brasier" (brazier) in his 1721 will and who may have been the William Taylor, scalemaker, who was registered as a freeman in 1716, described his brother as an "oyle man, living in Fryday street at the Sign of the Lamp" in London.[37] James Sibbitt, a cooper, who was granted freemanship in 1723/24, was undoubtedly the same James Sibbit, widower of London, who married a widow in New York City's Dutch Reformed Church in 1723.[38] James Foddy, a "Looking Glass-Maker, late from London" advertised his wares in the *New-York Gazette* in 1729.[39]

Though there was a large complement of Londoners among English newcomers during the first three decades of the eighteenth century, immigrants from other parts of England also gravitated toward New York City. Given the lack of passenger lists or other systematic data, it is impossible to rank in order the places of origin of these non-Londoners. What is striking, however, is the diversity of home places represented among newcomers. Immigrants originated in the north and west of England as well as the home counties, in both rural areas and urban centers. Men and women from the counties of Essex, Kent, Worcestershire, Warwickshire, Herefordshire, Yorkshire, Hampshire, Devon, Sussex, Somerset, and Cornwall, as well as the cities of Bristol, Norwich, Dorchester, Plymouth, and Exeter all found their way to New York City.

Henry Pincher, a "Servant Man . . . about 26 years of age . . . by trade a House Carpenter, a Mason and a Pump Maker . . . a West Country Man, [who] speaks pretty good English . . . of middle stature" escaped from his master, a New York City brewer, in 1730.[40] Another runaway servant, John Ivey, was described by his master, a merchant, as "aged about 30 Years born in Barnstaple in the West of England, by trade a Cooper."[41]

John Chasy, late of the Parish of Butleidge in the County of Somerset in Great Britain apprenticed himself to a New York City tanner and currier in 1718.[42] Several years later, in 1724, John Spicer, a husbandman from Bristol, also indentured himself in New York City.[43] In 1726, Hester Crudge, "late of Plymouth in the Kingdom of Great Britain, but now of the City of New York," indentured herself to a victualler for five years.[44] Thomas Stokum, a young man of Exeter in Old England, married a young woman from Bermuda in the city's Dutch Reformed Church in 1706.[45]

In 1715, butcher George Norton bequeathed his real estate to the son of his eldest brother who lived at the Forrest of Fechnam in Worcestershire, England.[46] John Burge, in his 1720 will, stated that he was late of Lemington in Hampshire, in England, and Joseph Leddell, a pewterer who registered as a freeman in 1716, bequeathed lands in Gosport, in Hampshire, that he had inherited.[47] Shipwright John Blake gave lands in the County of Devon in Great Britain to his son in his 1730 will.[48]

In 1722, George Cock, a merchant, left to his wife "the sum of £70 out of all the farmhouses and lands in the County of Sussex in England, which my father, Dean Cock, hath promised to settle upon me in case I survive him, and shall descend to me as heir at law."[49]

William Smith, the father of the man who penned *The History of the Province of New-York*, arrived in the city from Newport Pagnel in Buckinghamshire with his father, a tallow chandler, in 1715. He graduated from Yale University in 1719, read law in London, and then conducted a legal practice in New York for many years.[50] Though he had been living in New York City since at least 1728, when he was chosen assessor of the North Ward, merchant James Searle named one brother and three sisters, "all of the Isle of Wight in old England" in his 1740 will.[51] Longtime tavern-keeper Obadiah Hunt came from "Birmingham in Warwick Sheir" while his wife Susannah was from "Credly in Heariford Sheir in Oldingland."[52] William Laight, who died at the age of 36 in 1728, was a native of Tewkesbury, England.[53]

Though evidence on this point is not plentiful, it is probable that English migration to New York City from 1700 to 1730 was not primarily a family migration. The frequency of marriages involving English-born men and women, whether single or widowed, in New York City's Dutch Reformed Church coupled with the sizable number of wills and apprenticeship agreements of English who remained unmarried suggests that New York City held a particular appeal for young English men and women who had not yet formed families.

It was not uncommon for a married man to immigrate without his family. When Abraham Brock, a merchant who had come to New York City from Bristol, died unexpectedly in 1714 on a trading voyage to the Madeiras, authorities recorded that he had left a wife and children in England.[54] In at least one case, the existence of a family in England failed to prevent a newcomer from marrying again in New York. Though vintner Edward Broomhead bequeathed his entire estate to his wife in New York when he made his will in 1727, affidavits were collected after his death the following year to prove that he had a wife and child in England. George Ducent stated that "while Edward Broomhead was butler to the Lord Byron, he, the deponent, was at said Lord's country seat in Nottinghamshire, waiting upon the Duke and Dutchess of Kingston; and that the said Edward Broomhead Courted the Dairy maid, and declared afterwards that he married her, before he left England, and that he told him upon his deathbed, that he had a wife and child in England."[55]

The English people who transplanted themselves to New York during the first third of the eighteenth century came from all levels of the social scale. When Governor John Montgomerie wrote to the Lords of Trade in 1731 recommending the appointment of Henry Lane to the colony's council, he described him as "a Gentleman who has resided, and carried on a considerable Trade here, upwards of Twenty years; . . . Perhaps some of your Lordships may know him, he being son to Sir Thomas Lane who was Lord Mayor of London soon after the Revolution."[56] Lane was not the only English immigrant whose father was a member of the gentry. In his 1703 will, John Graham, a merchant, identified himself as the "son of Sir Richard Graham, of Norton Coynors in Yorkshire, England."[57]

Skilled workers, laborers, merchants, professionals, and gentlemen with patronage appointments sought improvement of their material circumstances in the city. So too did a widow named Susannah Oruck who, in 1727, contracted with newly appointed Governor Montgomerie to transport herself from London to New York City to work as his maid servant.[58]

Commercial ties between New York City and the islands of the West Indies facilitated another strong current of English migration. Immigrants, many of them merchants and mariners, flowed along the same routes as trade. Wealthier newcomers retained property and family members in the islands as they continued to exploit their trading connections with the West Indies after settling in New York City.

Most immigrants from the West Indies came from either Barbados or Jamaica. Newcomers from Jamaica included several men of substance. William Ricketts, a gentleman whose daughter married Stephen van Cortlandt, possessed a valuable sugar plantation in Jamaica.[59] Merchant William Bowyer who identified himself in his 1706 will as "late of the Island of Jamaica, in the West Indies, but now of the city of New York" owned a Negro boy named Richmond.[60] John Ashley, a former resident of Jamaica, was referred to as "a Gentleman" in a 1724 document.[61] William Carr, a Jamaican émigré who died intestate in the early 1720s, was a vintner.[62]

Nicholas Flanders, who died in 1726, described himself as "late of Kingston in the Island of Jamaica, Planter, but now in New York." Flanders's daughter was married to another Jamaican emigrant, William Crow, who called himself a "tayler" in his 1740 will. Crow's eldest son, Thomas Flanders Crow, then an apprentice in Boston, stood to inherit "certain lands and tenements in the Island of Jamaica, in the Parish of Clarendon, called by the name of Tobias Abbot's land, and two negroes . . . in Jamaica."[63]

Not all Jamaicans who transplanted themselves to New York City held assets in their homeland. Germanicus Andrews, an upholsterer who became a freeman of the city in 1714, left Jamaica under puzzling circumstances in 1711.[64] Youths with limited prospects on the island were sent to the city to learn a profitable trade. Sixteen-year-old David Wyatt was apprenticed to a cooper in 1719 with the consent of the New York City merchant "unto whose care he was committed by his father James Wyatt of Kingston in the Island of Jamaica, Barber surgeon."[65] In 1726, Leonard Barton, the son of widow Rebecca Barton of the Island of Jamaica, was apprenticed to a shipwright for seven years.[66]

Emigrants from Barbados also trickled into the city in the early eighteenth century. Henry Harding referred to himself as "of the Parish of St. Georges in the Island of Barbados, Esqr. at present residing in the city of New York" in his 1704 will.[67] Deeds recorded in 1722 mention two former Barbadians, Warner Richards, gentleman, and Philip Kirten, Esquire.[68]

The occupational background of Barbadians was diverse. Nicholas Croxton, "late of Bridgetown in the Island of Barbados," who drafted his will in New York City in 1706, was a mariner.[69] John Kelly's 1727 petition for admission to the New York City bar casts considerably more light on his career history:

> Whilst he . . . Resided in the Island of Barbados which was in orabout . . . one Thousand Seven Hundred & Twelve he lived with one Mr. William Verman who was then a Lycenced Attorney at Law of that Island . . . for about the Space of Two or three years . . . he . . . had the Opportunity of being Employed in Variety of practice belonging to the business of an Attorney . . . Since he . . . Left . . . Barbados and Trading in Merchandising, he . . . hath from time to time Drawne Variety of writings in the Law Between Sundry Persons of this Province.[70]

In 1721, Thomas Bowil, "late of the Island of Barbados, but now residing in the city of New York," apprenticed himself to a cordwainer for seven years.[71] Other Barbadians may have come to the city as servants, as the case of William Grout mentioned earlier suggests.

Few Welsh people were found in New York City. Charles Owen, a mariner, described himself in his 1702 will as "of the Parish of Ousen in Pembroke County, in South Wales."[72] In 1732, an advertisement in the *New-*

York Gazette proclaimed, "Just arrived from Great Britain, and are to be sold on board the ship Alice and Elizabeth . . . several likely Welch and English Servant Men, most of them Tradesmen."[73]

The Scottish presence grew more visible in New York City during the first third of the eighteenth century owing not only to the increased immigration of Scots but to the more prominent role Scots began to play in public affairs during the administrations of Governors Hunter and Burnet, who were themselves of Scottish birth.[74] The coalescing of a Scottish community in the city was accelerated by the gathering of a Presbyterian meeting after a decade of fruitless efforts.[75] In the summer of 1716, "att the desire of a few especially Scots people," visiting Presbyterian minister James Anderson "preached each Sabbath." Soon after came "a call from this small handfull with some few others" for Anderson to serve as pastor of the city's first Presbyterian church, which conducted worship in the manner of the Church of Scotland.[76] But, as Anderson reported in 1717, "The people here who are favorors of our church & perswasion . . . are yet but few & none of the richest. . . . Some are already come to live in the city & more are expected."[77]

The Scots who settled in New York City during the first three decades of the eighteenth century were predominantly lowlanders, as were most of the Scots who emigrated to the American colonies before the 1760s.[78] Some arrived indirectly by way of East New Jersey, where Scottish proprietors had encouraged the settlement of fellow countrymen from the late seventeenth century on.[79] Several men of Scottish ancestry such as John Johnstone and David Lyell held property and office in both New Jersey and New York City.

Perhaps New York's most famous Scottish immigrant—scientist and government official Cadwallader Colden (figure 7)—migrated from Philadelphia where he had settled first. Lured by Governor Hunter's promise of lucrative appointments, Colden arrived in New York City with his wife and infant son in 1718. Ten years later, Colden transferred his family's residence to a country home near Newburgh, New York.[80]

Scots migrated to New York City as individuals in search of opportunity. Receiver General of Customs Archibald Kennedy, attorney James Alexander, and Hugh Munro, a lieutenant in one of the Independent Companies, all reached the upper rungs of early eighteenth-century New York society. Munro's 1736 obituary highlighted the fact that "he was born in the North of Scotland; and allied to a considerable Family there of that Name, some of which now have or lately had, Honourable Stations in the Parliament of Great-Britain, and have bore several important Offices under the Crown."[81] Alexander Malcolm, a schoolmaster from Aberdeen, received a stipend from the city for conducting the Public School for the

Figure 7. Cadwallader Colden (1688–1776), a graduate of the University of Edinburgh, embarked on his political career in New York with patronage appointments from fellow Scotsman Governor Robert Hunter. Colden later achieved fame as a scientist and author. This portrait was painted by John Wollaston. Courtesy of The Metropolitan Museum of Art, Bequest of Grace Wilkes, 1922. (22.45.6)

"Teaching of Latin Greek and Mathematicks" established by the Assembly in 1732.[82]

Merchants dominated the Scottish immigrant community and the maturation of commercial ties between New York City and Scotland paved the way for a steady stream of immigrants. Reverend Anderson observed that "Severall of our Scots merchants trade hither, & I doubt not, more will, when before now they have come, they understanding neither Dutch nor French were oblidged either to stay att home or goe to ye church of E: or worse which has been ye occasion of some mischeifs wickednesse

& inconveniencies."[83] However, not all Scottish immigrants were men of substance. In 1735, the New York City churchwardens complied with the request of John Yorston, a blind man who had been supported in the poorhouse for over four years, for passage money to England to return to relatives in Scotland.[84]

Snapshots of individual Scots add to our impression of a growing Scottish community in the city. In 1726, Benjamin Gordon, the son of Mr. George Gordon, merchant of Aberdeen in North Brittain, was apprenticed to a pulleymaker in New York City.[85] In 1723, Patrik Miller and Elisabet Makneel, both from Scotland and living in New York City, were united in marriage in the Dutch Reformed Church.[86] Mariner Andrew Bisset's ties to Scotland were uppermost in his mind when he made his will in 1728. He bequeathed to his son "one house which is situated in a towne called Queensbury, in North Britain, and now in possession of Helen Turnbull, mother of me the said Andrew Bisset."[87]

Scots in New York City were distinguishable by their speech patterns. An advertisement in the *New-York Gazette* in 1729 described a runaway "servant Man who went by the Name of John Smith" as "aged 25 years of short stature, a fresh Ruddy complexion and short brown Hair; He walks Limping, speaks like a North Britain [Briton]; he has been used to the sea."[88]

Despite the growing numbers of Scots on the streets of New York, the major Scottish immigration to the city did not occur until after the third decade of the eighteenth century. It was only in 1744 that "some Gentlemen, Merchants and others of the Scots Nation, residing in New-York" banded together to form the Scots Society of New-York to dispense charity to "their indigent countrymen in these Parts."[89] Lasting until 1753, this association was the precursor of the better-known St. Andrew's Society, which was established in 1756.[90]

Until recently, historians have assumed that the vast majority of Irish immigrants to the American mainland colonies were Protestants and primarily Scots-Irish Presbyterians.[91] However, the pioneering investigations of David Doyle and Kerby Miller have demonstrated that Irish Catholics constituted a significant minority (20 to 33 percent) of eighteenth-century Irish immigrants to America.[92] Miller's research has also brought into question the customary linkage between geographic origins and religious affiliation by establishing that in the eighteenth century there were Protestants who lived in the south of Ireland and Catholics who lived in the North.[93] Consequently, an immigrant's port of embarkation (which may not even have been his birthplace or home), constitutes an imperfect guide to his religion.

How many Irish Catholics found homes in New York City during the first three decades of the eighteenth century is impossible to estimate. The only reference to the presence of Catholics from Ireland in the city was made in a 1700 letter of Governor Bellomont: "The recruits that came from Ireland are a parcel of the vilest fellows that ever wore the King's livery, the very scum of the army in Ireland and several Irish papists amongst 'em, who have stirred up a general mutiny among the soldiers."[94] Since people born into the Catholic church in Ireland experienced little toleration for their beliefs in New York after the administration of the Catholic Governor Dongan in the 1680s, they had no choice but to worship with the city's Protestants. As a result, they became indistinguishable from other Irish immigrants.

New York City was not the primary destination for the growing number of immigrants from Ireland in the first third of the eighteenth century.[95] Accounts of Irish migration to the American colonies make clear that the earliest wave of emigrants, those who departed between 1717 and 1720, headed for New England, and those who followed during the next peak period of emigration (1724–1730) had their eyes set on the Pennsylvania region.[96] Though the major streams of Irish migration were directed both north and south of New York, a substantial minority of Irish-born individuals made their way to the city. Thomas Truxes has concluded that "in spite of the small scale of the servant trade, New York served as entry point for a significant flow of Irish immigration in the half century before the Revolution."[97]

By the time officials first noted the flow of immigration from Ireland to New York in 1720–21, more than a few Irish had already settled in the city. Responding to a British government query regarding New York's population in 1720, Governor Hunter, then resident in London, noted that "the Inhabitants increase day [daily?] chiefly from New England & of late from the North of Ireland."[98] Irish immigrants did not arrive in New York City en masse before the late 1720s, the one exception being the contingent of Irish soldiers sent as part of the British garrison in 1700.[99] During the first quarter of the eighteenth century, persons of Irish birth trickled into the port along with other British newcomers.

Fragmentary evidence allows us to do little more than document the presence of Irish immigrants in early eighteenth-century New York City. Scanning the names of grooms in the marriage registers of the city's Dutch Reformed Church, while not an infallible guide to ethnic identity, offers impressionistic evidence of an influx of Irish men between 1700 and 1730. In twenty cases, however, Ireland is specified as the groom's birthplace. Archibald Gelaspy, a victualler who was enrolled as a freeman in 1729, was noted as "Asbil Gelesby, jong man van Ierlandt" when he married a young woman from New York in the Dutch Reformed Church in 1725.[100]

New York City residents' ties to Ireland are also specified in apprenticeship agreements and wills. In 1721, Thomas Neely, Jr., was apprenticed to a joiner with the consent of his father, Thomas Neely, late of the Kingdom of Ireland.[101] A year later, Thomas Moore, the son of "James Moore late from Ireland, Deceased," was apprenticed to a cordwainer.[102] Thomas Scurlock, a vintner who had been registered as a freeman of the city in 1702 while serving as a soldier, bequeathed £100 to his "sister, Mary Karby, late Mary Scurlock, of Dublin in Ireland" in his will dated 1747.[103]

The Irish origins of early eighteenth-century New Yorkers occasionally emerge in other sources. A deposition in the Lord Mayor's Court of London in 1719/20 mentioned "Anthony Lynch of Galloway, Ireland, and since of New York, merchant."[104] When merchant Thomas Tarpey, a resident of New York City since at least 1711, died in 1750, the obituary in a local newspaper identified him as a native of Ireland.[105] Most is known about the early history of Anthony Duane (figure 8), who was born in Cong, county Galway, in 1682. Orphaned as a boy and brought up by an uncle who was the Anglican vicar-general of Tuam, he joined the British navy at the age of eighteen. He was the purser of Her Majesty's man-of-war *Seaford* which docked in New York in 1713. Impressed with the opportunities available in the city and eager to settle down, Duane resigned from the navy a few years later and returned to New York to embark on a career as a merchant. He was made a freeman of the city in July 1717, two months after marrying Eve Benson, the daughter of a local family.[106]

That the nucleus of an Irish community could be found in the city as early as 1716 is suggested by the intriguing comments of John Fontaine, a Huguenot with kin in Dublin. During the course of his brief stay in New York City in 1716, Fontaine established friendly ties with New Yorkers and shared their convivial social life. On October 27, 1716, he recorded in his journal that "at night I went to the tavern and was there with the Irish club until ten." On the evening of October 30, he again spent time with the Irish club.[107]

Scholars date the regular traffic of passenger ships from Dublin and other ports in Ireland to New York City from 1728.[108] But at least two, and possibly three, vessels arrived in the city from Irish ports in 1718. One ship transported passengers from Londonderry to New York City in 1718. According to John Paterson, whose case was heard in the Mayor's Court, Samuel Gordon, the Master of "a Certain Ship . . . Called the Hart then Riding at Anchor in the harbour of Londonderry in Ireland and then bound on A Voyage to some part of America as the Majority of Passengers Should Vote In Consideration that the said John would provide and procure twenty Passengers to go on board the said ship and go the Voyage

Figure 8. Anthony Duane (1682–1747) was born in Galway, Ireland. After a stint in the British navy, he settled in New York City where he engaged in trade. Duane owned a pew in Trinity Church, where he served on the vestry. Courtesy of The New-York Historical Society, N.Y.C.

Aforesaid and should go on board the said Ship himself and be A Passenger for the Voyage . . . and that . . . John would pay . . . for the Passage of Every Passenger for the Voyage . . . the Majority of the Passengers on board the said ship did Vote that she should Come to New York."[109] Presumably Paterson intended to sell the indentures of the servants for whose transportation he had paid.

In its October 27, 1718, issue, the *Boston News-Letter* reported the arrival in New York of "a Ship from Ireland with about 100 Passengers."

Two weeks later, on November 10, the newspaper noted "Arrived here [New York] a Pink from Ireland, with Passengers, John Read, Master." Whether the same vessel was reported twice or these were separate vessels is unclear.[110]

While on the Atlantic Ocean in September 1726, Benjamin Franklin sighted "a snow from Dublin, bound to New York, having upwards of fifty servants on board, of both sexes; they all appeared upon deck, and seemd very much pleased at the sight of us." Franklin, who was en route from London to Philadelphia, remarked on "the miserable circumstances of the passengers on board . . . they live, confined and stifled up with such a lousy stinking rabble in this sultry latitude."[111] The arrival of this vessel in New York City has not been documented.

Four ships carrying servants sailed from Ireland to New York City in 1728 and 1729 while three others did so in 1732. Two of the ships—the *Thomas* and the *Betty and Hannah*—were listed as departing from Cork, while the other four vessels embarked from Dublin.[112] According to Audrey Lockhart, the large emigration at this time resulted from a recession in the linen trade in the late 1720s and famine in Ireland.[113] Most vessels sailed from Dublin for Philadelphia, but several transported Irish servants to New York City.

A total of 388 servants arrived on the six vessels for which statistics exist, the largest number (100) on the *George and John* and the fewest (25) aboard the *Betty and Hannah*.[114] Their geographic origins and prior histories in Ireland remain obscure.[115]

Both men and women were represented among these presumably young servants and many of the men were skilled workers. The persons who sought to sell the indentures of the 55 men and women servants transported on the *Eagle* in 1729 advertised in the *New-York Gazette* that "most of the Men are Handy-crafts as Weavers, Taylors, Coopers, Blacksmiths, Cordwainers, Felt-makers, Brasiers, Brewers, Butchers and the rest are Farmers and Labourers."[116] Not all servants waited until arrival to obtain labor contracts. In 1729, the indenture of service of "William Presland, tailor, to John Colgan, merchant, for four years, at New York, executed in the presence of Hen. Burrowes, lord mayor of Dublin" was recorded in colony records.[117]

Those engaged in the Irish servant trade made a point of assuring prospective employers that these workers were voluntary immigrants. In the advertisement for the servants carried by the *Thomas*, a disclaimer was included that "Master and Mate make oath that none of them [the servants] are convicted criminals but that they are Persons that freely and voluntarily engaged themselves by Indentures, to serve a certain time for their Passage."[118]

A chance remark of Elizabeth Ashbridge, an English-born woman who arrived in New York in 1732 after a nine-week voyage from Dublin with a group of 60 Irish servants, suggests that the primary language of Irish newcomers was Gaelic. In her memoir, Ashbridge, who later became a convert to the Quaker faith, noted that she was the only English passenger who could understand the Irish language spoken by the servants.[119] Instrumental in foiling a mutinous plot by these Irish servants, Ashbridge related that "at length they found out that I understood Irish, by my smiling at a story they were telling in that language."[120]

What proportion of the Irish servants landed at New York remained in the city is unclear. Thomas Truxes asserts that "some of the incoming Irish contributed to the city's growing population, but most who remained in the colony found their way into the Hudson River Valley, particularly after the close of the Seven Years War."[121] During the early years of Irish immigration to New York, however, many servants probably were sold to masters in the city or its environs. In 1729, New York City's church-wardens were ordered to provide relief for "a woman from Ireland lately Transported into this City in the Snow Speedwell John Ray Master whose name is Nancy Killpatrick now being big with Child and near her delivery, and her Husband sold A servant somewhere in New Jersey to her unknown."[122]

Advertisements for runaway Irish servants in the *New-York Gazette* document the presence of Irish workers in the city in the early 1730s: "A Servant Man named Hugh Agen, is Run away from his Master John Blake of New-York. He is a Tall Slender Man, and much given to talk. He pretends to be a Doctor and to let Blood. He wears a light coloured blew Coat, and is an Irish man."[123] Cordwainer Thomas Hall advertised for two runaway Irish servant men, "the one named Thomas Holland, of a middle Stature black Complexion and a Black Beard, aged about 35 Years . . . and the other named John Sulivan, a short well sett Fellow, of a fair complexion and fresh colour, . . . he wears his own Hair which is light colour'd and curl'd, . . . He is . . . about 18 Years of Age, and has very thick Legs."[124] Those Irish who arrived in New York City during the first third of the eighteenth century were the forerunners of a far more substantial migration. By the eve of the American Revolution, Irish immigration to New York had increased dramatically.[125]

In 1709, the British government undertook to resettle hundreds of impoverished refugees from the German territory of the Palatinate to the colony of New York.[126] Inspired by a combination of economic and humanitarian motives, statesmen envisioned the Palatines as a convenient source of labor for manufacturing naval stores, which were much in demand by the Royal

Navy. New York City, as the port of entry for the Palatine immigrants, could not fail to be affected by this massive transplantation of human beings. But the impact of the migration on the city's population was minimal.

City officials reacted with alarm to the arrival of the fleet carrying the main body of Palatines in 1710. Fearing that the contagious diseases that had enveloped the ships and decimated the passengers would spread among local residents, municipal authorities ordered the survivors of the voyage to be quarantined on Nutten (Governor's) Island in New York harbor.[127] After they recovered their health, the great majority of the German newcomers left the city to begin the next phase of their trouble-filled odyssey as workers on the government's naval stores project located up the Hudson River on Robert Livingston's land. Approximately 100 Palatines, primarily widows and their children, remained in New York City. Under Governor Hunter's direction, 41 boys and girls (some orphans and others with one surviving parent) were apprenticed to masters in the city.[128]

Between 1711 and 1728, 111 German newcomers joined the city's Dutch Reformed congregation, but most remained in the the church for only a short while.[129] Other Germans appear in the records of the Lutheran church.[130] The stay of most Palatines in New York City was abbreviated. As people accustomed to living on the land, they preferred the familiarity of a rural environment. Some widows remarried and accompanied their new husbands to the Palatine settlements up the Hudson River. By 1716–17, a score of Palatine families had left the city and settled in the Raritan Valley of New Jersey.[131]

The handful of German immigrants who became residents of New York City were skilled workers. In 1723, Hans Yure Bloom, "son of Andrew Blom, Pallentine [sic]," was apprenticed to Johannes Lesser, a cordwainer.[132] German newcomers Bartel Miller, a cordwainer, Jacob Miller and Daniel Miller, both sadlers, John Reupel, a baker, and Henry Schleydon, a taylor, also took apprentices.[133] Other German immigrants include Johannes Roorback, a baker, John Schutz, a barber and perriwig maker, and Michael Pfeffer, a laborer. On April 1, 1727, the city's Lutheran minister recorded that "Michel Pfeffer was buried in our church—a deacon of the church, about 56 years old. . . . A funeral sermon was preached for him, with a large attendance of Germans."[134] Christian Kocherthal, a tallow chandler, who emigrated to New York as a boy with his father, the Reverend Josua Kocherthal, a Lutheran minister, was married by the city's Lutheran pastor to the daughter of a local Dutch family in 1729. Soon after, in September 1732, he was buried in the Lutheran churchyard.[135]

John Peter Zenger, New York City's most celebrated Palatine immigrant, arrived with his widowed mother and sister and was apprenticed to the printer William Bradford. After a stint in Maryland, he returned to the city and embarked on his notable career as editor and publisher of the *New-York Weekly Journal*.[136]

But John Peter Zenger was not surrounded by hundreds of his countrymen in New York City. Though newcomers periodically arrived from Germany in the decades following 1710, and some of the children of the original immigrants trickled back into the city from rural areas, the Palatine Germans never constituted a sizable segment of New York City's population during the first three decades of the eighteenth century.[137] Only fifteen recognizably German names can be identified on the city's 1730 tax list.

The Jewish immigrants who joined their coreligionists in New York City during the first three decades of the eighteenth century assembled from places all over the map of Europe as well as in the West Indies.[138] In 1712, Anglican chaplain John Sharpe cited as one of the advantages of New York City that "it is possible also to learn Hebrew here as well as in Europe, there being a Synagogue of Jews, and many ingenious men of that nation from Poland, Hungary, Germany, & c."[139] Ashkenazim outnumbered Sephardim among these newcomers, since by 1728 they formed a majority of the congregation Shearith Israel. The preeminent historian of colonial New York City's Jewish community has concluded that "as early as 1728 the Ashkenazim were somewhat more numerous in New York, more recently immigrated, and therefore predominantly younger than the Sephardim, while the Sephardim were more settled, more prosperous, and more influential."[140] The shifting ratio did not escape the notice of Sephardic Jews in Curaçao who were benefactors of the synagogue under construction in New York City in 1728: "The Members of this Holy Congregation . . . as they Know that the (asquenazum) or Germans, are more in Number than Wee there, they desire of you not to Consent not Withstanding they are the most, to let them have any More Votes nor Authority then they have had hitherto."[141]

Though only 20 Jewish taxpayers (men and women) are found on the 1730 tax list, an estimate of the city's Jewish population based on contributors to the cemetery and synagogue funds, suggests that there were 75 Jewish families or 225 Jews in New York City in 1730, the year that the Mill Street Synagogue opened.[142] These figures may be too high, since the Mill Street Synagogue, only 35 foot square and 21 feet high, was able to house New York City's entire Jewish community.[143]

Ample biographical information on Jewish New Yorkers enables us to identify many of the newcomers.[144] Most immigrants engaged in some form of trade but Valentine Campanal was a butcher and Uriah Hyam was

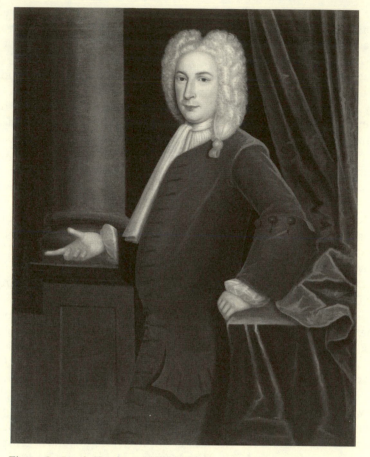

Figure 9. Jacob Franks (1688–1769) was one of the foremost figures in eighteenth-century New York City's Jewish community. In 1712, soon after his arrival from England, he married Abigail Levy, the daughter of a wealthy local merchant. American Jewish Historical Society. Gift of Captain N. Taylor Phillips. Photo, Courtesy, Museum of Fine Arts, Boston.

a tallow chandler.[145] Two merchant clans that put down roots in the city in the early years of the eighteenth century towered over other recent arrivals—the Franks family and the Gomez family. Jacob Franks (figure 9), an Ashkenazic Jew who was born in England, settled in the city about 1708 or 1709 and commenced his mercantile career.[146] Franks prospered, attaining high status in the city and serving in a number of important offices. With property assessed at £140 on the 1730 tax list, Franks ranked in the top 5 percent of the economic elite.

After spending several years in the West Indies, Lewis Moses Gomez, a Sephardic Jew, moved to New York City about 1703.[147] He and his five sons soon established a trading empire that brought them great wealth. In 1730, the taxable property of Lewis, Mordecai, Daniel, and Moses Gomez totaled £305. The eminence of the Gomez family is graphically illustrated by the fact that a special enclosure of the synagogue gallery was reserved for the Gomez women.[148]

New York City's slowly accelerating curve of population growth was abruptly halted near the end of the eighteenth-century's third decade by the reappearance of epidemic disease and the onset of economic decline. In early 1729, measles spread through the city. The seriousness of the outbreak was conveyed by James Alexander to Cadwallader Colden:

> There never was So great a mortality here Since I came to this place as now, theres no day but what theres numbers of buryings, Some of the measles but most of the pain of the Side there's hardly a house in town but what had severals [sic] Sick of the one or other of these Distempers.[149]

Theophilus Ellsworth, who operated the ferry between Manhattan and Long Island, noted "the great loss and damage [he had] sustained by the Disease Called the Measles which lately afflicted this City, by Means whereof, the . . . Ferry was almost unfrequented for a long time."[150]

While disrupting the city's commerce and causing suffering particularly among the city's children, the measles epidemic apparently did not claim many lives.[151] A far greater crisis was in store for New Yorkers in 1731. In Ellsworth's words, "it hath pleased Almighty God for several months past to visit this City with a More Fatal Disease Called the Small Pox, which now prevails in a most Deplorable manner to the great Terrour of all the Neighbouring Colonys and Countys, by means whereof there is Very little Intercourse between this City and Country, the Country People being so terrified with the Danger of Catching that loathsome and Malignant disease, that they wholy Neglect, not only Comeing to Market, but also Comeing to Negotiate their Urgent and lawfull Occasions."[152]

Smallpox was first detected in June 1731 and the number of cases increased rapidly during the summer. By August, the city was devastated: "Here is . . . nothing but the melancholy Scene of little Business, and less Money, The Markets begin to grow very thin; the Small-Pox raging very violently in Town, which in a great measure hinders the Country People from supplying this place with Provisions."[153] James Alexander detailed the personal impact of the disease: "The Small pox have taken from me my Son James & my negro jupiter all the rest of my family I hope are past Danger tho they are afflicted with Boyles, the Small pox was at the height on Sunday Last on the Last of my family."[154]

The death toll from the epidemic continued to climb, reaching 549 (478 whites and 71 blacks) by its end in mid-November.[155] Furthermore, official reports may have underestimated deaths in the city during these awful months. At a minimum, 8 percent of the city's population died in 1731. The survivors faced a gloomy prospect, not only as a result of the massive loss of lives, but because of the downturn in the economy.[156] The decade ahead was a time of exodus from New York City.

Chapter Eight

THE THIRD GENERATION

T

HE GRANDCHILDREN of New York City's original families came of age in a society whose ethnic composition
differed markedly from that of New Amsterdam. The expand-
ing ranks of immigrants from the British Isles in the early decades of the
eighteenth century, in tandem with the maturation of the second-generation of early English families, resulted in the British climbing from 29.5
percent of the city's white population in 1695 and 36 percent in 1703 to
49.5 percent in 1730.[1] While residents of British ancestry made up an increasing share of the city's population, the proportion of Dutch and
French inhabitants declined. In 1730, the Dutch constituted only 39.4
percent of New York City's white population, down from 58 percent in
1695 and 52 percent in 1703. The French dropped from 11 percent in
both 1695 and 1703 to 8 percent in 1730. The Jews constituted 1.8 percent and the Germans 1.4 percent of the white population in 1730.

The sheer number of English, Scots, and Irish residents in New York by
the third decade of the eighteenth century is not in itself indicative of the
reallocation of wealth and power in the city. Historians of colonial New
York customarily have linked changes in ethnic ratios to the transformation of the social structure, but as the evidence presented in chapter 4 has
shown, the position of the Dutch in the framework of urban life remained
notably secure throughout the seventeenth century, despite the influx of
English immigrants.[2] Whether the augmentation of the British population
during the early eighteenth century adversely affected the economic and
political status of the Dutch in New York City can only be ascertained by
examining the ethnic distribution of occupations, wealth, and officeholding in the years up to 1730.

For the purposes of this analysis, New Yorkers of British descent have
been classified as one group despite the fact that significant numbers of
Scots, Scots-Irish, and Irish had now joined their English compatriots in
the city. Given the dearth of information on the backgrounds of all but the
better-known British immigrants, identifying Scots, Scots-Irish, and Irish
is extremely difficult. Only 24 non-English men can be identified with cer-
tainty on the 1730 tax list, though undoubtedly more were present. Even
if the proportion of non-English men were as high as 10 percent of the
538 British male taxpayers, however, placing them in a separate category
would needlessly complicate the statistical profile, while failing to shed

TABLE 8–1
Occupations and Ethnic Identity of Male Taxpayers, 1730

Occupation	Dutch	British	French	Jews	Germans	Total
Merchants & retailers	64	47	20	14	1	146
Professionals						
Physicians	5	6	1	—	—	12
Ministers	—	2	—	—	—	2
Attorneys	—	12	1	—	—	13
Government officeholders	1	4	—	—	—	5
Printers	—	1	—	—	1	2
Schoolmasters	1	3	—	—	1	5
Service trades						
Victuallers & tavernkeepers	4	22	2	—	—	28
Bakers & bolters	30	11	—	—	1	42
Brewers	4	1	—	—	—	5
Butchers	—	7	—	1	—	8
Barbers	1	11	—	—	1	13
Combmaker	—	—	1	—	—	1
Confectioner	—	—	1	—	—	1
Gardeners	—	—	1	—	1	2
Distillers	1	2	1	—	—	4
Painters	4	1	—	—	—	5
Maritime trades						
Mariners	19	54	5	—	1	79
Ship carpenters	2	16	2	—	—	20
Sailmakers	1	2	1	—	—	4
Cloth & leather workers						
Cordwainers	28	13	3	—	3	47
Tanners	1	1	—	—	—	2
Tailors	1	7	3	—	1	12
Weavers	3	—	1	—	—	4
Feltmakers	3	6	—	—	—	9
Glovers	—	3	—	—	—	3
Wood, metal, & stone workers						
Carpenters	18	12	2	—	—	32
Joiners	3	6	2	—	—	11
Turners	5	3	—	—	—	8
Blockmakers	3	—	—	—	—	3
Coopers	13	13	2	—	—	28
Masons	4	2	—	—	—	6
Blacksmiths	8	2	1	—	—	11
Farrier	—	1	—	—	—	1
Gunsmiths	8	2	—	—	—	10
Locksmith	—	1	—	—	—	1
Braziers	—	1	1	—	—	2

Table 8–1 (*cont.*)

Occupation	Dutch	British	French	Jews	Germans	Total
Wood, metal, & stone workers (*cont.*)						
Glazier	1	—	—	—	—	1
Tallow chandlers	1	1	—	1	—	3
Silversmiths	8	—	4	—	—	12
Pewterers	—	1	2	—	—	3
Jeweler	—	—	1	—	—	1
Clockmaker	—	1	—	—	—	1
Laborers						
Carmen	15	13	—	—	—	28
Totals	260	291	58	16	11	636

much light on the fortunes of members of these groups. What can be said is that individual Scots, Scots-Irish, and Irish, like men of all ethnic groups, varied in their economic prowess. Scotsman James Alexander, a prominent attorney, was taxed for property assessed at £215 in 1730, but the property of fellow Scot, Andrew Bisset, a mariner, was rated at only £30. Similarly, Irish-born merchant Anthony Duane held property worth £90, while another Irish immigrant, Dennis Mahany, who served as the city's public whipper, possessed merely £5 of property.

The shift in the city's ethnic demography is reflected in the placement of ethnic groups in the occupational structure as shown in table 8–1.[3] The occupations of 636 of the 1,087 men on the 1730 tax list (59 percent) have been identified. This group forms the basis of the following generalizations. The British registered substantial gains from their position in 1695 in six of the seven occupational categories, with the sharpest increases occurring in the maritime trades and the cloth and leather trades. The Dutch experienced a corresponding reduction of their share of these six occupational categories, the steepest decline being in the cloth and leather trades. The French also lost ground in all but one occupational category, and, most significantly, in the maritime trades.

Comparing the proportion of each ethnic group in an occupational category with its proportion of the city's population, however, puts the dimensions of change in proper perspective. (See table 8–2.) As late as 1730, the British exceeded their proportion of the population in only two occupational categories—professionals and maritime workers. Moreover, they continued to be underrepresented among merchants, cloth and leather workers, and wood, metal, and stone workers.

For the Dutch, by contrast, the only glaring disparities between their share of the total population and their proportion of an occupational cate-

TABLE 8–2
Ethnic Composition of Occupational Categories, 1730

Ethnic Group	Merchants & Retailers	Professionals	Service Trades	Maritime Trades	Cloth & Leather Workers	Wood, Metal, & Stone Workers	Laborers	Proportion of Taxable Population
Dutch	44% (N=64)	18% (N=7)	40% (N=44)	21% (N=22)	47% (N=36)	54% (N=72)	54% (N=15)	39.4%
British	32% (N=47)	72% (N=28)	50% (N=55)	70% (N=72)	39% (N=30)	34% (N=46)	46% (N=13)	49.5%
French	14% (N=20)	5% (N=2)	6% (N=6)	8% (N=8)	9% (N=7)	11% (N=15)	—	8.0%
Jews	10% (N=14)	—	1% (N=1)	—	—	1% (N=1)	—	1.7%
Germans	1% (N=1)	5% (N=2)	3% (N=3)	1% (N=1)	5% (N=4)	—	—	1.4%
TOTAL	100% (N=146)	100% (N=39)	100% (N=109)	100% (N=103)	100% (N=77)	100% (N=134)	100% (N=28)	

gory occurred in these same fields—the professions and the maritime trades. The Dutch predictably were at a disadvantage in the professions since being an attorney required training in English law, and appointment to imperial offices depended on connections in England.[4] As New York's shipping came under English control, the substitution of British seamen for Dutch was inevitable. Already facing stiff competition in the new maritime environment, older Dutch seafaring men may have advised their sons not to follow in their footsteps.

Despite their diminishing share of most occupations, the Dutch in 1730 still dominated the basic productive trades (cloth and leather; wood, metal, and stone) that they had controlled since the days of New Amsterdam. Between 1718 and 1727, Dutch master artisans such as hatter Henry Brestede, gunsmith Henry van de Water, and turner Aron Bogart, trained 38 British apprentices, whereas only 16 Dutch youths arranged to learn a trade with a British master.[5] City officials contracted with carpenter Teunis Tiebout for a variety of municipal projects in the early eighteenth century.[6] Tiebout, along with masons Cornelis Turck, Peter Brouwer, and Jan Bogardus, and glazier Hendrick van der Spiegel, were among the Dutch artisans engaged to construct the new Dutch Reformed Church in 1727–28.[7]

In the all-important field of commerce, the Dutch managed to maintain the same level of involvement—44 percent of merchants and retailers—as they had in 1695, even though their share of the population had declined to slightly less than 40 percent. On the other hand, the British, who now constituted close to one-half of the city's population, still numbered only 32 percent of merchants and retailers—the same as 1695. The success of the Dutch in preserving their position in mercantile ranks must be attributed in large part to the strength of their kinship networks.

Slightly more than half of the 54 merchants identified as Dutch in 1730 descended from the city's old settler families.[8] Second- and third-generation members of prominent merchant clans—the Bayards, Van Cortlandts, De Peysters, Philipses, and Van Hornes—dominated the group. The remaining Dutch merchants were primarily sons or grandsons of Dutch families that initially settled in other areas of New Netherland. Some had moved to New York City before 1700 and others after the turn of the century. Families with ties to Albany included the Abeels, Van Dams, Rutgerses, Cuylers, Schuylers, and Tellers. A few had roots in Long Island—the Brinckerhoffs, Leffertses, and Van Wycks. Several had emigrated from the Netherlands or the West Indies. But the great majority came from families that had been in the colony before the conquest.

Longevity in New York was more pronounced among British merchants than might be expected, given the acceleration of British migration after 1700. Roughly half of the 43 British men identified as merchants in

Figure 10. Nathaniel Marston, Jr. (1704–1778), whose English immigrant father was a barber and wigmaker, rose to prominence as one of eighteenth-century New York City's principal merchants. John Wollaston painted this portrait. Courtesy Museum of the City of New York.

1730 had roots that stretched back to seventeenth-century New York City. Several were older men who had appeared on the 1695 tax list. Robert Lurting and Robert Walters, both of whom served as mayor, are examples. Quaker Edward Burling had come to New York from England as a boy with his parents. But at least 17 of these merchants were born in the city, most of them to English fathers and Dutch mothers. Included in this group were Philip French, Richard Ashfield, David and Matthew Clarkson, Thomas Thong, John Walters, John Spratt, Jeremiah Tothill, Jacob and William Walton, and Nathaniel Marston, Jr. (figure 10). Marston, the

TABLE 8–3
Ethnic Distribution of Taxable Property, 1730

Ethnic Group (Males)	Total Taxable Wealth (in pounds)	Proportion of Taxable Wealth (in percent)	Proportion in Population (in percent)
Dutch			
(N = 428)	13,925	46.0	39.4
British			
(N = 538)	12,285	40.6	49.5
French			
(N = 87)	3,110	10.3	8.0
Jews			
(N = 18)	745	2.5	1.7
Others[a]			
(N = 16)	220	0.7	1.5
TOTAL			
(N = 1,087)	30,285	100.1	100.1

[a] Includes Germans and one free black.

son of a barber, was among the five men whose fathers were not merchants or government officials.

The proliferation of men from the British Isles in New York City during the first three decades of the eighteenth century and their diffusion in the occupational structure did not dislodge wealthy Dutch merchants from their position. That the Dutch outnumbered other ethnic groups among merchants in 1730, notwithstanding their decline in the total population, indicates that they retained a considerable measure of economic power in the city during the first third of the eighteenth century. This is borne out by the data in table 8–3 on the relative shares of the city's taxable wealth in 1730 held by the men of each ethnic group. New York City's wealth was not distributed proportionally among its ethnic groups in 1730 as it had been in 1695. Dutch men, who numbered 110 fewer than British men in 1730, controlled 46 percent of the taxable wealth. In contrast, British men controlled only 40.6 percent of the city's taxable wealth, even though they constituted 49.5 percent of the population. Though French and Jewish men held more wealth than their proportion of the population, the disparity was less than 2.5 percent in both cases.

Though New York City's wealth distribution profile in 1730, as seen in table 8–4, largely resembled that of 1695, some differences are noteworthy.[9] In 1730, the top tenth controlled 43.8 percent of the taxable wealth, compared to 45.2 percent in 1695, whereas the lowest 30 percent, which had held only 3.6 percent of the wealth in 1695, now held 6 percent

TABLE 8–4
Distribution of Wealth Based on the 1730 Tax List

Wealth Bracket (in percent)	Assessments of Persons (in pounds)	Total Assessed Wealth (in pounds)	Percent of Wealth	Cumulative Percent of Wealth
0–10	0–5	555	1.6	1.6
11–20	5	655	1.9	3.5
21–30	5–10	865	2.5	6.0
31–40	10	1,310	3.8	9.8
41–50	10–15	1,500	4.3	14.1
51–60	15–20	2,010	5.8	19.9
61–70	20–25	2,745	7.9	27.8
71–80	25–35	3,855	11.0	38.8
81–90	35–60	6,120	17.5	56.3
91–100	60–610	15,295	43.8	100.1
0–30	0–10	2,075	6.0	
31–60	10–20	4,820	13.9	
61–90	20–60	12,720	36.4	
91–100	60–610	15,295	43.8	

Note: The tax list is for the five urban wards. The total number of persons on the tax list is 1,308 (with 130 persons in the top two brackets and 131 in the bottom eight). The total assessed wealth for all 1,308 persons is £34,910.

of the wealth. The contrast between the two years was most striking in the case of the richest 5 percent, who held 32 percent of the city's wealth in 1695 but only 25.4 percent thirty-five years later. Those residents in the bottom half of the wealth spectrum now controlled 14.1 percent of the taxable wealth whereas their counterparts in 1695 held only 10.3 percent.

The direction of change was toward a slightly more equitable division of property, but too much significance should not be attributed to this trend. New York City had just entered a period of serious economic depression when the tax roll was compiled in 1730.[10] In the short run, at least, the resources of artisans, especially those in shipbuilding and associated crafts, would be severely depleted. Though municipal expenditures for the city's most impoverished residents—old people, orphans, the ill, the handicapped, and women whose husbands had died, deserted them, or become incapacitated—rose only gradually during the first third of the eighteenth century and an almshouse was not constructed until 1736, it is essential not to overlook the scores of people who regularly existed in precarious financial circumstances.[11] Only when misfortune deprived these individuals of an accustomed source of income, and they faced immediate hardship, do they appear as petitioners in the public record. In 1704, Susannah Walgrave's

> husband George Walgrave being lately Seized with an unreasonable & extream melancholy laid violent hands on himself of which he immediately dyed Leaving Your . . . poor petitioner and two Children in a most miserable and forlone condition without any thing to Support or Subsist them, the little which [she] otherwise might have Received being . . . forfeit to her Majesty. That her said husband being a mason by trade maintained himself and his family by his dayly labor, and all the personall estate he had consisted of a few inconsiderable debts . . . without which (or the Charity of her Neighbors) shee and her poor children must inevitably perish the ensueing Winter.

Susannah went on to request authority from the governor to receive her husband's debts "that therewith and her own Labor and industry Shee may be enabled to provide sustenance for herself and her . . . Children without becoming a burthen to the Citty."[12]

Not infrequently the failure of the government to promptly pay for services it had contracted caused laboring men great distress. Daniel Ebbetts "a poor man [who] getts his livelihood by working as a Bricklayer by day work mostly and is weekly paid" had completed work on Fort Anne and received a warrant from New York authorities for £41 2s 7d "which is a very great sume your petitioners circumstances considered." Unable to collect the funds owed him, he was "everyday threatened to be arrested and put in prison for the victualls he and his family eat while he was working . . . & for the materialls he used about this work."[13]

While the poor struggled to stay afloat, the well-to-do were increasing their assets. Tax assessors invariably underestimated the actual wealth of city residents, particularly those at the upper end of the social scale, because certain forms of property were not taxable nor were landholdings outside the city.[14] By 1730, affluent New Yorkers were well along in the process of accumulating country estates, slaves, silver plate, furniture, and jewels, not to mention urban real estate.

The division of wealth within each of the city's major ethnic communities in 1730 was quite similar. (See tables 8–5, 8–6, and 8–7.) The upper 10 percent of each group controlled between 42 and 44.5 percent of the group's wealth, while the bottom 30 percent held between 5.2 and 6.4 percent. Poor French men were relatively most disadvantaged, as they had been in 1695, with the bottom half of the French group holding only slightly more than 12 percent of the group's total wealth.

The impressive display of Dutch economic power in early eighteenth-century New York City was matched in the political realm. In fact, the

TABLE 8–5
Distribution of Wealth for Dutch Men Based on the
1730 Tax List

Wealth Bracket (in percent)	Assessments of Persons (in pounds)	Total Assessed Wealth (in pounds)	Percent of Wealth	Cumulative Percent of Wealth
0–10	0–5	200	1.4	1.4
11–20	5–10	235	1.7	3.1
21–30	10	430	3.1	6.2
31–40	10–15	460	3.3	9.5
41–50	15	645	4.6	14.1
51–60	15–20	815	5.9	20.0
61–70	20–30	1,065	7.6	27.6
71–80	30–45	1,640	11.8	39.4
81–90	45–75	2,490	17.9	57.3
91–100	80–315	5,945	42.7	100.0
0–30	0–10	865	6.2	
31–60	10–20	1,920	13.8	
61–90	20–75	5,195	37.3	
91–100	80–315	5,945	42.7	

Note: The tax list is for the five urban wards. The total number of persons on the tax list is 428 (with 42 persons in the top two brackets and 43 in the bottom eight). The total assessed wealth for all 428 persons is £13,925.

Dutch were so successful in maintaining their political power at the local level that men of Dutch background dominated the most important offices of municipal government between 1708 and 1730.[15] The overwhelming number of men elected as alderman and assistant alderman during these years were Dutch. (See table 8–8.) Of the 115 alderman positions for the five urban wards (1708 to 1730), 102 (89 percent) were filled by Dutch men, 12 (10 percent) by British men and one (1 percent) by a French man. Of the 115 assistant alderman positions for the five urban wards (1708 to 1730), 95 (83 percent) were held by Dutch men, 11 (10 percent) by British men, and 9 (8 percent) by French men. In other words, a much greater proportion of Dutch men held municipal office at the highest level than their percentage of the city's population in 1730—39.4 percent. By contrast, British immigrants, despite their increasing numbers, did not rapidly move into positions of civic leadership during the early decades of the eighteenth century. Englishmen had fared better in the years between 1687 and 1707, when they held 32 percent of the positions as alderman and 28 percent of the positions as assistant alderman.

TABLE 8–6
Distribution of Wealth for British Men Based on the
1730 Tax List

Wealth Bracket (in percent)	Assessments of Persons (in pounds)	Total Assessed Wealth (in pounds)	Percent of Wealth	Cumulative Percent of Wealth
0–10	0–5	240	2.0	2.0
11–20	5	270	2.2	4.2
21–30	5	270	2.2	6.4
31–40	5–10	515	4.2	10.6
41–50	10	540	4.4	15.0
51–60	10–15	755	6.1	21.1
61–70	15–20	945	7.7	28.8
71–80	20–30	1,385	11.3	40.1
81–90	30–55	2,190	17.8	57.9
91–100	55–330	5,175	42.1	100.0
0–30	0–5	780	6.4	
31–60	5–15	1,810	14.7	
61–90	15–55	4,520	36.8	
91–100	55–330	5,175	42.1	

Note: The tax list is for the five urban wards. The total number of persons on the tax list is 538 (with 53 persons in the top three brackets and 54 in the bottom seven). The total assessed wealth for all 538 persons is £12,285.

Aldermen and assistants tended to hold on to their posts for many years. Jacobus Kip served as alderman of the North Ward from 1709 to 1726, John Cruger filled the office of alderman of the Dock Ward from 1712 to 1730, and Harmanus van Gelder was reelected as alderman of the West Ward from 1715 to 1730. Long terms such as these were not uncommon and, consequently, turnover in these offices was extremely low. Between 1708 and 1730, just 18 men filled the 115 alderman positions while 28 men filled the 115 assistant alderman positions.[16]

Dutch men also served as assessor, the next most important office in city government, in far greater numbers than their proportion in the population warranted. Turnover in this position was more frequent than in those of alderman and assistant alderman, but still the 230 positions were filled by only 142 men. Of the 230 assessor positions for the urban wards in the years 1708 to 1730, 165 (72 percent) were held by Dutch men, 47 (20 percent) by British men, and 18 (8 percent) by French men.

The ethnic distribution of tax collectors came closest to corresponding with the ratio of ethnic groups in the city's European population, though

TABLE 8–7
Distribution of Wealth for French Men Based on the
1730 Tax List

Wealth Bracket (in percent)	Assessments of Persons (in pounds)	Total Assessed Wealth (in pounds)	Percent of Wealth	Cumulative Percent of Wealth
0–10	5	45	1.4	1.4
11–20	5	45	1.4	2.8
21–30	5–10	75	2.4	5.2
31–40	10	90	2.9	8.1
41–50	10–15	130	4.2	12.3
51–60	20–25	195	6.3	18.6
61–70	25–35	270	8.7	27.3
71–80	40–50	365	11.7	39.0
81–90	50–85	510	16.4	55.4
91–100	90–610	1,385	44.5	99.9
0–30	5–10	165	5.2	
31–60	10–25	415	13.4	
61–90	25–85	1,145	36.8	
91–100	90–610	1,385	44.5	

Note: The tax list is for the five urban wards. The total number of persons on the tax list is 87 (with 8 persons in the top three brackets and 9 in the bottom seven). The total assessed wealth for all 87 persons is £3,110.

TABLE 8–8
Ethnic Distribution of Municipal Officeholders, 1708–1730

Office	Number of Positions Available	Number of Positions Held by				
		Dutch	British	French	Jews	Germans
Alderman	115	102 (89%)	12 (10%)	1 (1%)	—	—
Assistant alderman	115	95 (83%)	11 (10%)	9 (8%)	—	—
Assessor	230	165 (72%)	47 (20%)	18 (8%)	—	—
Tax collector	115	56 (49%)	42 (37%)	14 (12%)	1 (1%)	2 (2%)
Constable	115	29 (25%)	67 (58%)	9 (8%)	7 (6%)	3 (3%)
TOTAL	690	447 (65%)	179 (26%)	51 (7%)	8 (1%)	5 (1%)

Dutch men formed the largest number of officeholders. Collecting taxes was not a sought-after job and reelection to office was the exception, not the rule. Over the years 1708 to 1730, 92 men filled the 115 available positions. The precipitous decline in the number of Dutch serving in this office—from 84 percent in the period 1687–1707 to 49 percent in the period 1708–1730—paralleled a sharp increase in the number of British serving—from 5 percent in 1687–1707 to 39 percent in 1708–1730. With the expansion of the British population, the need for tax collectors of Dutch extraction receded.

Only in the odious office of constable, which men often chose to avoid by paying a large fine, were British men overrepresented. No person was expected to serve as constable more than once in fifteen years and, in fact, no individual repeated in this office between 1708 and 1730.[17] Dutch men were elected to the post of constable only 29 out of 115 times (25 percent), while British men were elected 67 times (58 percent). Members of other ethnic groups were elected to the remaining posts. Perhaps British men were perceived as best suited to enforce "English" laws.

Ethnic identity alone does not explain the pattern of officeholding in early eighteenth-century New York City. The men elected to the most powerful positions in municipal government—those of alderman and assistant alderman—had to meet the voters' expectation that they possess a substantial amount of property or be a member of a family of high social rank. Aldermen, whatever their ethnic background, tended to be merchants, as were 83 percent of the incumbents between 1708 and 1730. (See table 8–9.) The one significant exception to this rule was bricklayer Harmanus van Gelder, who filled the office for sixteen terms between 1715 and 1730. Though Van Gelder had roots in the artisan community, he had actually become a building contractor, employing workmen in various projects that he supervised. His property was assessed at £80 in 1730, which placed him in the top tenth of the city's wealth structure. Moreover, Van Gelder was considerably older than two of his counterparts on the Common Council who belonged to leading New York families. Van Gelder was 49 when first elected as alderman, whereas Philip van Cortlandt was 34 and Frederick Philipse (the second) only 21.

Assistant aldermen were drawn from a broader range of occupations, but almost twice as many merchants served in this office as artisans. Artisans, however, outnumbered merchants as assessors, tax collectors, and constables. The role of artisans in city government, overall, lessened by the second and third decades of the eighteenth century. Between 1687 and 1707, artisans had held 38 percent of offices, virtually the same proportion as merchants, who held 38.5 percent. However, in the years between 1708 and 1730, artisans held 34 percent of municipal offices (233 out of 690) compared to 39 percent for merchants (268 out of 690).

TABLE 8–9

Occupational Distribution of Municipal Officeholders, 1708–1730

Office	No. of Positions Available	Number of Positions Held by						
		Merchants	Professionals & Govt. Employees	Bakers, Bolters, Brewers, Butchers	Tavern-keepers	Artisans	Mariners	Unknown
Alderman	115	95 (83%)	—	4 (3%)	—	16 (14%)	—	—
Assistant alderman	115	58 (50%)	2 (2%)	20 (17%)	4 (3%)	31 (27%)	—	—
Assessor	230	86 (37%)	5 (2%)	21 (9%)	2 (1%)	98 (43%)	4 (2%)	14[a] (6%)
Tax collector	115	29 (25%)	8 (7%)	6 (5%)	7 (6%)	43 (37%)	11 (10%)	11[b] (10%)
Constable	115	20 (17%)	4 (3%)	10 (9%)	10 (9%)	45 (39%)	5 (4%)	21 (18%)
TOTAL	690	288 (42%)	19 (3%)	61 (9%)	23 (3%)	233 (34%)	20 (3%)	46 (7%)

[a] Includes 4 farmers.
[b] Includes 1 farmer.

In New York City between 1708 and 1730, the pool of potential aldermen and assistant aldermen was defined by social standing. But when the
voters came to choose the men who would run the city, they overwhelmingly picked persons of Dutch ancestry.

Surveying the ethnic distribution of occupations, wealth and officeholding
furnishes compelling evidence that New York City remained a Dutch
stronghold during the first three decades of the eighteenth century, notwithstanding the swelling of the British population and the engrafting of
English institutions. Statistical profiles, however, do little to elucidate the
sequence of decisions that, in the aggregate, resulted in the Dutch preserving their unique place in the social structure. Ascertaining why descendants of the city's old settler families, most of whom were Dutch, persisted
in the city, followed particular occupations, and reinforced their ethnic ties
through marriage requires an alternate vantage point. Focusing on third-
generation members of the cohort, who, in essence, are surrogates for the
preconquest population, enables us to see how the city's core families
adapted to the changing urban environment.

Of the 113 cohort members who had sons who survived to adulthood,
105 remained in New York City. These 105 men produced 237 traceable
sons.[18] Of these 237 second-generation men, 56 moved away from the
city, 13 died unmarried, and 52 married but did not have (traceable) sons
who survived to adulthood. The remaining 116 second-generation men
fathered the 237 third-generation men who form the subjects of the following analysis.

Though the birthdates of these men ranged from 1659 to 1726, nearly
three-quarters were born between 1680 and 1710, and 59 percent were
born betwen 1685 and 1705.[19] The median birth year was 1694. Evidence
on the date of first marriage, available for 174 third-generation men, further assists in locating the group in time. Of these men, 72 percent were
wed for the first time between 1700 and 1729, with the median marriage
year falling at 1718. Thus, most of the grandsons of cohort members came
of age betwen 1700 and 1730. With respect to longevity, the men of the
third generation illustrate the fact that death could strike at any age in
colonial America. The ages at death of the 133 men for whom reliable
information exists ranged from 20 to 101, with the median at 67. Their
average age at death, however, was 57.

Since most third-generation men survived long enough to make decisions about their future, focusing on their choice of residence presents an
initial means of determining attitudes toward the urban society in which
their families were rooted. For the grandsons of cohort members to remain in New York City was to register the perception that, despite ongoing change, they still had a niche in the city of their birth. Accustomed

to the English presence in New York, they were confident that they could shape their private lives in satisfactory ways. Deciding to relocate, on the other hand, might indicate dissatisfaction with the evolution of city life or a desire to improve the lot of one's family. Approximately the same number of third-generation cohort males migrated from New York City as had second-generation males. Of the 237 third-generation men, 59 (25 percent) left Manhattan at some point in their lives, whereas 56 out of 237 second-generation men (24 percent) did so. Examining the circumstances under which men left the city and their destinations makes clear that migration in the third generation was primarily a search for economic betterment rather than a consequence of despair.

The destinations of geographically mobile third-generation New Yorkers can be explained in terms of family biographies and regional patterns of migration in the eighteenth century. The great majority of these men relocated in newly opened rural areas where land was readily available to people with capital. In some families, fathers had already purchased land or moved out of the city themselves. The greatest number of migrants relocated to New Jersey. Of the 59 third-generation men who left New York City, 31 (53 percent) carved out new homes in New Jersey, particularly in the counties of Bergen, Essex, Monmouth, and Somerset—all in East New Jersey. Investigators of the transplantation of Dutch families to New Jersey in the early eighteenth century have trained their vision on the Kings County farmers who were propelled by population pressure on the land.[20] But city men were also attracted by New Jersey's proximity and the high quality of its land.

The next most popular places—Westchester County and Dutchess County, New York, each with 6 migrants or 10 percent of the total—trailed far behind. Several men of the group moved to Orange County, Queens County, and Richmond County (Staten Island), New York. Other destinations included Albany and Kingston, the primary targets of second-generation migrants, as well as Suffolk County, Kings County, New Castle (Delaware), Philadelphia, New Haven, Bermuda, and Jamaica in the West Indies.

It is tempting to attribute this migration to the constriction of opportunity in the city or more generally the search for economic betterment. But a close examination of the evidence reveals a more complex pattern. Migration occurred throughout the social structure and at different stages of the life cycle. Sons of artisan as well as merchant families departed from New York City as did young men on the eve of marriage and men in their forties and fifties. For some men, wealth acquired in commerce provided the means to retire in the country.

Migration from New York City was not entirely random, however, since the 59 individuals who left the city came from only 27 families. The decision of second-generation cohort member Johannes Meyer to transplant his family to Tappan in Orange County when he was in his early forties had obvious repercussions for the future of his offspring. Meyer, a carpenter, seized the opportunity to settle in the new farming community after his wife inherited her father's share in the venture. Ide van Vorst, who died in 1683, had been one of the original patentees of Tappan.[21] The move to Orange County altered the lives of the third generation of the Meyer family. All of Johannes's surviving sons and daughters, including his last two children born at Tappan, chose to marry and establish their own families there. Johannes Meyer (third generation) was approximately ten years old at the time of the family's relocation in Tappan, his brother Ide Meyer was about seven, and his youngest brother, Andries Meyer, was born at Tappan in 1697. Thus, the destinies of the third-generation sons of Johannes Meyer became linked with the farming settlement of Tappan rather than New York City.

Another second-generation family in which the father's mid-life migration from New York City decisively influenced the course of his sons' (and daughters') lives was the Leonard Lewis family.[22] Lewis, a merchant and alderman, as well as a member of the New York General Assembly, moved to Poughkeepsie in Dutchess County soon after he purchased land there in 1710. He represented Dutchess County in the General Assembly from 1713 to 1726. His family is counted on the 1714 Dutchess County census. Though his eldest son Thomas Lewis, who was about sixteen at the time of the family's move, married and had his first child in the city, he soon relocated to Poughkeepsie as did three other brothers, Leonard, Barent, and Johannes. A fourth brother, Gerardus, moved from the family home in Poughkeepsie to Kingston when he married in 1720. Because they did not reach maturity in New York City, Leonard Lewis's sons cast their lots in the Hudson Valley.

Some young men of the third generation left the city to capitalize on investments in rural land made by their fathers. Henry van der Burgh's move to Poughkeepsie had its genesis in the land purchases of his father, Dirck van der Burgh.[23] The elder van der Burgh, a mason who had become a merchant and amassed considerable wealth as a building contractor, died on his plantation in the Highland Schillyck at the beginning of September 1709, at the age of about 48 according to the records of the Lutheran minister.[24] Henry van der Burgh, with his wife and young family, left the city after inheriting land from his father.

Migration might also have its genesis in the example of an older brother or other kinsman, economic incentives proffered by a father-in-law settled elsewhere in the region, or the compulsion of an adventurous spirit.

Most commonly, third-generation migrants left the city shortly after reaching adulthood, their move often coinciding with their marriage or

Figure 11. Jacobus Stoutenburgh (1696–1772), a third-generation Dutch New Yorker whose father was a bricklayer, moved out of the city, settling first in Westchester County, where he was a merchant, and then in Dutchess County, where he had obtained land in the Great Nine Partners patent. Courtesy Museum of the City of New York.

soon following it. A few changed their residence a bit later, but still as young fathers. Jacobus Stoutenburgh (figure 11), for example, left New York City in his late twenties after he had married and started a family.[25] He moved to Philipsburgh, in Westchester County, where he engaged in trade. More children were born there. In 1742, he moved again to lands he had acquired in Dutchess County.

But the timing of migration in the life cycle varied. Several third-generation men left the city at mid-life. Frederick Woertendyck transplanted his wife and children in his early forties when he purchased land in Tappan, Orange County, New York, and became a farmer. Apparently, he sought to take advantage of attractive economic opportunities not available to him in New York City.[26]

A few wealthy men regarded their mid-life move to a country estate as retirement after attaining economic and political status in New York City. About 1750, merchant Stephen Bayard transplanted himself to a farm in Bergen County, New Jersey, where he had accumulated considerable property.[27] At the time of his move, Stephen was a widower with three children, his wife Alida Vetch Bayard having died in 1743. But his wife's death did not precipitate his move, since he served as mayor of New York City from 1744 to 1747 and as a council member in 1747. In his will, made in 1753, he styled himself Stephen Bayard, of Bergen County, yeoman, and instructed that he have a private funeral with none but his close relatives in attendance. Stephen Bayard exchanged the responsibilities of public life for a more private family-centered existence in the country.

Another member of a prominent New York City mercantile family, James van Horne, retired to Middlesex County, New Jersey, about the middle of the eighteenth century, when he was entering his forties. At the time he made his will in 1760, he styled himself a "Gentleman" and disposed of property including real estate, mines, minerals, coal pits, and twenty-two slaves, gold, jewels, plate, furniture, and linen.[28]

By the time second-generation fathers were ready to set their sons on their future paths in the early eighteenth century, the members of old settler families faced increasing competition from English and French newcomers in the New York City marketplace. But the third-generation descendants of these predominantly Dutch families who remained in the city did not experience any discernible setbacks in their occupational standing. Their pattern of occupational mobility replicated that of their fathers. Whereas 37.5 percent of second-generation sons performed the same work as their fathers, 42 percent of the 118 third-generation sons for whom adequate data are available held the same occupation as their father. Those third-generation sons who practiced different trades than their fathers usually entered an occupation that was roughly similar in terms of wealth and status.

Occupational continuity was most prominent in mercantile families. Among the Bayards, De Peysters, Richards, and Van Hornes, sons almost invariably followed in their fathers' footsteps. Merchants facilitated their sons' entree into the world of commerce by providing special education for them, arranging for them to begin their careers under the supervision of other merchants, and extending them capital to begin trading. Second-generation cohort member Johannes de Peyster, intent on preparing his son to trade in the trilingual Atlantic world, took young Johannes with him to Boston at the beginning of the eighteenth century and arranged for him to study English and French.[29] Though no formal apprenticeship documents survive for merchant families of the cohort, fathers undoubtedly placed their sons with their colleagues for a period of time. When Geertruyd van Cortlandt, the widow of merchant Stephanus van Cortlandt, made her will in 1718, she noted that "my eldest son, Johanes Van Cortlandt [also deceased], was considerably indebted to my husband, and I, as a tender mother, did advance and pay several sums for him."[30]

Not all sons of merchants elected to engage in trade as their life's work. Though one of merchant Isaac de Riemer's sons carried on his father's occupation, the other became a gunsmith. Scions of successful merchant families sometimes gave up commerce for the life of the gentleman. James van Horne, who had moved to an estate in New Jersey by the mid-eighteenth century, envisioned his youngest son as entering a profession. His 1760 will stipulated that

> The best education [is] to be given to my son James that the Province of Pennsylvania affords, either at the Academy or Mr Dove's English School, and there to remain till he is 16 or 17, and then put either to the study of Physick or Law, which shall best suit his capacity or inclination, and there to remain 4 or 5 years, either with the most eminent Physician or Lawyer. If his inclination should lead him to Physick, and he is desirous of going to one of the Colleges in Scotland to complete his studies, It is left to the discretion of my executors.[31]

Medical knowledge remained the province of one cohort family over the generations. Four of surgeon Hans Kierstede's five sons—Hans, Jr., Jochem (who moved to Maryland), Roelef (who moved to Kingston), and Jacobus—followed in their father's footsteps. Hans, Jr., and Jacobus both practiced medicine in New York City. Hans Jr.'s eldest son, Hans, also became a surgeon, but Jacobus died before his two surviving sons were old enough to study with him. His inventory lists a set of old chirurgy books.[32]

Specialized trades requiring a significant measure of artistic skill were also concentrated in certain families. Evert Duycking, who was well known in New Amsterdam and early New York City as a glazier and painter, had two sons, one of whom took to the sea and the other of whom practiced his father's trade.[33] In March 1680, Jasper Danckaerts noted in his journal that "they had built a new church in the Hysopus [Esopus], of which the glass had been made and painted in the city by the father of our

Figure 12. Gerrit Duycking (1660–c. 1710), seen here in a self-portrait, represents the second generation in a Dutch family of painters. His father Evert made stained glass windows in New Amsterdam while his son Gerardus catered to the taste of well-to-do New Yorkers in the mid-eighteenth century. Courtesy of The New-York Historical Society, N.Y.C.

mate, Evert Duiker, whose other son, Gerrit Duiker did most of the work. . . . [Gerrit] promised to teach me to draw."[34]

Gerrit Duycking (figure 12) trained in his craft not only his own son Gerardus but also his nephew Evert, the son of his brother who had gone to sea. Gerrit and other family members painted portraits of many eighteenth-century New Yorkers.[35] Word of mouth was sufficient to attract customers to the first two generations of Duycking artists, but by the third generation Gerardus found it necessary to advertise his skills: "Lookinglasses new Silvered, and the Frames plaine Japan'd or Flowered, also all sorts of Picktures, made and Sold, all manner of painting Work done. Likewise Lookinglasses, and all sorts of painting Coullers and Oyl sold at reasonable Rates."[36] When Gerardus died, consumers were assured by his son, Gerardus II, that he "continues to carry on the Business of his late Father, deceas'd. Viz. Limning, Painting, Varnishing, Japanning, Gilding, Glazing, and Silvering of Looking-Glasses."[37]

The kinship ties between New York City's silversmiths have been well documented.[38] One of silversmith Jacob Boelen's sons also became a silversmith.

In families where the breadwinner had received an appointment to a particular city job such as carman, this privilege was passed on to succeeding generations.[39] Cohort member William Koeck was a carman and his son Teunis was a laborer. His grandson Dirck, however, became a carman. Two third-generation members of the Blanck family also were carmen.

Occupational mobility occurred most frequently in artisan families, but this mobility was horizontal rather than vertical. Sons of artisans tended to remain skilled craftsmen, but often in trades different than their fathers. From early days in New Amsterdam, the Ten Eycks were associated with shoemaking and tanning.[40] All but one of Coenraet Ten Eyck's sons who remained in New York City became shoemakers. But by the third generation, Ten Eycks were found as a baker, a bolter, and a mariner. The two sons of ship carpenter Isaac de Milt, whose father Anthony had been a baker, became a carpenter and a mason.

Three of mariner Theophilus Ellsworth's four sons shared their father's affinity for the sea and became ship carpenters.[41] But only two of the five sons of Clement, John, and William Ellsworth continued the family occupational pattern as ship carpenters; the others took up the trades of shoemaker, mason, and gunsmith. Ellsworth's fourth son, George, was a butcher, and the occupations of two of his four sons are known—one was a vintner and the other a chairmaker.

Artisan fathers commonly settled their sons in different occupations of equivalent status. House carpenter Abraham van Gelder, a second-generation New Yorker, deliberately chose different trades for three of his sons. In 1724, Cornelius van Gelder was apprenticed to a blacksmith and his brother Isaac was apprenticed to a shipwright.[42] Their brother Abraham became a gunsmith. The oldest brother, whose occupation is unknown, moved to New Jersey at about the age of 30.

Not every artisan family, however, experienced occupational change. The two sons of cordwainer Abel Hardenbroeck were both cordwainers and the one surviving third-generation male was a tanner. Three generations of Van Hoecks also remained in the cordwaining trade.

It was unusual, but not impossible, for third-generation men to move up the occupational ladder in New York City. Third-generation members of the Bosch (Bush) family clung to the blacksmith trade of their father and grandfather, but at least one Bosch—Justus—gave up his blacksmith tools to become a merchant. Justus received the freemanship in 1698 as a blacksmith, when he was 24, but by 1717 he was referred to as a merchant.[43] In 1703 he was living in the North Ward and owned one slave. Sometime after 1720, when his last child was baptized in the city's Dutch Reformed Church, he transplanted his family to Rye in Westchester County. In his 1737 will, in which he called himself a merchant, he noted that he had already given his eldest son £500 and his eldest daughter £200. His assets included one-eighth ownership of a copper mine in Farmington, Connecticut, and land in Newtown, Connecticut.[44]

Another third-generation New Yorker who believed he had advanced in social status was John van Gelder. The son of a carpenter, he practiced his father's trade most of his life. He was referred to variously as a turner (1713), a carpenter (1718), and a wood turner (1750). But when he drafted his will in 1756, at the age of 67, John van Gelder called himself a gentleman. Perhaps he felt that retirement from active work entitled him to that appellation. Yet his artisan background was not far from his mind, since he bequeathed "my vise and hand saw and all my tools" to his youngest son.[45]

Though movement up the social scale was possible in eighteenth-century New York City, on the whole artisans and merchants remained socially distinct groups. There was little intermarriage between their families. Men who worked with their hands seemed content if they could accumulate sufficent property to maintain their family in comfort.[46]

How closely did the economic standing of third-generation men who remained in New York City resemble that of their fathers? Using occupations as a yardstick, young men of the third generation, for the most part, retained and reinforced the status of their fathers.[47] Few appear to have lost ground. The fact that the two sons of silversmith Jeuriaen Blanck, Jr., became carmen may have had more to do with a lack of talent than shifting social position.

Comparing the occupations of third-generation men with those of their grandfathers confirms substantial upward mobility in a few families. Merchants Abraham and Gerrit Keteltas had surpassed their grandfather, schoolteacher Evert Pietersen Keteltas. Third-generation members of the Van Horne mercantile clan had accumulated a great deal more property than their grandfather, fisherman Cornelis Jansen van Hoorn. Abraham Boelen and Henricus Boelen, two grandsons of tailor Boele Roelofsen, had risen to be, respectively, a merchant and a silversmith. On the other hand, an occasional family slid down the occupational ladder. Bartholdus Maan had been a trader but his son and grandson were cordwainers.

In general, however, the position of cohort members in the world of work remained stable over the generations. Third-generation men were ensured an occupational foundation by their parents, but ultimately skill, temperament, opportunity, and luck determined how successful they would be in their careers.

Choosing a bride offered third-generation men an opportunity to express their feelings about their cultural identity.[48] A man with a strong sense of belonging to a particular ethnoreligious group presumably would be unlikely to select his life partner from young women of a different cultural background. Consequently, the extent of ethnically exogamous marriages among third-generation men should indicate how deeply "Anglicization" had penetrated the personal lives of Dutch and French men. Large-scale intermarriage would suggest that group consciousness was waning. Transcending ethnic boundaries in marriage might be the prelude to or concomitant with crossing boundaries in other critical areas of personal life— religion, education of children, or language.

New York City's third-generation cohort men tended to marry at a relatively advanced age. Judging from the median marriage age of 25 and the mean marriage age of 25.7, it was customary for young men to postpone marriage until they had established themselves in their trades.[49] Scrutinizing their marriage patterns offers a way to assess the importance they attached to ethnic ties.

This analysis of marriage patterns is based on all 159 third-generation cohort males whose first marriage was contracted in New York City. Not included are men who never married or whose marriages are untraceable. However, out-migrants are included in this analysis if they married in New York City before moving elsewhere. Also, a few men whose marriage ceremony was conducted outside the city (for example, in the bride's hometown) but who continued to dwell in New York City are included.

Interpreting the marriage patterns of cohort grandchildren is a complex matter because surnames become an unreliable index of ethnic or cultural identity by the third generation. In early eighteenth-century New York City, an English surname might conceal the fact that an individual had a Dutch mother. It might mask an English bridegroom's Batavianization. In order to reveal the intricate nature of mate selection in New York's multiethnic society, it is essential to delve into the family histories of representative individuals.

Classifying third-generation cohort members according to their parents' ethnicity lays the groundwork for this analysis. Men whose fathers and mothers both were Dutch constituted the largest group of third-generation men (152 men). Only four second-generation Dutch men had married exogamously—Bernardus Hardenbroeck, Jacobus de Key, Jacobus Kierstede, and Jesse Kip. Bernardus Hardenbroeck had married Elizabeth Cooley, the daughter of John Cooley, an early English immigrant, and Jannetje van Dyck, who was of Dutch descent. The couple had no surviving sons. Thomas de Key, the only surviving son of Jacobus de Key and his half-English wife Sarah Willett, married Christina Duncan, whose father George had been born in Scotland, and moved to Orange County sometime after 1735, when he sold his property in the city's Out Ward.[50] Jacobus Kierstede, who had married Anna Holmes of Gravesend, Long Island, had two sons who survived him, Samuel and Jacobus, both of whom moved to Staten Island. Samuel married Lydia Deny and had three children baptized in the Port Richmond Dutch Reformed Church. Jacobus died unmarried.[51] Jesse Kip married Maria Stevens, the daughter of Thomas and Elizabeth Lawrence Stevens of Newtown, Long Island. Three of his sons died unmarried while the other three married women of English background.[52]

The progeny of the few English and French cohort members (19 men) must be treated as a separate group because of the pattern of exogamous marriages in these families in earlier generations. The Ellsworth, Brasier, Lewis, Richard, and D'Honneur families had become ethnically mixed either in the first or second generation. The two "pure" English families of the second generation, the Lawrences and the Merritts, did not produce third-generation males who lived in New York City.[53]

Of the 152 third-generation "Dutch" men, 115 married "Dutch" women, 31 married English or part-English women, four married French or part-French women, and two married German women. Thus, 76 percent married endogamously while only 24 percent married exogamously.[54] The men who chose their brides from within the ethnic fold came from throughout the social and occupational structure. Merchant Abraham van Horne, feltmaker Henry Brestede, mason Anthony de Milt, and shoemaker Johannes Man all married Dutch women.

Several men married the granddaughters of cohort members, some wed women from other old New York City Dutch families, while still others chose brides from families with roots in the outlying regions of Dutch settlement. Johannes van Gelder, a carpenter, selected Neeltje Oncklebag, the daughter of second-generation cohort member Gerrit Oncklebag, a silversmith, for his bride.[55] Two third-generation offspring of wealthy merchant families were brought together when Abraham de Peyster married Margarita, the daughter of Jacobus van Cortlandt in 1711.[56] Blacksmith Cornelius van Gelder, a cousin of Johannes, married Elizabeth Mesier, a third-generation New Yorker whose ancestor was not included in the cohort because of problems related to nomenclature.[57] Catharina Roosevelt, who became the wife of third-generation cohort member Steenwyck de Riemer, a gunsmith, was the fourth-generation of a family with deep roots in the region. Though the family's progenitor had settled in New Amsterdam, he had died before 1664. His son, Nicholas Roosevelt, resided in Ulster County for a number of years before returning to New York City where Catharina's father, also named Nicholas, was born.[58]

The 115 brides with Dutch surnames almost certainly were the offspring of Dutch fathers and mothers because second-generation Dutch men in New York City or elsewhere in the region rarely married outside the group. The ancestry of many of these women can be traced in family genealogies.

The marriages of third-generation men to women with English surnames must be looked at more closely to ascertain the ethnic and cultural identity of the bride. In at least one case, an English-sounding name turned out not to be English at all. Judged by her surname, Angenietje Bennet, the woman whom Johannes Schoute Thomassen selected for his bride c. 1718 seems to be English. But genealogists have documented that Angenietje, who was born in Brooklyn in 1700, was one of the Dutch Bennets (the telltale spelling of the name Bennet with one "t" instead of two is an important clue to the family's identity), a family that may have been of Huguenot ancestry but came to New Netherland directly from the Netherlands.[59] It is understandable, then, that all of the couple's children were baptized in the Dutch Reformed church.

More commonly a bride's English surname concealed the fact that she had a Dutch mother. It is critical to distinguish half-English women from fully English women. Whether or not the fathers of half-English brides had been Batavianized, the chances were great that the girls had been socialized in Dutch family networks. Molded by Dutch mothers who customarily embraced their faith wholeheartedly, these daughters more than likely adhered to the Dutch Reformed church. At least seven "English" brides are identifiable as communicants of the Dutch Reformed church. The fact of an English surname, then, could easily disguise a woman's cultural identity.

Tracing the daughters of marriages between second-generation cohort women and English immigrants who settled in New York City in the 1670s and 1680s is easier than pinpointing women of similar mixed background from the outlying region. Genealogists have documented some of these hybrid families, but it is likely that even more third-generation brides with English surnames had Dutch mothers. Hannah Earle, the woman whom Pieter Stoutenburgh married about 1712, had an English father and a Dutch mother. Her father Edward Earle, Jr., the son of an English immigrant who had purchased land and settled in Secaucus, New Jersey, after living in Maryland, married Elsie Vreeland, whose family was Dutch.

Hannah Earle was baptized in 1695 in the Dutch Reformed Church of Bergen, New Jersey. The couple's one child was baptized in the New York City Dutch Reformed Church in 1714.[60]

Unions that, on the basis of surname analysis, appear to be clearcut cases of Dutch-English intermarriage, frequently turn out to be more complex in nature. When Cornelius van Horne, a merchant of Dutch ancestry, chose Elizabeth French as his bride in 1718, he may have thought it more significant that he was marrying the granddaughter of the legendary Frederick Philipse than the daughter of an English merchant named Philip French. Moreover, Elizabeth French's religious loyalty had been shaped by her mother, Anna Philipse, a member of the Dutch Reformed church. Though Philip French had purchased a pew in Trinity Church in 1703, his daughter Elizabeth and her new husband together joined the Dutch Reformed Church in 1720.

Additionally, some ethnically exogamous marriages were actually intra-cohort marriages. When Isaac Bedloo and Susanna Brasier wed in 1705, they represented the third generation of New York City cohort families. Though Susanna Brasier had an English surname, her mother, Maryken van Alst, was Dutch and her father, Henry Brasier, was English. The ethnically distinct surnames of the partners mattered little in light of the close group ties and cultural similarities that had developed among cohort families by the third generation.

Analysis of the few marriages of third-generation Dutch men to women with French surnames also reveals the mixed ancestry of these brides. Martin Clock married a French woman, judging by her surname—Margaret D'Honneur. But, in reality Margaret was three-fourths Dutch. Her father, Johannes D'Honneur had a French father (born in Brussels) and most probably a Dutch mother. Her mother, Johanna Meynardt, was born in Utrecht and moved to New York with her parents. In his will, her father, a glover, who had two brothers in Utrecht, asked to be buried in the city's Dutch Reformed Church.[61] "Margrita de Honeur, wife of Marte Clock" joined the New York City Dutch Reformed Church in 1731.

Of course, a few Dutch men of the third generation did marry "pure" English women. In 1738, Stephen van Cortlandt, Philip van Cortlandt's son, married Mary Walton Ricketts, the daughter of William Ricketts, a Jamaican planter who had immigrated to the city a few years earlier. Ricketts was affiliated with Trinity Church.[62] But at least 19 of the 31 unions categorized as exogamous by using surnames turn out not to be cases of Dutch men marrying "pure" English or French women. If a significant number of the "English" and "French" women chosen as mates by third-generation Dutch men actually were half-Dutch, then their cultural identity is open to question. Given the pivotal role of mothers in educating their daughters, Dutch grooms may have perceived their brides to be fundamentally Dutch. On closer inspection, then, these "intermarriages" suggest that Dutch men may have been more reluctant to cross cultural boundaries in marriage than previously thought.

Pondering the cultural consequences of "intermarriages" leads us to consider the site of the children's baptism and religious education. When a Dutch man chose a bride of English or part-English descent, it did not automatically mean that the couple's offspring would be raised in an English church. Two third-generation cousins who bore the name Hendrick van de Water married sisters of the Skillman family of Newtown, Long Island, in the Newtown Presbyterian church. Hendrick (born 1692), the son of Johannes van de Water, married Elizabeth Skillman in 1715, and Hendrick (born 1698), the son of Albertus van de Water, married Anne Skillman in 1719. But the Skillman sisters, though of English descent on their father's side, had a Dutch mother (Annetje Aten) and the infants of both couples were baptized in New York City's Dutch Reformed Church.[63] Moreover, the Skillman girls' parents affiliated with the Newtown Dutch Reformed Church after it was built in 1731.[64]

Several non-Dutch brides of third-generation cohort men became communicants of the Dutch church. A few years after she wed Frederick van Cortlandt in 1723/24, Frances Jay, the daughter of Huguenot merchant Augustus Jay and Anna Maria Bayard, transferred her membership from the French church, where she had been baptized, to the Dutch Reformed church, which her husband had joined prior to their marriage. The couple's first five children were baptized in the Dutch church in New York City.[65]

When third-generation members of English and French cohort families married, loyalty to their ethnic group was a low priority. Cohort members Henry Brasier, a turner, and his wife Susanna, whom he wed in New Amsterdam's Dutch Reformed Church in 1644 were both of English ancestry.[66] Their three sons reached maturity in the still largely Dutch settlement of New York City in the years prior to Leisler's Rebellion and married women whose roots were Dutch. Like their father, the second-generation Brasier men never became communicants of the Dutch Reformed church, though their children were baptized there and two of their wives were members.

In contrast to their fathers, the male Brasiers of the third generation grew up in mixed Anglo-Dutch households. Their first marriages, contracted between 1711 and 1740 in the Dutch Reformed church, disclose their propensity to select spouses with little regard to ethnic background. Of the seven male cousins, none of whom affiliated with the Dutch Reformed church, three married Dutch women, three married French women, and just one married an English woman. The Brasier family of artisans had merged into the predominantly Dutch culture of the cohort, but its male members freely crossed ethnic boundaries when selecting a mate.

The grandsons of Theophilus Ellsworth, the Englishman who had married in Amsterdam before emigrating to New Amsterdam, were similarly eclectic in their choice of spouse. Marrying between 1704 and 1733, these nine men had no difficulty meeting women of diverse backgrounds. Five married Dutch women, three married women of English ancestry, and one wed a woman who was part French and part Dutch. Their fathers had not ranged so widely in their unions. Perhaps because their choices were more limited in the years between 1680 and 1694, three of Theophilus Ellsworth's four sons had taken Dutch wives, while the fourth married the daughter of a Swedish man and an English woman.[67]

Third-generation males of the Richard clan of merchants emulated their grandfather in crossing ethnic lines when choosing a bride.[68] Frenchman Paul Richard, the progenitor of the family, had married a widow from Denmark in the Dutch Reformed Church in New Amsterdam in 1664. Richard's wife had become a member of the church just prior to her marriage in 1664. Richard had joined the church in 1663 but he later transferred his membership to the French church. Only his wife was listed on the 1686 church roll and his contribution to the Dutch Reformed Church's building fund in 1688 was made in the name of his wife. Richard's only surviving son, Stephen, chose Maria van Brugh, the daughter of Dutch merchant Johannes van Brugh, for his bride in 1696. Richard joined the Dutch Reformed Church in 1699, where his wife was already a member.

Of Stephen Richard's five surviving sons, however, only one reinforced the family's developing Dutch identity through marriage—John Richard, who married Elizabeth van Rensselaer. Three of John's brothers married women of English descent, while a fourth brother, Henry, remained single. Paul Richard, who in 1715 as a young man of 18 had joined the Dutch congregation where his parents worshiped, later switched his affiliation to Trinity Church, the likely site of his marriage to Elizabeth Garland (figure 13), also an adherent of Trinity Church. Elizabeth was "the only daughter and heiress of Thomas Garland, Gentleman" who had been granted the freemanship in 1714 and died in 1725.[69] Though the names of Stephen and Elic Richard's brides are not known, the evidence suggests that they were not Dutch. Stephen's wife was Presbyterian and Elie married in Bermuda.

Thus, the marriage patterns of third-generation sons of Dutch parents of the second generation differed from those of the sons of the mixed families of English and French cohort members. Men from mixed families, having adapted to their marginal place in New York City's multiethnic society, paid scant attention to the ethnic background of their brides. Men

Figure 13. Elizabeth Garland Richard (1700–1774) a London-born heiress who immigrated to New York City with her parents, became the wife of merchant and mayor Paul Richard, the grandson of a French immigrant to New Amsterdam. Her portrait was painted by John Singleton Copley after she was widowed. Courtesy of The Museum of Fine Arts, Houston; Bayou Bend Collection, Gift of Miss Ima Hogg.

from Dutch families did. Mate selection among the third-generation reveals the continuing salience of ethnic identity in the private life of Dutch New Yorkers.

Unlike their fathers, the third-generation Dutch men who remained in New York City had the opportunity to marry women outside their ethnic group. Steady immigration from Britain, the proliferation of second-generation Anglo-American and French-American families in the city, and more frequent contacts between Dutch city dwellers and their English

Figure 14. Catharina Ten Eyck van Zandt (1692–1772) a third-generation member of a Dutch family of cordwainers, married Dutch widower Wynant van Zandt, a blockmaker, when she was eighteen and bore fifteen children. Courtesy of The New-York Historical Society, N.Y.C.

neighbors in the hinterland expanded the pool of potential brides for men maturing in the early eighteenth century. In light of the increased availability of non-Dutch women, the findings that more than three-quarters of third-generation Dutch men still married endogamously and other Dutch men chose brides who were part Dutch suggest that the Dutch community still looked with suspicion on men crossing ethnic lines at the altar.

For Dutch women, communal sanctions against intermarriage were not as strong. Perhaps because women could be counted upon to perpetuate the religious traditions of the homeland, Dutch parents allowed their daughters to accept the proposals of British suitors. Economic incentives undoubtedly carried considerable weight in a family's decision making. Exercising ethnic preferences in selecting a mate may have become a luxury that some families could ill afford. If there was latitude in this matter, it may have been understood that it was most important for males to preserve the ethnic integrity of the family line.

The life histories of third-generation cohort members, as far as they can be reconstructed from available evidence, graphically illustrate the staying power of New York City's original families. Despite mortality and migration, scores of families with roots in New Amsterdam, most of them Dutch in ancestry, survived into the early decades of the eighteenth century. Dutch grandsons pursued their careers against the altered backdrop of English rule and amidst an increasingly British cast of characters, but their opportunities to practice trades and accumulate wealth were not significantly diminished. The Dutch artisans who formed the heart of the city's productive community in the seventeenth century passed on their trades to their sons and nephews while Dutch mercantile families grew more firmly entrenched with each generation. Eligible to hold office in both municipal and provincial government, men of Dutch ancestry filled more than their share of the seats of power in early eighteenth-century New York.

New York City's Dutch families not only prospered in the reshaped urban arena, but did so without sacrificing control over their private life. Men persisted in selecting brides whose upbringing would ensure continuity in the ways of the household and they adhered to communal norms in disposing of their property after death. In doing so, they did not hesitate to use new means to accomplish traditional ends. By the final years of the seventeenth century, the customary Dutch mutual will had been replaced by the English will written solely by the husband, but the goal of the mutual will—to guarantee the widow oversight of the entire estate during her lifetime—was upheld by Dutch men well into the eighteenth century.[70] It was only when the value of tradition was questioned that the Dutch began to lose their place in New York City.

Chapter Nine

CULTURE AND COMMUNITY IN

NEW YORK CITY, 1700–1730

ESTABLISHING English dominion over New York City entailed much more than displaying the symbols of sovereignty. English men had to be installed as leaders of economic and political life, the public environment had to be transformed to reflect British traditions and institutions, and subjugated groups had to be brought into conformity with English values. By the early eighteenth century, as we have seen, the English had made only limited progress in dislodging the Dutch from powerful positions in the city's economy and government. Greater success attended English efforts to reshape the framework of public life. Trade was now conducted within the guidelines imposed by British imperial policy, English legal precedents guided court proceedings, the municipal government was patterned after an English model, and English had become the language of public discourse.[1] Not all of these changes had been accomplished swiftly. In 1703, Lord Cornbury informed the Lords of Trade that the New York Assembly had just passed "an Act to bring the weights and measures of this place, which hitherto have been according to the standard of Holland, to that of England," but it was not until 1714 that the New York City Common Council instructed the city's treasurer to "Send to London for A sett of Weights and Measures According to the Standard of her Majesties Exchequer in England to be a Standard of Weights and Measures for this Corporation."[2] After 1710, however, few would have disputed the fact that the English controlled the rules of the game.

Symbolic of the English triumph in the public arena was the institutionalization of the English calendar of celebration. Starting at the turn of the century, officially designated holidays marked signal events in English history such as Gunpowder Treason Day (Guy Fawkes Day) and the birthdays and accession and coronation days of British monarchs. On these occasions, amusement was coupled with patriotic indoctrination, as the populace was treated to bonfires and wine by the New York City Common Council.[3]

Outside the marketplace and the courtroom, the diffusion of English practices and beliefs proceeded slowly and unevenly. Despite decades of English rule, the burgeoning of the British population, and the frequency of interethnic contact, French, and especially Dutch, city residents remained reluctant to alter the traditional values that anchored their private life. Family, church, and ethnic community stood as barriers to English influence.

Nevertheless, the seeds of change were planted during the first third of the eighteenth century and began to germinate, first among the French, and eventually among the Dutch. As the English language and customs insinuated their way into the everyday life of the French and Dutch, previously insulated group members found common ground. Ethnic communities predicated on distinctive tongues, religions, and histories found it harder to claim the undivided loyalty of individuals who had yielded to the pressures of acculturation. Though the ultimate triumph of English culture in New York City still lay at least two decades off, the developments of the first third of the eighteenth century set the stage for the demise of ethnic pluralism.

For the average New Yorker of European ancestry, the greatest pressure to adapt to the Anglicized environment was felt in the area of language. With people of British ancestry crowding the city's streets and the news and commercial notices being printed in English, the ability to comprehend English became a prerequisite to full participation in civic life.[4] Though there is little direct evidence on French linguistic behavior, the case of the Dutch is well documented. Gradually, but ineluctably, Dutch New Yorkers acquired facility in the English language during the early decades of the eighteenth century. Even conservative churchmen conceded in 1726 that

> inasmuch as we are living in a Province where the English language is the common language of the inhabitants: there cannot but be a general agreement by each and all of us that it is very necessary to be versed in this common language of the people, in order properly to carry on one's temporal calling.[5]

While Dutch city dwellers recognized that command of English was essential for conducting daily life, they did not unilaterally convert to English. Dutch was not rejected; it was retained as the language of intimate communication and of worship. The ancestral tongue was preserved because it was the foundation of family and religious life. What ensued, then, was an era of bilingualism, with Dutch remaining the first language of New Yorkers of Netherlands ancestry and English becoming their auxiliary language. Had problems in securing instruction in Dutch not arisen during the first three decades of the eighteenth century, bilingualism might have been sustained indefinitely. As it was, by the 1740s, English had become the primary language of Dutch young people, portending the rapid decline of Dutch thereafter.

As the eighteenth century opened, adults in the Dutch community spoke primarily Dutch; their skills in English were minimal. When Nicholas Bayard accused the men who were to be the jurors in his 1702 treason trial of not being able to understand English or recite the Lord's Prayer in English, his perception of the linguistic abilities of his fellow Dutchmen, though exaggerated, had the ring of truth.[6] In 1713, Jacob Swan was sued by Dirck Coeck for uttering "in Dutch" the "false and scandalous words" that "dat Dirck Coock gestoolen Heeft de hollandse Clinckers Vande grondt and dat hij de brengen Cond die hem gesien had dat hij Se in Elsie Meyers plaes gebraaght had (which being Translated are . . . Dirick Cook . . . had Stole the Hollands Clinkers off of the Ground and that he cou'd bring them that had seen him carry them into Elsie Meyers Yard)."[7] The passage of years did little to convert Dutch speakers into English speakers. Responding to a political attack on Rip van Dam and Abraham van Horne in 1729, Lewis Morris, Jr., characterized the targets of the criticism as "two Ancient Dutch Gentlemen, one of about sixty, and the other nigh or above 70 years of age; and all our world knows, they never were perfect masters of the English tongue, nor never will be; and if they understood the common discourse, 'tis as much as they do."[8]

Several interrelated circumstances ensured the vitality of Dutch in early eighteenth-century New York City. In the home, Dutch was the language of family worship as well as ordinary conversation. Copies of the States-General Bible (*Statenvertaling*), the 1637 translation of the Bible into the Dutch vernacular authorized by the States General, were cherished possessions in Dutch families from which the father read aloud to family members.[9] These large Dutch house Bibles, which continued to be imported into New York until the 1750s, traditionally were bequeathed to the eldest son, just as psalters were transmitted from generation to generation in the female line.[10] The Dutch also inscribed the dates of family births, marriages, and deaths in their Bibles. A copy of a Bible published in Dordrecht and Amsterdam in 1702 that belonged to Samuel Kip contains the Kip family's vital records in Dutch.[11] Weekly worship at the Dutch Reformed Church was conducted in the ancestral tongue as well and congregants remained able to comprehend lengthy sermons delivered in Dutch.

Reinforced in the family circle and at church, Dutch remained a living language in New York City well into the eighteenth century. A sizable market for Dutch-language works existed since Dutch books were not only sold but published in the city. Between 1693 and 1794, one hundred books, pamphlets, and almanacs were printed in the Dutch language in America.[12] The majority of these publications dealt with religious matters, but almanacs and textbooks were also issued.[13] No Dutch-language newspaper ever appeared, however. New York City printers William Bradford and John Peter Zenger, a Palatine immigrant who was a member of the Dutch Reformed church, were the key figures in Dutch-language printing until midcentury, with Zenger producing twenty titles on his own.[14] Bookseller Jacobus Goelet marketed Zenger's Dutch-language titles and other city booksellers also sold Dutch publications imported from the Netherlands. In 1747, James Aarding advertised for sale Dutch works such as *Bruyns Reizen, Holmes Woordenbook, Beginsehn Van Euclides,* and *Werdadize Meethoust*.[15] The city's Dutch Lutheran congregation depended on church officials in Amsterdam to send Bibles, psalters, and other religious works. Though the Amsterdam Consistory had shipped books to the congregation in 1713, Reverend Wilhelm Berkenmeyer reported in 1725 "a universal complaint about the scarcity of hymn-books, catechisms and Bibles. Nearly all the last-named we have here are those sent by the Rt. Worshipful Consistory of Amsterdam . . . They know little of catechisms; Bibles are found with the older families, but the new families have to borrow one from another."[16]

Perpetuating the Dutch language in New York City at a time when the advantages of fluency in English were increasingly apparent hinged on the educational choices parents made for their children. These choices, in turn, were constricted by an unanticipated breakdown in the instructional arm of the Dutch church between 1702 and 1726, a situation engendered by the deliberately repressive policies of Lord Cornbury's administration. Hard-pressed to arrange formal schooling under the tutelage of a Dutch teacher during these years, Dutch parents, reluctantly or not, placed their offspring in the hands of English schoolmasters, thereby setting in motion an irreversible sequence of events that spelled the end of bilingualism in New York City.

The Dutch Reformed church had sponsored education in the the Dutch language throughout the seventeenth century and undoubtedly intended to carry on in the eighteenth century.[17] But the death of longtime schoolmaster Abraham Delanoy in 1702 coincided with the arrival of Lord Cornbury, who perceived Dutch schools as nurseries of anti-Anglican sentiment. Cornbury sought to curtail instruction in the Dutch language by instituting a rigorous licensing procedure that infringed on the right granted the New York City Dutch Reformed Church in its charter to appoint a Dutch schoolmaster. In 1705, Jacobus Goelet and Johannes Kerfbyl "had by personal petition solicited permission to hold a Dutch school from my lord Cornbury, and had been refused."[18] "It is true there is a Dutch Schoolmaster in the State," the church admitted in 1706, "but we have use for another and still more, of greater qualifications."[19] Cornbury's attempts to restrict the number of Dutch schoolmasters in the city won him few friends in the Dutch community, and particularly among

Dutch church leaders, who realized the gravity of the situation: "If things are to proceed in this fashion, practically holding back the training schools of the Dutch, in which alone our children could be educated in our religion, is not the hope of expecting a rich harvest and fruitage destroyed?"[20]

By placing sanctions on Dutch educational institutions Cornbury hoped to steer Dutch male youth to English schoolmasters.[21] Promoting an English-style education for the city's children of Dutch and French descent would not only accelerate the pace of language shift in the Dutch and French communities but pave the way for the reception of Anglicanism.[22] Cornbury took the first concrete steps toward establishing a city school, which functioned from 1704 to 1712. This grammar school, first taught by George Muirson and then by Andrew Clarke,[23] was aimed at bringing non-English boys under the tutelage of orthodox Anglican schoolmasters. According to the provincial act of 1702 which authorized its foundation, the school was intended for "the Education and Instruction of Youth and Male Children of Such Parents as are of French and Dutch Extraction, as well as of the English."[24]

Cornbury's efforts to undermine ethnic allegiance through educational ventures were not confined to the grammar school. The governor also eagerly embraced the cause of the Anglican Society for the Propagation of the Gospel in Foreign Parts (S.P.G.), which soon began to sponsor a charity school in the city. In an age when virtually all forms of education involved some financial burden, the lure of a charity school was capitalized upon by Anglican missionaries bent on altering the city's preexistent pattern of ethnically enclosed education. The fact that the S.P.G. was about to start a charity school in the city was publicized "in the English, Dutch & French Churches of this place," in order to entice poor parents of all nationalities to place their offspring under Anglican supervision.[25] S.P.G. missionaries were aware of the widespread usage of non-English tongues in New York and deliberately distributed religious materials in the French and Dutch languages.[26] In 1709, the S.P.G. promised to send its teacher in New York City "50 Copies of the Translation of the Common Prayer in Dutch."[27] When Anglican chaplain John Sharpe drafted a plan for a school in New York City in 1712, he pointed out that if "the Person to whom the care of the School is committed . . . understands Dutch and French, it will be of great advantage to him."[28] But the heart of the S.P.G.'s program for bringing foreigners into conformity with the Church of England was linking instruction in the English language with Anglican religious indoctrination.[29]

Dutch and French children attended the S.P.G. charity school. William Huddleston, who had been holding classes in the city since 1689 and had become the master of the city's S.P.G.-supported charity school in 1710, was known for his insistence that "all that send their Children of what Nation soever [to his school] . . . buy them Common Prayer books & that they should attend ye Divine Service refusing otherwise to receive them into his School."[30] Huddleston prided himself on his successful efforts to anglicize New York City's Dutch youth, reflecting in a 1715 letter on "the Service I have done almost Thirty Years in that green Colloney where almost nothing was Spoken but Dutch when I first came there." As a postscript, he added "I Lookt over my list lately and can make Appeare that I have taught and am now teaching 650 of the Dutch and French to read and write English Since I began to teach."[31] Lists of pupils at the city charity school periodically submitted to the S.P.G. in London by Huddleston and his son Thomas, who succeeded him following his death in 1723, reveal that several Dutch and French students were regularly enrolled in the institution thus making it likely that they acquired facility in English.[32]

During the first three decades of the eighteenth century, schoolmasters of British ancestry greatly outnumbered those of Dutch or French background. Of the 39 men known to have taught in the city during these years, 30 were either English or Scottish, while four were French, three were Dutch, and two were German.[33] In 1703 Lord Cornbury licensed André Foucautt to teach "an English and ffrench school within the City of New York and to instruct all Children . . . in the said Languages, as alsoe in ye art of Writeing Arethmetick &c."[34] Prudent de la Fayole was granted a license to teach a French school in New York City in 1705.[35] Another Frenchman, Peter Bontecou, called himself a schoolmaster when he registered as a freeman in 1702.[36] After acquainting Governor Hunter that the "youth brought up in this citty are at a loss in goeing to sea without a sufficient Instruction in writing and Arithmetick and in the Art of Navigation with other usefull parts of the Mathematicks," Allane Jarrett, a man of French ancestry, received a license to teach these subjects in 1710.[37]

Two Dutch men, Jacobus Goelet and Pieter van der Lyn (Vanderlyn), were identified in city records as teachers during the decade of the 1710s, but nothing is known about their classes.[38] Goelet was a bookseller and the clerk of the Dutch Reformed Church while Van der Lyn was an artist who migrated to Kingston in 1722.[39] Third-generation cohort member Pieter Stoutenburgh, who listed his occupation as schoolmaster when he became a freeman in 1735, might have plied his trade in the city earlier, but he seems to have resided in New Jersey prior to 1730.[40] Jewish religious instruction commenced at about the time the Mill Street synagogue opened in 1730.[41]

The proliferation of British schoolmasters in New York City diversified the educational options of Dutch and French parents. Some pedagogues confined themselves to basic subjects. James Weeks, who kept a school on Duke Street in the Dock Ward in 1723, instructed "Children and Others in reading writing and arithmetick."[42] Others offered a broad-ranging curriculum. George Brownell, in addition to teaching "Reading, Writing, and Cyphering," offered instruction in "Merchants Accompts, Latin, [and] Greek" as well as "Dancing, Plain-Work, Flourishing, Imbroidery, and various sorts of Works." The latter skills apparently were taught by Mrs. Brownell.[43] Alexander Malcolm, who became master of the grammar school established in New York City in 1732, concentrated on more advanced subjects such as Latin, Greek, mathematics, geometry, algebra, geography, navigation, and merchant-bookkeeping.[44] In 1723, James Walton, a Yale graduate who aimed at recruiting "Young Gentleman of the City" as well as the sons of country gentlemen, advertised a rigorous course of study in the liberal arts comprised of "the Same Things which are commonly Taught in Colledges." The curriculum included "Geometry, Surveying, the Latin Tongue, and Greek and Hebrew Grammars, Ethicks, Rhetorick, Logick, Natural Philosophy and Metaphysicks" as well as "Reading, Writing, Arethmatick, whole Numbers and Fractions, Vulgar and Decimal, the Mariners Art, Plain and Mercators way."[45]

Technical subjects were offered not only by Malcolm, Walton, and Allane Jarrett, but by James Lyne, who advertised in 1730 that during winter evenings he would teach "Aritmetick in all its parts, Geomotry, Trigonometry, Navigation, Surveying, Guaging, Algebra and sundry other parts of Mathematical Knowledge."[46]

Schoolmasters who offered instruction in classical languages, mathematics, and navigation undoubtedly expected their students to be male. Other teachers probably intended their classes for males as well. In 1708, William Huddleston reported that Andrew Clarke, who was in charge of the city's grammar school, had 33 students and "Mr. Cornelius Lodge hath about 20 Scholars; Mr. John Stevens 28 Scholars; Mr. John Bashford 8 scholars and I have about 30. . . . you may see that there are but 119 Boys taught by all the five Masters."[47]

What kind of education the sisters of the 119 boys received is a matter of conjecture. James Weeks unwittingly revealed that he admitted female pupils to his school in the course of describing a violent incident that occurred in 1723. A woman "broke in the school house & assaulted one Sarah Thatcher, beat & wounded her, threw her on the ground & trampled her with her feet to the great Terror and fright of all the Schollars then and there being."[48]

George Brownell also accepted female students, among them Phila Franks and Molly, the daughter of provincial secretary George Clarke.[49] In 1731 "young Gentlewomen" who wished to learn "the following curious

Works ... Artificial Fruit and Flowers, and other Wax-Work, Nuns-Work, Philligree and Raising of Paste, as alsoe to Paint upon Glass, and Transparent, for Sconces" were invited to study with Martha Gazley, who had recently arrived from Great Britain.[50]

The role ethnic considerations played in parental decisions concerning their children's formal schooling cannot be determined without information on the ethnic identity of the pupils of the city's private schoolmasters. However, the preferences of parents and guardians making vocational plans for their youngsters come to light by analyzing the ethnic background of masters and apprentices in a group of 199 apprenticeship contracts executed in New York City between 1718 and 1727.[51]

As they had in the years 1694 to 1707, the English were more likely than any other group to avail themselves of formal apprenticeship contracts in arranging their children's training. Over two-thirds of the apprentices (134 of 199, or 67 percent) were English, while only 19 percent were Dutch (37 of 199), 8 percent were French (16 of 199), and 4.5 percent were German (9 of 199). Three apprentices were free Negroes (1.5 percent).

Ethnic compartmentalization was less prominent in the indentures contracted between 1718 and 1727 than in those formalized between 1694 and 1707. Whereas 67.5 percent of the earlier group of apprenticeships paired members of the same ethnic group, only 53 percent (106 of 199) of the later group involved people of the same background. Nonetheless, Dutch parents remained wary of apprenticing their children to a master of a different heritage. Only 10 percent (20 of 199) of the agreements made between 1718 and 1727 linked a Dutch youth to an English, French, or German master (the comparable figure for the 1694–1707 group was 11 percent).

Whatever the ethnic origins of masters and apprentices, the terms of indenture frequently mandated that the apprentice receive instruction in reading and writing. Though the English language was only occasionally specified in these provisions, there is little question that the night schools patronized by the city's apprentices provided instruction in English.[52]

Dutch parents, however desirous of educating their offspring in the traditional manner, may have had little choice but to send the children to an English schoolmaster during the entire period from 1702 to 1726, for there is no evidence that the Dutch church reinvigorated its educational institutions in the years following Cornbury's departure in 1708. Thus, at the critical point in time when the third generation was coming of age, the educational apparatus of the Dutch community ceased to function. The existence of what might be called a generation lost to Dutch education was admitted by the Dutch Reformed Church consistory in 1726:

Most of those who belong to us . . . have now for some years neglected to have their children receive instruction in the Netherlandish tongue. Are not our youth, now growing up among us, living witnesses of this?[53]

In this year, the leaders of the city's Dutch Reformed church tried to pick up the threads of Dutch education, but a crucial link in the linguistic chain had never been forged. The diligent efforts of the church to provide instruction for boys and girls of Dutch families, commencing with the appointment of Barent de Forest as schoolmaster in 1726, extended so far as to subsidize the lessons of indigent youngsters.[54] But ground lost could never be regained and the work of De Forest and his successors merely slowed the inevitable loss of facility in the Dutch language by the majority of the population.[55]

Focusing on the language behavior of three generations of De Peysters illuminates the role of the family in determining the language preferences of Dutch New Yorkers. Cohort member Johannes de Peyster and his wife spoke Dutch and knew very little English. In 1677, Johannes de Peyster asked to be "excused from [the] place of Deputy Mayor and to continue an Alderman for this Citty (by reason of his not well understanding ye English Tongue)."[56] Over forty years later (in 1721), a dispute hinging on the linguistic skills of Cornelia de Peyster, Johannes's widow, elicited illuminating testimony from Mary Blood, a former employee in Mrs. De Peyster's shop:

> Mrs. Cornelia De Peyster did understand some English words, and but few, but she could not understand a whole discourse, or not a whole sentence. And . . . [Mary Blood] was often called upon to assist in the shop, when any English people were there, and used commonly to talk to them, and interpret to her, when none of her relations were there to interpret. That she could speak but some words of English.[57]

Letters in Dutch from Johannes de Peyster (born 1666) to his older brother Abraham (born 1657) written between 1699 and 1703 indicate that private communication among second-generation De Peysters was carried on in their first language. However, the fact that Abraham de Peyster's correspondence contains letters in English as well as Dutch suggests that he was conversant in both tongues.[58]

The decisions members of the De Peyster family made regarding the education of third-generation children highlight the part played by gender in preserving Dutch. Abraham de Peyster provided his daughter Catharina (born 1688) with instruction in the Dutch language. In 1698, young Catharina was enrolled in the Dutch Reformed church school where students were taught in the Dutch language. Catharina's ability to write

Dutch is evident from a brief letter that she wrote about this time to "Myn lieve Papa" and signed "Dochter Catharina."[59]

Abraham's younger brother Johannes had different ideas respecting his own son's education. He arranged for the boy to study English while they were in Boston in 1702 and 1703 and wrote to his brother in Dutch about his sons's progress in English. While the father praised his son's mastery of English, the boy's mother was fearful that he had lost his ability to understand Dutch and thereby his link to family and church. Mrs. De Peyster's dismay when "she could not get a single Dutch word" out of their nine-year-old son upon visiting him in Boston stands in sharp contrast to her husband's exuberance.[60]

Dutch mothers, as guardians of tradition in the home, knew that the Dutch language was at the heart of Dutch culture, the link to memory and the means of communicating with God. Always less proficient in English than men, owing to their less frequent exposure to English speakers, women could not afford to stand by and allow their native tongue to become extinct. They felt compelled to ensure that their children remained fluent in Dutch. Considerations such as these presumably influenced the educational choices made by Abraham and Johannes de Peyster's sister. Maria de Peyster Spratt, the widow of a Scottish immigrant, placed her children, Johan and Cornelia Spratt, in the same Dutch catechism class in which their cousin Catharina was enrolled.[61] Her younger daughter, Mary Spratt (figure 15), who achieved prominence as a shopkeeper and as the wife of attorney James Alexander, undoubtedly received training in Dutch as well, since her correspondence in later life included letters written from Amsterdam in the Dutch language.[62] The continued use of Dutch in the personal correspondence of New York City families is confirmed in a rare letter penned by Elizabeth Romme to her husband, who was implicated in the Negro plot of 1741. Written in what Judge Daniel Horsmanden called "female Dutch," the letter, which was intercepted in New Jersey, advised Johannis Romme to stay away from the city where authorities were searching for him.[63]

However committed New Yorkers were to preserving Dutch as their primary means of communication, they were powerless to prevent changes in the language itself. Ongoing contact with English speakers led to alterations in syntax as well as the incorporation of English words.[64] The divergence of the Dutch spoken in New York from the mother tongue was apparent to clergymen who arrived from Holland.[65]

While New York City's Dutch men and women sustained the Dutch language at home and in church during the first third of the eighteenth century, they became increasingly conversant with English and saw to it that their children learned it. Unlike their elders (people like the Widow De Peyster, Rip van Dam, and Abraham van Horne), who made little

Figure 15. Mary Spratt Provoost Alexander (1693–1760), the off-spring of a Dutch mother and a Scottish father, kept a shop in New York City. Attorney James Alexander, a native of Scotland, was her second husband. John Wollaston painted this portrait when she was in her late fifties. Courtesy Museum of the City of New York.

progress in their knowledge of English, and the very young, whose education was almost exclusively in English, they became masters of two languages. The deposition of Edward Pennant, an English scribe summoned to the deathbed of Abraham Splinter in 1721 to record his will, offers evidence of bilinguality in a Dutch family: "[Ann]etie Lackerman mother of the testators wife told [Pennant] what he should write[,] speaking to Mr. Splinter in Dutch & then telling [Pennant] from him what he should write and so through the whole Course of taking the will."[66]

The author of a bilingual reader published in 1730 was keen enough to identify this transitional stage in language behavior. Earmarked for Dutch people who wanted to improve their command of English, "The English and Low-Dutch School-Master containing Alphabetical Tables of the most Common Words in English and Dutch. With certain Rules and Directions whereby the Low-Dutch Inhabitants of North America may (in a short time) learn to Spell, Read, Understand and Speak proper English. And by the help whereof the English may also learn to Spell, Read, Understand and Write Low-Dutch" addressed the dilemma of descendants of the early Dutch settlers who now lived in an English world.[67]

Bilingualism was a temporary phenomenon in New York City, associated with a particular generation. It could only be sustained if Dutch youth could be persuaded that their ancestral tongue was functional in eighteenth-century New York. But the pressure to speak English in all contexts was becoming overwhelming. As one writer put it in the early 1750s:

> The Dutch tongue is . . . almost entirely become Useless. It is scarce necessary in an Office, Business, Condition or Employment; and there are therefore comparatively few Families amongst us, especially among the younger People, but are better acquainted with the *English* than the *Dutch* Language; and few also are the Instances, even among ourselves, of those who take any Pains to have their Children taught either to read or speak Dutch.[68]

By the 1740s, facility in the Dutch tongue was waning and English had become the first language of most Dutch New Yorkers, except the elderly. As Cornelius van Horne, the grandson of a New Amsterdam settler, summed it up in 1743, "the Dutch tongue Declines fast among Us Especially with the Young people. And All Affairs are transacted in English and that Language prevails Generally Amongst Us."[69] Once parents no longer had grounds for insisting that their offspring master the language of the Netherlands, the demise of Dutch in New York City was assured. When the council of the city's Lutheran church delivered the opinion in 1749 that "even in the homes of the Dutch only English is spoken," they were only confirming the view enunciated two years earlier by Dominie John Ritzema that "(English) is ever more natural to our inhabitants and even to the members of our congregation."[70] Peter Kalm's observation in the same year (1749) that there were "many homes [in New York City] in which Dutch was commonly spoken, especially by the elderly people" was immediately qualified by the assertion that "the majority . . . who were of Dutch descent, were succumbing to the English language."[71] William Livingston's 1754 pronouncement that "the Dutch tongue, which, though once the common dialect of this province, is now scarcely understood, except by its more ancient inhabitants" was not far off the mark with respect to New York City.[72]

Betweeen 1730 and 1750, the English language triumphed among the Dutch residents of New York City. Michael Christian Knoll, the minister of the city's Lutheran church, may have exaggerated when he asserted in 1749 that "as late as 20 years ago most everything was still Dutch." But his subsequent comment that "since that time everything seems to have turned to English" accurately reflects the course of development after 1730.[73]

As long as Dutch and French New Yorkers remained linguistically differentiated from their neighbors of British ancestry, the chances of their worshiping side by side were slim. The connection between language and faith in colonial New York City was articulated no more clearly than in the Dutch Reformed Church consistory's 1733 statement that "a good Dutch school" was necessary "for the Christian rearing, teaching and training of our youth, in order to gain them, from the earliest period, to the language of our Church, and to a love for the Dutch Reformed worship."[74] But the movement of various segments of the city's population toward a uniform language is not sufficient to explain the development of a voluntaristic religious system.

New York City's ethnically centered configuration of congregational life began to fracture in the early decades of the eighteenth century, but not until midcentury did a more complex ordering crystallize.[75] Personal predilection, social class, family, and education now played a greater part than ethnic identity in formulating religious preferences. The decreasing salience of ethnicity in determining church affiliation has been linked to the concerted efforts of educational missionaries of the Anglican Society for the Propagation of the Gospel in Foreign Parts (S.P.G.), dissension within the French church, an upsurge of pietist sentiment among the Dutch Reformed, and religious divisions within the English community, as well as the ongoing adaptation of the Dutch and French to the English language and culture.[76] But the dimensions and timing of shifts in church membership in the period up to 1730 have not been examined systematically until recently. Microscopic analysis of congregational records and family religious biographies illuminates the process of religious change and, by exposing its anomalous aspects, makes clear that it was neither as smooth nor as ineluctable as has been thought.[77]

The most clear-cut evidence of alterations in religious allegiance comes from the Huguenot church. Strong disagreement among members over the unorthodox behavior of their minister, Louis Rou, split the congregation and precipitated an exodus during the 1720s. This dispute, along with linguistic shift and intermarriage among the French, especially those of the second generation, ensured that, by 1730, the majority of Huguenots no longer worshiped in the French church. The high level of exogamy of French Huguenots, already evident in the seventeenth century, persisted in the early decades of the eighteenth century. Evidence assembled by Jon Butler showing that French men and women of all social ranks selected mates from among the Dutch and English underscores the fragility of ethnic ties among the French in early eighteenth-century New York City.[78] Only forty-six men affiliated with the church have been identified among city taxpayers in 1730.[79] Thereafter, the congregation dwindled in size and importance.[80]

The majority of the French transferred to the Anglican church, but a considerable number chose to cast their lot with the Dutch Reformed. Incomplete Trinity Church records prevent us from specifying the exact dimensions of this shift, but sixteen Huguenot men appear on the lists of Trinity Church vestrymen and pewholders before 1730, and seven French names are found on subscription lists for the assistant minister. More than a few French Protestants remained unchurched.[81]

During the first third of the eighteenth century, while Quakers and Jews continued along the paths they had charted in the seventeenth century, Lutherans, whose numbers remained small, underwent a metamorphosis from an ethnically mixed congregation to a predominantly German one—owing principally to inflows of migrants from the Palatinate in and after 1710—even though services continued to be conducted exclusively in Dutch until the 1740s.[82] As the church council put it in 1742, "Our Church owes its existence to the gifts of our sainted ancestors who were Dutchmen and who kept us united with God from generation to generation through the Dutch language."[83]

The Dutch Reformed church experienced no major diminution in size or influence during this period. Between 1700 and 1730, 1,259 people were admitted, one-third of them in the decade of the 1720s.[84] By the mid-1720s the church was struggling to accommodate its growing congregation. In 1726 the consistory brought to the notice of members "the increase of the number of those who have no seats in our church" and requested their advice as to whether to build a new church or enlarge the old.[85] In 1729, Governor John Montgomerie granted the church a license to seek voluntary contributions from city residents for completing the new edifice and reported that "the said Congregation is now become so numerous that very often their present Church will not contain all the members of it, so that many of them are obliged to Refraine from coming to the Publick Worship for want of room."[86] The new building, seating a thousand to twelve hundred people, was opened in 1729.[87] New York City's male taxpayers in 1730 included 485 men who were affiliated with the

Dutch church.[88] The size of the congregation in that year can be estimated as approximately 1,450 adults.[89]

New communicants comprised a mixture of descendants of old New York City Dutch families and migrants from Dutch communities in the area. The accession of 111 German immigrants between 1711 and 1728 constituted the only significant alteration in the customary pattern of recruitment. These German men and women of the Reformed faith, many of whom remained in the church only briefly, formed part of the much larger Palatine immigration to New York colony in the early eighteenth century.[90] Small numbers of French and English also joined the Dutch Reformed congregation between 1700 and 1730.

Nevertheless, the adherence of Dutch New Yorkers to the Reformed church could no longer be taken for granted at a time when the cumulative impact of decades of exposure to the English language and English customs was taking its toll. In 1726, church leaders castigated congregants for a "general apathy, or a sad indifference to evangelical truth as well as to true piety," that had led to failure to educate their children in the Dutch language, the prerequisite for worship in the Dutch Reformed church. In order to reverse this ominous trend and avert the loss of members among the younger generation, the church instituted a school, even providing financial assistance for families unable to pay the schoolmaster.[91] Women continued to predominate, accounting for nearly two-thirds of new members, 1700–1730. This disproportion suggests that the apathy spoken of by church leaders in 1726 was centered among males and was more likely to translate into religious indifference than to reflect a shift in religious affiliation.

The possibility of Dutch communicants switching to other churches was recognized as early as 1712 when new seating regulations included a provision regarding "any person now or hereafter holding seats in the Church [who] shall go over and enter into fellowship with other congregations not in fellowship with our Church."[92] A more urgent tone is evident in a 1729 document requesting financial support to complete a new church building. The lack of seats in the old church had to be remedied so that "every appearance of pretext for withdrawing from our congregation may be removed."[93]

The dimensions of disaffection from the Dutch church before 1730 are not clear. In 1741 Gualtherus Du Bois (figure 16), the minister of the city's Reformed congregation, was reporting as fact the loss of communicants to other churches throughout the colonies: "Certain ones, apparently only for worldly reasons, have united with the Episcopalians. Among them there is no confession demanded of one's faith, nor is there any discipline among them, as among us. Certain others have gone over to the Independents. Their ministers are running all over the country, and

Figure 16. Rev. Gualtherus Du Bois (1666–1751) graduated from the University of Leyden in the Netherlands and subsequently settled in New York, where he served as minister of the city's Dutch Reformed church from 1699 to 1751. Courtesy Collegiate Reformed Protestant Dutch Church of the City of New York. Photo by Tim Adams.

preaching, after their fashion, two or three times a day . . . [A]lthough to our sorrow we lose one another from time to time, nevertheless our Church remains in a fairly good condition, and thus far we have lost none who have at heart the real welfare of God's Zion."[94]

Dutch New Yorkers of pietist inclination may have contemplated a move to New Jersey, where evangelical preachers had made spectacular inroads into Dutch congregations, but systematic data on the migration of city church members to New Jersey is lacking.[95] A more likely destination for dissatisfied Dutch churchgoers was Trinity Church. The expectation of social betterment, the lure of English language services, and the endeavors of S.P.G. missionaries and schoolmasters to gather converts among the Dutch all pulled Reformed church members in this direction.[96]

"It's not an easy task to perswade men to change their Religion" wrote Lewis Morris, an advocate of the Anglican cause, in 1711. "As the bringing over the Dutch will be of great use in this part of America, where their Numbers are so considerable, so to accomplish it will be difficult and a work of time. Most of them are ignorant of our Religion, many of them take the Character of it from our Enemies, whose practice it is to misrepresent it."[97] Morris noted optimistically that "one of the most considerable dutch families in New York [had] embraced the Religion of the Church of England," but he recognized, as did Elias Neau, the S.P.G.'s catechist of Negroes in New York City, that winning members of the Dutch Reformed church to the Anglican communion was a long-term and complex enterprise.[98] Gratified by the sympathetic response of some Huguenots to the Church of England, Neau had speculated in 1709 that "in time the Dutch themselves may be brought to conform; they are very well pleased with the Liturgy's I lend them; . . . if God would unite these Churches, it would be a great good. I know that this must be managed with prudence for fear of exasperating people's minds."[99]

Though the lack of membership records for Trinity Church before the Revolution precludes constructing a precise chronology of change, lists of vestrymen and pewholders, along with subscription lists for the support of the assistant minister, disclose that few Dutch New Yorkers worshiped at Trinity before 1730.[100] The prosperous members of the city's Anglican communion, whose names appear on these documents, were almost exclusively English and French through the 1720s. A voluntary subscription list for the Reverend James Wetmore in 1725 contains only four recognizably Dutch surnames out of ninety-one.[101] Only in the final days of 1728 did Thomas Colgan, Trinity's assistant minister, report that "our congregation greatly increases; we have of late receiv'd Several conformists from the ffrench Dutch & English dissenters who are indeed but a small body Some of which Conformists are the most Considerable Traders in the City."[102]

By midcentury, contemporaries were agreed that a large-scale removal of Dutch to Trinity Church had taken place. William Smith, Jr., the early historian of New York, noted in 1756 that Trinity Church, "partly by the arrival of strangers from Europe, but principally by proselytes from the Dutch churches, is become so numerous, that though the old building will contain 2000 hearers, yet a new one was erected in 1752."[103] James Birket, a West Indian merchant who visited the city in 1750, offered a similar assessment: "Here are two Episcopal Churches, which are Large and Strong Buildings of Hewn Stone, and as it must be Allowed to be the most fasionable, So it Seems to me here as well as in most other parts of

North America to Prevail[.] [H]ere is also Four Dutch Churches Two of the Lutheran the Other of the Calvinistical Order, All which are Large & formerly were very much crowded but many of the young people fall of[f] to the National form."[104]

The exact timing and scope of the massive transfer of Dutch Reformed communicants to Trinity Church remains in doubt, but the statements of a variety of observers point to the 1740s as the critical decade of realignment. "The Dutch Reformed church was once the leading and predominant church," Lutheran pastor Henry Muhlenberg noted in his journal in 1751, "but in a very few years the English church has had an increase of many thousands, with the result that a very large building can no longer contain the members and the second large church is now in the process of construction and will be completed in the near future. The reason for this is that the Dutch children forget their mother tongue and learn English. Since they cannot hear English in their own church, they go over to the other to hear what they understand and like."[105] Muhlenberg's comment echoed that of Swedish traveler Peter Kalm, who wrote in 1749 that "most of the young people now speak principally 'English' and go to the 'English' church; and would even take it amiss if they were called 'Dutchmen' and not 'Englishmen'" and anticipated the line of argument of Presbyterian polemicist William Livingston, who in 1754 attributed the 'visible decay' of the Dutch Reformed churches to their unwillingness to substitute English for Dutch as the language of worship.[106] Livingston realized that considerations of social status as well as language disposed Dutch young people to change churches:

> Whatever is modish, captivates juvenile misunderstandings; and the Church of England might, for that reason, expect a further accession of the Dutch youth. The sticklers for the hierarchy, do not value themselves more upon their orthodoxy, than the fashionableness of their profession; and setting themselves up for patterns of true taste in religion; they would doubtless glean all those among the Dutch, who are fond of being reckoned among the 'beau monde'.[107]

Members of the Dutch Reformed community were sensitive to these developments. In 1747, Dominie John Ritzema reported "the close connection by marriage of many of our people with those of other churches. If they are denied (private) baptism, they threaten to leave our church and go to the others. Indeed, their language (English) is ever more natural to our inhabitants and even to the members of our congregation than the Dutch. Going elsewhere is also often done for less reasons."[108] The elderly Dominie Du Bois also recognized the inevitable course of events. "The Dutch churches here are gradually beginning to languish," he wrote in 1748, "both on account of internal strife in some of them, and because of the distaste for true piety in others; and not less on account of the fact that the Dutch language is gradually, more and more being neglected. On this account, in the New York church, several begin to speak of calling a minister, after my death, to preach in the English language, but in accordance with our manner and doctrine."[109] When 87 church members petitioned for services in English in 1754, they remarked that "for many years past, their Congregations have been, and at present are, in a very melancholy declining State, and that their Youth daily fall off to other Churches." In their view, "this sad Declension . . . is justly, and only to be ascribed, not to Objections against their Worship, Doctrine or Government, but to the General Disuse of the Dutch and the Prevailing Use of the English language."[110]

Since accessions to Trinity in the years between 1730 and 1750 cannot be documented, one must search other records for evidence of the shifts discussed by commentators. Trinity's marriage records, which begin in 1746, include only a smattering of recognizably Dutch names, and Dutch names are conspicuously absent from the vestry minutes and the roster of vestrymen and churchwardens. However, 14 percent of the 183 names on a 1737 subscription list for the church building fund are Dutch.[111] The membership lists of the Reformed church for this period yield few clues to the changing church affiliations of Dutch New Yorkers. Admissions to the church remained near the level of previous decades, and Germans continued to join the congregation at regular intervals. Only two references to individual transfers of membership to Trinity Church—one in 1752 and the other in 1753—are found in these records.[112]

The impression conveyed by Thomas Colgan's comment that the earliest Dutch converts to the Anglican communion in New York City came from the upper ranks of the social structure, a notion put forward by scholars as well, may be misleading.[113] Stressing the appeal of Anglicanism to ambitious members of the Dutch elite tends to discount the cumulative accomplishments of S.P.G. schoolmasters in educating poor non-English children in the Anglican faith. Changes in Dutch religious preferences may have first occurred not at the highest but at the lowest end of the social spectrum.

The modest size of Trinity's congregation during the first quarter of the eighteenth century also supports the contention that few Dutch transferred their membership there before 1730. In 1724, Trinity's rector, William Vesey (figure 17), reported that the Sacrament of the Lord's Supper was administered "once in six weeks, and the usual number of Communicants is one hundred and upwards. But on the thre[e] great festivals of Christmas, Easter & Whitsontide more than two hundred."[114] In 1730, 178 male taxpayers were identified with Trinity Church.[115] Although the

Figure 17. Rev. William Vesey (1674–1746), the first rector of Trinity Church, actively promoted the Anglican cause in New York City during a career that lasted almost half a century. Courtesy of the Parish of Trinity Church.

church edifice was enlarged during the 1720s, the major expansion did not occur until 1737.[116] The congregation grew rapidly thereafter. In 1748, Henry Barclay, Vesey's successor as rector, reported that "we have . . . resolved to lay the foundation of a Large Chapel of Ease to Trinity Church Early in the Spring, our Congregation becoming so Numerous that the Church cannot contain them."[117]

In 1702 Trinity's rector, in an enthusiastic report to the S.P.G. on the progress of Anglican educators in New York, wrote that he hoped "out of different nations, to compose the most glorious church in America."[118] But the goal of an ethnically diverse Trinity Church was realized only in a limited way in the first third of the eighteenth century through the accession of estranged French Huguenots and a few Dutch. Furthermore, Trinity experienceed a schism provoked in part by Vesey's imperious style. The hostility of some English residents toward Vesey, disclosed in depositions taken following the desecration of the church in 1713 by unknown parties, was capitalized on by Governor Robert Hunter, who created an alternative center for worship. He refurbished the chapel in the fort and directed that regular services be conducted there by the Anglican chaplain, John Sharpe.[119]

Notwithstanding their internecine disputes, New York's Anglicans possessed a virtual monopoly of the religious institutions serving the city's English population well into the second decade of the century. "Although the Presbiterians have made several attempts," a prominent Anglican layman exulted in 1714, "they have not been able to break in upon us[,] a happiness no city in North America can boast of besides ourselves."[120] But the demands of dissenters for a place to worship could not be forestalled indefinitely, and in 1716 a Presbyterian meeting was organized in New York City.[121]

Scots formed the mainstay of the congregation in the view of its minister, James Anderson, who related that "the people here who are favorers of our church & perswasion . . . are yet but few & none of the richest. . . . Some are already come to live in the city & more are expected whose langwage would not allow them to joyn with the Dutch or French churches, & whose consciences would not allow them to joyn in the service of the English church."[122] Dissenters from England and New England affiliated with the new Presbyterian church as well, but their dissatisfaction with the Scottish way of conducting worship led to a brief separation in 1722–23 and, more significantly, to lasting tension within the congregation.[123] Baptists had also begun to hold regular meetings in the city in 1716.[124]

Though the leaders of Trinity looked with trepidation upon these competitors for English souls, referring to "this Critical Juncture" in 1722, "when the Dissenters here have United their forces, & by Encouragemt & Liberal Contributions from abroad, have been enabled to build two meeting houses & support Ministers to preach in them according to their different opinions," their alarm was premature.[125] New York's Quakers and Baptists remained small groups, and the Presbyterians only gradually added to their numbers after Ebenezer Pemberton assumed the ministry in 1727.[126] In the 1730s the Presbyterian meeting comprised at most 70 to 80 members, about the number it had started with in 1716.[127] Most of its adherents were drawn not from Trinity Church or the Dutch Reformed church but from dissenting backgrounds in the British Isles and New England.[128] Pemberton's decision to allow George Whitefield access to his pulpit in 1739, when the city's other ministers denied the evangelist a forum, dramatically affected the subsequent history of the Presbyterian congregation. In the words of Henry Muhlenberg, writing in 1751, "Mr. Whitefield . . . preached in [Pemberton's] church several times, which resulted in a very large increase in the congregation. Divine services are held three times on Sundays—morning, afternoon, and evening. Great emphasis is put upon real Christianity and the English are eager to hear it."[129] The influx of members necessitated the enlargement of the Presbyterian meeting house in 1748, and the congregation grew rapidly thereafter, reaching 1,200 to 1,400 by 1756.[130]

That New York City's religious landscape altered between 1700 and 1730 is indisputable. The once burgeoning congregation of French Protestant refugees, rent by internal conflict, rapidly declined until it was reduced to parity with the small congregations of Lutherans, Quakers, and Jews. Concurrently, a notable vacuum in the religious spectrum was finally filled with the organization of Presbyterian and Baptist churches to meet the needs of British dissenters. The city's preeminent religious institutions, the Dutch Reformed Church and Trinity Church, while remaining on solid footing, worked vigorously to preserve and enlarge their constituencies in an environment of increasing denominational competition. Both expanded during this period, while at the same time diversifying their membership rolls, the Dutch by admitting a sizable group of Germans and a smattering of English and French, and the Anglican church by taking in numbers of French and a few Dutch. The distribution of New York City's population among its religious institutions now transcended ethnic lines, but large-scale shifts of church affiliation had not yet taken place.

Church membership profiles furnish an overview of patterns of religious allegiance in New York City between 1664 and the mid-eighteenth century and enable us to plot the direction and timing of change and estimate its extent. But when we shift the angle of vision from the congregation to the family, anomalies come into focus that caution against facile generalizations about shifts in religious affiliation. Religious biographies of interethnic families reveal that the choices people made regarding church membership, the site of their children's baptisms, and their own burial places did not always mesh with the patterns outlined in aggregate statistics.

The movement away from ethnic exclusivity in the choice of marital partners in New York City had become increasingly common after 1700. The propensity of the French to marry outside the group has already been noted. If the marriage patterns of third-generation Dutch cohort members discussed in chapter 8 are representative of the city's Dutch, then it is clear that Dutch men finally began to select mates from outside their group in the early eighteenth century. However, the fact that the majority of these

Dutch men still preferred brides who were familiar with their traditional culture suggests the continuing salience of ethnicity among Dutch New Yorkers. Dutch women, perhaps because of their greater numbers, frequently intermarried with English and French men.

New York's English, already a diverse group in the seventeenth century, fragmented further in the early eighteenth century as substantial numbers of Scots, Scots-Irish, and Irish entered the city. Under these circumstances, ethnic unity was unrealizable. The extent of ties between British and non-British city residents remains problematical. Given the lack of marriage records from Trinity Church and the incompleteness of civil marriage records for this period, systematic data on the proportion of exogamous marriages among the English and other British New Yorkers cannot be compiled. Yet scanning the marriage records of the Dutch Reformed church and extant civil marriage licenses leaves no doubt that during the first third of the eighteenth century scores of British men continued to marry outside the ethnic fold and primarily to Dutch women. Of the 43 British merchants on the 1730 tax list, at least 15 were married to women of Dutch or part-Dutch background.

Research on Anglo-Dutch families highlights the impressive loyalty of Dutch women to the church in which they were raised. In the late seventeenth and early eighteenth centuries, the Dutch Reformed church contained a sizable group of female communicants whose husbands were English. In 1686, twenty-five women in the congregation were married to English men, but only five of the men were members themselves.[131] Between 1698 and 1730, sixty Dutch women already married to English men joined the Reformed church. Sixteen of their husbands can be definitely identified as adherents of Trinity Church, and probably more were.[132] An additional number of Trinity men were married to Dutch women who had joined the Reformed church before 1698.

Examining the sequence of religious choices in ethnically mixed families enhances our understanding of the roles of husband and wife in defining the family's religious identity. In some cases, the timing of a wife's affiliation with the Dutch Reformed church looks like a statement expressing her resistance to her husband's religious preference. For example, in 1724 John McEvers bought a pew in Trinity Church. The next year, his wife Catharina van Horne entered into communion with the Reformed church. That a wife may have enjoyed considerable power in the arena of religious decision making seems evident from the site chosen for the baptism of the couple's children, for between 1723 and 1734 Catharina and John McEvers had seven children baptized in the Dutch church.

The obstinacy of Dutch wives of English men in matters of religion is illustrated in the case of Catharine DeHardt Symes, wife of Captain Lancaster Symes. During the period when Symes served as vestryman of Trinity Church (1699–1705), his wife chose to join the Dutch church (1701). Catharine maintained her loyalty to that church throughout her long life, rejoining the congregation in 1728, after an absence, with a certificate from the Albany Dutch church. Her will made in 1749 specified that "my body is to be decently buried in the Old Dutch Church near my mother and brethren there."[133] In her 1748 will, another Dutch woman, Anna Clopper, the wife of John Thompson and the widow of Patrick Mac-Knight—neither of whom were Dutch—directed that her body "be buried in the old Dutch church." She also left money for "such and so many poor widows, being communicants of the Protestant Dutch church of New York, as my executors shall judge best."[134]

Public life in New York City had taken on a decidedly English cast by the early eighteenth century, and scores of Dutch had undoubtedly mastered the rudiments of the English language and were familiar with English business practices. But most Dutch, reluctant to join Trinity Church, still gave their support, nominal or not, to the Dutch Reformed church, which managed to flourish even as the city's religious makeup changed. Given the characteristic pragmatism of the Dutch and their willingness to govern their conduct in the secular realm by English standards, this pattern seems puzzling until one remembers that Dutch religion traditionally centered in the home, where women exerted a powerful influence.[135]

Preoccupied with business and civic affairs, many Dutch men must have ceded the religious leadership of the family to their wives. Not inclined to strong feelings about religious issues, they allowed their spouses to define family religious choices. This is not to say that they ceased to attend Reformed services, because ingrained habits are slow to erode, but rather that many men did not bother to join the church. Neither did they press their wives into transferring to the Church of England, for religion had become an indifferent matter to them.

Dutch women carried on the religious traditions of the family along with other customs of the homeland. Their lives were bounded by the known and the tried. Limited in experience and education, and having only occasional contact with English society, Dutch housewives sought continuity in a world full of uncertainty. As the English colonial government chipped away at the egalitarian inheritance practices and other legal safeguards of women's rights that had been transplanted from the Netherlands, the Reformed church came to symbolize those aspects of Dutch experience that elevated the status of women.[136] No wonder women kept the Reformed faith, joining the church in large numbers and early in their life course.[137] Churchgoing reinforced the values that gave meaning to their existence.

The loyalty of Dutch women to a church that, after all, was organized on a patriarchal model need not be explained solely by reference to the strength of tradition. Concrete benefits lured them to worship. Extended Sabbath-day services gave them opportunities to cement social connections that could be mobilized in time of need. Sitting together in the separate women's pews or conversing between sermons, women shared mutual concerns, passed on practical advice, and comforted each other in times of sorrow. The communal event of worship thus assumed a special and positive significance for women required to spend most of their hours in the narrow confines of the home.

The continuing allegiance of Dutch women to the Reformed church enabled the church to sustain itself well past 1730. Though denied an active role in church governance, female communicants constituted a valuable group of allies for a minister who resisted modifications in church practice. In fundamental agreement with the clerical policy of preserving traditional ways, women reinforced the conservatism of the Reformed church as it defined its response to the accelerating pace of cultural change in eighteenth-century New York City.

Not all Dutch women married to Trinity Church men rejected the religious preference of their husbands. Janneken de Key, the wife of Jeremiah Tothill, accommodated to a change in church membership. De Key, who had joined the Reformed church at the age of sixteeen, married Tothill, an English merchant, in 1686. Their eight children were baptized in the Dutch church, the last in 1701. Before then, however, Tothill cast his lot with Trinity Church, serving as one of the original church managers and as a vestryman from 1698 to 1705, the year of his death. When Jane Tothill, as she styled herself, made her will in 1720, she left Trinity £10 "for opening my husband's grave for me."[138] The Tothills' daughter, Mary, married John Reade, a member of a prominent Trinity family whose sister was the wife of Trinity's rector, William Vesey. John Reade and his brother Joseph Reade (figure 18), both leading merchants, served numerous terms as vestrymen of Trinity Church.

The offspring of Anglo-Dutch couples did not invariably follow their fathers into the Anglican church. Matthew Clarkson, Jr., son of the secretary of New York colony and Catharina van Schayck Clarkson, was baptized in the Dutch Reformed church in 1699. Both parents had become Reformed communicants in the early 1690s, but the father shifted to Trinity Church, where he purchased a pew in 1698 and served as vestryman for several years. In 1718, the younger Clarkson joined the Dutch church; he and his wife, Cornelia de Peyster, had ten children baptized there between 1721 and 1738. His brother David did not become a member of the Dutch church, but David's wife, Anna Margareta Freeman, did.[139] The

Figure 18. Joseph Reade (1694–1771), a second-generation English merchant and a long-time vestryman of Trinity Church, was married to a granddaughter of Frederick Philipse, one of seventeenth-century New York City's premier Dutch merchants. Reade's portrait was painted by John Wollaston. Courtesy of The Metropolitan Museum of Art, Gift of Mrs. Russell Sage, 1948. (48.129.1)

couple had six children baptized in that church, three of them after it was noted in the Trinity vestry records on May 22, 1728, that Clarkson was "to have [a] patent for half of [the] pew his father had partially paid for upon his paying £9."[140]

The quickening pace of linguistic shift and the general substitution of English ways for traditional practices in the early part of the eighteenth century led inexorably to the weakening of ethnic ties and the reconfiguring of social institutions. In the case of the French, the absence of countervailing forces accelerated the process of change. As relatively recent immigrants, the Huguenots had tenuous ties to the locality and to each other and therefore were more susceptible to English ways. Their negative attitude toward their homeland coupled with the indebtedness they felt toward the English government for permitting them to settle in the colonies, paved the way for the acceptance of English values. Equally important, they lacked guidance from their native land and, after the untimely death of their minister Pierre Peiret in 1704, a strong spiritual leader in their new home. Centrifugal pressures became difficult to withstand and individuals broke away as opportunities arose.

For the Dutch, incentives to alter customary behavior were evaluated in a far different context. With a shared history that reached back over half a century and a core of common values that still constituted a reliable compass to the world around them, Dutch New Yorkers approached change cautiously.[141] Embedded in durable social networks that fused kinship and ethnic bonds, with their group identity bolstered by the venerable institutional structure centered in the Dutch Reformed church, they continued to nourish their cultural roots.

The most tangible evidence of the reluctance of the Dutch to stray from familiar paths comes from the realm of architecture. For more than half a century after the imposition of English rule, dwelling houses built in New York City reproduced forms originated in the towns of the Netherlands. Tall, narrow structures with stepped gables facing toward the street, these houses were constructed with the specially fabricated Holland brick that was the hallmark of Dutch urban architecture.[142] Holland brick continued to be used in New York long after the conquest, prompting one mason to complain in 1703 of "the Brichmakers in this province, making their Bricks not according to the standard of England."[143]

Dutch New Yorkers' preference for living in houses reminiscent of the Netherlands was matched by their adherence to the norms of their forebears in arranging the interiors of their dwellings. Accumulating evidence on Dutch colonial material culture, while not plentiful enough to document specific developments in New York City, leaves little doubt of the Dutch imprint on furniture, silver, and ceramics.[144] The prominent place in New York households of the *kas*, a large cupboard in which Dutch housewives stored their linen and on which they displayed prized plates and cups, was, in a rare instance, articulated by a New York City cordwainer. When second-generation cohort member Evert van Hoeck made his will in 1711, among the items he reserved to his wife if she remarried were "a new cupboard, that is now amaking by Mr. Shaveltie and three great and twelve small earthen cups, that stand on top of said cupboard."[145]

In light of the prevalence of domestic motifs in seventeenth-century Dutch culture, it is not surprising that New Yorkers of Netherlands descent were slow to alter their living environments.[146] Even as English-style dwellings multiplied in the city's new neighborhoods, only the exceptional Dutch family accommodated to the changing canons of taste. But, as in the case of language and religion, a watershed was reached in the 1740s that marked a turning away from the past. The impressions of travelers enable us to trace this progression.

In the years following the conquest, impermanent wooden structures in the small Dutch settlement at the tip of Manhattan Island gradually were replaced by brick and stone houses covered with red and black tile.[147] That local builders drew on prototypes from the Netherlands is evident from Labadist Jasper Danckaerts's 1679 prospect of the city revealing an unbroken line of Dutch-style houses, with the gable ends faced toward the street.[148]

"Multitudes of buildings [were] going forward" in New York City when Boston physician Dr. Benjamin Bullivant visited in 1697, graphic testimony of the wealth flowing into the city from the trade with pirates. Though some of these structures introduced new architectural elements, the majority replicated traditional designs. As might be expected, "the English church, new from the ground, of good brown square stone & brick" was "exactly English fashion with a large square steeple at the west end, not yet carried up." Among the "greate and Costly buildings erected since [Governor Fletcher's] arrivall about 4 years since . . . none appeared more Considerable than that of Coll. Abr. Depeisters a noble building of the newest English fashion, and richly furnished with hangings and pictures. The stair case Large, & Noble, ye whole built out of the Sea or Sound within this 2 yeares past, as are abundance of Lofty brick & stone buildings on the same range, theyr back doores & wharfes, warehouses & gardens Lookeing into the Sound, & Harbour."[149] Yet Abraham de Peyster's penchant for English architecture was not shared by many of his countrymen, since the most recent additions to the city's architectural landscape looked very much like Dutch townhouses:

> Most of theyr new buildings are magnificent enough, ye fronts of red and yallow (or flanders) brick Lookeing very prettily, some of them are 6 stories high & built with a Gable end to ye front, & so by Consequence make Very narrow garratts, the 3d story is usually a warehouse and over it a Crane for hawleing up goods, the Lower part is comonly Very substantiall & neate. . . . The windows are high & large as are the stories, ten or 12 foot ye first the casements of wood at bottom of the windows, and without, strong and thick shutters.[150]

Sarah Kemble Knight, another Bostonian who visited the city a few years later, emphasized the differences between New York's architectural styles and those of her hometown: "The Buildings Brick Generaly, very stately and high, though not altogether like ours in Boston. The Bricks in some of the Houses are of divers Coullers and laid in Checkers, being glazed look very agreeable."[151] Three distinctively Dutch features caught Knight's eye when she described the interior of the city's houses—their jambless fireplaces, the use of tiles for decoration, and the overall cleanliness:

> The inside of them are neat to admiration, the wooden work, for only the walls are plasterd, and the Sumers and Girt are plained and kept very white scowr'd as so is all the partitions if made of Bords. The fire places have no Jambs (as ours have) But the Backs run flush with the walls, and the Hearth is of Tyles and is as farr out into the Room at the Ends as before the fire, wch is Generally Five foot in the Low'r rooms, and the peice over where the mantle tree should be is made as ours with Joyners work, and As I supose is fasten'd to iron rodds inside. The House where the Vendue was, had Chimney Corners like ours, and they and the hearths were laid wth the finest tile that I ever see, and the stair cases laid all with white tile which is ever clean, and so are the walls of the Kitchen wch had a Brick floor.[152]

In the second decade of the eighteenth century, despite the proliferation of English-style dwellings, New York City's distinctively Dutch appearance still was singled out by Huguenot John Fontaine: "The town is compact, the houses for the most part built after the dutch manner, with the gable ends toward the street."[153] But the Burgis view of New York, dating from about 1717, depicts architecturally distinct sections of the city, the older part below Wall Street with its characteristically Dutch dwellings forming a striking contrast to the newer neighborhoods to the north dotted with English houses.[154]

As late as 1744, Dr. Alexander Hamilton reported that "the houses are more compact and regular and in generall, higher built [than those in Philadelphia], most of them after the Dutch modell with their gavell ends fronting the street. There are a few built of stone, more of wood, but the greatest number of brick, and a great many covered with pan tile and glazed tile with the year of God when built figured out with plates of iron upon the fronts of severall of them."[155]

From the 1740s on, however, observers agreed that recent construction followed English models.[156] Swedish traveler Peter Kalm stated in 1748 that "Most of the houses are built of brick, and are generally strong and neat, and several stories high. Some had, in the old style, turned the gable end toward the street; but the new houses were altered in this respect. . . . The roofs are commonly covered with tiles or shingles."[157]

In 1750 James Birket elaborated on the shift in building styles signaled by Kalm: "Neither their streets nor their houses are at all Regular Some being 4 or 5 Story high & Others not above two, Not any of the Modern houses are built wth the Gable End to the Street as was formerly the fashion amongst all the old Dutch Settlers, but are many of 'em Spacious Genteel houses Some are built of hewn stone Others of English & Also of the Small white Hollands Brick, which looks neat but not grand, their houses are Generally neat within and well Furnished, Notwithstanding there Still remains too many of the Old Dutch houses which prevents its Appearing to Advantage."[158]

Thomas Pownall, who viewed the city in 1753, noted that "since [New York City] came into the hands of the English New Churches & New Houses have been built in a more modern taste & many of the Gabel-ends of ye old houses, just as is done in Holland, have been new fronted in the Italian stile." Nevertheless, Pownall concluded that "the City still retains the general appearance of a Dutch town with its row of Gabel-ends & the rows of Trees on the sides of the Streets. It is Cheifly in its publick as well as private buildings built with brick and neatly paved."[159]

While the dichotomous character of New York City's architecture was still apparent at midcentury, the future trend was unmistakable. New buildings emulated the latest English fashions and older houses were being remodeled to conform with English styles. English taste had infiltrated the Dutch community and the contents of Dutch households would increasingly reflect prevailing British norms. Members of the Dutch elite stood in the vanguard of change, but average Dutch families could not long resist the flood of British consumer goods. The bulwark of tradition had been breached and the decades ahead would witness the receding influence of Dutch culture in New York City.

In 1853, two hundred years after New Amsterdam's official incorporation, a correspondent describing the changing face of New York City for *Putnam's Monthly* recalled with obvious pleasure the demolition of an antiquated structure on Broad Street about 1830: "We never waste a tear over the death of an old Fogy, especially a Dutch one, which . . . must be admitted to surpass in desolation all the other varieties of conservatism extant."[160] Architectural remnants of another age, such buildings offended the sensibilities of forward-looking New Yorkers of the nineteenth century. Yet as physical expressions of the taste of generations of Dutch urban dwellers, these houses stood as vivid reminders of the long-lasting cultural imprint of New York's original settlers.

CONCLUSION

THE OUTSTANDING sociological feature of colonial New York City, its melange of peoples, presents historians with a challenge of considerable magnitude. Asked to explain how settlers of diverse backgrounds worked out a basis for coexistence following the English conquest of New Netherland, they soon concede the inadequacy of conceptual models drawn from the era of mass immigration. Theories of assimilation that postulate a sequence of events in which immigrants enter a well-defined host society with a unified culture and gradually modify their actions and values to harmonize with those of the majority fail to account for the behavior of English newcomers in this historical context. Since men of their nation had seized the reins of government, English immigrants had no intention of adopting the ways of the majority Dutch population. In short, the predicted roles of the players in the process of ethnic interaction do not mesh with the social experience of early New York City.

An alternative explanation of the social and cultural rearrangements that occurred following the commencement of English rule takes as a point of departure the fact that imperial expansion entails the subduing of an indigenous population. Displacing the vanquished involves not only seizing their privileges but reducing their culture to an inferior status. Ample evidence of English cultural imperialism in the early modern era exists in the cases of Wales, Scotland, and Ireland.[1]

In New York historiography this scenario, dubbed "Anglicization," depicts the revamping of the local social order after the English takeover as Dutch men were ousted from the heights of wealth and power by newly arrived English men who rapidly installed their culture in the city. But, as this study has shown, the course of social and cultural development in the city did not follow this pattern for a variety of reasons.

The numerical ratios and consequently the positions of host society and immigrant group were reversed in seventeenth-century New York City. Unlike voluntary immigrants, the Dutch had not chosen to place themselves under English dominion but had been forced to recognize the authority of a victorious foreign power in an imperial contest. Expecting the city's Dutch majority to be absorbed by the few English newcomers and to accept their culture not only defies the logic of assimilation theory, but discounts the impress of decades of settlement in New Amsterdam. The Dutch "charter group" had deep roots in a society where its culture was dominant.[2]

Though New York's English rulers never doubted the superiority of their own culture, they acknowledged the difficulty of imposing their values on the Dutch. Coercion, in the form of punitive laws, might have been a suitable tactic to bring about cultural uniformity in Wales or Ireland, but the circumstances of New York's conquest mitigated against its use there. The large resident population was an offshoot of a formidable economic and naval power and a Protestant nation to boot. Forcing the Dutch colonists to adhere to English norms was never seriously considered.

Realism led the English to endorse a policy of toleration in New York and to rely instead on strategies of cooptation and conversion to wean foreigners from their compatriots. Despite the ethnocentric strain in English culture, precedents existed for the toleration of cultural diversity. England had allowed foreign groups—communities of Dutch and French Protestants and even a small number of Jews—to flourish in its midst for religious and economic reasons.[3] Furthermore, during the late seventeenth century, England was moving toward a more liberal religious settlement— formalized in the Act of Toleration of 1689—in which dissenters were to be left unmolested. Proprietary New York was, in a sense, a testing ground for some of these advanced notions.[4] When Virginian William Byrd visited the city in 1685, he was struck by the fact that "they have as many Sects of religion there as at Amsterdam, all being tolerated."[5] It is not surprising, then, that a new pattern of social relations was forged in New York City, one that could accommodate the interests of diverse groups while affirming the supremacy of English law and institutions.

The pluralism that took shape in seventeenth-century New York City was the product of an age of toleration, not an age of equality. Guaranteeing the right to express beliefs without persecution was a great step forward in the seventeenth century, but it was light years away from the notion of celebrating cultural differences which forms the underpinning of modern theories of cultural pluralism. The pluralism that emerged in New York City lacked an ideological backbone. Though not all contemporaries shared the goal of cultural uniformity implicit in Charles Lodwick's assessment that New York City was "too great a mixture of nations," his opinion was closer to the mainstream than the philosophy of tolerance and inclusion implemented by William Penn in Pennsylvania.[6] In the eyes of English imperial authorities, pluralism was not an ideal to be treasured, but a condition to be endured.

Their predecessors on Manhattan Island shared this view. But the administrators of the Dutch West India Company had forestalled the appearance of a genuine pluralism in the settlement by upholding the orthodoxy of the Reformed church and prohibiting the small groups of foreigners from founding religious institutions of their own. Despite New Amsterdam's heterogeneous makeup, cultural change had essentially flowed in one direction as individuals of diverse nationalities gradually conformed to Dutch culture. By the time of the conquest many of the town's Germans, Scandinavians, French, and English had become culturally Dutch. After England assumed power, however, the agglomeration of diverse peoples that had been loosely bound together by the institutions of a trading company in New Amsterdam was transformed into a pluralistic society divided along ethnic and racial lines.

The open economic and political environment of the new English city along with the latitude granted the Dutch and other groups in cultural matters set the stage for social processes that eventuated in the crystallization of ethnic groups and ultimately a pluralistic society. Obliged to make only minimal concessions to the fact of English governance and secure in their family and church life, most Dutch saw little reason to break with the ways of the past. Contact with the English, however, energized the Dutch population to defend its own customs and values.

Confronted with an alternative culture, Dutch men and women did not seek to emulate it, but instead realized the necessity of defining their own way of life. What resulted was the discovery and expression of Dutch ethnicity. Self-consciousness was accompanied by a resolve to retain the most meaningful parts of the Dutch ancestral heritage. Differences of origin and experience were submerged as the common bonds of language and religion were reinforced in the altered environment. In short, the city's Dutch coalesced into an ethnic group in a process resembling that labeled "ethnicization" by historians of nineteenth- and twentieth-century immigrant groups.[7] Typically, the process of ethnicization involved immigrant men and women whose attachments to particular European localities were transmuted in the United States into loyalties to newly defined ethnic groups unified by language and, in some cases, religion. Ethnic cohesion enabled members of the group to retain strong links with the past as well as to mobilize resources to face the future. The Dutch ethnic group in colonial New York City, however, was primarily the creation of Dutch creoles (people born or raised in the colony) and not immigrants from the Netherlands. Moreover, it was the creation of a majority group, not a minority.

The concept of ethnicization better fits the experience of early New York City's other cultural groups. English immigrants from a variety of backgrounds, cognizant of their position as a minority in New York City society, were drawn together gradually and with difficulty over the course of the seventeenth century. The delayed founding of the Church of England in New York City epitomizes the tortuous path of English "ethnicization" in New York City. Until the forging of an English ethnic group under the Anglican banner, New York indeed seemed to English residents "rather like a conquered Foreign Province held by the terrour of a Garrison, than an English Colony, possessed and settled by people of our own Nation."[8] Even so, divisions between English, Scots, and Irish as well as Anglicans, Presbyterians, Baptists, and Quakers may have impeded the diffusion of English culture in New York City.

In contrast to the English, the French Huguenots rapidly took their place in New York City's pluralistic social order. Already a self-conscious minority as a result of persecution and exile, the Huguenots easily organized a church upon arrival in the city. French ethnicity in New York City centered around religion. The newly formed French ethnic group was more fragile than other groups, since its attachment to French culture was tenuous as a result of negative associations with Catholic France. Added to the immigrants' sense of gratitude to English benefactors, this made the maintenance of French culture in New York City problematic.

Religion was the linchpin of the city's Jewish community as well. Wherever they settled around the world, Jews always came together to practice their faith. The ethnicization of New York City's Jews involved the merging of Sephardim and Ashkenazim in one community.

Though the denial of freedom to African newcomers set them apart from the city's Europeans, one can detect a parallel process of ethnicization at work here as well. Excluded from white society, but able to open channels of communication among themselves in the compact settlement, people of African origin began to discover common ground.

The sharpening of ethnic boundaries in seventeenth-century New York City and the emergence of ethnic communities brought a degree of order to a diverse society otherwise lacking in sources of cohesion. Forces that might have united New Yorkers across ethnic lines were barely perceptible in this vertically organized society. The social cement that naturally bound homogeneous populations had to be fabricated in New York City's ethnic communities.

Ethnic institutions flourished in early eighteenth-century New York City, but individual French and Dutch men, largely from the upper ranks, found their interests converging with British men of similar economic standing. Inevitably, their ties to their ethnic communities became more attenuated. Concurrently, the more aggressive Anglicanism of the early eighteenth century, epitomized by the S.P.G., lured increasing numbers of foreigners into the English fold. For most Dutch and some French, however, newly reinforced traditions proved more durable even as conditions changed. Ethnic identity would become less salient for them only as supra-ethnic loyalties were generated by the wave of evangelical religion of the 1740s and the republicanism of the revolutionary era.

Though individuals might desert their ethnic communities, the ethnic institutions created in early New York City and sustained through three generations constituted a model for future groups of newcomers to the city. The legitimacy of pluralism, though yet to be articulated, was not the least part of the historical legacy of the earliest New Yorkers.

NOTES

ABBREVIATIONS USED IN THE NOTES

CEM   *Calendar of English Manuscripts, 1664–1776*, vol. 2 of *Calendar of Historical Manuscripts in the Office of the Secretary of State, Albany, New York*, ed. E. B. O'Callaghan, 2 vols. (Albany, 1865–66)

CNYHS   *Collections of the New-York Historical Society*

DHNY   *The Documentary History of the State of New York*, ed. E. B. O'Callaghan, 4 vols. (Albany, 1850–51)

Doc. Rel.   *Documents Relative to the Colonial History of the State of New York*, ed. E. B. O'Callaghan, 15 vols. (Albany, 1856–1887)

Ecc. Rec.   *Ecclesiastical Records of the State of New York*, ed. Edward T. Corwin, 7 vols. (Albany, 1901–1916)

GQS   Court of General Quarter Sessions of the Peace for the City and County of New York (microfilm)

MCC   *Minutes of the Common Council of the City of New York, 1675–1776*, ed. Herbert L. Osgood, 8 vols. (New York, 1905)

N.Y. Col. MSS   New York Colonial Manuscripts, New York State Archives, Albany, New York

RNA   *The Records of New Amsterdam from 1653 to 1674*, ed. Berthold Fernow, 7 vols. (New York, 1897)

S.P.G.   Society for the Propagation of the Gospel in Foreign Parts

INTRODUCTION

1. Charles Lodwick, "New York in 1692," *CNYHS*, 2d ser., vol. 2, (New York, 1849), 244.

2. The standard histories of New York City in the colonial era are replete with references to different segments of the city's population, but this information is grafted onto a political narrative. The best account of New York City in the seventeenth century, Mariana Griswold van Rensselaer's *History of the City of New York in the Seventeenth Century*, intersperses an abundance of material on the various cultural groups with a basically chronological outline of the city's history from its founding to 1691. In one topical chapter entitled "Dutch and English in New York," the author expounds on the pertinacity of Dutch influence after the fall of New Netherland and the links between Dutch traditions and later American ones. Mariana Griswold van Rensselaer, *History of the City of New York in the Seventeenth Century*, 2 vols. (New York, 1909). See also M. L. Booth, *History of the City of New York from Its Earliest Settlement*, 2 vols. (New York, 1859); Martha J. Lamb, *History of the City of New York* (New York, 1877); James Grant Wilson, ed., *Memorial History of the City of New York from Its First Settlement to the Year 1892*, 4 vols. (New York, 1892–93).

Early studies of New Amsterdam similarly combine social with political history but also fail to deal with the town's ethnic makeup in more than a superficial fashion. See William R. Shepherd, *The Story of New Amsterdam* (New York, 1926); and Henry Kessler and Eugene Rachlis, *Peter Stuyvesant and His New York* (New York, 1959).

3. Patricia U. Bonomi, *A Factious People: Politics and Society in Colonial New York* (New York, 1971); Robert C. Ritchie, *The Duke's Province: A Study of New York Politics and Society, 1664–1691* (Chapel Hill, N.C., 1977); Thomas J. Archdeacon, *New York City 1664–1710: Conquest and Change* (Ithaca, N.Y., 1976). See also Steve J. Stern, "Knickerbockers Who Asserted and Insisted; The Dutch Interest in New York Politics, 1664–1691," *New-York Historical Society Quarterly*, 58 (1974), 113–138. On the relationship between ethnicity and political behavior in colonial New York City, see also Gary B. Nash, "The Transformation of Urban Politics 1700–1765," *Journal of American History*, 60 (1973), 605–32; Gary B. Nash, *The Urban Crucible: Social Change, Political Consciousness, and the Origins of the American Revolution* (Cambridge, Mass., 1979); John Murrin, "English Rights as Ethnic Aggression: The English Conquest, the Charter of Liberties of 1683, and Leisler's Rebellion in New York," in William Pencak and Conrad Edick Wright, eds., *Authority and Resistance in Early New York* (New York, 1988), 56–94; and Adrian Howe, "Accommodation and Retreat: Politics in Anglo-Dutch New York City, 1700–1760" (Ph.D. diss., University of Melbourne, 1984).

4. Oliver A. Rink, *Holland on the Hudson: An Economic and Social History of Dutch New York* (Ithaca and Cooperstown, N.Y., 1986); Cathy Matson, "Commerce After the Conquest: Dutch Traders and Goods in New York City 1664–1764," *de Halve Maen*, 59 (March 1987), 8–12; 60 (June 1987), 17–22.

5. Alice Morse Earle, *Colonial Days in Old New York* (New York, 1896); Esther Singleton, *Dutch New York* (New York, 1909); Esther Singleton, *Social New York Under the Georges 1714–1776: Houses, Streets and Country Homes, with Chapters on Fashions, Furniture, China, Plate and Manners* (New York, 1902). Also noteworthy is J. H. Innes's microcosmic study of New Amsterdam. Innes meticulously reconstructed the early community, supplying detailed biographical sketches of the town's culturally diverse populace. J. H. Innes, *New Amsterdam and Its People: Studies, Social and Topographical, of the Town Under Dutch and Early English Rule* (New York, 1902). Though written from a literary standpoint, Ellis Lawrence Raesly's *Portrait of New Netherland* (New York, 1945) also sheds light on cultural motifs in the Dutch colony's history.

6. Thomas Jefferson Wertenbaker, *The Founding of American Civilization: The Middle Colonies* (New York, 1938).

7. Michael Zuckerman, "Introduction: Puritans, Cavaliers and the Motley Middle," in Michael Zuckerman, ed., *Friends and Neighbors: Group Life in America's First Plural Society* (Philadelphia, 1982), 16. See also Douglas Greenberg, "The Middle Colonies in Recent American Historiography," *William and Mary Quarterly*, 3d ser., 36 (1979), 416–17.

8. Stephanie Grauman Wolf, *Urban Village: Population, Community, and Social Structure in Germantown, Pennsylvania, 1683–1800* (Princeton, 1976; Stephanie Grauman Wolf, "Hyphenated America: The Creation of an Eighteenth-Century German-American Culture," in Frank Trommler and Joseph McVeigh, eds., *America and the Germans: An Assessment of a Three-Hundred-Year History*, 2 vols.

(Philadelphia, 1985), 1:66–84; Laura Becker, "Diversity and Its Significance in an Eighteenth-Century Town," in Zuckerman, ed., *Friends and Neighbors*, 196–221; Ned C. Landsman, *Scotland and Its First American Colony, 1683–1765* (Princeton, 1985). See also Bernard Bailyn, *The Peopling of British North America: An Introduction* (New York, 1986).

9. Recent review essays help chart the vast historical and sociological literature on ethnic groups in the United States. See John Higham, "Current Trends in the Study of Ethnicity in the United States," *Journal of American Ethnic History*, 2 (1983), 5–15; Rudolph J. Vecoli, "Return to the Melting Pot: Ethnicity in the United States in the Eighties," *Journal of American Ethnic History*, 5 (1985), 7–20; John Ibson, "Virgin Land or Virgin Mary? Studying the Ethnicity of White Americans," *American Quarterly*, 33 (1981), 284–308; J. Milton Yinger, "Ethnicity," *Annual Review of Sociology*, 11 (1985), 151–80; and Charles Hirschmann, "America's Melting Pot Reconsidered," *Annual Review of Sociology*, 9 (1983), 397–423. See also Anya Peterson Royce, *Ethnic Identity: Stategies of Diversity* (Bloomington, Ind., 1982) and Werner Sollors, *Beyond Ethnicity: Consent and Descent in American Culture* (New York, 1986). The standard reference work on ethnic groups in the United States is Stephan Thernstrom, ed., *Harvard Encyclopedia of American Ethnic Groups* (Cambridge, Mass., and London, 1980).

10. David Evan Narrett, "Patterns of Inheritance in Colonial New York City, 1664–1775: A Study in the History of the Family" (Ph.D. diss., Cornell University, 1981); Linda Briggs Biemer, *Women and Property in Colonial New York: The Transition from Dutch to English Law, 1643–1727* (Ann Arbor, Mich., 1983); Ronald William Howard, "Education and Ethnicity in Colonial New York, 1664–1763: A Study in the Transmission of Culture in Early America" (Ph.D. diss., University of Tennessee, 1978).

11. For an extended discussion of the literature on the colonial Dutch, see Joyce D. Goodfriend, "The Historiography of the Dutch in Colonial America," in Eric Nooter and Patricia U. Bonomi, eds., *Colonial Dutch Studies: An Interdisciplinary Approach* (New York, 1988), 6–32.

12. Alice P. Kenney, *Stubborn for Liberty: The Dutch in New York* (Syracuse, N.Y., 1975); Gerald F. De Jong, *The Dutch in America, 1609–1974* (Boston, 1975); Rink, *Holland on the Hudson*; Nooter and Bonomi, eds., *Colonial Dutch Studies*; Roderic H. Blackburn and Ruth Piwonka et al., *Remembrance of Patria: Dutch Arts and Culture in Colonial America 1609–1776* (Albany, 1988). See also *New Netherland Studies: An Inventory of Current Research and Approaches*, in *Bulletin KNOB* 84, nos. 2 and 3 (June 1985), 46–181; and Roderic H. Blackburn and Nancy A. Kelley, eds., *New World Dutch Studies: Dutch Arts and Culture in Colonial America 1609–1776* (Albany, N.Y., 1987). The work of the New Netherland Project, based at the New York State Library in Albany, in translating Dutch documents and disseminating research on the colonial Dutch deserves special mention in this connection.

13. Jon Butler, *The Huguenots in America: A Refugee People in New World Society* (Cambridge, Mass., and London, 1983); David de Sola Pool, *Portraits Etched in Stone: Early Jewish Settlers, 1682–1831* (New York, 1952); David and Tamar de Sola Pool, *An Old Faith in the New World: Portrait of Shearith Israel, 1654–1954* (New York, 1955).

14. Thomas J. Davis, "Slavery in Colonial New York City" (Ph.D. diss., Columbia University, 1974); Vivian L. Kruger, "Born to Run: The Slave Family in Early New York, 1626–1827" (Ph.D. diss., Columbia University, 1985); Joyce D. Goodfriend, "Burghers and Blacks: The Evolution of a Slave Society at New Amsterdam," *New York History*, 59 (1978), 125–44. See also Edgar J. McManus, *A History of Negro Slavery in New York* (Syracuse, N.Y., 1966).

15. D. W. Meinig, *The Shaping of America: A Geographical Perspective on 500 Years of History* (New Haven and London, 1986), vol. 1, *Atlantic America, 1492–1800*, 225.

16. Randall Balmer, *A Perfect Babel of Confusion: Dutch Religion and English Culture in the Middle Colonies* (New York, 1989); Richard W. Pointer, *Protestant Pluralism and the New York Experience: A Study of Eighteenth-Century Religious Diversity* (Bloomington and Indianapolis, 1988).

17. Joyce D. Goodfriend, "The Social Dimensions of Congregational Life in Colonial New York City," *William and Mary Quarterly*, 3d ser., 46 (1989), 252–78. See also Laura L. Becker, "Ethnicity and Religion," in Charles H. Lippy and Peter Williams, eds., *Encyclopedia of the American Religious Experience: Studies of Traditions and Movements*, 3 vols. (New York, 1988), 3:1477–91; and Harold J. Abramson, "Religion," in Thernstrom, ed., *Harvard Encyclopedia of American Ethnic Groups*, 869–75.

18. Archdeacon, *New York City 1664–1710*. See also Thomas J. Archdeacon, "The Age of Leisler—New York City, 1689–1710: A Social and Demographic Interpretation," in Jacob Judd and Irwin H. Polishook, eds., *Aspects of Early New York Society and Politics* (Tarrytown, N.Y., 1974), 68–82; Bruce Martin Wilkenfeld, *The Social and Economic Structure of the City of New York 1695–1796* (New York, 1978). Archdeacon's book is confined to the first half century of the city's history, while Wilkenfeld's spans the years 1695 to 1796.

On the pace of social and cultural change see also Michael Kammen, *Colonial New York: A History* (New York, 1975).

19. The term "charter group" is used in T. H. Breen, "Creative Adaptations: Peoples and Cultures," in Jack P. Greene and J. R. Pole, eds., *Colonial British America: Essays in the New History of the Early Modern Era* (Baltimore and London, 1984), 204–5.

20. The term "Batavianization" comes from Murrin, "English Rights as Ethnic Aggression."

CHAPTER ONE
NEW AMSTERDAM BECOMES NEW YORK CITY

1. Evarts B. Greene and Virginia D. Harrington, *American Population Before the Federal Census of 1790* (New York, 1932; reprinted 1966), 93.

2. Oliver A. Rink, *Holland on the Hudson: An Economic and Social History of Dutch New York* (Ithaca and Cooperstown, N.Y., 1986); *The Birth of New York: Nieuw Amsterdam 1624–1664* (exhibition catalogue: New York, Amsterdam, 1982; 1983); Thomas J. Condon, *New York Beginnings: The Commercial Origins of New Netherland* (New York, 1968). Older studies include William R. Shepherd,

The Story of New Amsterdam (New York, 1926); Ellis Lawrence Raesly, *Portrait of New Netherland* (New York, 1945); Mariana Griswold van Rensselaer, *History of the City of New York in the Seventeenth Century*, 2 vols. (New York, 1909); J. H. Innes, *New Amsterdam and Its People: Studies, Social and Topographical, of the Town Under Dutch and Early English Rule* (New York, 1902); Edmund B. O'Callaghan, *History of New Netherland*, 2d ed., 2 vols. (New York, 1855); and John Romeyn Brodhead, *History of the State of New York*, 2 vols. (New York, 1853–1871).

3. See W. J. van Hoboken, "The Dutch West India Company: The Political Background of Its Rise and Decline," in J. H. Bromley and E. H. Kossman, eds., *Britain and the Netherlands: Papers Delivered to the Oxford-Netherlands Historical Conference 1959* (London, 1960), 41–61; P. C. Emmer, "The West India Company, 1621–1691: Dutch or Atlantic," in Leonard Blusse and Femme Gaastra, eds., *Companies and Trade: Essays on Overseas Trading Companies during the Ancien Regime* (Leiden, 1981), 71–95; Van Cleaf Bachman, *Peltries or Plantations: The Economic Policies of the Dutch West India Company in New Netherland, 1623–1639* (Baltimore, 1969); D. W. Davies, *A Primer of Dutch Seventeenth Century Overseas Trade* (The Hague, 1961); Charles R. Boxer, *The Dutch Seaborne Empire: 1600–1800* (New York, 1965); Cornelis C. H. Goslinga, *The Dutch in the Caribbean and on the Wild Coast 1580–1680* (Assen, the Netherlands, 1971); Jonathan I. Israel, *Dutch Primacy in World Trade, 1585–1740* (New York, 1989).

4. Harold C. Syrett, "Private Enterprise in New Amsterdam," *William and Mary Quarterly*, 3d ser., 11 (1954), 536–50. See also Rink, *Holland on the Hudson*.

5. Langdon G. Wright, "Local Government and Central Authority in New Netherland," *New-York Historical Society Quarterly*, 57 (1973), 7–29; Philip L. White, "Municipal Government Comes to Manhattan, " *New-York Historical Society Quarterly*, 37 (1953), 146–57.

6. Charles H. Wilson, *Profit and Power: A Study of England and the Dutch Wars* (London, 1957).

7. Allen W. Trelease, *Indian Affairs in Colonial New York: The Seventeenth Century* (Ithaca, N. Y., 1960); Ronald D. Cohen, "The Hartford Treaty of 1650: Anglo-Dutch Cooperation in the Seventeenth Century," *New-York Historical Society Quarterly*, 53 (1969), 311–32.

8. Rink, *Holland on the Hudson*. See also Ernst van den Boogaart, "The Servant Migration to New Netherland, 1624–1664," in P. C. Emmer, ed., *Colonialism and Migration: Indentured Labour Before and After Slavery* (Dordrecht, 1986), 55–81.

9. Simon Schama, *The Embarrassment of Riches: An Interpretation of Dutch Culture in the Golden Age* (New York, 1987); J. L. Price, *Culture and Society in the Dutch Republic During the 17th Century* (New York, 1974); Charles Wilson, *The Dutch Republic and the Civilisation of the Seventeenth Century* (New York, 1968); K. H. D. Haley, *The Dutch in the Seventeenth Century* (London, 1972); Paul Zumthor, *Daily Life in Rembrandt's Holland*, trans. Simon Watson Taylor (London, 1962; original French edition, 1959); J. H. Huizinga, *Dutch Civilisation in the Seventeenth Century and Other Essays* (London, 1968), 9–104 (this title essay was first published in 1941). See also Pieter Geyl, *The Netherlands in the Seventeenth Century*, 2d ed., 2 vols. (London, 1961–1964).

10. George L. Smith, *Religion and Trade in New Netherland: Dutch Origins and*

American Development (Ithaca, N.Y., 1973), and George L. Smith, "Guilders and Godliness: The Dutch Colonial Contribution to American Religious Pluralism," *Journal of Presbyterian History*, 47 (1969), 1–30.

11. In addition to the works cited in note 9, see John J. Murray, *Amsterdam in the Age of Rembrandt* (Norman, Okla., 1967) and Violet Barbour, *Capitalism in Amsterdam in the 17th Century* (Baltimore, 1950).

12. Rink, *Holland on the Hudson*, 233–35; Jacob R. Marcus, *The Colonial American Jew 1492–1776*, 3 vols. (Detroit, 1970), 1:215–48; 3:1418–22.

13. For an overview of the Dutch slave trade, see Johannes Menne Postma, *The Dutch in the Atlantic Slave Trade 1600–1815* (Cambridge, 1990). See also P. C. Emmer, "De Slavenhandel van en naar Nieuw Nederland," *Economisch en Sociaal-Historisch Jaerboek*, 35 (1972), 94–147.

14. On blacks in New Amsterdam, see Joyce D. Goodfriend, "Burghers and Blacks: The Evolution of a Slave Society at New Amsterdam," *New York History*, 59 (1978), 125–44, and Joyce D. Goodfriend, "Black Families in New Netherland," *Journal of the Afro-American Historical and Genealogical Society*, 5 (1984), 95–108.

15. Reginald Pelham Bolton, "New York City in Indian Possession," *Indian Notes and Monographs*, 2, no. 7 (New York, Museum of the American Indian, Heye Foundation, 1920), 238–39, 242–43, 272; Trelease, *Indian Affairs in Colonial New York*, 7–8. On Dutch attitudes toward the Indians, see Allen W. Trelease, "Dutch Treatment of the American Indian, with Particular Reference to New Netherland," in Howard Peckham and Charles Gibson, eds., *Attitudes of Colonial Powers Toward the American Indian* (Salt Lake City, 1969), 47–59.

16. On the Dutch Reformed church in New Netherland, see John Pershing Luidens, "The Americanization of the Dutch Reformed Church" (Ph.D. diss., University of Oklahoma, 1969); and Gerald Francis De Jong, *The Dutch Reformed Church in the American Colonies* (Grand Rapids, Mich., 1978).

17. On Megapolensis, see Gerald Francis De Jong, "Dominie Johannes Megapolensis: Minister to New Netherland," *New-York Historical Society Quarterly*, 52 (1968), 7–47. See also Gerald Francis De Jong, "The 'Ziekentroosters' or Comforters of the Sick in New Netherland," *New-York Historical Society Quarterly*, 54 (1970), 339–59.

18. Harry J. Kreider, *The Beginnings of Lutheranism in New York* (New York, 1949), 19–20, 22–23.

19. Kreider, *The Beginnings of Lutheranism in New York*, 25–30, 38–42.

20. "Letter from Hendrick Bosch to the Consistory at Amsterdam" (August 19, 1664), Arnold J. H. van Laer, trans., *The Lutheran Church in New York 1649–1772: Records in the Lutheran Church Archives at Amsterdam, Holland* (New York, 1946), 47–48. Though no estimate of the number of Lutherans in New Amsterdam exists, a 1659 petition of the Lutherans in New Netherland claimed that "at Fort Orange there are from 70 to 80 families, here at the Manhatans and on Long Island also fully that many, including permanent residents and mechanics, but mostly farmers." "Petition of the Lutherans in New Netherland to the Directors of the West India Company" (May 20, 1659), Van Laer, trans., *The Lutheran Church in New York*, 39.

21. Marcus, *The Colonial American Jew*, 1:215–43.

22. Ibid., 1:231–34. For background on Jews in Europe during this era, see Jonathan I. Israel, *European Jewry in the Age of Mercantilism 1550–1750* (Oxford, 1985).

23. Joyce D. Goodfriend, "The Historiography of the Dutch in Colonial America," in Eric Nooter and Patricia U. Bonomi, eds., *Colonial Dutch Studies: An Interdisciplinary Approach* (New York, 1988), 6–32. See also Alice P. Kenney, *Stubborn for Liberty: The Dutch in New York* (Syracuse, N.Y., 1975); and Gerald F. De Jong, *The Dutch in America, 1609–1974* (Boston, 1975).

24. On the transfer of power to the English, see Robert C. Ritchie, *The Duke's Province: A Study of New York Politics and Society, 1664–1691* (Chapel Hill, N.C., 1977).

25. See Lawrence Stone, "Prosopography," *Daedalus* (Winter 1971), 46–79, for a related method.

26. The inhabitants described themselves as "about fifteen hundred innocent souls, only two hundred and fifty of whom are capable of bearing arms." "Remonstrance of the People of New Netherland to the Director-General and Council" (September 5, 1664), *Doc. Rel.* 2:248.

27. This estimate of the number of blacks in New Amsterdam is based on information presented in Goodfriend, "Burghers and Blacks."

28. "A cohort may be defined as the aggregate of individuals (within some population definition) who experienced the same event within the same time interval." Norman B. Ryder, "The Cohort as a Concept in the Study of Social Change," *American Sociological Review*, 30 (1965), 845.

29. "Remonstrance of the People of New Netherland to the Director-General and Council" (September 5, 1664), *Doc. Rel.*, 2:240–50; "Names of the Dutch Who Swore Allegiance After the Surrender of New York" (October 21, 22, 24, 26, 1664), *Doc. Rel.*, 2:74–77; *RNA*, 5:220–25.

30. Seventy persons appeared on all three lists; 108 persons were on any two of the lists; and 172 persons appeared on one list only.

31. Many different sources were consulted to compile data on members of the conquest cohort. Among the most important were government and church records, wills, and genealogies.

32. Oliver A. Rink, "The People of New Netherland: Notes on Non-English Immigration to New York in the Seventeenth Century," *New York History*, 62 (1981), 5–42; David Steven Cohen, "How Dutch Were the Dutch of New Netherland?" *New York History*, 62 (1981), 43–60.

33. Cohen, "How Dutch Were the Dutch of New Netherland?" 49, 60.

34. Jan de Vries, "The Population and Economy of the Preindustrial Netherlands," *Journal of Interdisciplinary History*, 15 (1985), 667–68.

35. Howard S. F. Randolph, "The Ellsworth Family of New York City," *New York Genealogical and Biographical Record*, 64 (1933), 154–66, 255–67.

36. On this point, see John Murrin, "English Rights as Ethnic Aggression: The English Conquest, the Charter of Liberties of 1683, and Leisler's Rebellion in New York," in William Pencak and Conrad Edick Wright, eds., *Authority and Resistance in Early New York* (New York, 1988), 58.

37. Quoted in Kreider, *The Beginnings of Lutheranism in New York*, 21.

38. Syrett, "Private Enterprise in New Amsterdam"; Rink, *Holland on the*

Hudson; David M. Riker, "Govert Loockermans: Free Merchant of New Amsterdam," *de Halve Maen*, 62, no. 3 (September 1989), 4–10. See also Philip L. White, *The Beekmans of New York in Politics and Commerce 1647–1877* (New York, 1956).

39. Classifying the data on the occupations of the conquest cohort in terms of the functional categories proposed by Jacob Price in his study of American port towns in the eighteenth century reveals that 17 percent of the cohort was employed in the governmental sector, 46 percent in the service sector, 15 percent in the industrial sector, and 22 percent in the maritime sector. The striking feature of this occupational distribution is the high proportion of men employed by the government. See Jacob M. Price, "Economic Function and the Growth of American Port Towns in the Eighteenth Century," *Perspectives in American History*, 8 (1974), 123–86.

40. The statistics on slave ownership are from Goodfriend, "Burghers and Blacks," 142–43.

CHAPTER TWO
THE SECOND GENERATION

1. "The Mesier Family of New Amsterdam and Wappingers Falls, N.Y.," *New York Genealogical and Biographical Record*, 58 (1927), 172–80.

2. Donald G. Shomette and Robert D. Haslach, *Raid on America: The Dutch Naval Campaign of 1672–1674* (Columbia, S.C., 1988).

3. "Rev. William van Nieuwenhuysen to the Classis of Amsterdam" (July 26, 1674), *Ecc. Rec.*, 1:653–54.

4. "Passengers in the Ship *Unity*," *New York Colonial Records, General Entries* (Albany, 1899), vol. 1, *1664–65*, 139–40.

5. "A Proclamation Enjoyning All Psons That Have Been Inhabitants Here Six Months, Having A Mind To Transport Themselves For Carolina, Or Any of His Maties New Plantacons To Enter Their Names at Ye Secretaryes Office in Time, & Take Thence Their Pass-Portes" (November 9, 1671), *Doc. Rel.*, 14:658; "Lyst of Ye Persons Who Have Had Passes to Goe For Porte Royall in Carolina in the Ships Blessing, Charles & Phoenix; All Bearing Date About ye 17th, 18th, 19th & 20th Dayes of November 1671, Ye Ships Setting Sayle Prsently After," *Doc. Rel.*, 14:658–59.

6. "Extracts of letters from Carolina in Locke's handwriting" (November 1671), *Calendar of State Papers, Colonial, America and West Indies, 1669–1674*, 277–80; "Locke from Carolina" (January 1672), Ibid., 324–35. See also Bertus Harry Wabeke, *Dutch Migration to North America 1624–1860* (New York, 1944), 69.

7. "English Summaries and translations of notarial documents in the Gemeente Archief at Amsterdam pertaining [to] North America" (Numbers N.l–N.743), Gemeente Archief, Amsterdam, Notariele Archieven (microfilm), Historical Documents Collection, Queens College, N.350.

8. *RNA*, 6:177.

9. "A Proclamation for the Observing a Genrll day of Humiliacon throughout his R. Highnes Territoryes" (September 4, 1668), Victor Hugo Paltsits, ed., *Min-*

utes of the Executive Council of the Province of New York, Administration of Francis Lovelace 1668–1673, 2 vols. (Albany, 1910), 1:191–92; John Duffy, A History of Public Health in New York City 1625–1866 (New York, 1968), 34–36. The 1668 outbreak was identified as dysentery by the Rev. Samuel Megapolensis. "Rev. Samuel Megapolensis to a Friend" (New York, September 7, 1668), Ecc. Rec., 1:597.

10. "Samuel Maverick to Colonel Richard Nicolls" (New York, October 15, 1669), Doc. Rel., 3:185.

11. RNA, 6:247–48.

12. Margareta de Riemer Steenwyck also noted in her Bible "on the 21st of Nov. 1684 died (Cor)nelius Steenwijck (58 years 8 months and 5 days old) unto his Lord, and lies buried with (his) daughter and 6 sons in New York in the church." "The De Riemer Family Bible Record," New York Genealogical and Biographical Record, 63 (1932), 289.

13. In order to avoid duplication of data, those cohort sons who were cohort members themselves have been excluded from the analysis of marriages presented here.

14. For a summary of findings on the marriage ages of men in the seventeenth- and eighteenth-century colonies, see James M. Gallman, "Determinants of Age at Marriage in Colonial Perquimans County, North Carolina," William and Mary Quarterly, 3d ser., 39 (1982), 181.

15. CNYHS for the Year 1892, 143–44. Will abstracts have been checked against the original wills whenever possible. On the Ten Eyck family, see Henry Waterman George, "The Ten Eyck Family in New York," New York Genealogical and Biographical Record, 63 (1932), 152–65, 269–85, 321–34. On inheritance practices in New York, see David Evan Narrett, "Patterns of Inheritance in Colonial New York City, 1664–1775: A Study in the History of the Family" (Ph.D. diss., Cornell University, 1981).

16. CNYHS for the Year 1892, 98. On the Van Cortlandt family, see L. Effingham DeForest, The Van Cortlandt Family (New York, 1930).

17. CNYHS for the Year 1892, 296. In her 1692 will, Sara Roeloffse Kierstede offered her bake house to her son, Lucas Kierstede (CNYHS for the Year 1892, 225–27). Lucas became a baker, the only one of surgeon Hans Kierstede's sons not to follow in his father's footsteps. See David M. Riker, "Surgeon Hans Kierstede of New Amsterdam," de Halve Maen, 57, no. 3 (August 1983), 11–13, 24; and Howard S. F. Randolph, "The Kierstede Family," New York Genealogical and Biographical Record, 65 (1934), 224–33; 329–38.

18. CNYHS for the Year 1893, 409.

19. Thirteen cohort sons remained single or at least there is no trace of their marriages. Sons of three prominent cohort members were unmarried: Oloff (Oliver), the son of Stephanus van Cortlandt; Adolphus, the son of Frederick Philipse; and Jacob Leisler, Jr.

20. Howard S. F. Randolph, "Jacob Boelen, Goldsmith, of New York and His Family Circle," New York Genealogical and Biographical Record, 72 (1941), 265–94.

21. See the discussion of these men in chapter 8.

22. It is likely that several more women were married to British-born men.

They are among the 20 cohort daughters whose husbands' names are known, but not their birthplaces. Only seven of the 190 cohort daughters identified do not appear to have married. A few may have married outside the city and some died young. Eleven cohort daughters married widowers.

23. Of these 36 men, seven were born on Long Island, 23 in either Albany, Kingston, or Schenectady, four in New Jersey, and two in a former Dutch settlement in New England.

24. Jan de Vries, "The Population and Economy of the Preindustrial Netherlands," *Journal of Interdisciplinary History*, 15 (1985), 665.

25. On the marriage ages of women in the seventeenth- and eighteenth-century colonies, see Gallman, "Determinants of Age at Marriage in Colonial Perquimans County, North Carolina," 181.

26. On the Boelen family, see Randolph, "Jacob Boelen, Goldsmith, of New York."

27. *CNYHS for the Year 1902*, 86–87.

28. On the Hellakers family, see Gwenn F. Epperson, "Jacob Hellekers Alias Swart and Some of His Descendants," *New York Genealogical and Biographical Record*, 121 (1990), 13–18.

29. *CNYHS for the Year 1892*, 342.

CHAPTER THREE
NEWCOMERS IN SEVENTEENTH-CENTURY NEW YORK CITY

1. Marcus Lee Hansen, *The Atlantic Migration 1607–1860* (New York, 1961; originally published 1940), 35–43; Emberson Edward Proper, *Colonial Immigration Laws: A Study of the Regulation of Immigration by the English Colonies in America* (New York, 1900), 39.

2. For background on early Dutch settlers in areas outside New York colony, see Thomas Jefferson Wertenbaker, *The Founding of American Civilization: The Middle Colonies* (New York, 1938; reprinted 1963), 29–118; Adrian C. Leiby, *The Early Dutch and Swedish Settlers of New Jersey* (Princeton, 1964); C. A. Weslager, *Dutch Explorers, Traders and Settlers in the Delaware Valley (1609–1674)* (Philadelphia, 1961); Christopher Ward, *The Dutch and Swedes on the Delaware, 1609–64* (Philadelphia, 1930); Jeanette Eckman, "Life Among the Early Dutch at New Castle," *Delaware History*, 4 (1951), 246–302.

3. At the end of 1684, the membership records of the New York City Dutch Reformed Church began to detail systematically the provenance of new members. Those adult men and women who were not admitted into the church on the basis of a confession of faith were denoted in the church rolls as possessing a certificate of attestation from their former church. For example, the first entry for December 5, 1684, is "Catharina de Peyster, wife of Abraham de Peyster." Next to her name is inscribed "met attestatie van Amsterdam," indicating that she was admitted into the New York City church by means of a certificate testifying to her membership in good standing in a church in Amsterdam. For the church membership records of the New York City Dutch Reformed Church between 1649 and 1715, see "Records of the Reformed Dutch Church in the City of New York—Church Members' List," *New York Genealogical and Biographical Record*, 9 (1878), 38–45, 72–79, 140–47, 161–68; 59 (1928), 69–76, 158–65, 259–66, 372–79.

4. Bertus Harry Wabeke, *Dutch Migration to North America 1624–1860* (New York, 1944), 61, 69–70; American Council of Learned Societies, "Report of Committee on Linguistic and National Stocks in the Population of the United States," in American Historical Association, *Annual Report: 1931*, 3 vols. (Washington, D.C, 1932), 1:363–70.

5. Gov. Thomas Dongan noted in 1687 that within the preceding seven years "from Holland are come several Dutch familys." "Governor Dongan's Report to the Committee of Trade on the Province of New-York" (February 22, 1687), *DHNY*, 1:103.

6. Ties between Dutch residents of New York City and correspondents in the Netherlands are documented in "English Summaries and translations of notarial documents in the Gemeente Archief at Amsterdam pertaining [to] North America," Gemeente Archief, Amsterdam, Notariele Archieven (microfilm).

7. "Number of Inhabitants in Albany, 1689," *Doc. Rel.*, 4: 420–21; Hansen, *The Atlantic Migration*, 43; Stella H. Sutherland, *Population Distribution in Colonial America* (New York, 1936), 76. See also Sung Bok Kim, *Landlord and Tenant in Colonial New York: Manorial Society, 1664–1775* (Chapel Hill, N.C., 1978), 57–58.

8. American Council of Learned Societies Report, *AHA Annual Report: 1931*, 1:370–71; 372; Sutherland, *Population Distribution in Colonial America*, 75.

9. On the Dutch in the West Indies see Cornelis C. H. Goslinga, *The Dutch in the Caribbean and on the Wild Coast 1580–1680* (Assen, the Netherlands, 1971), and Cornelis C. H. Goslinga, *The Dutch in the Caribbean and in the Guianas, 1680–1791* (Assen/Maastricht, the Netherlands, 1985).

10. Jacob R. Marcus, *The Colonial American Jew 1492–1776*, 3 vols. (Detroit, 1970), 1:245–48 (quote on 248). On Asser Levy, see also Harriet (Mott) Stryker-Rodda, "Asser Levy," *New York Genealogical and Biographical Record*, 102 (1971), 129–35, 240–47; and Malcolm L. Stern, "Asser Levy—A New Look at Our Jewish Founding Father," *American Jewish Archives*, 26 (1974), 66–77.

11. Marcus, *The Colonial American Jew*, 1:244–45, 286–87, 306.

12. Ibid., 1:307; "Answers of Governor Andros to Enquries About New York" 1678, *Doc. Rel.*, 3:262. On the Jews in seventeenth-century New York City, see also Jacob Rader Marcus, *Early American Jewry: The Jews of New York, New England and Candada 1649–1794*, 2 vols. (Philadelphia, 1951), 1:34–54.

13. Marcus, *The Colonial American Jew*, 1:307.

14. Ibid., 1:308.

15. Ibid., 1:307.

16. Jon Butler, *The Huguenots in America: A Refugee People in New World Society* (Cambridge, Mass., 1983), 1.

17. Warren C. Scoville, *The Persecution of the Huguenots and French Economic Development 1680–1720* (Berkeley, 1960), 122–28.

18. Butler, *The Huguenots in America*, 49. See also American Council of Learned Societies Report, Annex B: "The Minor Stocks in the American Population of 1790," by Marcus L. Hansen (ch. 3, "The French") *AHA Annual Report: 1931*, 1:381–82.

19. Wesley Frank Craven, *The Colonies in Transition 1660–1713* (New York, 1968), 289. An official count reported 438 Huguenots in South Carolina in 1699 (cited in Converse D. Clowse, *Economic Beginnings in Colonial South Carolina 1670–1730* [Columbia, S.C., 1971]), 74.

20. See chapter 4 for a discussion of New York City's population in the seventeenth century.

21. John A. F. Maynard, *The Huguenot Church of New York: A History of the French Church of Saint Esprit* (New York, 1938), 75. The 1698 census of the town of New Rochelle, populated mainly by Huguenots at this time, along with their Negro slaves and servants, enumerates 230 names, of which 43 are labeled as Negroes. The remaining 187 persons were primarily recent Huguenot refugees to New York. "The Census of 1698 for Mamaroneck, Morrisania, and New Rochelle, Westchester County, New York," *New York Genealogical and Biographical Record*, 59, (1928), 105–7. See also *Records of the Town of New Rochelle, 1699–1828*, transcribed, translated, and published by Jeanne A. Forbes (New Rochelle, N.Y., 1916). A brief overview of French settlers in New York colony is found in Sutherland, *Population Distribution in Colonial America*, 84–85.

22. See chapter 5.

23. "M. De Denonville to the Minister" (Quebec, November 16, 1686), *DHNY*, 1:139.

24. "Gov. Dongan's Report on the Province of New York, 1687," *DHNY*, 1:103. In 1688, a Dutch clergyman on Long Island apprised the Classis of Amsterdam that "the French congregation increases by daily arrivals from Carolina, the Carribean Islands and Europe." "Rev. Rudolphus Varick to the Classis of Amsterdam" (September 30, 1688), *Ecc. Rec.*, 2:956. The minister of the Dutch church in New York City also informed the Amsterdam Classis of the arrival of many French exiles in 1688 but failed to specify their places of origin. "Rev. Henry Selyns to the Classis of Amsterdam" (New York, October 10, 1688), *Ecc. Rec.*, 2:959. A Huguenot residing in England in 1689 informed the Bishop of London that "200 French [Protestant] families about New York . . . will be put to the torture if the french takes itt. They came out of Caroline St. Christophes and London." "Peter Reverdye to the Bishop of London" (December 30, 1689, from the downs), *Doc. Rel.*, 3:650–51. I have found almost no evidence of Huguenot emigration from South Carolina to New York to support these observations.

25. Charles W. Baird, *History of the Huguenot Emigration to America*, 2 vols. (New York, 1885), 1:231–33.

26. See William A. Shaw, ed., *Publications of the Huguenot Society of London*, vol. 18, *Letters of Denization and Acts of Naturalization for Aliens in England and Ireland, 1603–1700* (Lymington, 1911), and vol. 27, *Letters of Denization and Acts of Naturalization for Aliens in England and Ireland, 1701–1800* (Manchester, 1923). Denizations and petitions for naturalization in New York colony are calendared in E. B. O'Callaghan, ed., *Calendar of Historical Manuscripts in the Office of the Secretary of State, Albany, New York*, 2 vols. (Albany, 1865–66), vol. 2, *English Manuscripts, 1664–1776*. For examples of denizations granted, see *CEM*, 140, 141, 143, 144, 145, 146. For a petition for naturalization, see *CEM*, 167. Charles W. Baird cites a document that has not been published: "An Act for the naturalizing of Daniell Duchemin and others, September 27, 1687. From (unpublished MSS.) 'Statutes at Large of New York: 1664–1691. From Original Records and Authentic Manuscripts.' Kindly communicated to me by Geo. H. Moore, LL.D." (Baird, *History of the Huguenot Emigration to America*, 1:232). Many of the original documents pertaining to the denization and naturalization of Huguenot immigrants

can be found in the New York Colonial Manuscripts and the Secretary of State Papers in the New York State Archives, Albany, New York. See also Kenneth Scott and Kenn Stryker-Rodda, *Denizations, Naturalizations, and Oaths of Allegiance in Colonial New York* (Baltimore, 1975), and James H. Kettner, *The Development of American Citizenship, 1608–1870* (Chapel Hill, N.C., 1978).

27. *Publications of the Huguenot Society of London*, vol. 49, A. P. Hands and Irene Scouloudi, eds., *French Protestant Refugees Relieved Through the Threadneedle Street Church, London 1681–1687* (London, 1971). On the Huguenots in England, see also Robin D. Gwynn, *Huguenot Heritage: The History and Contributions of the Huguenots in Britain* (London, 1985); Robin D. Gwynn, "The Arrival of Huguenot Refugees in England 1680–1705," *Proceedings* of the Huguenot Society of London, 21 (1969) 366–73; Robin D. Gwynn, "The Distribution of Huguenot Refugees in England," *Proceedings* of the Huguenot Society of London, 21 (1970), 404–36; and W. Cunningham, *Alien Immigrants to England*, 2d ed., (New York 1969; originally published 1897), 223–49.

28. Other sources consulted in preparing this profile of New York City's Huguenots include Rev. Alfred V. Wittmeyer, ed., "Registers of the births, marriages and deaths of the 'Eglise Françoise à la Nouvelle York,' from 1688–1804; and historical documents relating to the French protestants in N.Y. during the same period," Huguenot Society of America, *Collections*, vol. 1 (New York, 1886); "Records of the French Church du St. Esprit, New York City, 1689–1710," and "Accounts of Collections and expenditures March 1693–April 1699 kept by Gabriel Le Boyteulx," MSS (photostatic copies), New-York Historical Society; "Records of the French Church at New Rochelle, N.Y.," *New-York Historical Society Quarterly*, 1 (1917) 77–81; "The List of the Towne of New Rochelle & c. XBR [December] 9th 1710," *DHNY*, 3:571–72; "Difficulties in the French Church," *DHNY*, 3:281–90; Gilbert Chinard, *Les Refugies Huguenots en Amerique* (Paris, 1925); Lucien J. Fosdick, *The French Blood in America* (New York, 1906); *Catalogue or Bibliography of the Library of the Huguenot Society of America*, compiled by Julia P. M. Morand, (New York, 2d ed., 1920; reprinted Baltimore, 1971); David Duncan Wallace, *The Life of Henry Laurens* (New York, 1915); George Adams Boyd, *Elias Boudinot: Patriot and Statesman 1740–1821* (Princeton, 1952); Sheldon S. Cohen, "Elias Neau, Instructor to New York's Slaves," *New-York Historical Society Quarterly*, 55 (1971), 7–27; William A. Bultmann, "The S.P.G. and the French Huguenots in Colonial America," *Historical Magazine of the Protestant Episcopal Church*, 20 (1951), 156–72; Arthur Henry Hirsch, *The Huguenots of Colonial South Carolina* (Durham, N.C., 1928).

29. On the Huguenots in Boston, see Baird, *History of the Huguenot Emigration to America*, 2:188–254; and Butler, *The Huguenots in America*, 71–90.

30. On the Huguenots in Rhode Island, see Baird, *History of the Huguenot Emigration to America*, 2:291–329; Elisha R. Potter, *Memoir Concerning the French Settlements and French Settlers in the Colony of Rhode Island* (Baltimore, 1968; originally published as *Rhode Island Historical Tract* No. 5, Providence, 1879); "Records of the French Church at Narragansett, 1686–1691," *New York Genealogical and Biographical Record*, 70 (1939), 236–41, 359–65; 71 (1940), 51–61.

31. "Further Complant and Remonstrance of Dr. Ayrault" (Greenwich [R.I.], August 20, 1705), printed in Potter, *Memoir Concerning the French Settlements and French Settlers in the Colony of Rhode Island*, 40.

32. On Auguste Jay, see Richard Morris, ed., *John Jay: The Making of a Revolutionary; Unpublished Papers 1745–1780* (New York, 1975), 29–30; Frank Monaghan, *John Jay* (New York, 1935), 13–22.

33. For a discussion of areas of Protestant strength in France, see Scoville, *The Persecution of the Huguenots*, 8–12.

34. On the background of English emigration in the seventeenth century see Mildred Campbell, "'Of People either too Few or too Many': The Conflict of Opinion on Population and Its Relation to Emigration," in William Aiken and Basil Henning, eds., *Conflict in Stuart England: Essays in Honour of Wallace Notestein* (London, 1960), 169–201. For a portrait of the city in 1676, see Thomas J. Archdeacon, "Anglo-Dutch New York, 1676," in Milton M. Klein, ed., *New York: The Centennial Years 1676–1976* (Port Washington, N.Y., 1976), 11–39.

35. "Colonel Nicolls to Lord Arlington: April 9, 1666, New Yorke," *Doc. Rel.*, 3:114.

36. *Doc. Rel.*, 3:407; William P. McDermott, "Susannah Vaughton: Caught in the Web of 17th Century Politics?" Dutchess County Historical Society *Year Book*, 66 (1981), 77–90.

37. John Duffy, *A History of Public Health in New York City 1625–1866* (New York, 1968), 34–35, and John Duffy, *Epidemics in Colonial America* (Baton Rouge, 1953), 73. On the 1689 illness, see note 39 below.

38. Bartlett Burleigh James and J. Franklin Jameson, eds., *Journal of Jasper Danckaerts 1679–1680* (New York, 1913), 239.

39. "Stephanus van Cortlandt to Maria van Rensselaer, N: Jorcke" (January 21, 1689). A. J. F. van Laer, trans. and ed., *Correspondence of Maria van Rensselaer 1669–1689* (Albany, 1935), 188.

40. Charles Lodwick, "New York in 1692," *CNYHS*, 2d ser., vol. 2, part 1 (New York, 1848), 248.

41. Richard Hyer, "Walter Hyer from Kingston, Surrey, and Some of His Descendants," *New York Genealogical and Biographical Record*, 74 (1943), 1–11.

42. On the influx of men representing London mercantile interests after 1674, see Robert C. Ritchie, *The Duke's Province: A Study of New York Politics and Society, 1664–1691* (Chapel Hill, 1977), 114–17.

43. "Governor Dongan's Report to the Committee of Trade on the Province of New-York" (February 22, 1687), *DHNY*, 1:103.

44. "Churchwardens and Vestry of Trinity Church, New-York, to Archbishop Tenison" (New York, May 22, 1699), *Doc. Rel.*, 4:526.

45. See Stanley McCrory Pargellis, "The Four Independent Companies of New York," in *Essays in Colonial History Presented to Charles McLean Andrews by his Students* (New Haven, 1931), 96–123; and Lawrence H. Leder, ed., "'Dam'me Don't Stir a Man': Trial of New York Mutineers in 1700," *New-York Historical Society Quarterly*, 42 (July 1958), 261–83.

46. On English lawyers in seventeenth-century New York City, see Paul M. Hamlin, *Legal Education in Colonial New York* (New York, 1970; originally published 1939).

47. Abbot Emerson Smith, *Colonists in Bondage: White Servitude and Convict Labor in America 1607–1776* (Chapel Hill, N.C., 1947), 317; Samuel McKee, Jr., *Labor in Colonial New York, 1664–1776* (New York, 1935), 93.

48. See *Bristol and America: A Record of the First Settlers in the Colonies of North America 1654–1685* (London, n.d.). Gordon Ireland, "Servants to Foreign Plantations from Bristol England, 1654–1686," *New York Genealogical and Biographical Record*, 89 (1948), 65–75, has located three servants on the "Bristol and America" list as headed for New York, all in 1678. For a breakdown of the Bristol and America list according to servants' destinations, see Richard Dunn, *Sugar and Slaves: The Rise of the Planter Class in the English West Indies, 1642–1713* (Chapel Hill, N.C., 1972; reprinted New York, 1973), 70. Other lists examined: Cregoe D. P. Nicholson, "Some Early Emigrants to America," *The Genealogists Magazine*, 12 (1955–1958), 11–14, 48–53, 89–92, 122–25, 157–62, 191–96, 228–33, 269–72, 303–09, 340–44, 379–82, 404–06, 440–42, 478–82, 516–20, 552–55, 13 (1959–1961), 10–13, 46–50, 78–80, 105–08, 145–58, 175–79, 209–12, 236. Nicholson states that these are 758 indentures recorded in 1683 and 1684, found in the Middlesex Guildhall, Westminster, and that the emigrants were bound for Maryland, Virginia, Barbados, and Jamaica. Also, *A List of Emigrants to America 1682–1692*, transcribed from the original records at the City of London Record office by Michael Ghirelli (Baltimore, 1968). The names on this list are primarily those of indentured servants and were recorded in the Lord Mayor's Waiting Books. A few passengers who paid for their own transport are included. Out of about 960 emigrants, nine persons destined for New York were identified. Also, *List of Emigrants to America from Liverpool 1697–1707* (Boston, 1913). This document lists servants destined for Virginia, Maryland, Pennsylvania, New England, and the West Indies. P. William Filby, ed., *Passenger and Immigration Lists Bibliography 1538–1900* (Detroit, 1981) is the basic guide to the various compilations of emigrants to America.

49. John Camden Hotten, ed., *The Original Lists of Persons of Quality . . . and Others Who Went from Great Britain to the American Plantations, 1600–1700* (London, 1874), 347–508. See Dunn, *Sugar and Slaves*, 111, for a breakdown of the destinations of the 593 persons who left Barbados in 1679.

50. Peter R. Christoph and Florence A. Christoph, eds., *The Andros Papers 1677–1678: Files of the Provincial Secretary of New York During the Administration of Governor Sir Edmund Andros 1674–1680* (Syracuse, N.Y., 1990), 358–59.

51. "Indentures of Apprenticeship Feb. 9th. 1694–5 to Jan. 29th. 1707–8," *CNYHS for the Year 1885*, 571–72.

52. "Names of the Roman Catholics in the City of New-York" (June 1696), *Doc. Rel.*, 4:166; "Governor Fletcher to the Lords of Trade" (New York, June 10, 1696), *Doc. Rel.*, 4:160; John Tracy Ellis, *Catholics in Colonial America* (Baltimore, 1965), 360–70. See also Thomas F. O'Connor, "A Jesuit School in Seventeenth Century New York," *Mid-America: An Historical Review*, 3 (1942), 265–68.

53. Leonard J. Trinterud, *The Forming of an American Tradition: A Re-examination of Colonial Presbyterianism* (Philadelphia, 1949), 25.

54. Joyce D. Goodfriend, "A New Look at Presbyterian Origins in New York City," *American Presbyterians*, 67 (1989), 199–207.

55. Morgan Dix, ed., *A History of the Parish of Trinity Church in the City of New York*, vol. 1 (New York, 1898); Clifford P. Morehouse, *Trinity, Mother of Churches: An Informal History of Trinity Parish in the City of New York* (New York, 1973); and Rev. William Berrian, *An Historical Sketch of Trinity Church, New York*

(New York, 1847) all deal with the founding of the church in New York City. For additional background, see Elizabeth H. Davidson, *The Establishment of the English Church in the Continental American Colonies* (Durham, N.C., 1936), 37–46; and John Webb Pratt, *Religion, Politics, and Diversity: The Church-State Theme in New York History* (Ithaca, N.Y., 1967), 26–48. Also useful is *Inventory of the Church Archives of New York City: Protestant Episcopal Church in the United States of America; Diocese of New York; Manhattan, Bronx, Richmond*, vol. 2 (New York: Historical Records Survey, WPA, 1940), 1–26; 46–48.

56. James and Jameson, eds., *Journal of Jasper Danckaerts*, 75–76.

57. Rufus Jones, *The Quakers in the American Colonies* (New York, 1966; originally published 1911), 215–62. See also John Cox, Jr., *Quakerism in the City of New York 1657–1930* (New York, 1930).

58. Arthur J. Worrall, *Quakers in the Colonial Northeast* (Hanover, N.H., and London, 1980), 171.

59. "Petition. Miles Forster, Richard Jones, William Bickley and James Mills, Quakers and merchants of New York, in relation to oaths (May 18, 1691), *CEM*, 208.

60. Members of the meeting can be identified through Quaker records and official government documents. See "Minutes of Monthly, Quarterly, and Yearly Meetings held on Long Island & in New York from 1672 to 1703," Haviland Record Room of the New York Yearly Meeting, New York City; "Records of the Society of Friends of the City of New York and Vicinity, from 1640 to 1800," *New York Genealogical and Biographical Record*, 3 (1872), 184–90; 4 (1873), 32–39, 94–98, 190–94; 5 (1874) 38–41, 102–7, 186–90; 6 (1875), 97–107, 192–93; 7 (1876), 39–43, 85–90; "Governor Fletcher to the Lords of Trade" (New York, June 10, 1696), *Doc. Rel.*, 4:159; "An Account of What Hath Been Taken From Our Friends in New Yorke Government Since the Arrivall of Governour Dongan and Upon What Acct.," *DHNY*, 3:608–9. See also William Wade Hinshaw, *Encyclopedia of American Quaker Genealogy* (Baltimore, 1969; originally published 1940), vol. 3, *New York*.

61. Dickinson, "A Journal of the Life, Travels, and Labours of Love, in the Work of the Ministry, of . . . James Dickinson," in William Evans and Thomas Evans, eds., *The Friends Library*, (Philadelphia, 1848), 12:393–94. Dickinson also recounts the disruption of this meeting by former Quaker William Bradford. In 1699, another visiting Quaker, Thomas Story, held two meetings in the house of Thomas Roberts, "a convinced man in the heart of the city" (Jones, *The Quakers in the American Colonies*, 238).

62. Alexander Wall, Jr., "William Bradford, Colonial Printer: A Tercentenary Review," *Proceedings* of the American Antiquarian Society, 73 (1963), 361–84; *Churchyards of Trinity Parish in the City of New York 1697–1969* (New York, 1969), 16. Pewterer Thomas Burroughs, Sr., came to New York City from Boston; see Helen Burr Smith, "A New IB Silversmith and Two Unrecorded Pewterers," *New-York Historical Society Quarterly*, 52 (1968), 81–85.

63. Of the 75 grooms, 56 came from England, 9 from Scotland, 2 from Ireland, 3 from the British West Indies, and 5 from the continental colonies. See *Marriages from 1639 to 1801 in the Reformed Dutch Church, New York* (New York, 1940).

64. Of the 36 English immigrants whose birthplace is specified, 17 came from London, while 19 came from other places in England. See *Marriages from 1639 to 1801 in the Reformed Dutch Church, New York*.

65. On Sharpe, see Hamlin, *Legal Education in Colonial New York*, 73, 84n4. On Delavall, see Peter Wilson Coldham, *English Adventurers and Emigrants, 1661–1733: Abstracts from Examinations in the High Court of Admiralty with Reference to Colonial America* (Baltimore, 1985), 18; and Ritchie, *The Duke's Province*, 44.

66. "Records of the Society of Friends of the City of New York and Vicinity, from 1640 to 1800," *New York Genealogical and Biographical Record*, 6 (1875), 98.

67. Hyer, "Walter Hyer from Kingston, Surrey"; John Ross Delafield, "Walter Thong and His Forefathers," *New York Genealogical and Biographical Record*, 83 (1952), 196–204; William Seton Gordon, "Gabriel Ludlow (1663–1736) and His Descendants," *New York Genealogical and Biographical Record*, 50 (1919), 34–55, 134–56; "Gabriel Ludlow Memorandum Book," New-York Historical Society; J. Robert T. Craine, comp., Harry W. Hazard, ed., *The Ancestry and Posterity of Matthew Clarkson (1664–1702)* (n.p., 1971).

68. Paul M. Hamlin and Charles E. Baker, *Supreme Court of Judicature of the Province of New York 1691–1704*, 3 vols. (New York, 1959), 3:196–99.

69. Coldham, *English Adventurers and Emigrants*, 51–52. On Wenham, see also Hamlin and Baker, *Supreme Court of Judicature*, 3:214–20. In 1745, Wenham's two surviving children, John Wenham, Esq., of the City of London, and Sarah Wenham, the wife of Samuel Powell, Esq., of the Inner Temple, London, were living in London. Deeds from the Secretary of State's Office, New York State Archives, vol. 14 (1739–1750), fols. 267–70.

70. Will of Roger Baker, *CNYHS for the Year 1892*, 339. See also Elizabeth Marting, "Dom. Rex vs. Roger Baker," *New-York Historical Society Quarterly*, 31 (1947), 139–47.

71. Dixon Ryan Fox, *Caleb Heathcote, Gentleman Colonist: The Story of a Career in the Province of New York 1692–1721* (New York, 1926), 4–9.

72. Ritchie, *The Duke's Province*, 79–80; Peter Gouldesborough, "An Attempted Scottish Voyage to New York in 1669," *Scottish Historical Review*, 40 (1961), 56–62. On Scottish migration to the American colonies in the seventeenth century, both voluntary and involuntary, see Ian Charles Cargill Graham, *Colonists from Scotland: Emigration to North America, 1707–1783* (Ithaca, N.Y., 1956), 9–12; and Smith, *Colonists in Bondage*, 152–59, 180–87. See also George S. Pryde, "Scottish Colonization in the Province of New York," *New York History*, 16 (April 1935), 138–57.

Regarding Scots-Irish emigration in the seventeenth century, see R. J. Dickson, *Ulster Emigration to Colonial America 1718–1775* (London, 1966), 19–20. On the Scots-Irish in New York, see James G. Leyburn, *The Scotch-Irish: A Social History* (Chapel Hill, N.C., 1962), 243–45.

73. Quoted in Hamlin and Baker, *Supreme Court of Judicature*, 3:110–11. Other prominent Scots in seventeenth-century New York City were James Emott and James Graham (see ibid., 3:74–78, 90–98). On the business, political, and military ventures of Samuel Vetch, a Scotsman who reached New York City in 1699, see G. M. Waller, *Samuel Vetch: Colonial Enterpriser* (Chapel Hill, N.C., 1960).

74. Jackson later was associated with the first Presbyterian church in New York City. Goodfriend, "A New Look at Presbyterian Origins in New York City." Spratt married the daughter of merchant Johannes de Peyster. "Sprat Family Bible," *New York Genealogical and Biographical Record*, 12 (1881), 174–75. Smith notes that at least ten Scottish rebels were taken to New York in 1684. Smith, *Colonists in Bondage*, 184.

75. Will of David Vilant, *CNYHS for the Year 1893*, 46. Vilant is probably the "David Violent" listed as one of East Jersey's Original Proprietors in Ned C. Landsman, *Scotland and Its First American Colony, 1683–1765* (Princeton, 1985), 277. At least six Scottish indentured servants came to New York City from East New Jersey in the late seventeenth century (ibid., 136).

76. See the 1691 petition of "Lawrence Read [*sic*], of New York, merchant, late of Barbadoes," in *CEM*, 205.

CHAPTER FOUR
ETHNICITY AND STRATIFICATION IN
SEVENTEENTH-CENTURY NEW YORK CITY

1. "William Byrd to Bro. Dan'l per Ruds" (Virginia, March 8, 1685 [1686]), *Virginia Historical Register and Literary Companion*, 2 (1849), 208 (misprinted as 108). The 1698 census is found in *DHNY*, 1:467. New Amsterdam's population in 1664 is discussed in chapter 1. For comments on the population of colonial New York City, see Ira Rosenwaike, *Population History of New York City* (Syracuse, N.Y., 1972), 1–13; Stella H. Sutherland, *Population Distribution in Colonial America* (New York, 1936), 64–96; Robert V. Wells, "Household Size and Composition in the British Colonies in America, 1675–1775," *Journal of Interdisciplinary History*, 4 (1974), 543–70.

2. "William Byrd to Bro. Dan'l per Ruds," 208 (misprinted as 108). There are a few other impressionistic comments on the ethnic composition of New York City's population in the seventeenth century. Charles Lodwick lamented in 1692 that New York City's problem was "too great a mixture of nations, and English ye least part." Charles Lodwick, "New York in 1692," *CNYHS*, 2d ser., vol. 2 (New York, 1849), 244. In 1696, New York agents William Nicoll and Chidley Brooke reported to the Board of Trade that "the Inhabitants in the Town of New York are one half Dutch, a quarter part French Protestants, and a Quarter part English." "Representation of Messrs. Brooke and Nicoll to the Board of Trade" (Whitehall, August 26, 1696), *Doc. Rel.*, 4:181–82.

3. For related discussions, see Thomas J. Archdeacon, *New York City 1664–1710: Conquest and Change* (Ithaca, N.Y., 1976); Thomas J. Archdeacon, "The Age of Leisler—New York City, 1689–1710: A Social and Demographic Interpretation," in Jacob Judd and Irwin H. Polishook, eds., *Aspects of Early New York Society and Politics* (Tarrytown, N.Y., 1974), 63–82; and Bruce Martin Wilkenfeld, *The Social and Economic Structure of the City of New York 1695–1796* (New York, 1978).

4. Marcus Lee Hansen estimated the Dutch population of New York City and county in 1698 to be 2,000 or 47 percent of the total white population. This estimate was based on an analysis of the 1703 city census, in which less than 50

percent of the heads of families were identified as Dutch. American Historical Association, *Annual Report; 1931*, 3 vols. (Washington, D.C., 1932), 1:364–65. Patricia Bonomi states that "by 1698 the English had drawn equal to the Dutch in numbers and would rapidly surpass them thereafter, giving the capital at New York City a strongly English aspect by the early years of the eighteenth century." Patricia U. Bonomi, *A Factious People: Politics and Society in Colonial New York* (New York, 1971), 25. Her source for this statement appears to be the assertion by Carl Bridenbaugh that "the Dutch of New Amsterdam constituted the only non-English group of any size, and by 1690 this strain was becoming diluted by the steady infiltration of Englishmen." Carl Bridenbaugh, *Cities in the Wilderness: The First Century of Urban Life in America, 1625–1742* (New York, 1964; originally published 1938), 5.

5. New York City's population was smaller in 1703 than in 1699 because of the mortality resulting from the yellow fever epidemic that hit the city in the summer of 1702.

6. The urban wards of New York City were the East, West, North, South, and Dock wards. I have included property owned in the Bowery ward by those listed as taxpayers in any of the five urban wards.

7. March 15, 1683/84, *MCC*, 1:136–37. For background on New York City's carmen, see Graham Russell Hodges, *New York City Cartmen, 1667–1850* (New York and London, 1986). Hodges mistakenly gives the date of this law as 1677 (ibid., 25).

8. See Samuel McKee, Jr., *Labor in Colonial New York, 1664–1776* (New York, 1935); and Edgar J. McManus, *A History of Negro Slavery In New York* (Syracuse, N.Y., 1966).

9. On female traders, see Jean P. Jordan, "Women Merchants in Colonial New York," *New York History*, 58 (1977), 412–39.

10. See Michael B. Katz, "Occupational Classification in History," *Journal of Interdisciplinary History*, 3 (1972), 63–88.

11. "Table 7: City of London within the Walls. 1692 Poll Tax sample. Occupations specified in the returns, divided into broad categories," in D. V. Glass, "Socio-economic Status and Occupations in the City of London at the End of the Seventeenth Century," in A. E. J. Hollaender and William Kellaway, eds., *Studies in London History Presented to Philip Edmund Jones* (London, 1969), 382–83.

12. Two important studies concerning New York City's economy in this period are Curtis Nettels, "The Economic Relations of Boston, Philadelphia, and New York, 1680–1715," *Journal of Economic and Business History*, 3 (1931), 185–215; and Curtis Nettels, "England's Trade with New England and New York, 1685–1720," in *Publications of the Colonial Society of Massachusetts* (Boston, 1930–1933), vol. 23, *Transactions*, 322–50. See also Cathy Matson, "Commerce After the Conquest: Dutch Traders and Goods in New York City 1664–1764," *de Halve Maen*, 59 (March 1987), 8–12; 60 (June 1987), 17–22.

13. Classifying the data on New York City's occupations in 1695 in terms of the functional categories used by Jacob Price in his study of American port towns in the eighteenth century allows us to compare the city's occupational profile of 1695 with that of 1795 as delineated by Price. Over the century the trend was toward decline in the maritime sector and growth in the service sector. However,

Sector	New York City, 1695 (in percent)	New York City, 1795 (in percent)
Governmental	5.0	3.49
Service	37.0	56.59
Industrial	17.0	16.67
Maritime	41.0	23.26

the magnitude of the change is exaggerated here because retailers are included in the maritime category rather than in the service category in the 1695 figures. See Jacob M. Price, "Economic Function and the Growth of American Port Towns in the Eighteenth Century," *Perspectives in American History*, 8 (1974), 123–86.

14. Wayne Andrews, ed., "A Glance at New York in 1697: The Travel Diary of Dr. Benjamin Bullivant," revised from *New-York Historical Society Quarterly* (January 1956), 11.

15. Bridenbaugh, *Cities in the Wilderness*, 147–48.

16. "Attorney-General Broughton to the Lords of Trade" (New York, September 3, 1701), *Doc. Rel.*, 4:914.

17. "Minutes of the board of managers for the building of the church," Trinity Church, New York City, 1695–1697, January 27–June 23 O.S. Original manuscript in possession of Trinity Church; photostat negative at New York Public Library, Manuscript Division.

18. *Journal of the Votes and Proceedings of the General Assembly of the Colony of New-York, 1691 . . . 1743*, vol. 1 (New York, 1764), 163.

19. For background on the taverns of New York City, see W. Harrison Bayles, *Old Taverns of New York* (New York, 1915); Bridenbaugh, *Cities in the Wilderness*, 267–68; and Kym S. Rice, *Early American Taverns: For the Entertainment of Friends and Strangers* (Chicago, 1983). See also Eugene P. McParland, "Colonial Taverns and Tavernkeepers of British New York City," *New York Genealogical and Biographical Record*, 103 (1972), 193–202; 104 (1973), 17–27, 99–104, 170–72, 205–12; 105 (1974), 27–32, 89–92, 155–62, 218–23; 106 (1975), 34–37, 157–61, 214–16; 107 (1976), 26–28, 150–53.

20. Statistics on the distribution of wealth in Boston and Philadelphia are cited in Gary B. Nash, *Red, White, and Black: The Peoples of Early America* (Englewood Cliffs, N.J., 1974), 233–34.

21. In this context, see Wells, "Household Size and Composition in the British Colonies in America, 1675–1775."

22. For background on the New York City government see Arthur Everett Petersen, *New York as an Eighteenth-Century Municipality Prior to 1731* (New York, 1917); and Bruce M. Wilkenfeld, "The New York City Common Council, 1689–1800," *New York History*, 52 (1971), 249–73. See also Jon C. Teaford, *The Municipal Revolution in America: Origins of Modern Urban Government, 1650–1825* (Chicago and London, 1975).

23. The actual election years were 1687, 1689, 1690–91, and 1692 through 1707. The office of tax collector was not started until 1697.

24. "New York Army List—1700," *DHNY*, 1:232–33.

CHAPTER FIVE
COMMUNITY AND CULTURE IN
SEVENTEENTH-CENTURY NEW YORK CITY

1. See Lawrence A. Cremin, *American Education: The Colonial Experience, 1607–1783* (New York, 1970), 19–21; Carl F. Kaestle, *The Evolution of an Urban School System: New York City 1750–1850* (Cambridge, Mass., 1973), 22; John Higham, "Immigration," in C. Vann Woodward, ed., *The Comparative Approach to American History* (New York, 1968), 93.

2. George L. Smith, *Religion and Trade in New Netherland: Dutch Origins and American Development* (Ithaca, N.Y., 1973), 190–219, 236–46.

3. David M. Schneider, *The History of Public Welfare in New York State 1609–1866* (Chicago, 1938), 3–28.

4. William Heard Kilpatrick, *The Dutch Schools of New Netherland and New York* (Washington, D.C., 1912)

5. Quoted in Kilpatrick, *The Dutch Schools of New Netherland and New York*, 68.

6. See George L. Smith, "Guilders and Godliness: The Dutch Colonial Contribution to American Religious Pluralism," *Journal of Presbyterian History*, 47 (1969), 1–30; and Smith, *Religion and Trade in New Netherland*.

7. *Ecc. Rec.*, 1:621–22. See also *Ecc. Rec.*, 1:662.

8. John Webb Pratt, *Religion, Politics, and Diversity: The Church-State Theme in New York History* (Ithaca, N.Y., 1967), 32; *Ecc. Rec.*, 1:622.

9. John Cox, Jr., *Quakerism in the City of New York 1657–1930*, (New York, 1930) 28–30.

10. David and Tamar de Sola Pool, *An Old Faith in the New World: Portrait of Shearith Israel, 1654–1954* (New York, 1955), 35, 39. "Rev. Henry Selyns to the Classis of Amsterdam" (October 28, 1682), *Ecc. Rec.*, 2:830.

11. "Rev. Henry Selyns to the Classis of Amsterdam" (October 21/31, 1683), *Ecc. Rec.*, 2:867. See also Nelson R. Burr, "The Episcopal Church and the Dutch in Colonial New York and New Jersey—1664–1784," *Historical Magazine of the Protestant Episcopal Church*, 19 (1950), 92–93.

12. John A. F. Maynard, *The Huguenot Church of New York: A History of the French Church of Saint Esprit* (New York, 1938); "Records of the French Church du St. Esprit, New York City, 1689–1710," and "Accounts of Collections and expenditures March 1693–April 1699 kept by Gabriel Le Boyteulx," MSS (photostatic copies), New-York Historical Society.

13. Pratt, *Religion, Politics, and Diversity*, 40–46.

14. The Ministry Act of 1693 was designed to ensure that ministers were settled and supported in certain populated areas of the colony. Vestrymen and church wardens were to be elected in six separate jurisdictions, including New York City, and were given the power to select the minister and levy assessments for his support. "An Act for Settling a Ministry, and Raising a Maintenance for them in the City of New York, County of Richmond, Westchester and Queen's County" passed September 22, 1693. *Ecc. Rec.*, 2:1076–79. The political issue at stake was whether an Anglican minister would be chosen in New York City.

15. Raymond Breton, "Institutional Completeness of Ethnic Communities and the Personal Relations of Immigrants," *American Journal of Sociology*, 70

(1964), 193–205; reprinted in Bernard Blishen, Frank E. Jones, Kaspar D. Naegele, John Porter, eds., *Canadian Society: Sociological Perspectives*, 3d ed., (Toronto, 1968), 77–94, it offers a suggestive formulation of a related problem.

16. "Document of Call to a second preacher for the service of the Dutch Reformed Church of Jesus Christ in the City of New York" (July 21, 1698), *Ecc. Rec.*, 2:1195.

17. "A Catalogue of the Members of the Dutch Church, with the Names of the Streets in the City of New York, A.D. 1686," from the original manuscript of Rev. Henry Selyns, in *CNYHS*, 2d ser., vol. 1 (New York, 1841), 389–99.

18. Maynard, *The Huguenot Church of New York*, 75. Also, see chapter 3.

19. "Wardens and Vestrymen of Trinity Church," Appendix L in Rev. William Berrian, *An Historical Sketch of Trinity Church, New York* (New York, 1847), 352–65.

20. These figures are, of course, approximations, as are several others included in the correspondence of New York City church officials with the Classis in Amsterdam. With one exception, however, these estimates seem plausible, especially when examined in sequence. In 1666 the Rev. John Megapolensis reported "between three and four hundred communicants" in his church. The Rev. William van Nieuwenhuysen wrote in 1674 that "our church consists of between four and five hundred members; of whom . . . more than one hundred have been received under our ministry." (Van Nieuwenhuysen arrived in New York City in 1671.) In October 1681, eight months after the consistory described the church as a "large congregation, numbering about four hundred and fifty members," the Rev. Caspar van Zuuren asserted that the Dutch Reformed congregation had increased to "about five hundred." Soon after the Rev. Henry Selyns arrived in New York in 1682 to assume pastoral duties, he wrote back to Amsterdam that "the number of members has increased to about six hundred in all." This figure is clearly too high in light of Selyns's own enumeration of his congregation in 1686, which totaled 556 members, and the 1698 report of the consistory, which stated that since Selyns's "coming among us [1682] the number of our members, under God's blessing, has increased from four hundred and fifty to fully six hundred and fifty." Undoubtedly, Selyns had not been present in the community long enough in 1682 to make an accurate estimate of his flock. "A letter from Rev. John Megapolensis, pastor at Manhattan in New Netherland, . . . dated August 16, 1666; Classis of Amsterdam, Acts of the Deputies" (October 18, 1666), *Ecc. Rec.*, 1:583; "Rev. William van Nieuwenhuysen to the Classis of Amsterdam" (July 26, 1674), *Ecc. Rec.*, 1:654; "The Church of New York City to the Classis of Amsterdam" (February 25, 1681), *Ecc. Rec.*, 2:760; "Rev. Caspar van Zuuren to the Classis of Amsterdam" (October 28, 1682), *Ecc. Rec.*, 2:829; "Document of Call to a second preacher for the service of the Dutch Reformed Church of Jesus Christ in the City of New York" (July 21, 1698), *Ecc. Rec.*, 2:1195. On the building of the new church in Garden Street, see *Ecc. Rec.*, 2:950–51, 1108, 1172. On the accuracy of Selyns's enumeration of his congregation in 1686, see note 24 below.

21. "Documents Relating to the Administration of Leisler," *CNYHS*, vol. 1 (New York, 1868), 409. For a comprehensive discussion of the effect of Leisler's Rebellion on the Dutch Reformed church, see Randall Balmer, *A Perfect Babel of Confusion: Dutch Religion and English Culture in the Middle Colonies* (New York,

1989), 28–50. On the history of the Dutch Reformed church in colonial America see Gerald F. De Jong, *The Dutch Reformed Church in the American Colonies* (Grand Rapids, Mich., 1978).

22. "The Revs. Selyns, Varick, and Dellius to the Classis of Amsterdam" (October 12, 1692), *Ecc. Rec.*, 2:1043.

23. "Rev. Henry Selyns to the Classis of Amsterdam" (November 14, 1694), *Ecc. Rec.*, 2:1108. On Selyns's career, see A. P. G. Jos van der Linde, "Henricus Selijns (1636–1701), Dominee, dichter en historicus in Nieuw-Nederland en de Republiek," in J. F. Heijbroek, A. Lammers, and A. P. G. Jos van der Linde, eds., *Geen Schepsel Wordt Vergeten: liber amicorum voor Jan Willem Schulte Nordholt ter gelegenheid van zijn vijfenzestige verjaardag* (Amsterdam/Zutphen, 1985), 37–60.

24. "A Catalogue of the Members of the Dutch Church with the Names of the Streets in the City of New York, A.D. 1686," from the original manuscript of Rev. Henry Selyns in *CNYHS*, 2d ser., vol. 1 (New York, 1841), 389–400 (hereafter cited as "Catalogue of the Members of the Dutch Church, 1686"); "Records of the Reformed Dutch Church in the City of New York—Church Members' List," *New York Genealogical and Biographical Record*, 9 (1878), 38–45, 72–79, 140–47, 161–68; 59 (1928), 69–76, 158–65, 259–66, 372–79; 60 (1929), 71–78, 156–63 (hereafter cited as "Records of the Reformed Dutch Church, Members' List"). Selyns's enumeration of his congregation in 1686 appears to be quite accurate when examined in the context of other community records. Selyns arranged his list by streets and family groups, noted every communicant by name, and included the names of spouses, living or deceased, when pertinent. The inability to trace the initial date of admission of 126 of the 556 church members is attributable to possible gaps in the membership records of the city's Dutch Reformed Church and to problems associated with Dutch nomenclature, specifically the frequent failure of people to use surnames in the early years of settlement.

25. See chapter 3.

26. See chapter 3; see also "Catalogue of the Members of the Dutch Church, 1686."

27. This figure was calculated as follows: There were roughly 1,141 Dutch adults in New York City in 1698 (55 percent of 2,076 white adults, using the ratio of Dutch adult males on the 1699 tax list). Thus, the 650 church members composed 57 percent of Dutch adults. For the New York City census of 1698 see Evarts B. Greene and Virginia D. Harrington, *American Population Before the Federal Census of 1790* (New York, 1932; reprinted 1966), 92.

28. "Rev. Henry Selyns to the Classis of Amsterdam" (October 28, 1682), *Ecc. Rec.*, 2:827–34.

29. See chapter 4.

30. "Reformed Dutch Church of New York. List of Ministers, Elders and Deacons, 1710–1740," *Ecc. Rec.*, 3:1444–49.

31. "Catalogue of the Members of the Dutch Church, 1686."

32. "Records of the Reformed Dutch Church, Members' List."

33. "Catalogue of the Members of the Dutch Church, 1686." I have omitted single men and women from this calculation because most of them were young adults who were attached to other families.

34. See chapter 3.

35. "An Act to Enable the Minister and Elders for the time being of the ffrench Protestant Church in the City of Newyork to build a Larger Church for the worship of Almighty God in that Congregation to hold them & their Successors for ever" (passed June 19, 1703), in *The Colonial Laws of New York from the Year 1664 to the Revolution*, 5 vols. (Albany, 1894–1896), 1:527.

36. Rev. Alfred V. Wittmeyer, ed., "Registers of the births, marriages and deaths of the 'Eglise Françoise à la Nouvelle York,' from 1688–1804; and historical documents relating to the French protestants in N.Y. during the same period," Huguenot Society of America, *Collections*, vol. 1 (New York, 1886), 101.

37. No list of the members of the French congregation is extant, but the names of adherents can be compiled from marriage, baptismal, and burial records as well as other church documents. See ibid., see also "Records of the French Church du St. Esprit, New York City, 1689–1710," and "Accounts of Collections and expenditures March 1693–April 1699 kept by Gabriel Le Boyteulx," MSS (photostatic copies) New-York Historical Society.

38. See chapter 4.

39. On the history of Trinity Church see Berrian, *An Historical Sketch of Trinity Church*; Morgan Dix, ed., *A History of the Parish of Trinity Church in the City of New York*, vol. 1 (New York, 1898); and Clifford P. Morehouse, *Trinity, Mother of Churches: An Informal History of Trinity Parish in the City of New York* (New York, 1973). See also Borden W. Painter, "The Vestry in the Middle Colonies," *Historical Magazine of the Protestant Episcopal Church*, 47 (1978) 5–36. Because the early records of the congregation were burned in the eighteenth century, one must generalize about its social composition before 1730 from information on churchwardens, vestrymen, pewholders, and parishioners contained in the manuscript vestry minutes and fragmentary burial records in the Trinity Church Archives, New York City, and in the correspondence of the S. P. G., Letter Books, Series A, B, C/AM, 1702–1800 (microfilm; East Ardsley, Wakefield, England, 1964).

40. Cited in Dixon Ryan Fox, *Caleb Heathcote, Gentleman Colonist: The Story of a Career in the Province of New York 1692–1721* (New York, 1926), 228. I have estimated the population of New York colony in 1714 using the figures for 1710 and 1720 given in John J. McCusker and Russell R. Menard, *The Economy of British America, 1607–1789* (Chapel Hill, N.C., and London, 1985), 203. The Rev. George Keith, who preached at Trinity in 1702, reported that "there is a brave congregation of people belonging to the Church here" (Dix, ed., *History of Trinity Church*, 144).

41. See chapter 3. The Rev. John Miller, Anglican chaplain in New York City from 1693 to 1695, stated that there were 40 families of English dissenters in the city in 1695, along with 90 Anglican, 450 Dutch Reformed, 30 Dutch Lutheran, 200 French, and 20 Jewish families. "A Description of the Province and City of New York; with Plans of the City and Several Forts as They Existed in the Year 1695" (first published 1843), reprinted in Cornell Jaray, ed., *Historic Chronicles of New Amsterdam, Colonial New York and Early Long Island*, 1st ser. (Port Washington, N.Y., 1968), 37. Miller's estimates, composed from memory, must be regarded with caution.

42. Trinity Church Vestry Minutes, passim. Recent research has modified the notion that Anglican churches in northern colonial cities were uniformly upper

class in makeup. See Bruce E. Steiner, "New England Anglicanism: A Genteel Faith?" *William and Mary Quarterly*, 3d ser., 27 (1970), 122–35; and Frederick V. Mills, Sr., *Bishops by Ballots: An Eighteenth Century Ecclesiastical Revolution* (New York, 1978), 79–80.

43. Trinity Church Vestry Minutes, September 15, 1718.

44. Ibid., May 14, 1724. The price of pews in Trinity was a cause of contention among Anglicans during the administration of Gov. Robert Hunter (1710–1720). See "Address from Gov. Hunter's Friends to the Bishop of London Against the Rev. Mr. Vesey, Circa 1714," *DHNY*, 3:267. See also Alison Gilbert Olson, "Governor Robert Hunter and the Anglican Church in New York," in Anne Whiteman, J. S. Bromley, and P. G. M. Dickson, eds., *Statesmen, Scholars, and Merchants: Essays in Eighteenth-Century History Presented to Dame Lucy Sutherland* (Oxford, 1973), 44–64.

45. Trinity Church Vestry Minutes, September 23, 1700.

46. Ibid., passim; Trinity Church Burial Records, passim.

47. Trinity Church Vestry Minutes, October 25, 1697.

48. Cox, *Quakerism in the City of New York*, 28–29.

49. Minutes of Monthly, Quarterly, and Yearly Meetings held on Long Island and in New York from 1672 to 1703, Haviland Records Room of the New York Yearly Meeting, New York City.

50. See the Quarterly Meeting records from 1696 to 1698 in Minutes of Monthly, Quarterly, and Yearly Meetings . . . 1672 to 1703.

51. De Sola Pool and de Sola Pool, *Old Faith in the New World*, 34–35, 39; "Rev. Henry Selyns to the Classis of Amsterdam" (October 28, 1682), *Ecc. Rec.*, 2:830. See also note 41 above.

52. De Sola Pool and de Sola Pool, *Old Faith in the New World*, 458–59.

53. See Harry J. Kreider, *The Beginnings of Lutheranism in New York* (New York, 1949); and Harry Julius Kreider, *Lutheranism in Colonial New York* (New York, 1942).

54. Kreider, *Lutheranism in Colonial New York*, 50. Estimating their constituency at about 100 in 1664, Lutheran leaders nevertheless expressed pleasure when 45 persons attended the first communion celebrated in the New York City church in 1669. In 1670 the elders informed the Amsterdam consistory that when the minister is at Albany "our congregation suffers. It seems that the good people would rather hear a sermon preached than have someone read to them." "Letter from the Lutherans at New York to the Amsterdam Consistory" (December 8/18, 1664), in Arnold J. H. van Laer, trans., *The Lutheran Church in New York: 1649–1772: Records in the Lutheran Church Archives at Amsterdam, Holland* (New York, 1946), 50; "Letter from the Lutherans at New York to the Amsterdam Consistory" (April 13/23, 1669), ibid., 68; "Letter from the elders of the Lutheran church at New York to the Amsterdam Consistory" (August 22, 1670), ibid., 78. See also note 26 above.

55. "Letter from the Rev. Justus Falckner and the Consistory of the Lutheran Church–New York, to the Amsterdam Consistory" (November 10, 1705), in van Laer, *The Lutheran Church in New York*, 99. Falckner also noted that the congregation was very small, the members ignorant of Lutheran doctrine, and the church building very dilapidated (ibid., 100).

56. Kreider, *Lutheranism in Colonial New York*, 53–58, and *The Beginnings of Lutheranism in Colonial New York*.

57. "Justus Falckner to August Herman Francke, New York in America, Anno 1704," in Julius F. Sachse, ed., "A Contribution to Pennsylvania History: Missives to August Herman Francke," *Proceedings* of the Pennsylvania German Society, 18 (1909), 17.

58. Albert I. Gordon, *Intermarriage: Interfaith, Interracial, Interethnic* (Boston, 1964), and Milton L. Barron, *The Blending American: Patterns of Intermarriage* (Chicago, 1972) provide useful background on the study of marital behavior. Historical works that emphasize the significance of marriage patterns in analyzing social structure include Edward Pessen, "The Marital Theory and Practice of the Antebellum Urban Elite," *New York History*, 53 (1972), 389–410; Daniel Scott Smith, "Parental Power and Marriage Patterns: An Analysis of Historical Trends in Hingham, Massachusetts," *Journal of Marriage and the Family*, 35 (1973), 419–28; Peter Dobkin Hall, "Marital Selection and Business in Massachusetts Merchant Families, 1700–1900," in Ruth I. Coser, ed., *The Family, Its Structure and Functions*, 2d ed., (New York, 1974), 226–40; Bernard Farber, *Guardians of Virtue: Salem Families in 1800* (New York, 1972); and John J. Waters, "Hingham, Massachusetts, 1631–1661: An East Anglian Oligarchy in the New World," *Journal of Social History*, 1 (1968), 351–70. See also, Richard M. Bernard, *The Melting Pot and the Altar: Marital Assimilation in Early Twentieth-Century Wisconsin* (Minneapolis, 1980).

59. In this analysis, persons of German background have been classified as Dutch. For insight into Dutch and English attitudes toward marriage, see Alice Clare Carter, "Marriage Counselling in the Early Seventeenth Century: England and the Netherlands Compared," in Jan van Dorsten, ed., *Ten Studies in Anglo-Dutch Relations* (Leiden and London, 1974), 94–127.

60. Jon Butler, *The Huguenots in America: A Refugee People in New World Society* (Cambridge, Mass., 1983), 158.

61. Bartlett Burleigh James and J. Franklin Jameson, eds., *Journal of Jasper Danckaerts 1679–1680* (New York, 1913), 29.

62. *CNYHS for the Year 1892*, 394.

63. In this connection, see Smith, "Parental Power and Marriage Patterns."

64. *CNYHS for the Year 1894*, 143.

65. Sarah Willett was actually half-Dutch. Rosalie Fellows Bailey, "The Willett Family of Flushing, Long Island," *New York Genealogical and Biographical Record*, 80 (1949), 1–9, 83–96. On the De Key family, see George E. McCracken, "The American DeKay Family," *The American Genealogist*, 33 (1957), 223–31; 34 (1958), 29–38.

66. See Sydney H. Croog and James E. Teele, "Religious Identity and Church Attendance of Sons of Religious Intermarriages," *American Sociological Review*, 32 (1967), 93–103 (reprinted in Barron, *The Blending American*, 310–27), for a discussion germane to this question.

67. See Cremin, *American Education: The Colonial Experience*, 113–37. Charles Edward Ironside, *The Family in Colonial New York: A Sociological Study* (New York, 1942), Arthur W. Calhoun, *A Social History of the American Family* (New York, 1960; originally published 1917), vol. 1, Colonial Period, 153–83, and

Paula Dorman Christenson, "The Colonial Family in New York: A Study of Middle and Upper Class Interpersonal and Institutional Relationships" (Ph.D. diss., State University of New York at Albany, 1984) are impressionistic treatments of the family in colonial New York.

68. "Rev. Henry Selyns to the Classis of Amsterdam" (October 28, 1682), *Ecc. Rec.*, 2:829.

69. "Rev. Henry Selyns to the Classis of Amsterdam" (October, 21–31, 1683), *Ecc. Rec.*, 2:866.

70. "Rev. Henry Selyns to Classis of Amsterdam" (September 14, 1698), *Ecc. Rec.*, 2:1233–40. The quotation is on 1233.

71. Kilpatrick, *The Dutch Schools of New Netherland and New York*, 142–149. See also Henry W. Dunshee, *History of the School of the Collegiate Reformed Dutch Church in the City of New York from 1633 to 1883*, 2d ed., enlarged (New York, 1883); and Jean Parker Waterbury, *A History of Collegiate School, 1638–1963* (New York, 1965).

72. James and Jameson, eds., *Journal of Jasper Danckaerts*, 63. The 1702 inventory of Delanoy's estate included a large number of schoolbooks. For information on specific titles, see Kilpatrick, *The Dutch Schools of New Netherland and New York*, 225.

73. Ibid., 177 n. 4.

74. See Farber, *Guardians of Virtue*, 96–108; Dorothy Crozier, "Kinship and Occupational Succession," *Sociological Review*, new series, 13 (1965), 15–43; Lawrence H. Leder, "Robert Livingston's Sons: Preparation for Futurity," *New York History*, 50 (1969), 235–49; Carl Bridenbaugh, *The Colonial Craftsman* (Chicago, 1961; first published 1950), 129–30. See also Bernard Bailyn, "The Beekmans of New York: Trade, Politics, and Families; A Review Article," *William and Mary Quarterly*, 3d ser., 14 (1957), 598–608.

75. "Indentures of Apprenticeship. February 9th. 1694–5 to January 29th. 1707–8," *CNYHS for the Year 1885*, 565–622. Not all the documents found in this collection were indentures of apprenticeship nor did they all deal with fathers and sons. Still, they are predominantly apprenticeship arrangements and as such merit analysis. For discussions of apprenticeship in New York City see Robert Francis Seybolt, *Apprenticeship & Apprenticeship Education in Colonial New England & New York* (New York, 1917); Samuel McKee, Jr., *Labor in Colonial New York, 1664–1776* (New York, 1935), 62–88; and Ronald William Howard, "Education and Ethnicity in Colonial New York, 1664–1763: A Study in the Transmission of Culture in Early America" (Ph.D. diss., University of Tennessee, 1978).

76. See Joshua A. Fishman, *Language Loyalty in the United States: The Maintenance and Perpetuation of Non-English Mother Tongues by American Ethnic and Religious Groups* (The Hague, 1966).

77. At the beginning of the eighteenth century, Dutch residents of Albany had to send their children to New York City if they wished them to learn to speak and write English. Alice P. Kenney, *The Gansevoorts of Albany: Dutch Patricians in the Upper Hudson Valley* (Syracuse, N.Y., 1969), 42. Writing in the 1750s, William Smith, Jr., asserted that "the Dutch dialect . . . is still so much used in some counties, that the sheriffs find it difficult to obtain persons sufficiently acquainted with the English tongue, to serve as jurors in the courts of law." William Smith, Jr., *The

History of the Province of New-York, ed. Michael Kammen, 2 vols. (Cambridge, Mass., 1972), 1:226. See also Charles Theodor Gehring, "The Dutch Language in Colonial New York: An Investigation of a Language in Decline and Its Relationship to Social Change" (Ph.D. diss., Indiana University, 1973); and Allen Walker Read, "Bilingualism in the Middle Colonies, 1725–1775," *American Speech*, 12 (1937), 93–99.

78. By the 1680s, there was little evidence of the Dutch language in the city's legal records. Richard B. Morris, ed., "Introduction" to *Select Cases of the Mayor's Court of New York City 1674–1784* (Washington, D.C., 1935), 43.

79. See Edgar Franklin Romig, "'The English and Low-Dutch School-Master' (New York: William Bradford, 1730)," *New-York Historical Society Quarterly*, 43 (1959), 153.

80. *MCC*, 1:424–25.

81. April 29, 1699. Quoted in William Webb Kemp, *The Support of Schools in Colonial New York by the Society for the Propagation of the Gospel in Foreign Parts* (New York, 1969; originally published 1913), 65.

82. "Earl of Bellomont to the Lords of Trade" (New York, April 27, 1699), *Doc. Rel.*, 4:508. Johannes Kip's difficulty in writing English is apparent in a 1678 letter, a portion of which reads, "Whi wil sie in tym what der will bie Sir my deseyer is of you that ef you maghdt sie eene Letters of N:Jorck belangen to my that you send mey thie met thee forst opertunety en I sal bee tanck full to you." "Letter from Johannes Kip to John Addams concerning Business Transactions, 'horekill 12 feb 1678/7,'" in Peter R. Christoph and Florence A. Christoph, eds., *The Andros Papers 1677–1678: Files of the Provincial Secretary of New York During the Administration of Governor Sir Edmund Andros 1674–1680* (Syracuse, N.Y., 1990), 251. For Jacob Leisler's imperfect command of written English, see Donna Merwick, "Being Dutch: An Interpretation of Why Jacob Leisler Died," *New York History*, 70 (1989), 397–99.

83. On Dutch nomenclature and naming practices, see Rosalie F. Bailey, "Dutch Systems in Family Naming: New York and New Jersey," *National Genealogical Society Quarterly*, 41 (1953), 1–11, 109–18; and Edward H. Tebbenhoff, "Tacit Rules and Hidden Family Structures: Naming Practices and Godparentage in Schenectady, New York 1680–1800," *Journal of Social History*, 18 (1985), 567–85. See also Daniel Scott Smith, "Child-Naming Practices as Cultural and Familial Indicators," *Local Population Studies*, 32 (1984), 17–27; Daniel Scott Smith, "Child-Naming Practices, Kinship Ties, and Change in Family Attitudes in Hingham, Massachusetts, 1641 to 1880," *Journal of Social History*, 18 (1985), 541–66; and Wilbur Zelinsky, "Cultural Variations in Personal Name Patterns in the Eastern United States," *Annals of the Association of American Geographers*, 60 (1970), 743–69.

84. For a discussion of patterns of charitable giving in colonial America see Kenneth A. Lockridge, *Literacy in Colonial New England* (New York, 1974).

85. Raymond A. Mohl, "Poverty in Early America, A Reappraisal: The Case of Eighteenth-Century New York City," *New York History*, 50 (1969), 8–10; Schneider, *The History of Public Welfare in New York*, 37–42, 64–69. See also Robert E. Cray, Jr., *Paupers and Poor Relief in New York City and Its Rural Environs, 1700–1830* (Philadelphia, 1988).

86. See Sheldon S. Cohen, "Elias Neau, Instructor to New York's Slaves," *New-York Historical Society Quarterly*, 55 (1971), 7–27.

87. Kenneth Scott, "Contributors to Building of a New Dutch Church in New York City, 1688," *National Genealogical Society Quarterly*, 49 (1961), 131–36; "Subscriptions Toward Building the Steeple," Appendix A in Berrian, *An Historical Sketch of Trinity Church*, 321–25.

88. Sarah Kemble Knight, *The Journal of Madam Knight*, "Introduction" by Malcolm Freiberg (Boston, 1972), 30.

CHAPTER SIX
AFRICAN-AMERICAN SOCIETY AND CULTURE

1. Joyce D. Goodfriend, "Burghers and Blacks: The Evolution of a Slave Society at New Amsterdam," *New York History*, 59 (1978), 125–44. Three major studies treating blacks in New Amsterdam and colonial New York City are Edgar J. McManus, *A History of Negro Slavery in New York* (Syracuse, N.Y., 1966); Thomas J. Davis, "Slavery in Colonial New York City" (Ph.D. diss., Columbia University, 1974); and Vivienne L. Kruger, "Born to Run: The Slave Family in Early New York, 1626–1827" (Ph.D. diss., Columbia University, 1985). See also Roi Ottley and William J. Weatherby, *The Negro in New York: An Informal Social History, 1626–1940* (New York, 1967).

2. Carl Nordstrom, "The New York Slave Code," *Afro-Americans in New York Life and History*, 4 (1980), 7–26; Edwin Olson, "The Slave Code in Colonial New York," *Journal of Negro History*, 29 (1944), 147–65. For municipal and provincial laws regarding slaves, see *MCC* and *The Colonial Laws of New York from the Year 1664 to the Revolution*, 5 vols. (Albany, 1894–1896). See also William M. Wiecek, "The Statutory Law of Slavery and Race in the Thirteen Mainland Colonies of British America," *William and Mary Quarterly*, 3d ser., 34 (1977), 258–80.

3. Sir John Werden to William Dyer, November 30, 1676, in Elizabeth Donnan, *Documents Illustrative of the History of the Slave Trade to America*, 4 vols. (Washington, D.C., 1932), 3:435. On the slave trade to New York see James G. Lydon, "New York and the Slave Trade, 1700–1774," *William and Mary Quarterly*, 3d ser., 35 (1978), 375–94.

4. Evarts B. Greene and Virginia D. Harrington, *American Population Before the Federal Census of 1790* (New York, 1932; reprinted 1966), 92.

5. "Answers of Governor Andros to Enquiries About New York" (1678), *Doc. Rel.*, 3:261.

6. *MCC*, 1:208–9.

7. Jacobus van Cortlandt Letter Book, 1698–1700, New-York Historical Society.

8. "Petition of the Royal African Company to the Court of Admiralty, 1687," Donnan, *Documents Illustrative of the Slave Trade*, 3:436–38.

9. On the Madagascar slave trade to New York see Virginia Bever Platt, "The East India Company and the Madagascar Slave Trade," *William and Mary Quarterly*, 3d ser., 26 (1969), 548–77; Jacob Judd, "Frederick Philipse and the Madagascar Trade," *New-York Historical Society Quarterly*, LV (1971), 354–74; and Robert C. Ritchie, *Captain Kidd and the War Against the Pirates* (Cambridge, Mass., 1986).

10. Jacobus van Cortlandt to Mr. Mayhew, April 15, 1698, in the Jacobus van Cortlandt Letter Book.

11. Quoted in Judd, "Frederick Philipse and the Madagascar Trade," 358.

12. Platt, "The East India Company and the Madagascar Slave Trade," 571. Platt suggests that Adolphus Philipse (Frederick Philipse's son) might have sent a ship to Madagascar for slaves in 1717. Most of this cargo was sold in Barbados, but six Negroes from the voyage were transported to New York in 1718, ibid., 564 n. 34.

13. "Lord Cornbury to the Board of Trade" (New York, July 1, 1708), *Doc. Rel.*, 5:57.

14. Donnan, *Documents Illustrative of the Slave Trade*, 3:444 n. 3.

15. Lydon, "New York and the Slave Trade."

16. "Isaac Bobin to George Clarke" (New York, August 2, 1720), *Letters of Isaac Bobin, Esq., Private Secretary of Hon. George Clarke, Secretary of the Province of New York, 1718–1730* (Albany, 1872), 35–36. On June 24, 1713, the recorder and aldermen of New York reported the arrival in "this Port from the Island of Jamaica the Hawk Galley Jacob Mauritz Master on board whereof are Several Negro Slaves one of which lyes ill of the Small Pox" (N.Y. Col. MSS, 58:133).

17. Lydon, "New York and the Slave Trade."

18. "An Act for relieving the Inhabitants of the Colony of South Carolina from the Dutys laid and paid in this Colony of New York for such Goods Slaves and Merchandizes as they shall Import into this Colony during the time of Six Months" (passed July 21, 1715), *The Colonial Laws of New York*, 1:884–85. See also "An Act to Exempt Hannah Martin, Doct'r Christian Cooper & Mr. George Smith from paying of the Tax for twelve Negroes Imported from South Carolina" (passed July 21, 1715), ibid., 1:873–75.

19. Lydon, "New York and the Slave Trade."

20. Greene and Harrington, *American Population Before the Federal Census of 1790*, 94–97.

21. *New-York Gazette.*

22. "Isaac Bobin to George Clarke" (January 27, 1722/23), *Letters of Isaac Bobin*, 116.

23. "Isaac Bobin to George Clarke" (October 21, 1723), ibid., 160.

24. On the tribal origins of New York's slaves, see Kruger, "Born to Run," 81. In 1660, Rev. Henricus Selyns reported that there were "forty negroes, from the region of the negro coast" at the Bowery. "Rev. Henry Selyns to the Classis of Amsterdam" (October 4, 1660), *Ecc. Rec.*, 1:488. For information on the Cormantines and Pawpaw (Popo) see Donnan, *Documents Illustrative of the Slave Trade*, 1:398 nn. 25 and 26.

25. *RNA*, 4:56–57. In 1665/66, it was recorded that Jan Angola, a Negro who was accused of stealing wood, "cannot speak Dutch," and it was ordered that the next court day he bring with him "Domingo the Negro as interpreter" (*RNA*, 5:337).

26. *Boston News-Letter*, July 24, 1704.

27. "Governor Hunter to the Lords of Trade" (New York, June 23, 1712), *Doc. Rel.*, 5:342.

28. Almon Wheeler Lauber, *Indian Slavery in Colonial Times Within the Present*

Limits of the United States (New York, 1913); Kruger, "Born to Run," 70–73. See also laws in *MCC* and *The Colonial Laws of New York*.

29. Petition of Sarah Robinsa a Free born Indian Woman, September 18, 1711, N.Y. Col. MSS, 56:96.

30. Petition of Anna Grevenraedt of the City of New York and Martha Simson of Kings County, May 16, 1717, N.Y. Col. MSS, 60:165.

31. "Some Early Records of the Lutheran Church, New York," *Year Book of the Holland Society of New York* (1903), 44. See Lauber, *Indian Slavery in Colonial Times*, 193.

32. Goodfriend, "Burghers and Blacks." According to Shane White, "free blacks in New York City in the seventeenth and eighteenth centuries . . . were of little significance. . . . Probably there were never more than one hundred free blacks in the city during the colonial period." White, "'We Dwell in Safety and Pursue Our Honest Callings': Free Blacks in New York City, 1783–1810," *Journal of American History*, 75 (1988), 448.

33. I. N. Phelps Stokes, *The Iconography of Manhattan Island, 1498–1909*, 6 vols. (New York, 1915–1928), 6:123–24 (in section entitled "Original Grants, and Farms").

34. *Third Annual Report of the State Historian of the State of New York, 1897* (New York and Albany, 1898), Appendix M, Colonial Muster Rolls, 441–43.

35. Bartlett Burleigh James and J. Franklin Jameson, eds., *Journal of Jasper Danckaerts 1679–1680* (New York, 1913), 65.

36. "Original Book of New York Deeds January 1st 1672/3 to October 19th 1675," *CNYHS for the Year 1912*, 42–43; Stokes, *Iconography*, 6:140. For other land transactions involving free blacks see Peter R. Christoph, "The Freedmen of New Amsterdam," *Journal of the Afro-American Historical and Genealogical Society*, 5 (1984), 116–17.

37. Peter R. Christoph and Florence A. Christoph, eds., *The Andros Papers 1674–1676: Files of the Provincial Secretary During the Administration of Governor Sir Edmund Andros 1674–1680* (Syracuse, N.Y., 1989), 349–50.

38. "Records of the Reformed Dutch Church, Members' List" and (see note 24 for chapter 5). "Catalogue of the Members of the Dutch Church, 1686" Several free blacks also were married in the church in the late seventeenth century.

39. *CNYHS for the Year 1893*, 293; Kruger, "Born to Run," 55.

40. Anthony John Evertse sold his property to Adrian van Schaick in 1697 (Stokes, *Iconography*, 6:140). On the history of the land grants to blacks, see Stokes, *Iconography*, 6:123–24 (in section entitled "Original Grants, and Farms"). See also Elizabeth Blackmar, *Manhattan for Rent, 1785–1850* (Ithaca, N.Y., 1989), 284–85 n. 12.

41. Firth Haring Fabend, "The Yeoman Ideal: A Dutch Family in the Middle Colonies, 1650–1800" (Ph.D. diss., New York University, 1988), 94; David Steven Cohen, *The Ramapo Mountain People* (New Brunswick, N.J., 1974).

42. Kruger, "Born to Run," 592–95.

43. Original will of Mary Jansen Loockermans (microfilm), Historical Documents Collection, Queens College, New York City.

44. Harry B. Yoshpe, "Record of Slave Manumissions in New York During

the Colonial and Early National Periods," *Journal of Negro History*, 26 (1941), 78–107.

45. Deeds from the Secretary of State's Office, New York State Archives, vol. 10 (1703–1712), fols. 202–6; *CNYHS for the Year 1885*, 84.

46. Yoshpe, "Record of Slave Manumissions in New York."

47. Yoshpe, "Record of Slave Manumissions in New York."

48. Kruger, "Born to Run," 595–96; Will of George Norton, *CNYHS for the Year 1893*, 151; "Governor Hunter to the Lords of Trade" (New York, November 12, 1715), *Doc. Rel.*, 5:461.

49. Will of Marten Clock, *CNYHS for the Year 1902*, 86–87; Will of Elizabeth Clock, *CNYHS for the Year 1895*, 436.

50. GQS, August 8, 1722; GQS, November 7, 1722. See also Kenneth Scott, comp., *New York City Court Records, 1684–1760: Genealogical Data from the Court of Quarter Sessions* (Washington, D.C., 1982), 36.

51. "Indentures of Apprentices, 1718–1727," *CNYHS for the Year 1909*, 158–59. John Fortune may have been the "Fortune, free Negro" who was assessed £5 in the North Ward on the 1730 tax list. "New York City Assessment Roll" (February 1730), *New York Genealogical and Biographical Record*, 95 (1964), 27–32, 166–74, 197–202. See also the indenture of Peter Jacobson, a free Negro, to Gerardus Stuyvesant made in 1718 ("Indentures of Apprentices, 1718–1727," 119).

52. For lists of Neau's pupils see "Mr. Neau to Mr. Chamberlayne" (New York, October 3, 1705), S.P.G., Letter Books A, vol. 2, #124; "A List of Negro Slaves Taught by Elias Neau enclosed in his letter of November 10, 1714" (ibid., vol. 10, fols. 220–23); "A List of Negroes instructed by Mr. Neau Since November 1714 inclosed in his letter of May 2, 1718" (ibid., vol. 13, fols. 422–23); "A List of Negroes taught by Mr. Neau, December 23, 1719 inclosed in his Letter of January 22, 1719/20" (ibid., vol. 14, fols. 141–43).

53. GQS, February 1714/15. On Peter the Doctor's role in the 1712 rebellion see Kenneth Scott, "The Slave Insurrection in New York in 1712," *New-York Historical Society Quarterly*, 45 (1961), 43–74.

54. Kruger, "Born to Run," 133–50.

55. Inventory of Roger Baker, 1704, Historical Documents Collection, Queens College, New York City.

56. "James Alexander to Cadwallader Colden" (New York, March 26, 1729), *The Letters and Papers of Cadwallader Colden*, vol. 1, *1711–1729*, in *CNYHS for the Year 1917*, 277. See also "James Alexander to Cadwallader Colden" (New York, March 14, 1728/29), ibid., 276. In 1731, Alexander noted the death of "my negro jupiter" from smallpox. "James Alexander to Cadwallader Colden" (New York, n.d. but c. 1731), *The Letters and Papers of Cadwallader Colden*, vol. 2, *1730–1742*, in *CNYHS for the Year 1918*, 24.

57. N.Y. Col. MSS, 41:23a, 41:23b.

58. "Cadwallader Colden to Captain Van pelt at North Carolina" (New York, December 17, 1726), *Letters and Papers of Cadwallader Colden*, 1:59.

59. Petition of Harmanus Burger, August 28, 1719, N.Y. Col. MSS, 61:176. In 1698, bricklayer Dirck Vanderburgh petitioned for the pardon of his slave Jack on the grounds that he cost him £60 and was "very assistant to [Vanderburgh] in

his trade." Petition of Dirck Vanderburgh, October 10, 1698, N.Y. Col. MSS, 42:72. See also ibid., 42:118a and 42:118b.

60. Petition of Richard Elliott (n.d., but c. 1693), N.Y. Col. MSS, 39:110. See also Petition of Susan Elliott, May 30, 1695, N.Y. Col. MSS, 40:21.

61. Helen Burr Smith, "A New IB Silversmith and Two Unrecorded Pewterers," *New-York Historical Society Quarterly*, 52 (1968), 83–84.

62. "Governor Hunter to the Lords of Trade" (New York, November 12, 1715), *Doc. Rel.*, 5:461.

63. "Cadwallader Colden to Dr Home" (New York, December 7, 1721), *The Letters and Papers of Cadwallader Colden*, 1:51.

64. *MCC*, 3:6. Remuneration was ordered for the City Marshall in 1716/17 for the "hire of a Negro to hang up the Ladders in the City Hall" and for the city's ferry man in 1720 for "Negroes Work for Repairing the ferry house" (*MCC*, 3:135, 238). In all probability, these workers were slaves.

65. "Isaac Bobin to George Clarke" (New York, October 16, 1723), *Letters of Isaac Bobin*, 157–58.

66. Joyce D. Goodfriend, "Black Families in New Netherland," *Journal of the Afro-American Historical and Genealogical Society*, 5 (1984), 95–107.

67. *RNA*, 6:286. When "Lewis Michiel and Stoffel, negroes" attempted to defend themselves after being accused of killing a white woman's pigs in 1668, the court ordered them "to keep still and quiet, so as to give no cause of complaint to their neighbours" (*RNA*, 6:146).

68. Mayor's Court Minutes, December 7, 1680 (microfilm), Historical Documents Collection, Queens College, New York City.

69. *MCC*, 1:276–77.

70. See the cases of Peter the Doctor (1714/15) and Tom Fauconnier (1724) in GQS.

71. See laws regarding assemblies of blacks in *MCC*.

72. GQS, August 20, 1696.

73. "A Law Appointing a Place for the More Convenient Hiring of Slaves," *MCC*, 2:458. The law was published again in 1731 (*MCC*, 4:85).

74. *CNYHS for the Year 1912*, 37–38. See also *MCC*, 1:134, 276–77; and "An Act against profanation of the Lords Day, called Sunday" (passed October 22, 1695), *The Colonial Laws of New York*, 1:356–57.

75. *CNYHS for the Year 1912*, 192; *MCC*, 2:102–3.

76. "Elias Neau to Mr. Hodges" (July 10, 1703), S.P.G. Letter Books A, vol. 1, #106.

77. GQS, February 3, 1718/19.

78. GQS, August 2, 1710; November 7, 1710; November 8, 1710. Numerous cases of whites being prosecuted for entertaining blacks and selling them liquor are found in the records of the Court of General Quarter Sessions.

79. GQS, November 4, 1718. There are other cases of whites buying stolen goods from blacks in the records of the Court of General Quarter Sessions.

80. Confession of Hannah, mulatto woman, for felony, July 3, 1716, N.Y. Col. MSS, 60:117.

81. GQS, August 1, 1699. For a discussion of slave crimes in colonial New

York, see Douglas Greenberg, *Crime and Law Enforcement in the Colony of New York 1691–1776* (Ithaca and London, 1976), 42–46, 149–53.

82. "Rev. John Sharpe's Proposals, March: 1713," *CNYHS for the Year 1880*, 355.

83. "Elias Neau to the Secretary" (May 2, 1718), S.P.G. Letter Books A, vol. 13, fols. 397–98 (my translation).

84. Albert J. Raboteau, *Slave Religion: The Invisible Institution in the Antebellum South* (New York, 1978), 83–85, 230–31; Mechal Sobel, *The World They Made Together: Black and White Values in Eighteenth-Century Virginia* (Princeton, 1988), 214–25; David R. Roediger, "Funerals in the Slave Community," *The Massachusetts Review*, 22 (1981), 163–83; John Michael Vlach, *The Afro-American Tradition in Decorative Arts* (Cleveland, 1978), 139–47.

85. "Rev. John Sharpe's Proposals," 355.

86. "A Law for Regulating the Burial of Slaves" (October 3, 1722), *MCC*, 3:296; "A Law for Regulating the Burial of Slaves" (February 18, 1731), *MCC*, 4:88–89.

87. On Peter Kalm's account, see George Piersen, *Black Yankees: The Development of an Afro-American Subculture in Eighteenth-Century New England* (Amherst, Mass., 1988), 82–83. On Pinkster, see Alice Morse Earle, *Colonial Days in Old New York* (New York, 1896), 195–201; David S. Cohen, "In Search of Carolus Africanus Rex," *Journal of the Afro-American Historical and Genealogical Society*, 5 (1984), 149–62; A. J. Williams-Meyers, "Pinkster Carnival: Africanisms in the Hudson River Valley," *Afro-Americans in New York Life and History*, 9 (1985), 7–17; and Shane White, "Pinkster: Afro-Dutch Syncretization in New York City and the Hudson Valley," *Journal of American Folklore*, 102 (1989), 68–75.

88. "Elias Neau to the Secretary" (May 2, 1718), S.P.G., Letter Books A, vol. 13, fols. 397–98 (my translation).

89. Will Liber 19B, 590; *CNYHS for the Year 1894*, 434–35.

90. *New-York Gazette*, August 24, 1730.

91. N.Y. Col. MSS, 36:114 (in Dutch).

92. On the 1712 slave rebellion, see Scott, "The Slave Insurrection in New York in 1712."

93. "John Sharpe to the Secretary" (June 23, 1712), S.P.G., Letter Books A, vol. 7, #33.

94. Donnan, *Documents Illustrative of the Slave Trade*, 3:444; *Doc. Rel.*, 5:814.

95. *New-York Gazette*, October 12, 1730. See also "Isaac Bobin to George Clarke" (April 19, 1723), *Letters of Isaac Bobin*, 129.

96. *New-York Gazette*, June 23, 1729. See also John Moor[e]'s advertisement for his runaway slave Cesar, who "reads and writes English, and its believed . . . has a sham Pass." *New-York Gazette*, August 12, 1728.

97. Petition of Abraham Santvoord, mariner, November 18, 1710, N.Y. Col. MSS, 54:109.

98. Petition of George Elsworth, June 25, 1710, N.Y. Col. MSS, 54:21.

99. Goodfriend, "Black Families in New Netherland." Pious Dutch slaveowners such as Judith Stuyvesant, the wife of New Netherland's director-general, made special provisions for the baptism of slave children. "Vice Director Beck to Pieter Stuyvesant. Curaçao, in Fort Amsterdam the 15 November. . . ," in E. B.

O'Callaghan, *Voyages of the Slavers St. John and Arms of Amsterdam, 1659, 1663: Together with Additional Papers Illustrative of the Slave Trade Under the Dutch* (Albany, N.Y., 1867), 226–27. See also Cohen, *The Ramapo Mountain People*; and Kruger, "Born to Run."

100. "Rev. Henry Selyns to the Classis of Amsterdam" (June 9, 1664), *Ecc. Rec.*, 1:548.

101. "Records of the Reformed Dutch Church, Members' List." "Den slave van Capt. Davidt Provoost" was baptized on March 10, 1708, upon confessing his faith. *Baptisms from 1639 to 1730 in the Reformed Dutch Church in New Amsterdam and New York* (New York, 1901). "Frans Abramse and Annetje Frans, negers," witnessed the baptism of Salomon, son of Pieter Luykasse And Marytje Willems on July 15, 1713. Between 1731 and 1743 the children of "Frans Franse, Neger van Harmanus van Gelder and Elisabet Bickers, Negerin van Gelyn Ver Planck" were baptized in the Dutch Reformed church. Witnesses to the 1743 baptism were "Jan Herris, Neger van Antony Rutgers and Anna Claase, Negerin" (ibid.). Black couples were married in the Dutch Reformed church in 1666, 1667, 1671, 1672 (two), 1680, 1681, 1682, 1683, 1688, 1689, 1691 (two), 1695, and 1697 (two). See *Marriages from 1639 to 1801 in the Reformed Dutch Church, New York* (New York, 1940).

102. "Directions for Jan de la Montagne, in reference to the Public Service of the Church, and Funerals . . . ," *Ecc. Rec.*, 2:931; In 1767, the sexton's instructions included a similar directive: "You are to prevent any disorders in the church by children, negroes, or dogs, either before and after service-time." Quoted in Gerald Francis De Jong, "The Dutch Reformed Church and Negro Slavery in Colonial America," *Church History*, 40 (1971), 427.

103. "Elias Neau to the Secretary" (New York, October 18, 1719), S.P.G., Letter Books A, vol. 13, fols. 479–82. Writing later in the century, Swedish traveler Peter Kalm observed that "the negroes or their other servants accompanied [Dutch Reformed women] to church mornings carrying the warming pans. When the minister had finished his sermon and the last hymn had been sung, the same negroes, etc. came and removed the warming pans and carried them home." Adoph B. Benson, ed., *The America of 1750: Peter Kalm's Travels in North America. The English Version of 1770*, revised from the original Swedish, 2 vols. (1937; reprinted, New York, 1966); 2:624. A similar custom was observed at the Albany Dutch Reformed church: "Foot stoves were then in vogue, and it was not an uncommon occurence to see, on a Sunday, from fifty to seventy-five colored servants or slaves, at the church door, awaiting the arrival of master or mistress, with two or more foot stoves in hand, filled with live hickory coals taken from an old Dutch fire-place." Quoted in Alice P. Kenney, *Stubborn for Liberty: The Dutch in New York* (Syracuse, N.Y., 1975), 127.

104. Arnold J. H. van Laer, trans., *The Lutheran Church in New York 1649–1772: Records in the Lutheran Church Archives at Amsterdam, Holland* (New York, 1946), 68, 70.

105. "Some Early Records of the Lutheran Church, New York," *Year Book of the Holland Society of New York* (1903), 40; "First Communions in the Lutheran Church of New York City 1704 to 1769," *New York Genealogical and Biographical Record*, 104 (1973), 111.

106. Harry Julius Kreider, *Lutheranism in Colonial New York* (New York, 1942). Other New York City denominations did not incorporate blacks in their congregations during this period. On the treatment of blacks in New York City's Presbyterian church in the 1760s, see Dorothy Ganfield Fowler, *A City Church: The First Presbyterian Church in the City of New York 1716–1916* (New York, 1981), 26, 29–30, 31. See also Andrew E. Murray, *Presbyterians and the Negro: A History* (Philadelphia, 1966). On the Quakers' treatment of blacks, see John Cox, Jr., *Quakerism in the City of New York 1657–1930* (New York, 1930), and Thomas E. Drake, *Quakers and Slavery in America* (New Haven, Conn., 1950).

107. "Rev. John Sharpe's Proposals," 357.

108. "Gov. Dongan's Report on the State of the Province" (February 22, 1687), *Doc. Rel.*, 3:415.

109. "Earl of Bellomont to the Lords of Trade" (April 27, 1699), *Doc. Rel.*, 4:510–11.

110. "An Act to Incourage the Baptizing of Negro, Indian and Mulatto Slaves" (passed October 21, 1706), *The Colonial Laws of New York*, 1:597–98. On opposition to the Christianization of slaves, see John C. Van Horne, "Impediments to the Christianization and Education of Blacks in Colonial America: The Case of the Associates of Dr. Bray," *Historical Magazine of the Protestant Episcopal Church*, 50 (1981), 243–69.

111. "Neau to Secretary" (April 30, 1706), S.P.G., Letter Books A, vol. 2, #167.

112. "Neau to Secretary" (July 24, 1707), ibid., vol. 3, #128.

113. "John Sharpe to Secretary" (June 23, 1712), ibid., vol. 7, #33.

114. "Neau to Secretary" (March 1, 1705/6), ibid., vol. 2, #159.

115. These statements are based on an examination of four lists of pupils submitted by Neau to the S.P.G. "Mr. Neau to Mr. Chamberlayne" (New York, October 3, 1705), ibid., vol. 2, #124; "A List of Negro Slaves Taught by Elias Neau enclosed in his letter of November 10, 1714," ibid., vol. 10, fols. 220–23; "A List of Negroes instructed by Mr. Neau since November 1714 inclosed in his letter of May 2, 1718," ibid., vol. 13, fols. 422–23; "A List of Negroes taught by Mr. Neau, December 23, 1719 inclosed in his Letter of January 22, 1719/20," ibid., vol. 14, fols. 141–43.

116. "Neau to Secretary" (October 8, 1719), ibid., vol. 13, fols. 479–82.

117. "Neau to Secretary" (n.d. but c. 1714), ibid., vol. 9, New York Letters #29.

118. "A List of Negroes taught by Mr. Neau" (December 23, 1719), ibid., vol. 14, fols. 141–43.

119. "Neau to Secretary" (October 8, 1719), ibid., vol. 13, fols. 479–82.

120. "Neau to Secretary" (June 6, 1709), ibid., vol. 5, #6.

121. "Neau to Secretary" (May 2, 1718), ibid., vol. 13, fols. 397–98 (my translation).

122. See Sheldon S. Cohen, "Elias Neau, Instructor to New York's Slaves," *New-York Historical Society Quarterly*, 55 (1971), 7–27; and Jon Butler, *The Huguenots in America: A Refugee People in New World Society* (Cambridge, Mass., 1983), 161–65; 168–69.

123. "Rev. John Sharpe's Proposals," 349.

124. "Certificate from the Governor & Clergy of New York in behalf of Mr. Neau Inclosed in Mr. Neau's Letter of July 2, 1718," S.P.G., Letter Books A, vol. 13, fol. 424.

125. "Rev. John Sharpe's Proposals," 350.

126. Ibid., 349.

127. "Neau to Secretary" (July 24, 1707), S.P.G., Letter Books A, vol. 3, #128.

128. Piersen, *Black Yankees*, 66; Charles Joyner, *Down by the Riverside: A South Carolina Slave Community* (Urbana and Chicago, 1984), 162.

129. "Neau to Secretary" (June 21, 1709), S.P.G., Letter Books A, vol. 4, #155.

130. Ibid.

131. "Neau to Secretary" (July 24, 1707), ibid., vol. 3, #128.

132. "Neau to Secretary" (February 27, 1708/9), ibid., vol. 4, #121.

133. "Neau to Secretary" (October 3, 1710), ibid., vol. 6, #43.

134. "Neau to Mr. Chamberlayne" (July 5, 1710), ibid., vol. 5, #134; Mechal Sobel, *Trabelin' On: The Slave Journey to an Afro-Baptist Faith* (Westport, Conn., 1979), 62–63.

135. "John Sharpe to Secretary" (June 23, 1712), S.P.G., Letter Books A, vol. 7, #33.

136. *New-York Gazette*, September 14, 1730; Will of William Ricketts, *CNYHS for the Year 1894*, 188–89.

137. "Neau to Mr. Chamberlayne" (November 22, 1715), S.P.G., Letter Books A, vol. 11, fols. 283–86.

138. "Neau to Secretary" (November 24, 1720), ibid., vol. 14, fols. 128–29.

139. Morgan Dix, ed., *A History of the Parish of Trinity Church in the City of New York* (New York, 1898), 1:113.

140. "Extract of a Letter from Mr. Elias Neau Catechist att New York to Doctor Sharpe at London" (November 22, 1715), S.P.G., Letter Books A, vol. 11, fols. 294–95.

141. "Neau to Secretary" (October 8, 1719), ibid., vol. 13, fols. 479–82.

142. "Neau to Secretary" (April 2, 1722), ibid., vol. 16, fols. 196–97.

143. "Neau to Secretary" (n.d. but after April 1722), ibid., vol. 16, fol. 204.

144. "Neau to Secretary" (May 2, 1718), ibid., vol. 13, fols. 397–98 (my translation). See also William Webb Kemp, *The Support of Schools in Colonial New York by the Society for the Propagation of the Gospel in Foreign Parts* (New York, 1969; originally published 1913), 248.

145. "Neau to Secretary" (March 1, 1705/6), ibid., vol. 2, #159.

146. "Rev. Samuel Auchmuty to Rev. John Waring" (New York October 7, 1761), in John C. Van Horne, ed., *Religious Philanthropy and Colonial Slavery: The American Correspondence of the Associates of Dr. Bray, 1717–1777* (Urbana and Chicago, 1985), 167.

147. "Rev. Samuel Auchmuty to Rev. John Waring" (New York, October 20, 1774), ibid., 322. In the same letter, Auchmuty noted that "many of [these Negroes] are now . . . qualified to instruct their own Children" (ibid., 323). On Gerard G. Beekman, see Philip L. White, *The Beekmans of New York in Politics and Commerce 1647–1877* (New York, 1956), 211–311.

CHAPTER SEVEN
IMMIGRANTS TO NEW YORK CITY, 1700–1730

1. "Lord Cornbury to the Lords of Trade" (New York, May 18, 1702), *Doc. Rel.*, 4:958–59. John Duffy is of the opinion that this was not a very significant outbreak of smallpox. John Duffy, *Epidemics in Colonial America* (Baton Rouge, 1953), 74–75.

2. "James Logan to William Penn" (Philadelphia, July 11, 1702), "Correspondence Between William Penn and James Logan," Vol. 1, in *Memoirs* of the Historical Society of Pennsylvania, 9 (Philadelphia, 1870), 134–35. See also Duffy, *Epidemics in Colonial America*, 145–46.

3. "Lt. Gov. Hamilton to William Penn" (Burlington, September 19, 1702), *Calendar of State Papers, Colonial, 1702–1703*, 27.

4. *MCC*, 2:203.

5. Council Minutes, September 17, 1702, in Berthold Fernow, ed., "Calendar of Council Minutes, 1668–1783," New York State Library, *Bulletin*, 58 (1902), 174.

6. "Lord Cornbury to the Lords of Trade" (Orange County, September 27, 1702), *Doc. Rel.*, 4:972.

7. "Lord Cornbury to Mr. Secretary Hedges" (New York, July 15, 1705), *Doc. Rel.*, 4:1152. See also Duffy, *Epidemics in Colonial America*, 145–46.

8. Duffy, *Epidemics in Colonia America*, 146.

9. Evarts B. Greene and Virginia D. Harrington, *American Population Before the Federal Census of 1790* (New York, 1932; reprinted 1966), 92, 94. A slightly different total of 4,375 people for 1703 also exists (ibid., 95).

10. "An Act for the better Support and Maintenance of the Poor in the City of New York for the future" (passed November 27, 1702), *The Colonial Laws of New York from the Year 1664 to the Revolution . . .*, 5 vols. (Albany, 1894–1896), 1:507.

11. On New York City population figures, see Greene and Harrington, *American Population Before the Federal Census of 1790*; Robert V. Wells, "The New York Census of 1731," *New-York Historical Society Quarterly*, 57 (1973), 255–59. See also Gary B. Nash, "The New York Census of 1737: A Critical Note on the Integration of Statistical and Literary Sources," *William and Mary Quarterly*, 3d ser., 36 (1979), 428–35.

12. On the small pox epidemic of 1731, see John Duffy, *A History of Public Health in New York City (1625–1866)* (New York, 1968), 53–54; and Duffy, *Epidemics in Colonial America*, 78–80. And see the discussion later in this chapter.

13. Smallpox was present in the city in 1716 and 1718, but its impact was not significant. Duffy, *History of Public Health in New York City*, 36; Duffy, *Epidemics in Colonial America*, 76–77. On the 1729 measles epidemic, see Duffy. *History of Public Health in New York City*, 58–59; and Duffy, *Epidemics in Colonial America*, 170–171. And see the discussion later in this chapter.

14. A. Roger Ekirch, "Bound for America: A Profile of British Convicts Transported to the Colonies, 1718–1775," *William and Mary Quarterly*, 3d ser., 42 (1985), 184–200.

15. David W. Galenson, *White Servitude in Colonial America: An Economic Analysis* (Cambridge, 1981); John Wareing, "Migration to London and Trans-

atlantic Emigration of Indentured Servants, 1683–1775," *Journal of Historical Geography*, 7 (1981), 356–78. John Wareing, *Emigrants to America: Indentured Servants Recruited in London 1718–1733* (Baltimore, 1985), which lists 1,544 servants transported to America, notes none going to New York.

16. Thomas M. Truxes, *Irish-American Trade, 1660–1783* (Cambridge, 1988), 142.

17. *Boston News-Letter*, September 7, 1713.

18. "Indentures of Apprentices, 1718–1727," *CNYHS for the Year 1909*, 136.

19. See the discussion later in this chapter.

20. Paying passengers are the group of immigrants about which historians know least. See John J. McCusker and Russell R. Menard, *The Economy of British America, 1607–1789* (Chapel Hill, N.C., and London, 1985), 219, 222.

21. Jon Butler, *The Huguenots in America: A Refugee People in New World Society* (Cambridge, Mass., 1983).

22. "The Oath of Abjuration, 1715–1716," *New-York Historical Society Quarterly Bulletin*, 3 (1919), 35–40; Richard J. Wolfe, "The Colonial Naturalization Act of 1740 with a List of Persons Naturalized in New York Colony, 1740–1769," *New York Genealogical and Biographical Record*, 94 (1963), 132–47; Kenneth Scott and Kenn Stryker-Rodda, *Denizations, Naturalizations, and Oaths of Allegiance in Colonial New York* (Baltimore, 1975); James H. Kettner, *The Development of American Citizenship, 1608–1870* (Chapel Hill, N.C., 1978), 65–128.

23. "Records of the Reformed Dutch Church, Members' List" (see note 24 for chapter 5). The Palatine Germans who joined the church during this period are excluded from this analysis. Not all Dutch newcomers joined the Dutch Reformed church or did so with a certificate, so this analysis underestimates the number of Dutch internal migrants. For background on Dutch migration patterns in the eighteenth century, see Bertus Harry Wabeke, *Dutch Migration to North America 1624–1860* (New York, 1944), 61–70; Gerald F. De Jong, *The Dutch in America, 1609–1974* (Boston, 1975), 39–40. See also American Council of Learned Societies, "Report of the Committee on Linguistic and National Stocks in the Population of the United States," Annex B: "The Minor Stocks in the American Population of 1790," by Marcus L. Hansen, in American Historical Association, *Annual Report: 1931*, 3 vols. (Washington, D.C., 1932), 1:363–79.

24. Herman Winkler's obituary is in the *New-York Weekly Journal*, March 24, 1734. On Floris van Taerling, see Waldron Phoenix Belknap, Jr., *The De Peyster Genealogy* (Boston, 1956), 40. Floris van Taerling's son, Jan, married Anna de Peyster, the daughter of merchant Johannes de Peyster, in 1724.

25. Wabeke, *Dutch Migration to North America*, 61; De Jong, *The Dutch in America*, 39.

26. Randall Balmer, *A Perfect Babel of Confusion: Dutch Religion and English Culture in the Middle Colonies* (New York, 1989,) 55–61.

27. "Lord Cornbury to the Board of Trade" (New York, July 1, 1708), *Doc. Rel.*, 5:56.

28. "Governor Hunter to the Lords of Trade" (Amboy, April 30, 1716), *Doc. Rel.*, 5:476.

29. The distinguishing features of British migrants to New York City between 1700 and 1730 must be pieced together from diverse and often intractable sources

such as the marriage records of the Dutch Reformed church, wills, indentures of apprenticeship, miscellaneous public records, and genealogies. Genealogical sources consulted include Michael Tepper, ed., *Immigrants to the Middle Colonies: A Consolidation of Ship Passenger Lists and Associated Data from the New York Genealogical and Biographical Record* (Baltimore, 1978); Peter Wilson Coldham, comp., *Lord Mayor's Court of London: Depositions Relating to Americans 1641–1736* (Washington, D.C., 1980); Peter Wilson Coldham, *English Adventurers and Emigrants, 1661–1733: Abstracts from Examinations in the High Court of Admiralty with Reference to Colonial America* (Baltimore, 1985). See also the sources on Scottish immigrants cited in note 44.

30. Peter Clark, "Migration in England during the late Seventeenth and early Eighteenth Centuries," *Past and Present*, 83 (1979), 57–90; Wareing, "Migration to London and Transatlantic Emigration of Indentured Servants."

31. Will of John Gee, *CNYHS for the Year 1893*, 227.

32. Wareing, "Migration to London and Transatlantic Emigration of Indentured Servants."

33. Regarding Thomas Davenport's will, see *CNYHS for the Year 1893*, 207–8.

34. Will of Thomas Cockerill, *CNYHS for the Year 1893*, 38. On Caleb Cooper, see Thomas J. Archdeacon, *New York City 1664–1710: Conquest and Change* (Ithaca, N.Y., 1976), 76; Will of William Glencross, *CNYHS for the Year 1893*, 74, 142.

35. Will of Jacob Regnier, *CNYHS for the Year 1893*, 142–43. On Regnier, see Paul M. Hamlin and Charles E. Baker, *Supreme Court of Judicature of the Province of New York 1691–1704*, 3 vols., (New York, 1959), 3:172–75.

36. "Indentures of Apprentices, 1694–5 to 1707–8," *CNYHS for the Year 1885*, 597–98; Will of Barne Cosens, *CNYHS for the Year 1893*, 31–32.

37. Will of William Taylor, *CNYHS for the Year 1893*, 242.

38. *Marriages from 1639 to 1801 in the Reformed Dutch Church, New York* (New York, 1940), 138.

39. *New-York Gazette*, October 6, 1729.

40. *New-York Gazette*, May 11, 1730.

41. *New-York Gazette*, October 23, 1732.

42. "Indentures of Apprentices, 1718–1727," 119.

43. Ibid., 163–64.

44. Ibid., 190.

45. *Marriages from 1639 to 1801 in the Reformed Dutch Church, New York* (New York, 1940), 105.

46. Will of George Norton, *CNYHS for the Year 1893*, 151.

47. Will of John Burge, *CNYHS for the Year 1893*, 225; Will of Joseph Ledell, *CNYHS for the Year 1895*, 467–68.

48. Will of John Blake, *CNYHS for the Year 1893*, 367.

49. Will of George Cock, *CNYHS for the Year 1893*, 256.

50. William Smith, Jr., *The History of the Province of New-York*, ed. Michael Kammen, 2 vols. (Cambridge, Mass., 1972), 1:181, 2:293.

51. *MCC*, 3:452; Will of James Searle, *CNYHS for the Year 1895*, 73.

52. *Churchyards of Trinity Parish in the City of New York 1697–1969* (New York, 1969), 32–33,

53. *Churchyards of Trinity Parish in the City of New York 1697–1969*, 36.

54. Letters of Administration for Abraham Brock, *CNYHS for the Year 1893*, 112–13; 140.

55. *CNYHS for the Year 1902*, 101–2.

56. "Governor Montgomerie to the Lords of Trade" (New York, June 20, 1731), *Doc. Rel.*, 5:920.

57. Will of John Graham, *CNYHS for the Year 1892*, 395–96.

58. "Guy Miller and ux: Late Susannah Oruck ver: Charles Home Adm. etc: of John Montgomerie Esqr Deceased" (January 11, 1731–32), in Richard B. Morris, ed., *Select Cases of the Mayor's Court of New York City 1674–1784* (Washington, D.C., 1935), 478–83.

59. Will of William Ricketts, *CNYHS for the Year 1894*, 188–89.

60. Will of William Bowyer, *CNYHS for the Year 1892*, 416.

61. Deeds from the Secretary of State's Office, New York State Archives, vol. 12 (1723–1735), fol. 45.

62. Letters of Administration for William Carr, *CNYHS for the Year 1893*, 263.

63. Will of Nicholas Flanders, *CNYHS for the Year 1893*, 371; Will of William Crow, *CNYHS for the Year 1894*, 301. See also Deeds from the Secretary of State's Office, New York State Archives, vol. 14 (1739–1750), fol. 219.

64. "Michael Bassett Ver Germanicus Andrews" (August 14, 1711), in Morris, ed., *Select Cases of the Mayor's Court of New York City*, 174–76.

65. "Indentures of Apprentices, 1718–1727," 128–29.

66. Ibid., 189–90.

67. Will of Henry Harding, *CNYHS for the Year 1892*, 443–44, 406.

68. Secretary of State Deeds, vol. 12 (1723–1735), fols. 503, 517.

69. Will of Nicholas Croxton, *CNYHS for the Year 1892*, 434.

70. Paul M. Hamlin, *Legal Education in Colonial New York* (New York, 1970; originally published 1939), 157.

71. "Indentures of Apprentices, 1718–1727," 183.

72. Will of Charles Owen, *CNYHS for the Year 1892*, 351.

73. *New-York Gazette*, August 28, 1732.

74. On Governor Hunter's Scottish inner circle, see Mary Lou Lustig, *Robert Hunter 1666–1734: New York's Augustan Statesman* (Syracuse, N.Y., 1983).

75. Joyce D. Goodfriend, "A New Look at Presbyterian Origins in New York City," *American Presbyterians*, 67 (1989), 199–207.

76. "James Anderson to the Right Reverend Mr John Stirling principal of the Colledge of Glasgow" (New York, December 3, 1717), in Charles Augustus Briggs, *American Presbyterianism: Its origin and early history together with an appendix of Letters and Documents*, Appendix, lxxviii. See also Dorothy Ganfield Fowler, *A City Church: The First Presbyterian Church in the City of New York, 1716–1976* (New York, 1981).

77. "James Anderson to Rev. John Stirling," in Briggs, *American Presbyterianism*, Appendix, lxxviii.

78. Ian Charles Cargill Graham, *Colonists from Scotland: Emigration to North America, 1707–1783* (Ithaca, N.Y., 1956). See also William R. Brock, *Scotus Americanus: A Survey of the Sources for Links between Scotland and America in the Eighteenth Century* (Edinburgh, 1972); George S. Pryde, "Scottish Colonization in the Province of New York," *New York History*, 16 (April 1935), 138–57. Some Scottish immigrants to New York City can be identified in David Dobson, *The Original Scots Colonists of Early America 1612–1783* (Baltimore, 1989).

79. Ned C. Landsman, *Scotland and Its First American Colony, 1683–1765.* (Princeton, 1985).

80. Brooke Hindle, "A Colonial Governor's Family: The Coldens of Coldengham," *New-York Historical Society Quarterly*, 45 (1961), 233–50.

81. See the obituary of Hugh Munro in the *New-York Weekly Journal*, March 15, 1735 (1735/36). In his will, Munro bequeathed to his son John "all my right of lands in Scotland." Will of Hugh Monro, *CNYHS for the Year 1894*, 215.

82. On Alexander Malcolm's career, see Leo Hershkowitz and Isidore Meyer, eds., *The Lee Max Friedman Collection of American Jewish Colonial Correspondence: Letters of the Franks Family (1733–1748)* (Waltham, Mass., 1968), 13 n. 8; and James R. Heintze, "Alexander Malcolm: Musician, Clergyman, and Schoolmaster," *Maryland Historical Magazine*, 73 (1978), 226–35. Another New York City schoolmaster, Andrew Clarke, also was a native of Scotland. Dobson, *The Original Scots Colonists of Early America*, 55.

83. "James Anderson to Rev. John Stirling," in Briggs, *American Presbyterianism*, Appendix lxxix.

84. Kenneth Scott, "The Church Wardens and the Poor in New York City, 1732–1735," *New York Genealogical and Biographical Record*, 101 (1970), 172.

85. "Indentures of Apprentices, 1718–1727," 187–88.

86. *Marriages from 1639 to 1801 in the Reformed Dutch Church, New York*, 138.

87. Will of Andrew Bisset, *CNYHS for the Year 1894*, 149–50.

88. *New-York Gazette*, April 21, 1729.

89. David Baillie Morrison, ed. and comp., *Two Hundredth Anniversary 1756–1956 of St. Andrew's Society of the State of New York* (1956), 7. See also Fowler, *A City Church*, 17.

90. Morrison. *Two Hundredth Anniversary*, 7–9; Fowler, *A City Church*, 17.

91. On the Scots-Irish immigrants, see R. J. Dickson, *Ulster Emigration to Colonial America 1718–1775* (London, 1966), and James G. Leyburn, *The Scotch-Irish: A Social History* (Chapel Hill, N.C., 1962).

92. David Noel Doyle, *Ireland, Irishmen, and Revolutionary America, 1760–1820* (Dublin, 1981), 51–76; Kerby A. Miller, *Emigrants and Exiles: Ireland and the Irish Exodus to North America* (New York, 1985), 137.

93. Miller, *Emigrants and Exiles*, 137–68.

94. "Earl of Bellomont to the Lords of Trade" (New York, October 28, 1700), *Doc. Rel.*, 4:770–71. According to Lawrence Leder, a 300-ton vessel carrying 129 soldiers, plus officers, had arrived in New York from Dublin, Ireland, in October 1700 after a twelve-week passage. Lawrence H. Leder, ed., "'Dam'me Don't Stir a Man': Trial of New York Mutineers in 1700," *New-York Historical Society Quarterly*, 42 (July 1958), 261–83. See also Stanley McCrory Pargellis, "The Four In-

dependent Companies of New York" in *Essays in Colonial History Presented to Charles McLean Andrews by his Students* (New Haven, 1931).

95. Miller, *Emigrants and Exiles*; Dickson, *Ulster Emigration to Colonial America 1718–1775*; Truxes, *Irish-American Trade*.

96. Dickson, *Ulster Emigration to Colonial America 1718–1775*, 19–47; Miller, *Emigrants and Exiles*, 152–53.

97. Truxes, *Irish-American Trade*, 142.

98. "Brigadier Hunter's Answers to Queries relating to New-York" (London, August 11, 1720), *Doc. Rel.*, 5:556.

99. See note 94.

100. List of Freemen in *CNYHS for the Year 1885, 112; Marriages from 1639 to 1801 in the Reformed Dutch Church, New York*, 143. For studies that rely heavily on surnames to identify Irish individuals, see Richard David Doyle, "The Pre-Revolutionary Irish in New York (1643–1775)" (Ph.D. diss., Saint Louis University, 1932), and Michael J. O'Brien, *Irish Settlers in America: A Consolidation of Articles from the Journal of the American Irish Historical Society*, 2 vols. (Baltimore, 1979).

101. "Indentures of Apprentices, 1718–1727," 148.

102. Ibid., 180–81.

103. Will of Thomas Scurlock, *CNYHS for the Year 1895*, 116.

104. Coldham, comp., *Lord Mayor's Court of London*, 45.

105. Michael J. O'Brien, *In Old New York: The Irish Dead in Trinity and St. Paul's Churchyards* (New York, 1928), 14–15.

106. Edward P. Alexander, *A Revolutionary Conservative: James Duane of New York* (New York, 1938), 3–8.

107. Edward Porter Alexander, ed., *The Journal of John Fontaine: An Irish Huguenot Son in Spain and Virginia 1710–1719* (Williamsburg, Va., 1972), 114, 116.

108. Audrey Lockhart, *Some Aspects of Emigration from Ireland to the North American Colonies between 1660 and 1775* (New York, 1976).

109. "John Paterson ver Samuell Gordon" (December 16, 1718), in Morris, ed., *Select Cases of the Mayor's Court of New York City*, 684–87.

110. *Boston News-Letter*, October 27, 1718; November 10, 1718.

111. Benjamin Franklin, "Journal of a Voyage, 1726," in *The Papers of Benjamin Franklin*, ed. Leonard W. Labaree, 28 vols. (New Haven, 1959), 1:90–91.

112. CO 5/1224 records consulted by Audrey Lockhart list the *Thomas* as sailing from Cork, but the *New-York Gazette* advertised "several English Men, Women and Boys, Servants" on this vessel and stated that the ship had arrived from London. Lockhart, *Some Aspects of Emigration from Ireland to the North American Colonies*, Appendix C: Emigrant Shipping; *New-York Gazette*, October 21, 1728.

113. Lockhart, *Some Aspects of Emigration from Ireland to the North American Colonies*, 44.

114. The seventh ship, the *Olive Branch*, was noted in *Faulkner's Dublin Journal* as departing from Dublin for Philadelphia and New York in July–August 1732. Lockhart, *Some Aspects of Emigration from Ireland to the North American Colonies*, Appendix C: Emigrant Shipping.

115. I have found only three instances where a specific birthplace is given for

an Irish immigrant to New York City in the late seventeeth and early eighteenth centuries. Anthony Duane of Cong, county Galway, and Anthony Lynch of Galway have already been mentioned. The other is Daniel Honan who, as of c. 1701, had lived in New York "for 7 years, but born at Elfin, Roscommon, Ireland, merchant, aged 33." Peter Coldham, *English Adventurers and Emigrants*, 89.

116. *New-York Gazette*, April 21, 1729.

117. *CEM*, 504.

118. *New-York Gazette*, October 21, 1728.

119. *Remarkable Experiences in the Life of Elizabeth Ashbridge. A True Account (Written mostly by herself)* (n.p., 1927), 11.

120. Ibid., 12

121. Truxes, *Irish-American Trade*, 142.

122. "M.C.M. [Minutes of the Mayor's Court]," (December 16, 1729), in Morris, ed., *Select Cases of the Mayor's Court of New York City*, 70.

123. *New-York Gazette*, July 19, 1731.

124. *New-York Gazette*, July 16, 1733.

125. Lockhart, *Some Aspects of Emigration from Ireland to the North American Colonies*; Doyle, *Ireland, Irishmen, and Revolutionary America*; Miller, *Emigrants and Exiles*.

126. Walter Allen Knittle, *Early Eighteenth Century Palatine Emigration: A British Government Redemptioner Project to Manufacture Naval Stores* (Philadelphia, 1936); Henry Z. Jones, Jr., *The Palatine Families of New York: A Study of the German Immigrants Who Arrived in Colonial New York in 1710* (Universal City, Calif., 1985). For a brief overview of German immigration to colonial New York, see Klaus Wust, *Guardian on the Hudson: The German Society of the City of New York 1784–1984* (New York, [1984]), 9–13. On German immigrants in the American colonies, see A. G. Roeber, "In German Ways? Problems and Potentials of Eighteenth-Century German Social and Emigration History," *William and Mary Quarterly*, 3d ser., 44 (1987), 750–74; and John B. Frantz, "The Awakening of Religion among the German Settlers in the Middle Colonies," *William and Mary Quarterly*, 3d ser., 33 (1976), 266–88.

127. Knittle, *Early Eighteenth Century Palatine Emigration*, 148.

128. Robert E. Cray, Jr., *Paupers and Poor Relief in New York City and Its Rural Environs, 1700–1830* (Philadelphia, 1988), 43.

129. "Records of the Reformed Dutch Church, Members' List."

130. Harry Julius Kreider, *Lutheranism in Colonial New York* (New York, 1942).

131. Using contemporary documents in conjunction with Jones's comprehensive genealogical study of the Palatine families of 1710, it is possible to trace the subsequent movements of many of the persons who resided in New York City in 1710. "List of the Palatines Remaining at New York, 1710," *DHNY*, 3:562–65; Jones, *The Palatine Families of New York*.

132. "Indentures of Apprentices, 1718–1727," 154.

133. Ibid., 143, 166, 178, 181, 185.

134. "Lutheran Church of New York City: Burials," *New York Genealogical and Biographical Record*, 105 (1974), 40.

135. "Some Early Records of the Lutheran Church, New York," *Year Book of*

the Holland Society of New York (1903), 15; "Lutheran Church of New York City: Burials," 81.

136. Jones, *The Palatine Families of New York*; Livingston Rutherfurd, *John Peter Zenger: His Press, His Trial* (New York, 1981; originally published 1904); Vincent Buranelli, ed., *The Trial of Peter Zenger* (New York, 1957); Stanley Nider Katz, ed., *A Brief Narrative of the Case and Trial of John Peter Zenger Printer of the New York Weekly Journal* by James Alexander (Cambridge, Mass., 1963).

137. For the arrival in New York City in 1726 of a ship from Rotterdam with 93 Palatine Germans, see "Smith V. Dern" (June 13, 1726), Morris, ed. *Select Cases of the Mayor's Court of New York City*, 689–691.

138. On Jews in Europe during this period, see Jonathan I. Israel, *European Jewry in the Age of Mercantilism 1550–1750* (Oxford, 1985).

139. "Rev. John Sharpe's Proposals, March: 1713," *CNYHS for the Year 1880*, 343.

140. David de Sola Pool, *Portraits Etched in Stone: Early Jewish Settlers, 1682–1831* (New York 1952), 171.

141. Quoted in D. de Sola Pool, *The Mill Street Synagogue (1730–1817) of the Congregation Shearith Israel* (New York, 1930), 49. The fact that congregational accounts and some other records were kept in Portuguese until the middle of the eighteenth century demonstrates the enduring influence of the Sephardim in the city's synagogue. David and Tamar de Sola Pool, *An Old Faith in the New World: Portrait of Shearith Israel, 1654–1954* (New York, 1955), 280.

142. Jacob R. Marcus, *The Colonial American Jew 1492–1776*, 3 vols. (Detroit, 1970), 1:309. The list of "Contributors Towards the Construction of the Mill Street Synagogue" is printed in de Sola Pool, *The Mill Street Synagogue*, 71–72. According to Leo Hershkowitz, New York City's Jewish community during the first third of the eighteenth century was about 1 to 2 percent of the city's total population. Leo Hershkowitz, "Some Aspects of the New York Jewish Merchant and Community, 1654–1820," *American Jewish Historical Society Quarterly*, 66 (1976–77), 10.

143. De Sola Pool, *Portraits Etched in Stone*, 119.

144. In addition to the works already cited, basic sources on New York City's Jews include Jacob Rader Marcus, *Early American Jewry: The Jews of New York, New England, and Canada, 1649–1794*, 2 vols. (Philadelphia, 1951); Hyman B. Grinstein, *The Rise of the Jewish Community of New York 1654–1860* (Philadelphia, 1947); "The Earliest Extant Minute Books of the Spanish and Portuguese Congregation Shearith Israel in New York, 1728–1786," American Jewish Historical Society, *Publications*, no. 21 (1913), 1–171; and Leo Hershkowitz, *Wills of Early New York Jews (1704–1799)* (New York, 1967). See also Joseph R. Rosenbloom, *A Biographical Dictionary of Early American Jews Colonial Times through 1800* (Lexington, Ky., 1960).

145. Valentine Campanal also served the Jewish congregation as *shammash*, an office resembling that of sexton. De Sola Pool and de Sola Pool, *Old Faith in the New World*, 285–86. Uriah Hyam's mention of a son in Jamaica and a brother in Bohemia in his 1740 will illustrates the far-flung connections of early New York Jews. Hyam's will is printed in Hershkowitz, *Wills of Early New York Jews*, 55–56. On the activities of New York's Jewish merchants, see Hershkowitz, "Some As-

pects of the New York Jewish Merchant and Community," and Marcus, *The Colonial American Jew*, vol. 2.

146. On the Franks family, see Hershkowitz and Meyer, eds., *The Lee Max Friedman Collection of American Jewish Colonial Correspondence*, and Leo Hershkowitz, "Abigail Franks and Jewish Education in Early New York," in Charles T. Gehring and Nancy Anne McClure Zeller, eds., *Education in New Netherland and the Middle Colonies: Papers of the 7th Rensselaerswyck Seminar of the New Netherland Project* (Albany, 1985), 43–49.

147. On the Gomez family, see de Sola Pool, *Portraits Etched in Stone*, 217–23, 234–37, 470, 474–75, 476–78.

148. De Sola Pool, *The Mill Street Synagogue*, 45.

149. "James Alexander to Cadwallader Colden" (New York, March 14, 1728–29), *The Letters and Papers of Cadwallader Colden*, vol. 1, *1711–1729*, in *CNYHS for the Year 1917*, 276. Alexander also reported that "our Supream Court was adjourned . . . for Six weeks because of the Sickness of the town" (ibid., 277).

On March 26, 1729, Alexander informed Colden that "My wife is brought Low with the Measles & dare not come out of her room yet, Johnie is ill of a Relapse after them, Mattie's measles were at the height yesterday but I think is in no danger, Jammee was dangerously ill, but now Sets up & plays, Billie was taken yesternight w[ith] a fever I suppose its the Measles, my children at Nurse have had them & are not quite recovered yet, four of our Negroes have the Measles, & one we are afraid is getting them this day, So that there is but davie & my Self of whites & one black wench that I can call well in our family" (ibid., 277).

150. *MCC*, 4:132–33. Governor Montgomerie noted that the chief justice was unwilling to come into the city "in the Time when the Measles raged lately in Town." "Governor Montgomerie to the Lords of Trade" (June 30, 1729), *Doc. Rel.*, 5:881.

151. Duffy, *A History of Public Health in New York City*, 58; *New-York Gazette*, February 18, 1728 (1728–29). However, the Great Consistory of the Dutch Reformed Church postponed critical business because of "the length of the winter, the very general sickness prevailing, and the many deaths." "Great Consistory meeting" (March 6, 1728–29, *Ecc. Rec.*, 4:2453.

152. *MCC*, 4:132–33.

153. Quoted in Duffy, *A History of Public Health in New York City*, 54. In September 1731, New York Council President Rip van Dam informed the Lords of Trade that "There is but a slender appearance of Members in the howse by reason of the Small pox which rage in the province, especially in the City which terrifies the rest, even some of those that mett in the beginning of the Session are returned home." "President Van Dam to the Lords of Trade" (New York, September 11), 1731, *Doc. Rel.*, 5:924.

154. "James Alexander to Cadwallader Colden" (New York, n.d, but c. 1731), *The Letters and Papers of Cadwallader Colden*, vol. 2, *1730–1742*, in *CNYHS for the Year 1918*, 24.

155. Duffy, *A History of Public Health in New York City*, 54.

156. Nash, "The New York Census of 1737," 433–34; Gary B. Nash, *The Urban Crucible: Social Change, Political Consciousness, and the Origins of the American Revolution* (Cambridge, Mass., 1979), 123–25. About 1735–36, according to

George Clarke, "nigh an hundred houses in the town [New York City] stood empty for want of Tenants and the rents of those that were tenanted were fallen considerably many people having left the Town and province." "Lieutenant-Governor George Clarke to the Lords of Trade" (New York, December 15, 1741), *Doc. Rel.*, 6:207. See also "Lieutenant-Governor George Clarke to the Lords of Trade" (New York, February 17, 1737–38), *Doc. Rel.*, 6:112.

CHAPTER EIGHT
THE THIRD GENERATION

1. Statistics on the ethnic distribution of New York City's population in 1730 are derived from analysis of the 1730 tax list, which is printed in "New York City Assessment Roll, February 1730," *New York Genealogical and Biographical Record*, 95 (1964), 27–32, 166–74, 197–202. On the development of New York City during the first third of the eighteenth century, see Gary B. Nash, *The Urban Crucible: Social Change, Political Consciousness, and the Origins of the American Revolution* (Cambridge, Mass., 1979); Gary B. Nash, "The Social Evolution of Preindustrial American Cities, 1700–1820," *Journal of Urban History*, 13 (1987), 115–45; Bruce Martin Wilkenfeld, *The Social and Economic Structure of the City of New York 1695–1796* (New York, 1978); and Bruce M. Wilkenfeld, "New York City Neighborhoods, 1730," *New York History*, 57 (1976), 165–82.

2. Thomas Archdeacon has argued that the English (along with the French) had displaced the Dutch in power and wealth by the end of the seventeenth century. Thomas J. Archdeacon, *New York City 1664–1710: Conquest and Change* (Ithaca, N.Y., 1976); Thomas J. Archdeacon, "The Age of Leisler—New York City, 1689–1710: A Social and Demographic Interpretation," in Jacob Judd and Irwin H. Polishook, eds., *Aspects of Early New York Society and Politics* (Tarrytown, N.Y., 1974), 68–82.

3. For background on the trades practiced in New York City during the first third of the eighteenth century see Rita S. Gottesman, comp., *The Arts and Crafts in New York, 1726–1776: Advertisements and News Items from New York City Newspapers*, in *CNYHS for the Year 1936* (New York, 1938); and Carl Bridenbaugh, *The Colonial Craftsman* (Chicago, 1961; originally published 1950). On various specific trades, see as follows: SILVERSMITHS: Kristan Helen McKinsey, "New York City Silversmiths and their Patrons, 1687–1750" (Master's thesis, University of Delaware [Winterthur Program], 1984); PRINTERS: Charles R. Hildeburn, *Sketches of Printers and Printing in Colonial New York* (New York, 1895); POTTERS: William C. Ketchum, Jr., *Potters and Potteries of New York State, 1650–1900*, 2d ed., (Syracuse, N.Y., 1987); METALWORKERS: James A. Mulholland, *A History of Metals in Colonial America* (University, Ala., 1981), ch. 5, "Metals Manufacture in the Colonial Period," 74–98; SHIP CARPENTERS: Joseph A. Goldenberg, *Shipbuilding in Colonial America* (Charlottesville, Va., 1976), and Richard W. Unger, *Dutch Shipbuilding Before 1800: Ships and Guilds* (Assen/Amsterdam, the Netherlands, 1978); BREWERS: Stanley Baron, *Brewed in America: A History of Beer and Ale in the United States* (Boston, 1962), 19–30, 68–71; TAVERNKEEPERS: W. Harrison Bayles, *Old Taverns of New York* (New York, 1915), and Eugene P. McParland, "Colonial Taverns and Tavernkeepers of British New York City," *New York*

Genealogical and Biographical Record, 103 (1972), 193–202; 104 (1973), 17–27, 99–104, 170–72, 205–12; 105 (1974), 27–32, 89–92, 155–62, 218–23; 106 (1975), 34–37, 157–61, 214–16; 107 (1978), 26–28, 150–53. Information on the city's carmen can be gleaned from Graham Russell Hodges, *New York City Cartmen, 1667–1850* (New York and London, 1986).

4. On the development of the legal profession in New York City, see Paul M. Hamlin, *Legal Education in Colonial New York* (New York, 1970; originally published 1939).

5. "Indentures of Apprentices, 1718–1727," *CNYHS for the Year 1909,* 113–99.

6. For examples, see *MCC,* 3:218, 227, 239, 280, 313, 318, 324.

7. *Ecc. Rec.,* 4:2378, 2390, 2415, 2438, 2440–41.

8. On New York City's Dutch merchants, see Cathy Matson, "Commerce After the Conquest: Dutch Traders and Goods in New York City 1664–1764," *de Halve Maen,* 59 (March 1987), 8–12; 60 (June 1987), 17–22. For background on New York City's merchants, see Wilkenfeld, *The Social and Economic Structure of the City of New York,* and Bruce M. Wilkenfeld, "The New York City Shipowning Community, 1715–1764," *American Neptune,* 37 (1977), 50–65. On the city's merchants in a later period, see Virginia D. Harrington, *The New York Merchant on the Eve of the Revolution* (New York, 1935; reprinted 1964).

9. On trends in wealth distribution in New York City, Boston, and Philadelphia, see Gary B. Nash, "Urban Wealth and Poverty in Pre-Revolutionary America," *Journal of Interdisciplinary History,* 6 (1976), 9–48.

10. Nash, *The Urban Crucible,* 123–25.

11. On municipal expenditures for the poor, see Nash, *The Urban Crucible,* 126–27, 402; Steven J. Ross, "Objects of Charity: Poor Relief, Poverty, and the Rise of the Almshouse in Early Eighteenth-Century New York City," in William Pencak and Conrad Edick Wright, eds., *Authority and Resistance in Early New York* (New York, 1988), 138–72; and the records printed in Kenneth Scott, "The Church Wardens and the Poor in New York City, 1693–1747," *New York Genealogical and Biographical Record,* 99 (1968), 157–64; 100 (1969), 18–26, 141–47; 101 (1970), 33–40, 164–73; 102 (1971), 50–56, 150–56. New York City's churches also assisted indigent parishioners. The Dutch Reformed church continued to maintain an almshouse (*Ecc. Rec.,* 3:1460–62, 1514, 1802).

Other studies of poverty in colonial New York City include Robert E. Cray, Jr., *Paupers and Poor Relief in New York City and Its Rural Environs, 1700–1830* (Philadelphia, 1988); Robert E. Cray, Jr., "Poverty and Poor Relief: New York City and Its Rural Environs, 1700–1790," in Pencak and Wright, eds., *Authority and Resistance,* 173–201; Raymond A. Mohl, "Poverty in Early America, A Reappraisal: The Case of Eighteenth-Century New York City," *New York History,* 50 (1969), 5–27; and David M. Schneider, *The History of Public Welfare in New York State, 1609–1866* (Chicago, 1938). For an overview of poverty in the eighteenth-century colonies, see Billy G. Smith, "Poverty and Economic Marginality in Eighteenth-Century America," *Proceedings* of the American Philosophical Society, vol. 132, no. 1 (1988), 85–118.

12. N.Y. Col. MSS, 50:41a.

13. N.Y. Col. MSS, 50:27.

14. Nash, "Urban Wealth and Poverty in Pre-Revolutionary America," 11–12.

15. Adrian Howe reaches a similar conclusion after analyzing patterns of municipal officeholding for the period 1701–1730. Adrian Howe, "Accommodation and Retreat: Politics in Anglo-Dutch New York City, 1700–1760" (Ph.D. diss., University of Melbourne, 1984), 167–70, 227–31. See also Bruce M. Wilkenfeld, "The New York City Common Council, 1689–1800," *New York History*, 52 (1971), 249–73.

On New York City government in the early eighteenth century, see Arthur Everett Petersen, *New York as an Eighteenth-Century Municipality Prior to 1731* (New York, 1917); Jon C. Teaford, *The Municipal Revolution in America: Origins of Modern Urban Government 1650–1825* (Chicago and London, 1975); Nicholas Varga, "The Development and Structure of Local Government in Colonial New York," in Bruce C. Daniels, ed., *Town and County: Essays on the Structure of Local Government in the American Colonies* (Middletown, Conn., 1978), 186–215.

Information on the background of New York City residents who sat on the provincial council is provided in Jessica Kross, "'Patronage Most Ardently Sought': The New York Council, 1665–1775," in Bruce C. Daniels, ed., *Power and Status: Officeholding in Colonial America* (Middletown, Conn., 1986), 205–31, 308–11.

16. Bruce Wilkenfeld emphasizes turnover on the Common Council between 1689 and 1733, but concedes that "the membership of the council remained relatively stable" from 1717 to 1728. Wilkenfeld, "The New York City Common Council," 254.

17. In October 1715, the Common Council ordered that "no Freeman or Inhabitant of this Corporation be Obliged to serve twice in the office of Constable of this City in less than fifteen years time." *MCC*, 3:112. Men frequently paid fines rather than serve as constable (for examples, see *MCC*, 3:18, 20, 48, 53). Some men appointed deputies to serve in their place (see, for example, *MCC*, 3:186). Other men provided valid reasons for not serving as constable. In 1721, Nicholas Eyres was "excused from serving as Constable because he is a Minister or preacher to a Congregation called Baptists" (*MCC*, 3:270).

18. Not included here are (1) cohort members who had no surviving children or only daughters who survived to adulthood and (2) cohort members who migrated from New York City, taking their sons (and daughters) with them. These second-generation sons who grew to adulthood outside the city are not included in this analysis.

19. Birthdates are available for 231 men.

20. On migration from Kings County to New Jersey see above, ch. 7, notes 26 through 28 and accompanying text.

21. Firth Haring Fabend, "The Yeoman Ideal: A Dutch Family in the Middle Colonies, 1650–1800" (Ph.D. diss., New York University, 1988), 253.

22. Howard S. F. Randolph, "The Lewis Family of New York and Poughkeepsie," *New York Genealogical and Biographical Record*, 60 (1929), 131–42, 245–54. Second-generation cohort member Jesse Kip's mid-life move to Newtown in Queens County, the home of his wife's family (the Stevenses), similarly affected the life course of his sons. Frederick Ellsworth Kip, *History of the Kip Family in America* (Morristown, N.J., 1928); John Marshall Phillips, "Identifying the Mys-

terious IK: Jesse Kip, New York Goldsmith," *Antiques* (July 1943). On the Stevens family of Newtown, see Jessica Kross, *The Evolution of an American Town: Newtown, New York, 1642–1775* (Philadelphia, 1983), 61, 94. On the marriages of Jesse Kip's sons, see the discussion later in this chapter.

23. Howard A. Thomas, comp., *Lucas Dircksen van der Burgh of New Amsterdam and his son Dirck, Progenitors of the Van der Burgh Family of Dutchess County, New York* (1951).

24. "Lutheran Church of New York City: Burials," *New York Genealogical and Biographical Record*, 105 (1974), 38.

25. "A Memorial to Jacobus Stoutenburgh," *Year Book of the Dutchess County Historical Society*, 20 (1935), 47–49.

26. Louise (Howes) Burnett, "The Wortendykes of Bergen County, New Jersey," *New York Genealogical and Biographical Record*, 103 (1972), 203–16.

27. Mrs. Anson Phelps Atterbury, *The Bayard Family* (Baltimore, 1928).

28. Will of James van Horne, *CNYHS for the Year 1897*, 123–24.

29. David E. Narrett, "Dutch Customs of Inheritance, Women, and the Law in Colonial New York City," in Pencak and Wright, eds., *Authority and Resistance*, 40–41.

30. Will of Geertruyd van Cortlandt, *CNYHS for the Year 1893*, 288–89.

31. Will of James van Horne, *CNYHS for the Year 1897*, 123–24.

32. Howard S. F. Randolph, "The Kierstede Family," *New York Genealogical and Biographical Record*, 65 (1934), 224–33, 329–38; David M. Riker, "Surgeon Hans Kierstede of New Amsterdam," *de Halve Maen*, 57, no. 3 (August 1983), 11–13, 24.

33. On the Duyckinck family, see Waldron Phoenix Belknap, Jr., "Notes on the Duyckinck Family," in *American Colonial Painting: Materials for a History* (Cambridge, Mass., 1959), 63–128; and R. W. G. Vail, "'Storied Windows Richly Dight,'" *New-York Historical Society Quarterly*, 36 (1951), 149–59.

34. Bartlett Burleigh James and J. Franklin Jameson, eds., *Journal of Jasper Danckaerts 1679–1680* (New York, 1913), 181.

35. On the Duyckinck family of painters, see also Roderic H. Blackburn and Ruth Piwonka et al., *Remembrance of Patria: Dutch Arts and Culture in Colonial America 1609–1776* (Albany, 1988), 215–16, 233–34.

36. Belknap, Jr., "Notes on the Duyckinck Family," 119.

37. Ibid.

38. McKinsey, "New York City Silversmiths and their Patrons"; Howard S. F. Randolph, "Jacob Boelen, Goldsmith, of New York and His Family Circle," *New York Genealogical and Biographical Record*, 72 (1941), 265–94.

39. Hodges, *New York City Cartmen*, 38.

40. Henry Waterman George, "The Ten Eyck Family in New York," *New York Genealogical and Biographical Record*, 63 (1932), 152–65, 269–85, 321–34.

41. Howard S. F. Randolph, "The Ellsworth Family of New York City," *New York Genealogical and Biographical Record*, 64 (1933), 154–66, 255–67.

42. "Indentures of Apprentices, 1718–1727," 165–66, 170–71.

43. Deeds from the Secretary of State's Office, New York State Archives, vol. 14 (1739–1750), fol. 25. Justus Bosch was classified among New York City's

shipowners in 1716. Wilkenfeld, "The New York City Shipowning Community," 57.

44. Will of Justus Bush, *CNYHS for the Year 1894*, 272–73.

45. Arthur Pine van Gelder, "Van Gelder Families in America," *New York Genealogical and Biographical Record*, 75 (1944), 15–24, 49–59; Will of John van Gelder, *CNYHS for the Year 1899*, 323–24.

46. On the limited aspirations of eighteenth-century artisans, see Gary B. Nash, "Up From the Bottom in Franklin's Philadelphia," *Past and Present*, #77 (November 1977), 61.

47. Inadequate data on wealth and slaveholding make intergenerational comparisons impossible except in isolated instances. Certain families remained large slaveholders.

48. Recent historical studies of intermarriage have focused on the twentieth century. See Richard M. Bernard, *The Melting Pot and the Altar: Marital Assimilation in Early Twentieth-Century Wisconsin* (Minneapolis, 1980); and Paul R. Spickard, *Mixed Blood: Intermarriage and Ethnic Identity in Twentieth-Century America* (Madison, Wis., 1989).

49. These statistics are based on an analysis of the marriage ages of the 171 third-generation cohort men for whom both birthdate and date of first marriage are available.

50. On the De Key family, see George E. McCracken, "The American DeKay Family," *The American Genealogist*, 33 (1957), 223–31; 34 (1958), 29–38; and Rosalie Fellows Bailey, "The Willett Family of Flushing, Long Island," *New York Genealogical and Biographical Record*, 80 (1949), 1–9, 83–96. For the sale of De Key's property in the Out Ward, see I. Phelps Stokes, *Iconography of Manhattan Island, 1498–1909*, 6 vols. (New York, 1915–1928), 6:98.

51. On the Kierstede family, see Randolph, "The Kierstede Family."

52. Kip, *History of the Kip Family in America*; Phillips, "Identifying the Mysterious IK." On the Stevens family of Newtown, see Kross, *The Evolution of an American Town*, 61, 94.

53. On the Lawrence family, see *Thomas Lawrence, Historical Genealogy of the Lawrence Family from their First Landing in this country, A.D. 1635 to the Present Date, July 4th, 1858* (New York, 1858); Paul M. Hamlin and Charles E. Baker, *Supreme Court of Judicature of the Province of New York 1691–1704*, 3 vols. (New York, 1959), 3:122–27. On the Merritt family, see Douglas Merritt, comp., *Revised Merritt Records* (New York, 1916).

54. At least 83 percent of 111 marriages involving the Dutch residents of Newtown, Long Island, between 1692 and 1723 were endogamous. Kross, *The Evolution of an American Town*, 172.

55. Van Gelder, "Van Gelder Families in America."

56. Waldron Phoenix Belknap, Jr., *The De Peyster Genealogy* (Boston, 1956).

57. Van Gelder, "Van Gelder Families in America"; "The Mesier Family of New Amsterdam and Wappingers Falls, N.Y.," *New York Genealogical and Biographical Record*, 58 (1927), 172–80.

58. Timothy Field Beard and Henry Hoff, "The Roosevelt Family," *New York Genealogical and Biographical Record*, 118 (1987) 193–202; 119 (1988), 19–34.

59. Wilson V. Ledley, "William Adriaense Bennet of Brooklyn and Some of His Descendants," *New York Genealogical and Biographical Record*, 92 (1962), 193–204.

60. Isaac Newton Earle, *History and Genealogy of the Earles of Secaucus with an Account of Other English and American Branches* (Marquette, Mich., n.d.).

61. Rosalie Fellows Bailey, "The De Honeur (D'Honeur or D'Honneur) Family with the Allied Families of Keteltas, Beekman, Strong and Nicoll," *New York Genealogical and Biographical Record*, 63 (1932), 169–79.

62. See the wills of William Ricketts and Mary Ricketts, *CNYHS for the Year 1894*, 188–89 and 379–80.

63. Wilson V. Ledley, "The Van De Waters of New York, the First Five Generations," *New York Genealogical and Biographical Record*, 98 (1967), 23–33, 95–98, 153–58, 212–21. William Jones Skillman, "The Skillmans of America and their Kin," *New York Genealogical and Biographical Record*, 37 (1906), 22–26, 91–96.

64. Skillman, "The Skillmans of America," 25. On the formation of the Dutch Reformed church in Newtown, see Kross, *The Evolution of an American Town*, 254–55.

65. Frances Jay's mother, Anna Maria Bayard, had joined the Dutch Reformed church in 1692. On the Van Cortlandt family, see L. Effingham DeForest, *The Van Cortlandt Family* (New York, 1930).

66. "Genealogy of the Family Named Brasier, Brasher, Breser, Bresart, Bradejor," *New York Genealogical and Biographical Record*, 27 (1890), 37–42.

67. Randolph, "The Ellsworth Family of New York City."

68. John Reynolds Totten, "Richaud and Richard Family Notes," *New York Genealogical and Biographical Record*, 66 (1935), 122–39, 245–57.

69. Deeds from the Secretary of State's Office, New York State Archives, Vol. 12 (1723–1735), fols. 150, 154; *CNYHS for the Year 1885*, 93. Both Paul and Elizabeth Garland Richard were buried in Trinity Church. Totten, "Richaud and Richard Family Notes," 139, 246. When Paul Richard wrote his will in 1749, he directed that £50 be given to the poor of Trinity Church and to the poor of the Dutch Reformed Church. New-York Historical Society *Collections*, 1896, 143–146.

70. David E. Narrett, "Men's Wills and Women's Property Rights in Colonial New York," in Ronald Hoffman and Peter J. Albert, eds., *Women in the Age of the American Revolution* (Charlottesville, Va., 1989), 101, 107.

CHAPTER NINE
CULTURE AND COMMUNITY IN NEW YORK CITY, 1700–1730

1. On the establishment of English institutions and practices in New York see Michael Kammen, *Colonial New York: A History* (New York, 1975), and Arthur Everett Petersen, *New York as an Eighteenth-Century Municipality Prior to 1731* (New York, 1917). On changes in the legal system see Richard B. Morris, ed., "Introduction" to *Select Cases of the Mayor's Court of New York City 1674–1784* (Washington, D.C., 1935); Herbert A. Johnson, *The Law Merchant and Negotia-*

ble Instruments in Colonial New York 1664 to 1730 (Chicago, 1963); and Julius Goebel, Jr., and T. Raymond Naughton, *Law Enforcement in Colonial New York: A Study in Criminal Procedure (1664–1776)* (New York, 1944).

2. "Lord Cornbury to the Lords of Trade" (July 12, 1703), *Doc. Rel.*, 4:1064–65; "Memorandum of Common Council" (March 24, 1713/14), *MCC*, 3:56–57. For the law, see "An Act to Assertain [*sic*] the Assize of Casks, Weights, Measures and Bricks within this Colony" (passed June 19, 1703), *The Colonial Laws of New York from the Year 1664 to the Revolution*, 5 vols. (Albany, 1894–1896), 1:554–57. In a case heard before the Mayor's Court in 1711, a Dutch man attempted unsuccessfully to repudiate an old debt by arguing that "Dutch weight is A forraign and Outlandish measure." "Christina Veenvos Ex[ecutri]x Ver Hendrick Gerrits" (January 16, 1710/11), in Morris, ed., *Select Cases of the Mayor's Court of New York City*, 171–73 (quote on 173).

3. On October 25, 1726, for example, the Common Council "Order'd there be a Bonfire at the usual place within this City at the Charge of this Corporation with the Usual quantity of good Wine on the fifth day of November Next being the Anniversary thanksgiving for the discovery of the horrid Gunpowder Plot" (*MCC*, 3:399–400). English New Yorkers undoubtedly celebrated Gunpowder Treason Day at local taverns as well. When innkeeper Roger Baker was presented by the grand jury in 1702 for "saying the 5 November last the King was made a nose of Wax and no longer King than the English please," a witness explained that "they were all very drunk it being Holy-day." "Proceedings of Chief Justice Atwood and of the Assembly of New-York" (May 4, 1702), *Doc. Rel.*, 4:757. In another account, Baker is reported to have said, "King William is but a Dutch King, and a Nose of Wax, and no longer King than we please." "The Case of William Atwood, Esq. 1703," in *CNYHS for the Year 1880*, 282. See also Elizabeth Marting, *"Dom. Rex vs. Roger Baker,"* New-York Historical Society Quarterly, 31 (1947), 139–47.

For instances of other celebrations, see *MCC*, 2:221 (Queen Anne's birthday); *MCC*, 2:442 (Queene Anne's coronation day); *MCC*, 3:92 (King George I's birthday); *MCC*, 3:212 (King George I's coronation day); and *MCC*, 3:320 (King George I's accession day). An account of "Funeral obsequies for Late Queen Anne" and the festivities following the proclamation of Prince George as king was published in the *Boston News-Letter*, October 11, 1714. For background on British holidays, see David Cressy, "The Protestant Calendar and the Vocabulary of Celebration in Early Modern England," *Journal of British Studies*, 29 (1990), 31–52.

4. Reading English was necessary if one was to avail oneself of business opportunities in the city. In February 1723/24, when the Ferry between New York and Nassau Island was to be let to farm, the Common Council ordered that "the Town Clerk cause printed Advertisements thereof forthwith to be Published." *MCC*, 3:337.

5. "Declaration of the Reverend Consistory to the Christian Congregation, that Mr. Barend de Forest has been appointed by them, together with the Great Consistory, to be Schoolmaster for one year, beginning with January 1, Anno 1726," *Ecc. Rec.*, 4:2340. Dutch pragmatism was also reflected in the decision of the Consistory of the New York City Dutch Reformed Church in December 1711

that "henceforth the [account] books of Elders, Deacons and Church Masters shall no longer be kept in guilders, but in pounds, shillings, and pence" (*Ecc. Rec.*, 3:1897).

6. Adrian Howe, "Accommodation and Retreat: Politics in Anglo-Dutch New York City, 1700–1760" (Ph.D. diss., University of Melbourne, 1984), 47–48.

7. Morris, ed., *Select Cases of the Mayor's Court of New York City*, 337.

8. "Lewis Morris, Jr., to the Lords of Trade" (New York, July 19, 1729), *Doc. Rel.*, 5:886.

9. Printed in the Netherlands by publishing firms such as Elsevier, these folio Bibles were "great volumes often illustrated with numerous engravings and ornamented with brass corners and clasps." Alice P. Kenney, "Neglected Heritage: Hudson River Valley Dutch Material Culture," *Winterthur Portfolio*, 20 (Spring 1985), 67. One scholar has noted that "the Dutch . . . saw virtue in leaving a Bible open to view, demonstrating to visitors the strength of family belief." Roderic H. Blackburn and Ruth Piwonka, *Remembrance of Patria: Dutch Arts and Culture in Colonial America 1609–1776* (Albany, 1988), 177.

10. Joyce D. Goodfriend, "Probate Records as a Source for Early American Religious History: The Case of Colonial New York City, 1664–1730" (Paper presented at the Dublin Seminar for New England Folklife, Deerfield, Mass., 1987). "Importation of Dutch Bibles continued through the 1750s and then appears to have nearly ceased" (Blackburn and Piwonka, *Remembrance of Patria*, 177).

11. The title page and pages containing family records from the Samuel Kip bible are reproduced in Frederick Ellsworth Kip, *History of the Kip Family in America* (Morristown, N.J., 1928), 387–89.

12. Hendrick Edelman, *Dutch-American Bibliography 1693–1794: A Descriptive Catalog of Dutch-Language Books, Pamphlets and Almanacs Printed in America* (Nieuwkoop, the Netherlands, 1974)

13. Thomas Jefferson Wertenbaker, *The Founding of American Civilization: The Middle Colonies* (New York, 1938), 106. William Heard Kilpatrick asserted that the only textbook published in the Dutch language in America was an arithmetic book written by Pieter Venema and published by Zenger in 1730. Kilpatrick, *The Dutch Schools of New Netherland and New York*, (Washington, D.C., 1912) 226. However, since the publication of Kilpatrick's study, another textbook in Dutch has come to light—"The English and Low-Dutch School-Master containing Alphabetical Tables of the most Common Words in English and Dutch. With certain Rules and Directions whereby the Low-Dutch Inhabitants of North America may (in a short time) learn to Spell, Read, Understand and Speak proper English. And by the help whereof the English may also learn to Spell, Read, Understand and Write Low-Dutch," by Frances Harrison. It was published in 1730 by William Bradford in New York City. Edgar Franklin Romig, "'The English and Low-Dutch School-Master' (New York: William Bradford, 1730)," *New-York Historical Society Quarterly*, 43 (1959), 149–50.

14. Of 1,100 Bradford imprints between 1693 and 1744, only ten were in Dutch. It was believed that in the years between 1726 and 1744, Zenger printed seventeen titles in Dutch. That figure has now been revised upward to twenty. Romig, "'The English and Low-Dutch School-Master,'" 150; Howe, "Accommodation and Retreat," 179–80.

15. Howe, "Accommodation and Retreat," 178, 180; Thomas J. Wertenbaker, *The Golden Age of Colonial Culture* (Ithaca, N.Y., 1959; originally published 1949), 46–47.

16. "Report of Rev. W. C. Berkenmeyer to the Amsterdam Consistory, October 21 / November 1, 1725," Arnold J. H. van Laer, trans., *The Lutheran Church in New York, 1649–1772: Records in the Lutheran Church Archives at Amsterdam, Holland* (New York, 1946), 140. On the shipment of "a large folio Bible, 50 psalters, 50 *Paradijshofkens*, and 50 Haverman's prayer books" to the congregation, see ibid., 104, 105, 107. In 1705, Rev. Justus Falckner apprised the Amsterdam Consistory of "the lack of Bibles, Catechisms, Psalm and Hymn books." "Letter from the Rev. Justus Falckner and the Consistory of the Lutheran Church—New York, to the Amsterdam Consistory" (November 10, 1705), ibid., 99.

17. On the Dutch Reformed school, see Kilpatrick, *The Dutch Schools of New Netherland and New York*; Henry W. Dunshee, *History of the School of the Collegiate Reformed Dutch Church in the City of New York from 1633 to 1883*, 2d ed., enlarged (New York, 1883); and Jean Parker Waterbury, *A History of Collegiate School, 1638–1963* (New York, 1965).

18. *Ecc. Rec.*, 3:1584.

19. *Ecc. Rec.*, 3:1654.

20. *Ecc. Rec.*, 3:1654, 1700. See also Kilpatrick, *The Dutch Schools of New Netherland and New York*, 149–50; William Webb Kemp, *The Support of Schools in Colonial New York by the Society for the Propagation of the Gospel in Foreign Parts* (New York, 1969; originally published 1913), 69; Carl F. Kaestle, *The Evolution of an Urban School System: New York City 1750–1850* (Cambridge, Mass., 1973), 22.

21. Apparently, Cornbury was not as concerned about the perpetuation of the French language in New York City, since he licensed a few French schoolmasters. See discussion later in this chapter.

22. See Ronald William Howard, "Education and Ethnicity in Colonial New York, 1664–1763: A Study in the Transmission of Culture in Early America" (Ph.D. diss., University of Tennessee, 1978).

23. Kemp, *The Support of Schools in Colonial New York*, 71–72.

24. "An Act For Encouragement of a Grammar Free School in the City of New York" (passed November 27, 1702), *Ecc. Rec.*, 3:1511. As early as 1691 a bill had been proposed "to appoint a schoolmaster for the educating and instructing of Children and youth, 'to read and write English,' in every town in the province" (cited in Kemp, *The Support of Schools in Colonial New York*, 70).

25. Kemp, *The Support of Schools in Colonial New York*, 83 n. 31.

26. William A. Bultmann, "The S.P.G. and the Foreign Settler in the American Colonies," in Samuel Clyde McCulloch, ed., *British Humanitarianism: Essays Honoring Frank J. Klingberg* (Philadelphia, 1950), 61–63; John Calam, *Parsons and Pedagogues: The S.P.G. Adventure in American Education* (New York, 1971), 91.

27. Kemp, *The Support of Schools in Colonial New York*, 82–83.

28. "Rev. John Sharpe's Proposals, March: 1713," *CNYHS for the Year 1880*, 343. In Sharpe's view, one of the advantages of living in New York City was the opportunity of "learning both Dutch & French which are very usefull accomplishments to scholars, as well as to travellers or traders" (ibid).

29. On the work of the S.P.G. in New York see Kemp, *The Support of Schools in*

Colonial New York; Frank J. Klingberg, *Anglican Humanitarianism in Colonial New York* (Philadelphia, 1940); and Howard, "Education and Ethnicity." See also Bultmann, "The S.P.G. and the Foreign Settler in the American Colonies"; Calam, *Parsons and Pedagogues;* and Carson I. A. Ritchie, *Frontier Parish: An Account of the Society for the Propagation of the Gospel and the Anglican Church in America. Drawn From the Records of the Bishop of London* (Rutherford, N.J., 1976).

30. "Caleb Heathcote to the Secretary, Mannor of Scarsdale" (November 14, 1705), S.P.G., Letter Books A, vol. 2, #118.

31. "William Huddleston to the Secretary" (New York, July 22, 1715), ibid., vol. 10, fols. 201–2. Elias Neau mentions the intriguing possibility that some of his slave pupils may have served as a conduit for the transmission of Anglican values to Dutch and French children: "Several Negroes learn at home the Catechism & some learn to read & that is a means also for the white Children of the dutch & ffrench to learn our Catechism." "Elias Neau to the Secretary" (c. April 1722), ibid., vol. 16, fol. 204. See also "Elias Neau to the Secretary" (April 2, 1722), ibid. vol. 16, fols. 196–97.

32. The seventeen lists of charity school pupils are found in S.P.G., Letter Books A, vol. 9, New York Papers #2, fols. 179–80; vol. 10, fol. 265; vol. 12, fols. 402–3, 408–10; vol. 13, fols. 485–86; vol. 15, fols. 111–13; vol. 16, fols. 239–42; vol. 17, fols. 312–13; vol. 18, fols. 232–33; vol. 19, fols. 199–200, 206–7, 428–30; vol. 20, fols. 221–22; vol. 22, fols. 40–42; vol. 23, fols. 96–97, 364–365. It is possible that William Huddleston inflated his estimate of the number of Dutch and French pupils he had taught, since the same names appear on several successive lists.

33. A list of schoolmasters active in New York City between 1700 and 1730 was compiled from the following sources: List of Freemen in *CNYHS for the Year 1885*, "Indentures of Apprentices, 1718–1727," *CNYHS for the Year 1909*; Daniel J. Pratt, *Annals of Public Education in the State of New York, from 1626 to 1746* (Albany, 1872); Robert Francis Seybolt, *Apprenticeship & Apprenticeship Education in Colonial New England & New York* (New York, 1917); Robert Francis Seybolt, "The Evening Schools of Colonial New York City (after 1664)" (ch. 14) and "New York Colonial Schoolmasters . . . 1664–1783" (ch. 15), in Thomas E. Finegan, *Free Schools: A Documentary History of the Free School Movement in New York State* in *Fifteenth Annual Report of the Education Department, University of the State of New York*, vol. 1, *1919* (Albany, 1921), 630–52, 653–69; Robert Francis Seybolt, *The Evening School in Colonial America* (Urbana, Ill., 1925); Robert Francis Seybolt, *Source Studies in American Colonial Education: The Private School* (Urbana, Ill., 1925); and Howard, "Education and Ethnicity." We know only the name of many of these schoolmasters.

34. Pratt, *Annals of Public Education in the State of New York*, 90.

35. Ibid., 92.

36. List of Freemen in *CNYHS for the Year 1885*, 83.

37. Pratt, *Annals of Public Education in the State of New York*, 93–94.

38. Seybolt, "New York Colonial Schoolmasters," 656.

39. On Van der Lyn, see Mary C. Black, "Pieter Vanderlyn and Other Limners of the Upper Hudson," in Ian M. G. Quimby, ed., *American Painting to 1776: A*

Reappraisal (Charlottesville, Va., 1971), 234–41. On Goelet, see "Editor's Note" to Will of Jacob Goelet, *CNYHS for the Year*, 1894, 37–39.

40. List of Freemen in *CNYHS for the Year 1885*, 127.

41. On Jewish education in New York City, see David and Tamar de Sola Pool, *An Old Faith in the New World: Portrait of Shearith Israel, 1654–1954* (New York, 1955), 212–13.

42. "James Weeks ver William Osburne et ux." (April 2, 1723), Morris, ed., *Select Cases of the Mayor's Court of New York City*, 402–3.

43. *New-York Gazette*, June 7, 1731. See also Leo Hershkowitz and Isidore Meyer, eds., *The Lee Max Friedman Collection of American Jewish Colonial Correspondence: Letters of the Franks Family (1733–1748)* (Waltham, Mass., 1968), 3, 4 n. 9, 13.

44. On Malcolm, see Hershkowitz and Meyer, eds., *The Lee Max Friedman Collection of American Jewish Colonial Correspondence*, 13 n. 8; and James R. Heintze, "Alexander Malcolm: Musician, Clergyman, and Schoolmaster," *Maryland Historical Magazine*, 73 (1978), 226–35.

45. Seybolt, *Source Studies in American Colonial Education*, 99.

46. *New-York Gazette*, August 24, 1730.

47. Kemp, *The Support of Schools in Colonial New York*, 72, 77.

48. "James Weeks ver William Osburne et ux." (April 2, 1723), Morris, ed., *Select Cases of the Mayor's Court of New York City*, 402–3.

49. Hershkowitz and Meyer, eds., *The Lee Max Friedman Collection of American Jewish Colonial Correspondence*; "Isaac Bobin to George Clarke" (New York, September 28, 1723), *Letters of Isaac Bobin, Esq., Private Secretary of Hon. George Clarke, Secretary of the Province of New York, 1718–1730* (Albany, 1872), 150.

50. *New-York Gazette*, December 13, 1731.

51. "Indentures of Apprentices, 1718–1727," 111–99.

52. Seybolt, "The Evening Schools of Colonial New York City (after 1664)," 633.

53. "Declaration of the Reverend Consistory," *Ecc. Rec.*, 4:2341.

54. Kilpatrick, *The Dutch Schools of New Netherland and New York*, 152.

55. On the subsequent history of the Dutch Reformed school in New York City, see Gerald F. De Jong, *The Dutch Reformed Church in the American Colonies* (Grand Rapids., Mich., 1978), 217.

56. *MCC*, 1:64.

57. *CNYHS for the Year 1902*, 37.

58. De Peyster Papers, 1695–1710, New-York Historical Society. Johannes de Peyster wrote his brother (in Dutch) from Boston in 1702, "I now know the way and understand the speech," indicating that he too had acquired proficiency in English. Quoted in Adrian Howe, "The Bayard Treason Trial: Dramatizing Anglo-Dutch Politics in Early Eighteenth-Century New York City," *William and Mary Quarterly*, 3d ser., 47 (1990), 75 n. 56. (Johannes was a second- not third-generation New Yorker, as Howe states.)

The Letterbook of Jacobus van Cortlandt, another second-generation Dutch New Yorker, for the period 1698–1700 also includes correspondence in Dutch and English. Jacobus van Cortlandt Letterbook 1698–1700 (photostat), New-York Historical Society.

59. *Ecc. Rec.*, 2:1234; De Peyster Papers, 1695–1710.

60. Quoted in David E. Narrett, "Dutch Customs of Inheritance, Women, and the Law in Colonial New York City," in William Pencak and Conrad Edick Wright, eds., *Authority and Resistance in Early New York* (New York, 1988), 41.

61. On the Spratt children, see chapter 5.

62. Jean P. Jordan, "Women Merchants in Colonial New York," *New York History*, 58 (1977), 417 n. 15. See also Nicholas Varga, "Mary Spratt Provoost Alexander" in Edward T. James, Janet Wilson James, and Paul S. Boyer, eds., *Notable American Women 1607–1950: A Biographical Dictionary*, 3 vols. (Cambridge, Mass., 1971), 1:35–36.

63. Daniel Horsmanden, *The New York Conspiracy*, ed. Thomas J. Davis, (Boston, 1971), 46–47.

64. Charles Theodor Gehring, "The Dutch Language in Colonial New York: An Investigation of a Language in Decline and Its Relationship to Social Change" (Ph.D. diss., Indiana University, 1973); Wertenbaker, *The Founding of American Civilization*, 107–8. It is probable that Dutch New Yorkers also switched to an English handwriting style, even when they continued to write Dutch. Gehring, "The Dutch Language in Colonial New York," 4–5.

65. De Jong, *The Dutch Reformed Church in the American Colonies*, 218.

66. N.Y. Col. MSS, 63:123. The growing familiarity of Dutch (and French) New Yorkers with English is confirmed in a letter of the Rev. William Williams, who visited the city in 1709: "Last week Dom Du Bois, ye Dutch minister, asked me to preach for him (for most of his Dutch congregation understand English); . . . the church was full as it could hold (as we say) of English, French, & Dutch, to hear a young Presbyterian preacher." "William Williams to John Winthrop" (New York, April 25, 1709), *Collections* of the Massachusetts Historical Society, 6th ser., vol. 5 (Boston, 1892), 185.

67. This book was written by Frances Harrison, a schoolmaster in Somerset County, New Jersey, and published by William Bradford in New York City in 1730. Romig, "'The English and Low-Dutch School-Master,'" 149–50. On the intended audience for this reader, see Gehring, "The Dutch Language in Colonial New York," 69–70.

68. From an essay c. 1754 in *The Occasional Reverberator*, quoted in Waterbury, *A History of Collegiate School*, 54 (italics in original). The 1764 will of Henry Barclay, the rector of Trinity Church, offers evidence of a bilingual couple's decision not to educate their son in Dutch. Rev. Barclay, who was fluent in Dutch as a result of his long residence in Albany, married Mary Rutgers, a member of a prominent Dutch family, in 1749. Fifteen years later, when he divided up his library in his will, he specified that his wife was to inherit "all my printed books in the Low Dutch language" and his eldest son, Thomas Barclay, was to have "all my printed books except those in the Dutch language." Will of Henry Barclay, *CNYHS for the Year 1897*, 351–52. On Henry Barclay, see Morgan Dix, ed., *A History of the Parish of Trinity Church* (New York, 1898), 1:237–42, 250, 305–6.

69. Narrett, "Dutch Customs of Inheritance," 41. Van Horne's decision to send his sons to the Anglican church, despite his own continuing affiliation with

the Dutch Reformed church, illustrates the turning point in family education. See Howe, "Accommodation and Retreat," 413 n. 94.

70. "Letter from the Church Council to the Revs. Wilhelm C. Berkenmeyer and Peter Nicholas Sommer, Giving a Detailed Account of the German-Dutch Language Problem" (August 2, 1749), in Simon Hart and Harry J. Kreider, trans., *Protocol of the Lutheran Church in New York City, 1702–1750* (New York, 1958), 421; "Baptisms in Private Houses [Paper read by Rev. John Ritzema]" (New York, August 20, 1747), *Ecc. Rec.*, 4:2971.

71. Adolph B. Benson, ed., *The America of 1750: Peter Kalm's Travels in North America. The English Version of 1770*, revised from the original Swedish, 2 vols. (1937; reprinted, New York, 1966), 2:626.

72. *Ecc. Rec.*, 5:3459.

73. "[Letter from the Rev. Michael Christian Knoll] to the Lutheran Consistory at Rothenburg on the Tauber, [Germany]" (December 21, 1749), in Hart and Kreider, trans., *Protocol of the Lutheran Church in New York City*, 465.

74. *Ecc. Rec.*, 4:2621.

75. Richard Wayne Pointer, "Seedbed of American Pluralism: The Impact of Religious Diversity in New York, 1750–1800" (Ph.D. diss., Johns Hopkins University, 1982); Richard W. Pointer, *Protestant Pluralism and the New York Experience: A Study of Eighteenth-Century Religious Diversity* (Bloomington and Indianapolis, 1988).

76. Pointer, "Seedbed of American Pluralism;" Pointer, *Protestant Pluralism and the New York Experience*; Randall Balmer, *A Perfect Babel of Confusion: Dutch Religion and English Culture in the Middle Colonies* (New York, 1989); John Pershing Luidens, "The Americanization of the Dutch Reformed Church" (Ph.D. diss., University of Oklahoma, 1969); Howard, "Education and Ethnicity."

77. Pointer suggests that critical changes in the organization of the city's religious life had taken place by 1730 and that third- and fourth-generation Dutch young people were apt to shift their church membership ("Seedbed of American Pluralism," 103–5).

78. Jon Butler, *The Huguenots in America: A Refuge People in New World Society* (Cambridge, Mass., 1983), 159–60.

79. Bruce M. Wilkenfeld, "New York City Neighborhoods, 1730," *New York History*, 57 (1976), 179.

80. Butler, *Huguenots in America*, 192–95. The size of the New York City parish between 1725 and 1735 has been estimated at three hundred. John A. F. Maynard, *The Huguenot Church of New York: A History of the French Church of Saint Esprit* (New York, 1938), 132.

81. Trinity Church Vestry Minutes, passim; "Certificate from the Governor the Rector Church Wardens & Vestry & other Gentlemen of Trinity Church New York in behalfe of Mr Jenny Inclosed in his Letter to the Archbishop of Canterbury September 1, 1716," S.P.G., Letter Books A, vol. 11, fols. 361–62; "Subscriptions to the Rev. Mr. Wetmore at New York inclosed in Mr Veseys Letter of the 6th of November 1724," ibid., vol. 18, fols. 230–31; "Subscriptions of the People in New York to Mr Wetmore as Assistant to Mr Vesey for two Years ending the 1st August 1726. Inclosed in their Letter of the 5th of July 1726," ibid., vol. 19, fols. 431–35; Butler, *Huguenots in America*, 194–95. See also Robert

M. Kingdon, "Why Did the Huguenot Refugees in the American Colonies Become Episcopalian?" *Historical Magazine of the Protestant Episcopal Church*, 49 (1980), 317–35.

82. In 1715 Falckner wrote that he served "four small Lutheran congregations [in New York province] & all these four consist in all of about one hundred constant communicants besides strangers going and coming in the city of N York." "Justus Falckner to Magister Sandel" (New York, September 28, 1715), in Julius Friedrich Sachse, *Justus Falckner, Mystic and Scholar* (Philadelphia, 1903), 93. Falckner's successor, Wilhelm Berckenmeyer, informed the Amsterdam consistory in 1725 that "the whole congregation . . . consists of from ten to twelve households, which either upon the male or the female side are of the reformed faith." "W. C. Berckenmeyer to the Amsterdam Consistory. October 21 / November 1, 1725," in van Laer, *The Lutheran Church in New York*, 138. In 1726 a church member placed the size of the congregation at "about 25 to 30 families." "Supplementary Information furnished by Johannes Sybrandt to the Amsterdam Consistory" (February 20, 1726), ibid., 155. Between 1704 and 1723, the years of Falckner's ministry, 78 people joined the congregation. This figure includes 35 Palatines admitted in 1710. From 1724 through 1731, only 15 persons became members. Harry Julius Kreider, *Lutheranism in Colonial New York* (New York, 1942), 51, 137, 138.

83. "Request for German Services. Minutes of the Church Council of October 17, 1742, continued," in Hart and Kreider, trans., *Protocol of the Lutheran Church*, 332. Ultimately, the language issue split New York City's Lutherans and a separate German Lutheran church was started in 1750 (Kreider, *Lutheranism in Colonial New York*, 58–64).

84. "Records of the Reformed Dutch Church, Members' List" (see note 24 for chapter 5).

85. *Ecc. Rec.*, 4:2343–44.

86. *Ecc. Rec.*, 4:2458.

87. William Smith, Jr., *The History of the Province of New-York*, ed. Michael Kammen, 2 vols. (Cambridge, Mass., 1972), 1:203.

88. Wilkenfeld, "New York City Neighborhoods, 1730," 179.

89. I use the sex ratio of persons admitted to the Dutch Reformed church between 1700 and 1730 to estimate the size of the congregation in 1730.

90. "Records of the Reformed Dutch Church, Members' List." The standard source on the Palatine immigration is Walter Allen Knittle, *Early Eighteenth Century Palatine Emigration* (Philadelphia, 1937). See also Kreider, *Lutheranism in Colonial New York*.

91. *Ecc. Rec.*, 4:2341. For a 1706 statement to the same effect see "The Consistories of New York . . . to the Classis of Amsterdam" (May 23, 1706), *Ecc. Rec.*, 3:1654.

92. *Ecc. Rec.*, 3:1903–5.

93. *Ecc. Rec.*, 4:2449–54 (quotation on 2451).

94. "Rev. Gualterus Du Bois to the Rev. Classis of Amsterdam" (May 14, 1741), *Ecc. Rec.*, 4:2757.

95. Balmer, *A Perfect Babel of Confusion*, 55–69. See also Randall H. Balmer, "The Social Roots of Dutch Pietism in the Middle Colonies," *Church History*, 53

(1984), 187–99. A survey of the records of New Jersey Dutch Reformed congregations might reveal transfers of membership from New York City. It is interesting to note that between 1700 and 1730 the city congregation admitted several new members from New Jersey Dutch churches.

96. On the work of the S.P.G. in New York see the sources cited in note 29 above.

97. "Lewis Morris to the Secretary, New York, New Years Day 1711," S.P.G., Letter Books A, vol. 7, fols. 159–61.

98. Ibid.

99. "Elias Neau to the Secretary" (New York, June 21, 1709), ibid., vol. 4, #155.

100. Trinity Church Vestry Minutes; Certificate from the Governor . . . September 1, 1716," S.P.G., Letter Books A, vol. 11, fols. 361–62; "Subscriptions to the Rev. Mr. Wetmore . . . 6th of November 1724," ibid., vol. 18, fols. 230–31; "Subscriptions of the People . . . 1st August 1726," ibid., vol. 19, fols. 431–35.

101. "Subscriptions of the People . . . 1st August 1726." Only a handful of Dutch names appear on the Trinity lists of vestrymen and pewholders before 1730 (Trinity Church Vestry Minutes).

102. "Thomas Colgan to the Secretary" (New York, December 23, 1728), S.P.G., Letter Books A, vol. 21, fols. 376–77.

103. Smith, Jr., *History of New-York*, ed. Kammen, 1:204. Smith also commented that "the Dutch congregation is more numerous than any other, but as the language becomes disused, it is much diminished; and unless they change their worship into the English tongue, must soon suffer a total dissipation" (ibid., 203).

104. *Some Cursory Remarks Made by James Birket in his Voyage to North America 1750–1751* (New Haven, Conn., 1916), 45. Travelers to New York were not always accurate in their identifications of the city's religious institutions. Birket erred when he spoke of two "Episcopal" churches; there was only one in 1750—Trinity Church. It is possible that he mistook the Presbyterian meetinghouse for an Anglican church. His reference to "Four Dutch Churches Two of the Lutheran the Other of the Calvinistical Order" is equally puzzling. In 1750, New York City had two Dutch Reformed ("Calvinistical") churches, a Dutch Lutheran church, and a newly formed German Lutheran church. Birket may have intended the term "Dutch" to refer to both German and Dutch institutions. For the observations of two other mid-eighteenth-century visitors to New York City see Peter Kalm, *Travels into North America*, trans. John Reinhold Forster (Barre, Mass., 1972), 131, and Carl Bridenbaugh, ed., *Gentleman's Progress: The Itinerarium of Dr. Alexander Hamilton 1744* (Chapel Hill, N.C., 1948), 44, 45, 178, 180, 182. See also William Smith's description of New York City's churches in 1756 (*History of New-York*, ed. Kammen, 1:203–8).

105. Theodore G. Tappert and John W. Doberstein, trans., *The Journals of Henry Melchior Muhlenberg*, 3 vols. (Philadelphia, 1942–1958), 1:283.

106. Kalm, *Travels into North America*, trans. Forster, 140; "The Reformed Dutch Church. Reasons for its Decline. By William Livingston, January 1754. Second Extract from Preface of the Independent Reflector," *Ecc. Rec.*, 5:3460.

107. "The Reformed Dutch Church. . . . By William Livingston," *Ecc. Rec.*, 5:3460.

108. "Baptisms in Private Houses [Paper read by Rev. John Ritzema]" (New York, August 20, 1747), *Ecc. Rec.*, 4:2971.

109. "Rev. Gualterus Du Bois to the Classis of Amsterdam" (November 2, 1748), *Ecc. Rec.*, 4:3038.

110. Quoted in Alexander J. Wall, "The Controversy in the Dutch Church in New York Concerning Preaching in English, 1754–1768," *New-York Historical Society Quarterly Bulletin*, 12 (1928), 40.

111. The marriage records of Trinity Church from 1746 to 1777 are found in "Records of Trinity Church Parish New York City," *New York Genealogical and Biographical Record*, 69 (1938), 158–62, 268–83, 369–78; 70 (1939), 41–54, 163–70, 271–76, 379–84. The only year before the Revolution for which a record of christenings in Trinity Church survives is 1759; Dutch names are also found here and there on this list. "Records of Trinity Church Parish New York City," ibid., 68 (1937), 66–78; Trinity Church Vestry Minutes, passim; and "Subscription Towards Enlarging the Church," in Rev. William Berrian, *An Historical Sketch of Trinity Church, New York* (New York, 1847), 340–42.

112. "Records of the Reformed Dutch Church, Members' List." Between 1731 and 1740, 391 people were admitted to the Dutch Reformed church; between 1741 and 1750, 489 were admitted.

113. See, for example, Balmer, *A Perfect Babel of Confusion*.

114. "Returns of the New York Clergy, 1724," Fulham Papers, Lambeth Palace Library (American colonial section, seventeenth and eighteenth centuries), vol. 41, fols. 109–12 (London, World Microfilm Publications). Another indication of the limited appeal of Anglicanism in the early years of the eighteenth century is William Bradford's dismal record in selling his first edition of the Book of Common Prayer. Bradford printed one thousand copies in 1706 but had sold only fifty by 1709. Beverly McAnear, "William Bradford and The Book of Common Prayer," *Papers of the Bibliographical Society of America*, 43 (1949), 103–4, 108.

115. Wilkenfeld, "New York City Neighborhoods, 1730," 179.

116. Smith, *History of New-York*, ed. Kammen, 1:204–5. See also Dix, ed., *History of Trinity Church*.

117. "Henry Barclay to the Secretary" (New York, November 7, 1748), S.P.G., Letter Books B, vol. 16, #55. When Dr. Alexander Hamilton worshiped at Trinity Church in 1744, he noted that there was "a large congregation of above a thousand" (Bridenbaugh, ed., *Gentleman's Progress*, 45).

118. Quoted in Kemp, *The Support of Schools in Colonial New York*, 81. For a biographical sketch of William Vesey see Clifford K. Shipton, *New England Life in the 18th Century: Representative Biographies from Sibley's Harvard Graduates* (Cambridge, Mass., 1963), 12–19.

119. *DHNY*, 3:269–77; Alison Gilbert Olson, "Governor Robert Hunter and the Anglican Church in New York," in Anne Whiteman, J. S. Bromley, and P.G.M. Dickson, eds., *Statesmen, Scholars and Merchants* (Oxford, 1973); Dix, ed., *History of Trinity Church*. See also "Journal of Rev. John Sharpe," *Pennsylvania Magazine of History and Biography*, 40 (1916), 257–97, 412–25.

120. "Caleb Heathcote to the Secretary" (New York, June 13, 1714), S.P.G., Letter Books A, vol. 9, New York Letters, #19.

121. After a visit to New York City in 1718, John Winthrop reported that "the Dissenters are now tollerated to preach publickly in the State House and are build-

ing a church in the citty, which has heretofore been denied them. Mr. Anderson, A Scotch gentleman, is the minister to this new-gathered Dissenting church, and their congregation increases dayly." "John Winthrop to Increase Mather" (July 2, 1718), *Collections* of the Massachusetts Historical Society, 6th ser., vol. 5 (Boston, 1892), 381–82. On earlier efforts to hold Presbyterian worship in New York City, see Joyce D. Goodfriend, "A New Look at Presbyterian Origins in New York City," *American Presbyterians*, 67 (1989), 199–207. See also Dorothy Ganfield Fowler, *A City Church: The First Presbyterian Church in the City of New York, 1716–1976* (New York, 1981).

122. Quoted in Theodore Fiske Savage, *The Presbyterian Church in New York City* (New York, 1949), 7–8.

123. Jon Butler, *Power, Authority, and the Origins of American Denominational Order: The English Churches in the Delaware Valley, 1680–1730* (American Philosophical Society, *Transactions*, vol. 68, part 2 [Philadelphia, 1978]), 62–63; Boyd Schlenther, ed., "The Presbyterian Church of New York vs. John Nicoll, M.D.," *Journal of Presbyterian History*, 42 (1964), 198–215, 272–85.

124. Nicholas Eyres, a brewer, preached to the small group of Baptists. I. N. Phelps Stokes, *The Iconography of Manhattan Island, 1498–1909*. 6 vols. (New York, 1915–1928), 4.473, 484, 501, 508, 510. Wm. Parkinson, *Jubilee: A Sermon, Containing a History of the Origin of the First Baptist Church in the City of New-York, and Its Progress, during the First Fifty Years since Its Constitution: (with Explanatory Notes) Delivered in the Meeting-House of Said Church, January 1, 1813* (New York, 1846).

125. "Ministers Churchwardens and Vestry [of Trinity Church, New York City] to the Secretary" (New York, December 18, 1722), S.P.G., Letter Books A, vol. 16, fols. 229–31.

126. In 1724 Quaker missionary Thomas Chalkley referred to "those few Friends at New-York." *A Collection of the Works of . . . Thomas Chalkley . . . To which is prefix'd A Journal of his Life, Travels, and Christian Experience, Written by Himself*. 4th ed., (London, 1766), 120. On Ebenezer Pemberton, see the biography in Clifford K. Shipton, *Biographical Sketches of Those Who Attended Harvard College in the Classes 1713–1721, with Bibliographical and Other Notes. Sibley's Harvard Graduates* vol. 6, *1713–1721* (Boston, 1942), 535–46.

127. Fowler, *A City Church*, 9. Fowler adds that "the building was in disrepair and the windows had been boarded over." Only 11 Presbyterians have been identified among New York City's taxpayers in 1730 (Wilkenfeld, "New York City Neighborhoods, 1730," 179).

128. Clifford M. Drury, "Presbyterian Beginnings in New England and the Middle Colonies (1640–1714)," *Journal of the Presbyterian Historical Society*, 34 (1956), 26. The earliest baptismal records of the First Presbyterian Church beginning in 1728 are virtually devoid of Dutch names. "Records of the First Presbyterian Church of the City of New York," *New York Genealogical and Biographical Record*, 4 (1873), 98–103, 140–43; 195–99. Patrick MacKnight, one of the founders of the Presbyterian church in New York City, was married to a Dutch woman and had three children baptized in the Dutch Reformed church between 1712 and 1715. William Jackson, an early Presbyterian supporter from Scotland, was married to a Dutch woman and had children baptized in the Dutch Reformed church.

129. Tappert and Doberstein, trans., *Journals of Muhlenberg*, 1:291. Fowler, *A City Church*, 9, 11; Gabriel Disosway, *The Earliest Churches of New York and Its Vicinity* (New York, 1864), 134.

130. Smith, *History of New-York*, ed. Kammen, 206–7; Fowler, *A City Church*, 12, 14.

131. "Catalogue of the Members of the Dutch Church, 1686" (see note 24 for chapter 5).

132. "Records of the Reformed Dutch Church, Members' List."

133. The will of Catherine DeHardt Symes is printed in *CNYHS for the Year 1895*, 318–20.

134. Will of Anna Thompson, *CNYHS for the Year 1895*, 278–80.

135. Paul Zumthor, *Daily Life in Rembrandt's Holland*, trans. Simon Watson Taylor (London, 1962; original French edition, 1959), 79–94. Wayne Framis, "The Family Saying Grace: A Theme in Dutch Art of the Seventeenth Century," *Simiolus*, 16 (1986), 36–49. A majority of the family bibles listed in the wills and inventories of city residents during this period were found in the estates of Dutch persons (Goodfriend, "Probate Records as a Source for Early American Religious History").

136. Several recent studies focus on the impact of the transition from Dutch to English law on the legal status of women in New York. See Linda Briggs Biemer, *Women and Property in Colonial New York: The Transition from Dutch to English Law, 1643–1727* (Ann Arbor, Mich., 1983); David Evan Narrett, "Patterns of Inheritance in Colonial New York City, 1664–1775: A Study in the History of the Family" (Ph.D. diss., Cornell University, 1981); Narrett, "Dutch Customs of Inheritance"; Joan R. Gundersen and Gwen Victor Gampel, "Married Women's Legal Status in Eighteenth-Century New York and Virginia," *William and Mary Quartery*, 3d ser., 39 (1982), 114–34; and Sherry Penney and Roberta Willenkin, "Dutch Women in Colonial Albany: Liberation and Retreat," *de Halve Maen*, 52 (Spring 1977), 9–10, 14–15, and (Summer 1977), 7–8, 15.

137. Joyce D. Goodfriend, "Dutch Women in Colonial New York" (Paper presented at the meeting of the American Society for Ethnohistory, Colorado Springs, 1981). For other discussions of the feminization of colonial religion see Patricia U. Bonomi, *Under the Cope of Heaven: Religion, Politics, and Society in Colonial America* (New York, 1986), 105–15; Mary Maples Dunn, "Saints and Sisters: Congregational and Quaker Women in the Early Colonial Period," in Janet Wilson James, ed., *Women in American Religion* (Philadelphia, 1980), 27–46; Gerald F. Moran, "'Sisters in Christ': Women and the Church in Seventeenth-Century New England," in ibid., 47–65; Gerald F. Moran, "'The Hidden Ones': Women and Religion in Puritan New England," in Richard L. Greaves, ed., *Triumph Over Silence: Women in Protestant History* (Westport, Conn., 1985), 125–49; and Richard D. Shiels, "The Feminization of American Congregationalism, 1730–1835," *American Quarterly*, 33 (1981), 46–62.

138. The will of Jane de Key Tothill is printed in *CNYHS for the Year 1893*, 228–30.

139. Anna Margareta Freeman was the daughter of Dominie Bernardus Freeman, the Dutch Reformed minister at Flatbush. See the will of Bernardus Freeman, *CNYHS for the Year 1894*, 361–62. This relationship explains her allegiance

to the Dutch Reformed church. Whether by choice or not, at her death in 1759, "Mrs. Anna Margareta Clarkson, Relict of Mr. David Clarkson, . . . [was] decently interr'd in the Family Vault, in Trinity Church." *The New York Mercury*, February 12, 1759, quoted in "Old New York and Trinity Church," *CNYHS for the Year 1870*, 174.

140. Trinity Church Vestry Minutes, May 22, 1728.

141. Dutch culture was distinctive in a number of respects not discussed here. On Dutch political culture, see Howe, "Accommodation and Retreat," and Donna Merwick, "Being Dutch: An Interpretation of Why Jacob Leisler Died," *New York History*, 70 (1989), 373–404. On Dutch foodways, see Peter G. Rose, trans. and ed., *The Sensible Cook: Dutch Foodways in the Old and the New World* (Syracuse, N.Y., 1989).

142. On Dutch urban architecture, see Aram Harutunian, "The Dutch-American Vernacular Style of Architecture," in *The Dutch and America* (Los Angeles, 1982), 9–16; and Roderic H. Blackburn, "Dutch Domestic Architecture in the Hudson Valley," *New Netherland Studies*, in *Bulletin KNOB*, 84, nos. 2 and 3 (June 1985), 151–65. For background on seventeenth-century Dutch architecture, see W. Kuyper, *Dutch Classicist Architecture: A Survey of Dutch Architecture, Gardens and Anglo-Dutch Architectural Relations from 1625 to 1700* (Delft, 1980). On architecture in the Dutch colonies, see Doreen Greig, *The Reluctant Colonists: Netherlanders Abroad in the 17th and 18th Centuries* (Assen/Maastricht, the Netherlands, 1987).

143. *Journal of the Votes and Proceedings of the General Assembly of the Colony of New-York, 1691 . . . 1743*, vol. 1 (New York, 1764), 163.

144. On colonial Dutch material culture, see Blackburn and Piwonka, *Remembrance of Patria*; Roderic H. Blackburn, "Transforming Old World Dutch Culture in a New World Environment: Processes of Material Adaptation," in Roderic H. Blackburn and Nancy A. Kelley, eds., *New World Dutch Studies: Dutch Arts and Culture in Colonial America 1609–1776* (Albany, N.Y., 1987), 95–106; Sondra Pratt, "Interiors and Decorative Arts" in *The Dutch and America*, 21–29; Kenney, "Neglected Heritage: Hudson River Valley Dutch Material Culture;" and Ruth Piwonka, "Dutch Colonial Arts," in Eric Nooter and Patricia U. Bonomi, eds., *Colonial Dutch Studies: An Interdisciplinary Approach* (New York and London, 1988), 78–94. On furniture, see Benno M. Forman, *American Seating Furniture 1630–1730: An Interpretive Catalogue* (New York, 1988). On silver, see Kristan Helen McKinsey, "New York City Silversmiths and their Patrons, 1687–1750" (Master's thesis, University of Delaware [Winterthur Program], 1984). On ceramics, see Charlotte Wilcoxen, *Dutch Trade and Ceramics in America in the Seventeenth Century* (Albany, 1987). See also Meta F. Janowitz, Kate T. Morgan, and Nan A. Rothschild, "Cultural Pluralism and Pots in New Amsterdam–New York City," in Sarah Peabody Turnbaugh, ed., *Domestic Pottery of the Northeastern United States, 1625–1850* (Orlando, Fla., 1985), 29–48.

145. Will of Evert van Hook, *CNYHS for the Year 1893*, 72. To illustrate "the persistence of the original Dutch habits in material culture many years after the Dutch of New York were politically anglicized," Charlotte Wilcoxen quotes Dr. Alexander Hamilton's comments on the Albany Dutch in 1744: "[The Dutch here] set out their cabinets and buffets much with china, [and] they hang earthen

or delft plates and dishes all around the walls, in manner of pictures, having a hole drilled thro' the edge of the plate or dish, and a loop or ribbon put into it to hang by" (Wilcoxen, *Dutch Trade and Ceramics in America*), 65.

On the *kas*, see Blackburn and Piwonka, *Remembrance of Patria*, 256–69. Blackburn suggests that the kas "represented a self-conscious symbol of cultural identity, the preservation of one's Dutch ways" (Blackburn, "Transforming Old World Dutch Culture," 99).

146. On the domestic motif in Dutch culture see Simon Schama, *The Embarassment of Riches: An Interpretation of Dutch Culture in the Golden Age* (New York, 1987), and Zumthor, *Daily Life in Rembrandt's Holland*.

147. Daniel Denton, "A Brief Description of New York formerly called New Netherlands with the Places Thereunto Adjoining" (London, 1670), reprinted in Cornell Jaray, ed., *Historic Chronicles of New Amsterdam, Colonial New York and Early Long Island*. 2d ser., (Port Washington, N.Y., 1978), 2. In 1678, Governor Andros reported that "our buildings most wood, some lately stone & brick, good country houses & strong of their severall kindes." "Answers of Governor Andros to Enquiries about New-York" (received April 16, 1678), *Doc. Rel.*, 3:261.

Bayrd Still's description of New Amsterdam is relevant here: "By the 1650's, a fairly compact flank of slim frame dwellings extended for some distance along the East River at the tip of [Manhattan] island; and occasional stone and brick structures, with ornamented gable ends facing the street and roofs of red or black pantile, fostered the impression that a Dutch town had been transplanted in New World soil." Bayrd Still, *Mirror for Gotham: New York as Seen by Contemporaries from Dutch Days to the Present* (New York, 1956), 7. Charles M. Andrews stated succinctly that "New Amsterdam bore no resemblance to a New England town. Instead of homesteads clustering about a church and a village green, the Dutch houses adjoined a fort, within which were the governor's house, the church, the barracks, a prison, the whipping post and gallows, while nearby were the two windmills." Charles M. Andrews, *The Colonial Period of American History*, 4 vols. (New Haven, 1937), 3:78.

148. The Danckaerts view of New York City c. 1679 is reproduced in Stokes, *The Iconography of Manhattan Island*, vol. 1, Plate 17.

149. Wayne Andrews, ed., "A Glance at New York in 1697: The Travel Diary of Dr. Benjamin Bullivant," revised from *New-York Historical Society Quarterly* (January 1956), 13, 10, 11. For a description of the interior of Abraham de Peyster's house, see Esther Singleton, *Social New York Under the Georges 1714–1776: Houses, Streets and Country Homes, with Chapters on Fashions, Furniture, China, Plate and Manners* (New York, 1902), 69–73.

150. Andrews, ed., "A Glance at New York," 13.

151. Sarah Kemble Knight, *The Journal of Madam Knight*, "Introduction" by Malcolm Freiberg (Boston, 1972), 28–29.

152. Knight, *The Journal of Madam Knight*, 29–30. On the Dutch fetish for cleanliness, see Schama, *The Embarassment of Riches*, 375–97.

153. Edward Porter Alexander, ed., *The Journal of John Fontaine: An Irish Huguenot Son in Spain and Virginia 1710–1719* (Williamsburg, Va., 1972), 115.

154. The Burgis view of the city is reproduced in Stokes, *The Iconography of Manhattan Island*, vol. 1, Plate 25. According to John Kouwenhoven, "The medi-

eval Dutch architecture of the old city below Wall Street, with its stepped gables and steep roofs, gave place in the upper town to Renaissance styles popular in England at the time." John A. Kouwenhoven, *The Columbia Historical Portrait of New York: An Essay in Graphic History* (New York, 1972; originally published 1953), 53.

According to Roderic Blackburn, in 1717 "the older half of New York City was still almost entirely composed of Dutch houses. From this time forward, however, most substantial buildings were in the English style although more modest dwellings of Dutch families might have been constructed in traditional Netherlandish style for another generation." Blackburn and Piwonka, *Remembrance of Patria*, 99.

155. Carl Bridenbaugh, ed., *Gentleman's Progress*, 44.

156. House construction accelerated in New York City in the late 1730s, according to George Clarke, and in the late 1740s, according to James Alexander. After noting that "nigh an hundred houses in the town stood empty [in 1735/36]," Clarke reported in 1741 that "the houses that stood empty are now all tenanted and now as many more since built as then were empty and even the houses that are now building are bespoke before they are finished." "Lieutenant-Governor Clarke to the Lords of Trade" (New York, December 15, 1741), *Doc. Rel.*, 6:207. Alexander stated that "in 1733 James Lyne, then my clerk, counted all the houses in New York, including churches, public buildings, store houses, stables, smith shops, etc., and there were 1473; that now [1752] in this present June my son has counted them and there are 2611 dwelling houses and that above 500 dwelling houses have been built since 1746." James Alexander to Mr. R. Peters of Philadelphia (June 22, 1752), quoted in Stokes, *Iconography*, 6:23.

157. Adolph B. Benson, ed., *The America of 1750: Peter Kalm's Travels in North America. The English Version of 1770*, 1:132. Kalm also comments on the decoration of the city's houses: "The walls were whitewashed within, and I did not anywhere see wall paper, with which the people of this country seem in general to be but little acquainted. The walls were covered with all sorts of drawings and pictures in small frames. On each side of the chimneys they had usually a sort of alcove, and the walls under the windows were wainscoted and had benches placed near them. The cupboards and all the wood work were painted with a bluish grey color" (ibid., 1:132).

158. *Some Cursory Remarks Made by James Birket in his Voyage to North America*, 43–44.

159. Thomas Pownall, *A Topographical Description of the Dominions of the United States of America*, ed. by Lois Mulkearn (Pittsburgh, 1949), 43. Of special value in analyzing colonial Dutch architecture is Blackburn, "Dutch Domestic Architecture in the Hudson Valley," 151–65.

160. "New-York Daguerrotyped," *Putnam's Monthly*, 1 (February 1853), 129. The article's author calls the old Dutch store, erected in 1689, a monstrosity: "Almost the last link which connected us with the sleepy days of old Peter Stuyvesant, [it] lingered till within twenty years like a bedridden great-grandmother among her stirring and bustling descendants, who at last, weary of her presence, and rendered desperate by her unflinching determination 'never to say die,' tore her limb from limb and scattered her bones far and wide." I obtained this reference from Kouwenhoven, *The Columbia Historical Portrait of New York*, 138.

CONCLUSION

1. Michael Hechter, *Internal Colonialism: The Celtic Fringe in British National Development, 1536–1966* (Berkeley and Los Angeles, 1975), 47–123.

2. For the term "charter group," see T. H. Breen, "Creative Adaptations: Peoples and Cultures," in Jack P. Greene and J. R. Pole, eds., *Colonial British America: Essays in the New History of the Early Modern Era* (Baltimore and London, 1984), 204–5.

3. See the growing literature on foreigners in early modern England: Andrew Pettegree, *Foreign Protestant Communities in Sixteenth Century London* (Oxford, 1986); Andrew Pettegree, "'Thirty Years On': Progress Towards Integration Amongst the Immigrant Population of Elizabethan London," in John Chartres and David Hey, eds., *English Rural Society, 1500–1800: Essays in Honour of Joan Thirsk* (Cambridge, 1990), 297–312; Ole Peter Grell, "The French and Dutch Congregations in London in the Early Seventeenth Century," *Proceedings* of the Huguenot Society, 24 (1987), 362–77; Ole Peter Grell, *Dutch Calvinists in Early Stuart London: The Dutch Church in Austin Friars 1603–1642* (Leiden, 1989); Robin D. Gwynn, *Huguenot Heritage: The History and Contributions of the Huguenots in Britain* (London, 1985); Jonathan I. Israel, *European Jewry in the Age of Mercantilism 1550–1750* (Oxford, 1985), 158–60.

4. John Webb Pratt, *Religion, Politics, and Diversity: The Church-State Theme in New York History* (Ithaca, N.Y., 1967), 26–37.

5. "William Byrd to Bro. Dan'l per Ruds" (Virginia, March 8, 1685/86), *Virginia Historical Register and Literary Companion*, 2 (1849), 208 (misprinted as 108).

6. Charles Lodwick, "New York in 1692," *CNYHS*, 2d ser., vol. 2 (New York, 1849), 244. Ironically, Lodwick himself was of Dutch origin. See John Murrin, "English Rights as Ethnic Aggression: The English Conquest, the Charter of Liberties of 1683, and Leisler's Rebellion in New York," in William Pencak and Conrad Edick Wright, eds., *Authority and Resistance in Early New York* (New York, 1988), 93 n. 87. On Penn's plan for Pennsylvania, see Sally Schwartz, *"A Mixed Multitude": The Struggle for Toleration in Colonial Pennsylvania* (New York and London, 1987), 1–35.

7. Jonathan D. Sarna, "From Immigrants to Ethnics: Toward a New Theory of 'Ethnicization'," *Ethnicity*, 5 (1978), 370–78; John Higham, "Integrating America: The Problem of Assimilation in the Nineteenth Century," *Journal of American Ethnic History*, 1 (1981), 8–9.

8. "Churchwardens and Vestry of Trinity Church, New-York, to Archbishop Tenison" (New York, May 22, 1699), *Doc. Rel.*, 4:526.